Public Policy and the Economy since 1900

JIM TOMLINSON

CLARENDON PRESS · OXFORD

Oxford University Press, Walton Street, Oxford OX2 6DP

Oxford New York Toronto
Delhi Bombay Calcutta Madras Karachi
Kuala Lumpur Singapore Hong Kong Tokyo
Nairobi Dar es Salaam Cape Town
Melbourne Auckland Madrid

and associated companies in
Berlin Ibadan

Oxford is a trade mark of Oxford University Press

Published in the United States
by Oxford University Press Inc., New York

British Library Cataloguing in Publication Data
Data available

Library of Congress Cataloging in Publication Data
Tomlinson, Jim.
Public policy and the economy since 1900 / Jim Tomlinson.
p.   cm.
Includes bibliographical references.
1. Great Britain—Economic policy. 2. Great Britain—Economic
conditions—20th century.   I. Title.
HC256.T56 1990   338.941—dc20   89-37444
ISBN 0-19-828658-9
ISBN 0-19-828774-7 (Pbk.)

3 5 7 9 10 8 6 4 2

Printed in Great Britain
on acid-free paper by
Bookcraft (Bath) Ltd.
Midsomer Norton, Avon

Acknowledgments

THIS is the sixth book typed for me by Mrs Christine Newnham. As always she has worked with a speed and efficiency for which I am extremely grateful.

Like British industry, British universities have been slow to 'rationalize' themselves, and in consequence I have had rather little opportunity to teach the subject matter of this book, thus being deprived of a fruitful means of development and clarification of ideas. Whatever merit the book does contain, however, owes much to the stimulus (direct and indirect) of the work of Alan Booth, Alec Cairncross, Tony Cutler, Barry Hindess, Paul Hirst, Athar Hussain, Grahame Thompson, John and Karel Williams, and Jonathan Zeitlin. None of these, of course, bears any responsibility for the way I have used his or her work.

Contents

List of Tables		ix
List of Abbreviations		xi
1	Public Policy and the National Economy	1
2	1900–1914: The World we have Lost	14
3	1914–1925: 'A World Shattered—and Rebuilt'?	42
4	1925–1931: The Old World Restored and Found Wanting	70
5	1931–1939: The Rise of Economic Management?	98
6	1939–1945: Planning the War and Plans for Peace	134
7	1941–1958: Reconstructing the World Economy	172
8	1945–1951: Domestic Reconstruction: Building a New Jerusalem?	203
9	1951–1973: The Long Boom	238
10	1973–1979: From Crisis to Crisis	277
11	1979–1988: Renaissance or Retrogression?	313
	References	348
	Index	377

List of Tables

2.1 Prices and Wages 1900–1913   17
2.2 Government Expenditure (Local and Central)
    1895–1913   24
2.3 Recorded Unemployment 1900–1913   40
3.1 The Budget 1913/14–1924/5   45
3.2 Unemployment 1914–1925   46
3.3 Price Indices 1913–1925   47
4.1 Budgetary Policy 1929/30–1932/3   78
5.1 Main Economic Indicators 1929–1939   99
5.2 Sterling Exchange Rates in the 1930s   100
5.3 Fiscal Stance in the 1930s   113
6.1 Britain's Cumulative Balance of Payments
    1939–1945   136
6.2 Import and Exports 1938–1945   139
6.3 Budgets 1939–1945   140
8.1 British Trade with the Dollar Area 1945–1952   208
8.2 British Trade and Payments 1946–1952   212
8.3 Budget Surplus or Deficit and Public Sector
    Savings 1946–1952   214
8.4 Change in Allocation of Resources 1945–1952   226
8.5 Gross Fixed Capital Formation in the United
    Kingdom 1946–1953   228
8.6 Main Economic Indicators 1945–1952   235
9.1 British Economic Performance 1950–1973   238
9.2 The Balance of Payments 1952–1973   242
9.3 Geographical Composition of Britain's Trade
    1955–1972   245
9.4 Government Finance 1952–1973   247
9.5 Unemployment in Great Britain 1951–1973   258
9.6 Inflation in the Long Boom   269
10.1 Effective Exchange Rate for the £ 1972–1979   278
10.2 The Balance of Payments 1972–1979   279
10.3 Standard of Living 1972–1979   282
10.4 Public Expenditure 1972/3–1978/9   285
10.5 PSBR 1972–1979   288

10.6	Monetary Growth 1972–1979	291
10.7	Government Support for Industry, Excluding Nationalized Industries, 1974/5–1979/80	294
10.8	Unemployment 1973–1979	295
10.9	Monetary Targets 1976–1979	300
11.1	Exchange Rates 1979–1987	319
11.2	Public Expenditure under the Conservatives 1979/80–1987/8	323
11.3	The First MTFS: Targets and Outcomes	324
11.4	GDP in the OECD 'Big 6', 1979–1988	334
11.5	Unemployment in the OECD 'Big 6', 1979–1988	334
11.6	Inflation in the OECD 'Big 6', 1979–1988	339
11.7	Fiscal Tightening in the OECD 'Big 6', changes in Budget Balancing 1979–1982	341
11.8	Rate of Monetary Growth in the OECD 'Big 6', 1979–1982	341
11.9	Manufacturing Productivity Growth in the OECD 'Big 6', 1979–1985	342
11.10	Private-Sector Productivity Trends in the OECD 'Big 6', 1979–1989	344
11.11	Britain's Current Balance of Payments 1979–1988	346

List of Abbreviations

AACP	Anglo-American Council on Productivity
BEQB	*Bank of England Quarterly Bulletin*
BID	Bankers' Industrial Development Corporation
BISF	British Iron and Steel Federation
BL	British Leyland
CEA	Chief Economic Adviser
CEI	Committee on Economic Information
CEPG	Cambridge Economic Policy Group
CEPS	Central Economic Planning Staff
DEA	Department of Economic Affairs
DM	Deutsche Mark
DTI	Department of Trade and Industry
EAC	Economic Advisory Council
ECOSOC	Economic and Social Council
ECSC	European Coal and Steel Community
EEA	Exchange Equalization Account
EFTA	European Free Trade Association
EMS	European Monetary System
EPU	European Payments Union
FBI	Federation of British Industry
FSBR	Financial Statement and Budget Report
GATT	General Agreement on Tariffs and Trade
GDP	Gross Domestic Product
GNP	Gross National Product
HCP	House of Commons Paper
IBRD	International Bank for Reconstruction and Development
ILO	International Labour Organization
ILP	Independent Labour Party
IMF	International Monetary Fund
IRC	Industrial Reorganization Corporation
IRI	Istituto Ricostruzione Italiana
IS/LM	Standard, two-equation Keynesian model of the macro-economy
ITO	International Trade Organization

JPC	Joint Production Committee
M3	Wide definition of money supply, including cash, sight, and time deposits
MFA	Multi-Fibre Agreement
MITI	Ministry of International Trade and Industry (Japan)
MTFS	Medium Term Financial Strategy
NCEO	National Confederation of Employers' Organizations
NEB	National Enterprise Board
NEDO	National Economic Development Council
OECD	Organization for Economic Co-operation and Development
OEEC	Organization for European Economic Co-operation
OPEC	Organization of Petroleum Exporting Countries
PESC	Public Expenditure Survey Committee
PSBR	Public Sector Borrowing Requirement
R. & D	Research and Development
RPE	Relative Price Effect
SDRs	Special Drawing Rights
SDP	Social Democratic Party
SIAS	Social Insurance and Allied Services
SWP	Sector Working Party
TUC	Trades Union Congress
UAB	Unemployment Assistance Board
UGC	Unemployment Grants Committee
VER	Voluntary Export Restraint

1

Public Policy and the National Economy

THIS book is an account of the major features and development of British economic policy since 1900. In style it is narrative and broadly chronological. It is also analytical, but that analysis is mainly concrete and specific rather than abstract and general. However concrete and narrowly focused, analysis must of course rest, explicitly or implicitly, on a wider framework which determines what is deemed relevant and important, and what glossed over or omitted. The purpose of this introductory chapter is to outline the framework which underlies the organization of this book. Those whose taste is for the empirical and who adhere to the saying that the 'proof of the pudding is in the eating' may skip directly to Chapter 2. But this introduction should make the menu offered in the rest of the book more explicable.

Framework

Frameworks for the analysis of public policy and the economy are numerous (for overviews see, for example, Hall 1986, ch. 1; Levacic 1987). To give a complete typology of such frameworks would be lengthy and tedious, so the approach here is to discuss only a few of the major approaches which form a background (or counterpart) to that adopted in this book.

The most intellectually insurgent of current approaches to policy-making is public choice theory (Downs 1957; Olson 1965; Niskanen 1971; Levacic 1987, part 2 gives a sympathetic survey). Broadly, this approach attempts to extend the neo-classical economists' a priori of individuals as rational maximizers to the actors in the policy-making process, to the governments, and to the bureaucrats. Governments are seen as attempting to maximize votes to obtain power, bureaucrats to maximize their bureaux to obtain the benefits (both financial and non-financial) which go with increased scale.

At the most abstract level such approaches seem to suffer from fatal weaknesses. First, they not only assume a general rationality on the part of all agents or actors, but more significantly 'that which is to count as rationality is uniquely defined within each category of actor defined by the model' (Hindess 1984, p. 263). In other words, it is assumed that all firms must maximize profits, all governments maximize votes, all bureaucrats maximize bureaux. This is a very strong assumption, not at all deducible from a general postulate of rationality.

But this general postulate of rationality (defined as actors having given and well-ordered ends, between which they choose in a consistent fashion and which link ends to means) is itself very problematic. If we think of actors as always individuals, most actors have competing rationalities which battle against each other, or in which one end is pursued in the knowledge that it is against a considered judgement—the action is 'incontinent' (Hindess 1984, pp. 264–5). So to call all actors rational in this strong sense is implausible—which is not of course to deny that human actors have reasons for their actions. Rather, the problem is that individuals can provide reasons for each of an array of different and contradictory actions.

In fact, for public-choice theorists, actors always are individuals: they are committed to 'methodological individualism'. This is linked to the presumption, noted above, that all bureaucrats will maximize bureaux etc.—that is to say, this approach ascribes the rationality to the actor, rather than the structure within which the actor operates. If we start from the assumption that the forms of rationality to be deployed by actors cannot simply be assumed to be homogeneous in this way, then rationality can be better related to *particular* forms of rationality or 'calculation', which may be deployed by individuals. But if rationality is related to the idea of an entity which (rationally) calculates in a variety of ways, varying with the institutional context, and acts on those calculations, why should we limit such rationality to individuals? Thus firms, government ministries, Cabinets, trade unions, and other collective bodies can equally be treated as sources of rational calculation, i.e. as making decisions on the basis of some assessment of their situation and taking action accordingly (Hindess, 1984, pp. 267–8).

These brief points by no means exhaust the problems of rational choice theory,[1] but enough has been said to suggest that this approach suffers fundamental weaknesses as a starting point for analysing public policy.[2] These weaknesses do not prevent the approach from having some positive features. First, much of the public choice literature starts from a hostility to the idea that states and governments pursue 'the public good' in a disinterested fashion. Though some of the opposition to this idea is crude political polemic (e.g. Buchanan *et al.* 1978) it nevertheless is right to challenge the rather cosy 'presuppositions of Harvey Road'[3] which have had a big impact on writing about public policy in Britain. Of course, the danger here is of throwing the baby out with the bath water; of replacing policy as guided by an ingenuous pursuit of the public good by policy as guided by rational 'self-interest', where the calculation of that interest is treated as obvious and unexamined.

Secondly, the public choice literature, paradoxically and un-intentionally, does focus attention on the diverse character of calculations amongst different participants in the policy process, and the potential conflicts between them. Most obviously such conflicts could arise between vote-maximizing by politicians and bureaux-maximizing by bureaucrats. But again this positive point is weakened by treating the rationality of each category as individualistic and 'natural', and the forms of calculation employed as unproblematic.

Whilst usually seen as being at the opposite end of the ideological spectrum, Marxism has certain analytical features in common with public choice theory. Above all both are 'reductionist'; whilst public choice theory reduces everything to the pre-given rationality of individuals, Marxism reduces everything (ultimately) to class interests and the class struggle.

---

[1] For general discussions of rationality see Hindess 1984, 1988*b*.

[2] Public choice work also often depends on the methodological postulate of Friedman (1953), which argues that theories should not be judged by the realism of their assumptions but solely by the accuracy of the predictions they produce. For problems in this see, for example, Hindess (1977) and Toye (1976).

[3] The 'presuppositions of Harvey Road' refer to Keynes's birthplace, and his work as the classic example of the idea that the public policy is made in pursuit of the public good, and the task is to make sure that the formulators of that policy act on the best possible advice (Harrod 1952, pp. 183, 192–3). For discussion, see Clarke (1988), 15–16, 191–2, 308–10.

Throughout its history Marxism has been torn by a conflict between its most basic postulate, of society as a unity grounded in the organization of the economy (the relations of production), and on the other hand the recognition that to relate all features of social life directly to the economy is unsustainable. This tension is there in Marx himself—between the programmatic reductionism of the *Communist Manifesto* or the *Preface to a Contribution to Political Economy*, and the subtle analysis of the 'autonomy' of politics in the *Eighteenth Brumaire* and other analyses of particular political conjunctures (Hindess 1988a, chs. 2, 6).

The key issue for Marxism is whether this tension can be satisfactorily resolved, or whether it points to a fundamental flaw in the whole enterprise. Cutler *et al.* (1977, 1978) have persuasively argued that this tension is irresolvable. Either politics is ultimately reducible to the economy or it is not. Or put the other way, what are the mechanisms whereby, in (say) a capitalist economy, politics are not directly representative of that economy, but nevertheless those politics are ultimately determined by the economy (except in a revolutionary situation)? It is the failure to specify these mechanisms satisfactorily which points to the ultimate sterility of the concept of 'relative autonomy'.

A number of points may be made about the implications of the rejection of the basic Marxist postulate of the ultimate reducibility of politics to the economy. First, it does not by any means imply the rejection of all Marxist political analysis, which like Marx's own has been characterized by extremely insightful discussions of particular situations, alongside the much more dubious programmatic statements, and with often only the most tenuous relation between the two.

Second is the question of class. What is at stake in the current discussion is the use of the category of class to explain politics and policy-making. The central point is that typically Marxists refer back from a particular decision-making agency (e.g. government, trade union, political party) to a class interest which is said to underlie that agency's decisions. This two-level analysis is necessary because Marxists recognize that classes *per se* do not (normally?) appear on the political stage, and therefore have to be 'represented'. But once there is a space for such representation we are back to the same problem as before—how is the interest of the class always to be secured unless the form of that representation is completely determined by what is represented? But this is unacceptable to the great bulk of Marxists, who reject this direct collapse of every agency into a simple representation of class interests. Again, it seems impossible to specify mechanisms which would allow such agencies 'relative autonomy' but still constrain them to represent a class's interests.

Of course, behind this notion of agencies representing class interests lies the idea of classes having interests simply as a consequence of their location in the 'relations of production' or social structure. This too raises insurmountable problems, because it attempts to substitute for quintessentially normative, political judgements (i.e. what are desirable forms of social organization) an assertion that the interests of a class arise *prior* to those political judgements i.e. an argument about desirable forms of social organization, how to bring them about and so on. In other words, arguments about class interest always involve a specific political discourse in which those formulations about interests are deployed.

Thus, for example, arguments about whether the British Labour Party 'really' represents the working class, always presuppose a political argument about what the interests of that class are. Political discourses which deploy concepts of class interest have on occasions been extremely important and influential in British (and other country's) politics. A rejection of class interest in this traditional Marxist sense as an analytical concept in no way involves a rejection of the importance of such discourses to understanding politics. But the influence of such discourses tells us nothing, of course, about their 'truth value'. An obvious parallel would be evangelical Christianity. This was an extremely important and influential ideology in nineteenth-century England. But recognition of this significance tells us absolutely nothing about the validity of that evangelicalism's theology.

Where does all this leave the concept of capitalism—can this term be used if we reject the notion of society as a unity ultimately shaped by the economy? The answer is that the concept still has value, but must necessarily be reformulated. One can still accept capitalism as describing, in classical Marxist formulations, a society in which ownership of the means of production is predominantly in private hands. But this must be uncoupled from the notion that this private ownership is the 'essence' of society, which ultimately everything relates back to. Equally, one can still talk about a socialist economy, but without any presumption that such an economy has any necessary forms of politics or ideology. (I will return to the pertinence of talking about a capitalist economy in the discussion of public policy in the second section below).

Marxist accounts of public policy must tend ultimately to limit the autonomy of the policy-making apparatuses by linking them back to classes and class interests outside themselves—though, of course, the *degree* of autonomy of 'the state' has been much debated within Marxism (Jessop 1982). A high level of autonomy of the state is emphasized by what may be called 'state-centric theories' (Hall 1986, pp. 15–17; Zeitlin 1985, pp. 25–31). These theories argue that policy is not primarily a reaction to pressure from interested social groups, but that the state has interests and policy preferences of its own.

Beyond this initial postulate, 'state-centric' theorists diverge on how to understand the state's actions. Some focus on the internal characteristics of the state often called 'bureaucratic politics'; others on the process of 'social learning'; others on the pre-existing institutional capacities of the state which are brought to bear on new policy problems (Hall 1986, pp. 16–17).

The state-centric approach has much to commend it, and has been used to illuminate several areas of historical analysis, for example Tolliday and Zeitlin (1985) on industrial relations, Evans *et al.* (1985) on the welfare state and related topics, and Cronin (1988) on the broad sweep of British politics. State-centric theories start from general postulates about the state, but it is less clear that they amount to a 'general theory of the state'. Rather, 'once it is acknowledged that states pursue goals which can be derived neither from the play of interest groups nor from the needs of the economy or the class structure, and that their autonomy and coherence vary greatly over time and space, a theoretical focus on states and distinctive structures with their own specific histories becomes unavoidable' (Zeitlin 1985, p. 25).

But in pursuing these specific histories one cannot avoid reference back to the institutions of 'civil society' in relation to which the state's objectives have to be pursued. Thus to assert the state's 'autonomy' is to emphasize it as a decision-making entity, irreducible to interests elsewhere in society. It is not to assert its calculations and capacities to be independent of the network of institutions (national and international) within which it operates.

This emphasis on the importance of institutions naturally leads to the 'institutionalist' approach to politics. This word is commonly used in extremely vague ways, but in the current context it can be given a quite specific meaning as the 'structural setting of the British state that had an important influence over policy' (Hall 1987, p. 279). Thus 'institutions' denotes a set of long-lived (but not permanent) features of British society which form that structure: 'the position of Britain within the international system, the organisational configuration of British society, the institutional structure of the state itself, and the nature of the wider political system, understood as the network of political parties and interest intermediaries that seek to influence policy' (Hall 1987, p. 279).

Institutionalist accounts of British economic performance are extremely powerful, and have provided the most persuasive general analysis of that much-debated phenomenon, the relative decline of the British economy (Elbaum and Lazonick 1987). However, one problem with this framework is its treatment of politics. Take as an example Hall's (1986, ch. 3) account of the failure of the British state to reverse industrial decline. This gives a persuasive account of the institutional relations that have blocked the necessary reformist policies. The analysis concludes with a discussion of the political system and of 'two post-war conjunctures', in which the policies of the British government at these two key periods are outlined. Nevertheless there is little sense of the impact of the broad political system (e.g. Gamble and Walkland 1984) or of the political ideologies and calculations of the governing parties, above all of the possibility that politically things might have been different. This downgrading of the importance of political argument and struggle seems an inherent danger of the institutionalist approach, with its emphasis on deep-laid institutional patterns and their longevity (Thompson 1987).

So far this introduction has focused on the frameworks for analysing public policy. The other issue is how the 'economy' is to be understood. Marxism and neo-classical economics, with all their other differences, start from analyses of the 'economy in general', i.e. independent of any particular national context. Thus Marxism's starting points are modes of production and their laws of motion, neo-classical economics factors of production, markets and the laws of their operation. The vast majority of Marxists and neo-classical economists then go on to analyse particular national economies, but these analyses are always likely to collapse back into the theoretically prior accounts of the economy in general (Cutler *et al.* 1978, ch. 8).

As an alternative we can start from the concept of a national economy (Cutler *et al.* 1978, pp. 243–57). National economies are a crucial level of analysis because

> they are the level at which certain crucial parameters and conditions of operation are determined; these determinations are various and are by no means necessarily 'economic' . . . The concept of 'national' economy does not designate an essence . . . What defines such an economy are the factors which operate to determine and delimit the forms and conditions of economic performance within a region. These factors are not given and may vary. (pp. 244–5).

Clearly such a notion of national economy limits the pertinence of designations such as 'capitalist'. Whilst this concept designates a set of features of the economy—private ownership of the means of production, the separation of the mass of producers from possession of the means of production—it is at a national economy (or other politically defined unit) that these features are determined. To take the most obvious example, whilst all capitalist economies are characterized by private ownership of the means of production, the form within which this operates differs significantly between different nations (or in Western Europe, between larger political jurisdictions like the EC and countries outside it).

For the discussion of twentieth-century public policy the national economy is the obvious unit of concern. Broadly through much of this century national states have augmented their capacities to delimit and regulate a national economy. But this, of course, has never been complete—some features of almost all economies, and certainly open economies like that of Britain, have never been amenable to control at the national level (the lack of national capacity to determine the level of exports would be an obvious example). Equally there is no reason to treat this trend as irreversible or permanent. Indeed some have argued that the capacities of nation states have been significantly eroded by structural changes in the world economy since 1945 (Holland 1975, 1983; Stewart 1983; Tomlinson 1988). Also, a focus on the national economy is not meant to suggest that public policy is wholly internally oriented. Indeed, precisely because national states cannot delimit and determine all the workings of the national economy acting independently, they co-operate to a greater or lesser extent with other states to secure their objectives.

This preliminary sketch of the frameworks which lie behind the organization of this book seeks to make sense of the divisions of the chapters (with the exception of Chapter 7) into 'Institutions', 'Agencies', 'Doctrine', and 'Politics and Policies'. How this division relates to the abstract points made above can perhaps best be shown by a (schematic) example. This example takes the form of a sketch answer to a question: why, by the post-1945 period, was the British economy managed in a manner inconceivable in 1900?

The Rise of the Managed Economy: A Sketch

Institutions

For the rise of a managed economy two kinds of institution are important—those that govern the insertion of a national economy into the world economy, and those that delimit the scope of domestic policy. On the first point, a managed economy emerged from an insertion of the national economy into the world economy governed by the twin institutions of the gold standard and free trade. A gold standard in its pure sense (where domestic and international money are interchangeable) rules out a national monetary policy, as domestic monetary action is automatically neutralized by gold flows into and out of the country. Free trade also restricts the effectiveness of national economic management, as crucial determinants of the level of domestic economic activity (imports and exports) are left unregulated.

The nature of budgetary policy also crucially defines the scope of economic management. If the level of public expenditure is low, and the budget is seen as purely concerned with financing expenditure, then the instruments available for regulation of expenditure flows in the domestic economy are greatly restricted.

Thus the 'pre-managed economy' rested on the institutions of the gold standard, free trade, and a small and balanced budget.

Agencies

This institutional structure was both supportive of and supported by the major policy-making state agencies. The Bank of England and the Treasury regarded these institutions as a bulwark against political intervention in the economy. The Treasury saw its concerns as dominated by defence of the 'fiscal constitution', basically the idea that politicians should not have scope for spending public money unless also willing to bear the political costs of imposing taxes (i.e. no budget deficits). The Bank of England in parallel saw the gold standard as a defender of financial probity and a defence against inflation.

Both the Bank of England and the Treasury were thus decision-making agencies separate from the elected government. They operated in a context dominated by the institutions sketched above on the one side, and the political pressures from government on the other. What 'broke' the pre-managed economy was a combination of the breakdown of the institutional environment and new pressures from the policy. Most importantly, gold, and later free trade, broke down in 1931 not through 'political choice' but through the conflict between maintenance of gold and domestic political objectives. The breakdown substantially destroyed the Bank of England's powers, whilst forcing the Treasury back onto a narrower defence of its traditional position, focused on budgetary policy. National economic management appears unambiguously in the 1930s, but narrowly focused on regulation of the exchange rate and interest rates.

After World War Two the repertoire of instruments of management was extended, notably to embrace fiscal policy. This became acceptable to the Treasury and the Bank of England when it became apparent in wartime that fiscal policy could be efficacious in pursuit of the traditional objective of counter-inflationary policy, and that in this context the use of the fiscal instrument involved no necessary break with the 'fiscal constitution'.

Doctrine

National economic management is a doctrine about the economy. It is a doctrine with many possible variants. In Britain, we know that the Keynesian variant became dominant after World War

Two, but many others were in play prior to that, especially in the 1930s and 1940s, ranging from the Empire protectionism of the 'Imperial Visionaries' to full collectivist planning, with many intermediate 'planning' programmes especially prominent in the 1930s.

The existence of managerialist doctrines is a necessary condition for economic management, but clearly not a sufficient condition. Such doctrines (and particular variants) will be deployed only when they seem to have purchase on current institutional arrangements. Hence the efflorescence of managerial doctrines in the 1930s when the breakdown of the gold standard and free trade undermined the purchase of the old doctrine of 'automaticity', and mass unemployment posed urgent political questions about how it could be reduced.

If we ask further why Keynesianism as a *particular* managerialist ideology triumphed in Britain, this would involve looking at both the internal dynamics of economics as a discourse and the conditions of Keynesianism's insertion into the policy-making process. On the first, we might note that Keynesianism was readily assimilable to existing doctrine as a macro complement to the core microeconomic doctrines of that discourse. Linked to this, Keynesianism was the dominant doctrine of the economists recruited to government service in World War Two, thus providing a channel for the doctrine into the major state agencies. In turn those agencies found Keynesianism congenial because, as already noted, in an environment of excess demand no real break with a non-interventionist strategy *vis-à-vis* the private sector was necessary, because in principle that approach only involved regulation of macro aggregates.

Politics and Policies

The above sketch of the interaction between institutions, agencies, and doctrine leaves out the most important agency of all— governments and their policies. It is important to stress that ultimately it is governments that make policy; we can paraphase Marx and say 'governments make policy, but not in circumstances of their own choosing'. What governments bring to bear are particular forms of political calculation which are in turn embedded in their internal structures (Thompson 1986*b*, ch. 1). At key moments these forms of political calculation were crucial in the movement to a managed economy. In 1929–31 the Labour government's incapacity to either deflate the economy or alternatively devise a programme of managing an expansionary economy doomed the gold standard (and themselves). This failure reflected, above all, the internal character of the Labour party as an unstable combination of profound intellectual conservatism in policy (though radical rhetoric) and defence of the interests of the working class. This generated quite different forms of political calculation and split the party.

After 1939 the Labour Party embraced management via economic planning, but after 1945 this planning was exposed as ill-specified and in conflict with the Labour government's political desire to co-operate with the private sector. The Treasury and its version of Keynesianism were thus able to assert themselves. Equally, for the Conservatives after 1945, the crucial political calculation was that their return to electoral success necessitated a commitment to economic management and full employment. This commitment (unlike in the 1970s and 1980s) was not politically problematic when the buoyant economic environment meant such policies were largely costless in terms of other objectives.

Conclusions

The above is not, of course, intended as more than the briefest thumb-nail sketch of the rise of economic management in Britain. The objectives of making this sketch in the introduction are two-fold. First, to put some, if rather thin, flesh on the abstract points of the section on Frameworks. Second, to provide a bridge from those abstractions to the substantive chapters that follow, where many of the issues raised are looked at in more detail.

One major issue raised again by this sketch is how relevant it is to this framework of analysis that Britain was during this period a capitalist economy. At the most general level the capitalist character (private ownership of the means of production) clearly did matter. One of the primary goals of the state agencies and governments during this period was to maintain private-sector confidence. This goal necessarily inhibited policy; private investment in general had to be maintained at a high level or the whole functioning of the economy would be threatened. More specifically, economic management had to take account of the possibilities of capital flight for example, if domestic policy was deemed 'irresponsible'; or 'gilt strikes' if 'excessive' budget deficits were generated. None of these problems would presumably exist if all capital were in public hands.

But beyond these points, the specification of the British national economy as capitalist tells us rather little about policy-making. The above constraints on policy-making have been counteracted and evaded with very variable degrees of success in a number of capitalist countries, so that little about policy development in capitalist economies would seem derivable from that capitalist character *per se*. Striking evidence of the limited pertinence of the designation capitalist is provided by Marxist writings on Britain's economic decline. These seem to rely strikingly little on general characteristics of capitalism, and to focus on the peculiarities of the British economy in a way which (other than in their rhetoric) makes them, for good or ill, almost indistinguishable from non-Marxist writings on the topic (Barratt-Brown 1988). This serves to reinforce the point already made, that the central concept with which to start talking about public policy should be the national economy.

2

1900–1914: The World we have Lost

At the turn of the twentieth century public policy on the economy was bounded by three institutions, 'the three pillars of the anti-collectivist temple' (Checkland 1983, p. 174)—the gold standard, free trade, and low and balanced budgets. In the period before the First World War these three came under varying degrees of challenge and strain, but, with qualification, they remained the crucial framework for events up to 1914. This chapter must therefore begin with an account of these three pillars of the late Victorian economy.

Institutions

The Gold Standard

Three basic features define the gold standard: (*a*) inter-convertibility between domestic money and gold at a fixed official price; (*b*) freedom for private citizens to import and export gold, and (*c*) a set of rules relating the quantity of money in circulation in a country to that country's gold stock (Eichengreen 1985, pp. 3–4).

Britain was *de facto* on such a standard from the early eighteenth century, when silver coins were driven from circulation, and on a full legal standard from 1821. But as an international system, the gold standard was strikingly short-lived—running only from around 1880 to 1914. Despite its transitory character the gold standard has attracted an enormous volume of academic discussion, especially on the question of how balance of payments adjustment took place under such a regime. Much of this discussion has mirrored changing fashion in economic theories—thus analyses focusing on price adjustment were challenged in the 1930s by Keynesian theories focusing on income adjustment, to be themselves challenged in the 1970s by theories developed from the revival of the quantity theory of money (Foreman-Peck 1983, ch. 6; Goodhart 1986, ch. 14; Eichengreen 1985; Bordo 1984).

From the point of view of British policy the crucial feature of the gold standard regime was its 'painless' character. It was a regime which seems to have imposed no substantial costs on any agent in the economy, and in consequence, and unlike in many other countries, came under no substantial challenge in this period. There was no serious balance of payments crisis in Britain between 1866 and 1914 (Matthews *et al*. 1982, p. 456), though it has been suggested that the system was already under pressure before 1914 as Britain's international financial predominance was eroded (de Cecco 1974).

Whatever their theoretical stance, most modern commentaries on the golden standard agree that its smooth working (from a British point of view) owed little to the internal logic of its mechanisms and much to the peculiarity of the British economy's relation to the world economy (Bloomfield 1968, pp. 26–30). Above all this relation was characterized by London's domination of world financial markets, involving very large-scale flows of short-term money into and out of London. Broadly put, this meant that the mechanism of the Bank Rate, whereby in times of unacceptable gold outflow the Bank of England would raise interest rates, largely affected the money markets and only the money markets. A small cessation of overseas lending would quickly offset the gold loss, and thus attain the policy of maintaining the desired level of gold reserves. Of course, for countries not in such favourable financial markets, such ease of adjustment was not available, and departure from gold was a fairly frequent occurrence for countries on the periphery of the system (e.g. de Cecco 1974).

In principle attachment to gold meant allowing the domestic economy to adjust to world events, rather than attempting to smooth its path either in terms of prices or output. Since a condition of the gold standard was that gold supplies were the ultimate determinant of the world money supply, prices world-wide would respond at least in part to fluctuations in the discovery and mining of gold. Such a fluctuation may be seen in the last quarter of the nineteenth century, when the general trend of prices in Britain and the world went down.

In many countries, just contemplating or just having joined the gold standard system, such deflationary pressures led to serious attacks on the standard, as the sufferers from deflation fought for an alternative monetary regime. But in Britain no such problem emerged on a serious scale. Whilst academic economists hotly debated the costs and benefits of the monetization of silver (e.g. Marshall 1926; C. 5512, 1888) there was no substantial political pressure for departure from gold—Britain was overwhelmingly a country of wage earners, with few of the agrarian mortgagees who provided the backbone of anti-gold-standard sentiment in other countries (Tomlinson 1981*a*, ch. 2; Ford 1962).

By 1900 price trends were moving clearly upwards, partly under the impact of gold discoveries in Australia and South Africa. After 1900 this trend continued, and was accompanied by substantial unrest, especially in the years immediately before the First World War.[1] However, whilst stagnant real wages formed part of the background to this unrest, as money wages lagged behind price increases (Table 2.1), this disparity did not lead to attacks on the monetary regime, but struggles over the level of money wages.

The question of money wages is important to our general understanding of the gold standard and its policy implications. In principle accepting international trends in prices will be painless if domestic costs fully adjust i.e. prices and wages adjust rather than output and employment. Such a nirvana of price and wage flexibility has probably never existed. But between the wars, some commentators saw a decline in wage flexibility during the First World War and after, and ascribed the conflict between the gold standard and employment to this new inflexibility (see discussion in Keynes 1981; Wright 1981, pp. 298–302).

Certainly, wages before the First World War did show a degree of flexibility. In the 'down' phases of the trade cycle in the period between 1860 and the War, money wages fell by an average of 0.48 per cent per annum (Phelps Brown and Browne 1968, p. 69). But there seems little clear relation between this flexibility and responses to international forces transmitted by the gold standard. Wages fell in the periods 1874–82, 1901–5, and 1907–9, and whilst each of these episodes was preceded by a sharp rise in Bank Rate, there seem to have been other rises which did not have this

---

[1] How far price trends in this period should be interpreted as a matter of gold supplies is highly controversial. Lewis (1978), ch. 4, for example, emphasizes changes in the terms of trade (manufacturing relative to commodity prices), which in turn depended upon an acceleration in demand for, but deceleration in supply of, primary commodities. Thus the price trends were a response to 'real' not monetary forces.

Table 2.1   *Prices and Wages 1900–1913* (1913 = 100)

	Retail prices	Average weekly wage rates	Average weekly wage earnings
1900	89	97	95
1901	88	95	94
1902	88	94	92
1903	89	93	92
1904	90	93	90
1905	90	92	90
1906	91	94	92
1907	91	94	97
1908	91	94	95
1909	92	94	95
1910	94	94	95
1911	95	95	96
1912	98	98	99
1913	100	100	100

Source: Feinstein (1972), Table 65, p. T140–1.

accompaniment—e.g. in 1864, 1866, and 1890. There was a strong trade cycle element in wages in this period, but no unambiguous relation to the gold standard (Phelps Brown and Browne 1968, ch. 1B; for the course of Bank Rate see Clapham 1944, appendix B; also generally, Bordo 1981).

From the point of view of analysing the policy regime the important issue is how far the gold standard was sustained by wage flexibility, and how far by the 'peculiar' international position of the British economy. The argument here is that it is the latter which is crucial (Eichengreen 1985, introduction). The effectiveness of the gold standard was tied to the status of London as a financial market, which in turn meant that the burden of adjustment fell largely on foreigners rather than British wage-earners.

For the governing classes, advocates rather than recipients of fluctuating incomes, the attraction of the gold standard lay primarily in two features. First, and least problematic of those, was its anti-inflationary character. Whilst the precise mechanisms may be disputed, the gold standard before 1914 did (and was widely perceived to) provide a defence against inflation in the national economy. Any substantial rise in domestic prices, unmatched elsewhere, would lead to gold loss and the need for remedy via measures which would deflate the domestic economy. This link between gold and inflation was seen as having been clearly demonstrated in the Napoleonic Wars, when wartime inflationary finance had only been sustainable by a suspension of gold payments (Fetter 1965).

Second in the attractions of the gold standard was its alleged automatic character. It was widely agreed, across a broad political spectrum, that the monetary system was too important to be in the hands of politicians. The dominant theory of the gold standard at this time, Hume's specie-flow mechanism (see Hume, 1985), implied just such a consequence, as it held that international gold flows would lead to domestic money supply and price adjustment which would equilibrate the system without recourse to any discretionary national action.

In fact the body charged with maintaining Britain on the gold standard had a substantial degree of discretion in how this was done (see section on the Bank of England below). Nevertheless this notion of automaticity was important. Whilst the Bank of England had room for manœuvre in its management of the gold standard, it nevertheless had to sustain that standard, and this put clear and narrow limits on the scope for discretionary national monetary management. Such national monetary management never came on to the agenda in this period, when the benefits of gold appeared so manifest and the costs so few. But events in many other countries had made clear before 1914 the threat of a clash between such management and the gold standard in less propitious circumstances.

Free Trade

The second crucial Victorian inheritance of the twentieth century was Free Trade. Unlike the gold standard, this had already come under challenge before 1900, and was to do so again in the pre-war years. But like the gold standard it was to endure in its pristine glory through to 1914.

We are not concerned here with how and why free trade became so firmly entrenched in Britain in the middle of the nineteenth century. Suffice to say in the current context that this should not be reduced to the manifestation of an unambiguous interest ('the interest of the middle classes') nor the simple triumph of a doctrine of *laissez-passer*, blood brother of *laissez-faire*. Such approaches should be at least qualified by a recognition of the political institutions within which the policy emerged, such as the short-term political calculations of Peel at the time of the repeal of the Corn Laws (Bentley 1985), or the pecularities of the ideology and practices of the Anti-Corn Law League (McCord 1968). More broadly the link between free trade and the distrust of the state should be noted, based on a perception of the state's corruption and inefficiency, which was so important to the Victorian world view. Finally one should note the interdependence of the revenue implications of free trade and small budgets, and consequently the way in which free trade emerged simultaneously with the reorganization of public finances to provide revenue from a very narrow range of customs and excise duties and a low income tax (see further below, section on the Budget).

This free-trade regime came under challenge in the 1880s. The challenge involved a double thrust both against the alleged economic consequences of free trade in terms of unemployment, and against its ideological trappings of 'cosmopolitanism' and its lack of a national economy consciousness. Whilst the 'Fair Traders' of the 1880s made arguments, especially on the state of Britain's balance of payments which we know to be extremely dubious, they forged a new link between the state of employment and trade which set an agenda of discussion which never subsequently disappeared. They did this in the 1880s, parallel to the emergence of a new concern with unemployment (see section below on Politics and Policies).

The policy offered by opponents of free trade was that of *managing* trade to achieve national economic objectives. A number of objectives were possible and emerged clearly in the renewed Tariff Reform controversy after 1903. One objective was full employment—as in the 1880s, tariff reformers at times stressed the priority of jobs over cheap imports: 'those who try to induce you to believe that everything depends upon the price of corn are deceiving you. What you have to find is employment— plenty of employment and the best wages you can get for that employment' (Chamberlain 1904).

At the same time Tariff Reformers were able to draw upon the newly emerging data on poverty to argue the ineffectual nature of free trade in generating national prosperity (e.g. Amery 1969, p. 267).

But the objectives of the would-be reformers were not confined to the economic objectives of employment and higher real incomes. For Chamberlain, the leader of the movement, one (perhaps *the*) central concern was tariff reform as an accompaniment to Imperial Preference, itself a support of a grand design of (White) Imperial Unity (Zebel 1967; Amery 1969; but compare Green 1985, who emphasizes the electoral reasons for Chamberlain's campaign). Thus for Chamberlain the claims of uniting the Empire largely predominated over the claims of cheap food and cheap raw materials to which his opponents gave priority, and predominated over the emphasis of his own leader (Balfour) on retaliatory tariffs (Zebel 1967, p. 155).

But probably most challenging to the existing policy regime was the third element of the Tariff Reformers' argument. This viewed tariff reform as a source of revenue for programmes of social welfare, the basis of a 'social imperialism' designed to link, via welfare, the working-class voter to the Conservative Party and its imperialism (Semmel 1960). There may well have been incoherence in such a proposal—how could tariffs simultaneously keep non-Empire goods out and generate large-scale state revenues? But economic rationality is not usually a pre-condition for the pursuit of a political programme, and in this instance what is important is how the strategy of social imperialism offered a way of 'squaring the circle' of a limited tax base and growing welfare expenditure which in many ways defined the predominant public policy concern of the era (Murray 1980, p. 19). It thus challenged simultaneously free trade and budgetary orthodoxy (see further below).

The Chamberlainite challenge to the free trade regime failed. At the broadest political level it failed to capture substantial working-class support, despite its emphasis on employment creation. Thus in 1906 the Conservatives suffered from the failure to 'adopt the party of privilege, property and aristocracy to the exigencies of democratic politics' (Green 1985, p. 692). This failure was in part highly contingent on immediate circumstance—the revival of the economy after 1904. In the absence of cyclical distress and unemployment, the Liberal linking of free trade to cheap food and cheap raw materials was compelling for many of the electorate. At a rather more sophisticated level, they could stress the efficiency effects on domestic producers of free trade, and the political dangers inherent in designing a tariff (see section on Doctrine below).

Free trade thus survived its Edwardian buffeting. But the legacy of that period also included a Conservative Party that, despite the electoral trauma of 1906, had become basically a tariff reform party, awaiting an electoral opportunity. In addition the controversy had made a linkage between the state of trade and the level of employment which was never, in the twentieth century, to disappear from the repertoire of public policy debate.

The Budget

As in the case of free trade, the emergence of the Victorian tradition of low and balanced budgets can only too readily be assigned to a facile monocausal reason—either one of interests ('the middle-class taxpayers') or of doctrine ('the ideology of *laissez-faire*'). This emergence is not the focus of concern here, but it is important to emphasize both the general complexity of the issue, and especially the linkages between this tradition and other facets of the Victorian policy regime. Roseveare (1969, p. 143) locates the tradition as follows:

> Hindsight makes this appear to be wholly Gladstonian, but of course it was not. The tradition was shaped by at least two fundamental obsessions of early nineteenth-century England—the elimination or reduction of the National Debt, and the attainment and preservation of free trade. The latter objective required, at its simplest, that public income and expenditure should balance at the lowest possible figure; the former, that there should be, if possible, some balance of income over expenditure. Taken together these requirements hedged budgetary policy into the narrow path of strict public parsimony. Of course other factors played their part . . . but the Debt and free trade were the major formative influences.

As already noted, the commitment to free trade had been coupled to a narrow tax base in a small range of commodity taxes, and a low income tax. Up to the fourth quarter of the nineteenth century this had provided an elastic tax base, with the general rise in incomes per head and the high income elasticities of the taxed commodities. Public expenditure was stable in absolute (constant price) terms from the 1820s to the 1870s, but was a falling share of National Income (Peacock and Wiseman 1967, p. 35). In this period we may helpfully think of the progress of the revenue determining expenditure, with little pressure from the expenditure side to strain against the volume of revenue gathering, indeed with a budget surplus as the norm.[2]

In the 1870s this happy compatibility came under pressure. Initially the problem appeared as one of the inelasticity of indirect tax revenues in the face of the depression of the early part of the decade. But in the face of continuous upward pressure thereafter from both social and especially defence expenditure the whole tenor of budgetary policy changed. (Defence spending rose from 33 per cent of the total to 41 per cent in 1905—a peacetime record, Hicks 1958, p. 14). No longer was the Chancellor in the position of not knowing 'what to do' with the revenues pouring in, but rather continuously looking for new ways to increase revenue (Roseveare 1969, pp. 190–1).

Most high Victorian tax revenue was raised from the consumption taxes on tea, coffee, sugar, beer, and spirits. Income tax was a subsidiary tax, perceived by many as a temporary expedient. This system rested on the presumption that paying taxes was part of citizenship. 'Victorians tended to regard taxes as a useful moral discipline in making the taxpayer recognise his responsibilities as a member of the body politic.' (Hicks 1958, p. 71.) Conversely graduated taxation, according to ability to pay, was regarded by Gladstone and Gladstonians as 'confiscation', as opening the path to socialism and communism (Roseveare 1969, p. 191).

But in the face of sustained upward pressure on the expenditure side, taxes on income and capital expanded their share of revenue, from 13 per cent in 1880 to 35 per cent by 1913 (Hicks 1958, p. 75, Table 6). In 1894 a crucial breakthrough to a new tax regime was made when Harcourt introduced progressive death duties. Such a step on the road to perdition in Gladstonian eyes was substantially reinforced by the growing current concern with the incidence of

---

[2] Robert Lowe, a disciple of Gladstone, said 'I would define a Chancellor of the Exchequer as an animal who ought to have a surplus; if except under extraordinary conditions he has not a surplus he fails to fulfil the very ends and object of his being'. (Cited Hicks (1953), p. 25.) For a modern general defence of the Gladstonian tradition, see Baysinger and Tollison (1980).

taxation, especially with indirect taxes in general and the impoverished Irish in particular (Rees 1921, pp. 170–1).

The principle of a substantial Sinking Fund to reduce the National Debt proved more resistant to challenge. This principle rested on three elements. First, the idea that posterity should not be burdened with the current generation's debts. Second, that payments of interest on the Debt were an undesirable transfer from active to inactive members of society. Finally, the fear that borrowing by the State would put the City in too powerful a position in determining interest on the Debt (Checkland 1983, p. 178).

Debt redemption out of budget surpluses under the 1875 Sinking Fund meant that, until the South African War, the National Debt was reduced substantially—from £724m. in 1886 to £635m. in 1899. In the last year of the nineteenth century, Hicks-Beach's proposal to reduce the contribution to the Sinking Fund from £7.5m. to £5.8m. (in a budget of £108m.) aroused a storm of protest (Mallett 1913, pp. 133–148). After the South African War had driven the Debt up to £798m. in 1903, the process of reduction continued, so that with all the expansion of expenditure and budgetary strain of the pre-war years, the Debt had fallen back to £706m. by 1914, including a redemption of an astonishing £16.6m. in 1907/8 (Checkland 1983, p. 178; Hargreaves 1930, pp. 222–8).

Even if the Sinking Fund had been abandoned—and it never looked likely—the upward pressure on expenditure would have necessitated a sharp rise in taxation to finance its approximate doubling between the (peacetime) budget of 1899 and the last peacetime budget before World War One (Table 2.2). As already noted, revenue came increasingly from direct rather than indirect taxes, and it was the attempt to expand this form of tax, and newly to include land, that precipitated the crisis over the 'People's Budget' of 1909.

From the point of view of the overall policy regime, as opposed to party politics (see below on Politics and Policies), the main importance of the 1909 budget was that it offered a way of financing social reform without breaking with free trade. This, indeed, was a reason for the depth of Unionist opposition to the budget (Murray 1980, pp. 13–14). Ultimately the struggle over the budget established that, for the time being, increasing welfare expenditure could be financed without tariff reform, albeit only by enhancing the progressivity of tax, and building on the distinction in Asquith's 1907 budget between earned and unearned income, which licensed an especial focus on a tax on increasing land values. Along the way it was established that the House of Commons would be sovereign in finance matters, with no effective constraint from the House of Lords.

Table 2.2   *Government Expenditure (Local and Central) 1895–1913*

	National Debt		Military		Social Services		Economic Services		Total	
	(a)	(b)	(a)	(b)	(a)	(b)	(a)	(b)	(a)	(b)
1895	22.7	1.5	43.1	2.9	39.7	2.6	18.4	1.2	156.8	10.4
1900	19.6	1.0	134.9	6.9	50.6	2.6	36.4	1.9	280.8	14.4
1905	24.4	1.2	63.1	3.2	68.3	3.5	39.4	2.0	241.7	12.3
1910	20.2	0.9	74.3	3.5	89.1	4.2	37.8	1.8	272.0	12.7
1913	18.7	0.8	91.3	3.7	100.8	4.1	39.5	1.6	305.4	12.4

(a) Expenditure in £m., current prices.
(b) % of G.N.P.
Source: Peacock and Wiseman (1967), tables A–15, A–17, pp. 184,190.

By 1914 no effective challenge had been mounted to the gold standard, the system had become 'a state of mind, almost unquestioned, within the Bank, throughout the City, and in the outlook of governments' (Checkland 1983, p. 167) though in retrospect some have seen serious weaknesses undermining its sustainability (de Cecco 1974). Free trade had been successfully defended from powerful challenge, although it no longer commanded the support of one of the two major political parties. The Victorian budgetary tradition in one crucial respect had disappeared—the growth of expenditure had for thirty years outpaced the growth of the National Income, and expenditure minimization was no longer seriously pursued. One crucial consequence of this change was the acceptance of the principle of tax progressivity. At the same time the desire to obtain a budget surplus to reduce the Debt remained as strong as ever. The budget was still a way of finding the resources to finance expenditure; it had become a weapon of redistribution but not yet of economic management.

Agencies

The Bank of England

As any account of the British economy's institutional context at this time must begin with the gold standard, so any account of the major agencies must begin with the Bank of England. This was the body charged, above all, with the maintenance of Britain's gold reserves and adherence to that standard.

The Bank remained throughout this period a private institution. Nevertheless, since the time of William III it had slowly acquired powers and responsibilities which turned it into a central bank. Founded initially to circumvent the monarchy's financial problems following Charles I's reneging on his debts, it had been greatly aided by the circumstances of the Napoleonic Wars in which it had expanded its credit to government in return for an effective promise to be bailed out of any crisis. The notes of the Bank were formally made legal tender in 1812, and an Act of 1826 put restrictions on other banks' note-issuing powers. By the Bank Charter Act of 1844 the Bank of England became the 'conduit' for regulating the money supply through its control of the note issue. Other banks were willing to cede this monopoly position to the Bank because by mid-century the rise of cheques meant that the note issue was becoming less important in the total money supply. On this monopoly of the note issue was founded the monopoly of the gold reserves (Clapham 1944, vol. i).

This growth of Bank pre-eminence was not smooth or without opposition. In the mid-nineteenth century part of the reason for Gladstone's policy of balanced or surplus budgets was to prevent the government being in a 'false' position in relation to the Bank and the City. Budget surpluses meant that 'a Chancellor now never had to beg' (Clapham 1944, vol. ii, p. 274; Morley 1903, vol. i, p. 650). However once the Bank was established as the monopolist of the note issue it was bound to be protected by the government. And as the government's borrowing expanded, despite Gladstone's best endeavours, the Bank enhanced its role as manager of the National Debt.

The Bank's private status but growing public responsibility unsurprisingly created tensions. Most important of these was the low level of gold reserves held, because unlike other assets these yielded no income to the Bank (see further below). But it cannot be said that in this period any clash arose between the Bank and public authorities. The politicians after 1900 were too pre-occupied elsewhere to concern themselves with the Bank's doings. The Bank was left 'singularly free of all legislative restriction of its operations' (Sayers 1936, p. 135), and conducted its activities in a highly secretive and largely unaccountable fashion.

Those activities centred on a single objective—to maintain the gold reserves. Most of the time this involved manipulation of the Bank Rate, but this was by no means a mechanical operation. The Bank was granted, and exercised, a great deal of discretion in how it defended the reserve, belying the expectations of early nineteenth-century monetary reformers: 'Some of the sponsors of the Bank Charter Act of 1844 thought they were reducing the art of central banking to a rule of thumb; how great would have been their surprise if they could have sat in the Bank parlour on a Treasury morning 60 years later'. (Morgan 1943, p. 227.)

A major concern of the Bank's weekly deliberations was how to make its Bank Rate effective in the money markets. In the third quarter of the nineteenth century Bank Rate had been largely passive—following rather than leading market rates. But over the next decades the Bank's leverage over market rates increased as it used Bank Rate more and more as a penal rate for borrowing by the discount houses. These houses were increasingly in the business of discounting international rather than domestic bills of exchange (the latter undermined by the growth of chequing), so that the Bank Rate impacted directly on international transactions (Sayers 1957, p. 13).

But this growing effectiveness of Bank Rate exposed the Bank to the criticism that it disrupted markets by excessively frequent adjustments of that rate. Unfavourable comparisons were drawn with French practice, where rate changes were much less frequent. This difference resulted from the small volume of gold reserves (about £40m. against an annual import bill of over £600m.), which meant that the Bank was operating on low margins of safety, and could not afford to see much gold loss before taking action (Sayers 1976, pp. 9–10; Lewis 1978, pp. 34–5).

Particularly in the period from the 1890s to the early 1900s this problem led to the frequent use of 'gold devices' as an alternative or supplement to Bank Rate manipulation. These devices included such action as the Bank offering above the official price in the gold market, or giving interest-free loans to gold imports (Sayers 1936, ch. 4). The gold devices were also useful as an alternative to raising the Bank Rate where such a rise would cause difficulties for the Bank's other major responsibility—managing the government debt. Thus in 1900 the Bank used them to avoid a Bank Rate increase cutting across the government's loan for fighting the South African war (Sayers 1936, p. 92). But it is important to note that, in this period, debt management was very much subsidiary to managing the gold reserve in the Bank's concerns.

In the new century the favourable position on the balance of payments increased the gold reserves, and the use of Bank Rate as the primary weapon reasserted itself in the years immediately prior to 1914. This was encouraged by the very successful use of the Bank Rate in 1907 to reverse the flow of gold at the time of financial crisis (Sayers 1936, pp. 93–5).

In conducting its operations the Bank's primary concern was always its responsibility to preserve the gold reserve. But it was not wholly insensitive to claims that Bank Rate changes had side effects on home trade. The Bank seems to have believed that such changes exhausted themselves in the money markets, but faced a growing (though never very large) volume of dissent from this view. Following complaints about the impact of the 1906/7 Bank Rate increase, in 1909 the Bank conducted an enquiry into how far Bank Rate charges impacted on traders and manufacturers via charges in overdraft rates. Sayers (1976, p. 44) summarizes the results of this survey as follows: 'on the whole . . . the impression is irresistible . . . movements in Bank Rate did not matter so very much outside the Banks and financial markets' (see also Ford 1969, pp. 106–14; Dutton 1984).

In the last years before the War the Bank's operations were much more straightforward than in previous decades. An atypical combination of circumstances—sustained trade activity, record volumes of lending, help from the joint-stock banks—allowed a limited and almost mechanical use of the Bank Rate to defend the gold position. This indeed seems to have been the period the Cunliffe Committee of 1918 (Cd. 9182) drew on in its rather idealized account of the pre-war gold standard (Sayers 1936, pp. 137–8). This provided an unhelpful benchmark against which to judge the desirability of a return to gold in the 1920s.

Overall the status of the Bank of England in policy-making in this period is extraordinary to modern eyes. Here was a private and largely unregulated body charged with the management of one of the primary institutions of public policy—the gold standard. And as should be clear from the above paragraphs, it was a question of management—the Bank was never simply a conduit of impulses from the international to the domestic economy. Such an 'anomaly' was only sustainable because of the conditions of the pre-war world economy. Once the insulation of external finance from the domestic economy was no longer possible, the status and powers of the Bank unavoidably came under attack.

The Treasury

Central to state policy on the economy during this period was the Treasury. However the range of concerns of this body, in comparison with a later age, was strikingly narrow. Its responsibilities lay almost entirely in the field of public finance, but were far from covering the whole of this field. The autonomy of the Bank of England, and the monetary orthodoxy that sustained it, meant that the Treasury had little to say in Bank Rate decisions. Debt management, not in any event a very important concern in this period, lay outside the Treasury's remit. The central concern of the Treasury was thus very much with the control of public expenditure and taxation.

In 1927 an ex-Treasury civil servant defined the Treasury as 'responsible for the administration of the public finances of the country' . . . 'in essence it is the one permanent institution which stands between the country and national bankruptcy' (Heath 1927, p. 1). This sense of both the importance and the narrowness of Treasury responsibility well summarizes its activities in late nineteenth- and early twentieth-century Britain.

In the third quarter of the nineteenth century the Treasury's Gladstonian role as minimizer of public expenditure was already clear, but not easy to perform. Control over departmental expenditure at this time was largely operated on an *ad hoc* and negative basis, that is, it came into play only when a department tried to increase its expenditure. The Treasury had no basis for calling for expenditure reductions, or looking at departmental efficiency (Roseveare 1969, p. 205). But the last decades of the century saw the Treasury role change to much more that of a co-ordinator, parallel with the growth of Parliamentary control over expenditure through the Public Accounts Committee and the Exchequer and Audit Department. This was especially so in the twenty-five years before the war, when Treasury control became effective over other government departments, threatening the use of Orders in Council against dissentients, and introducing uniform procedures into departmental financial administration (Wright 1972, pp. 224–6).

This did not of course make the Treasury omniscient. Its role could be reduced if it faced a powerful enough political combination at Cabinet level. And its writ was especially difficult to enforce on the service departments, notably when the periodic naval scares of the late nineteenth century were used as political leverage for higher expenditure. Nevertheless, the centrality of the Treasury in the state machine, implicit in its role as defender of the public purse, was largely realized before World War One.

There was a substantial paradox in this, because the extension of the Treasury's effective powers coincided with a rapid expansion of public expenditure which ran directly against the continuing ethos of that body as 'defender of the taxpayer'. For proponents of enhanced expenditure this posture of the Treasury was seen as an 'anomaly and usurpation' administered by 'inexperienced young pedants' (Roseveare 1969, p. 185). This conflict was particularly sharp in relation to those who proposed grand schemes of imperial expenditure. Salisbury, the Prime Minister, was moved in 1900 to mount a public attack on this state body for holding back many desirable developments especially in the imperial field by its control of the purse strings (Roseveare 1969, p. 183).

The Treasury, then, was perceived by many to be carrying Gladstonian traditions of public expenditure into a new age which rendered those traditions inappropriate. This assessment seems fair, given the powerful pressures for enhanced expenditure both for warfare and welfare that the new century brought. And in this struggle the Treasury in aggregate can't be said to have been very successful, given the scale of growth of public expenditure that occurred.

However one should not exaggerate the break with Gladstonian tradition, nor too much emphasize the weakening of the Treasury.

First, whilst the Treasury's Gladstonian obsession with debt reduction abated in the two decades before the First World War, as already noted the policy on the Sinking Fund was continued. This was important in restricting the size of impact of public borrowing—this was not yet on a large enough scale to form an instrument of economic management. (And the bulk of what debt did exist was not monetized, so that any impact on the money supply was very limited.)

Second, the Treasury attachment to free trade as an accompaniment to budgetary responsibility was one of the reasons for Chamberlain's failure in the pursuit of Tariff Reform. Treasury civil servants were widely believed to have been unconstitutionally avid in their campaign to defeat anti-free-trade proposals (Roseveare 1969, pp. 220–3).

Despite, then, the rise in public expenditure, other parts of the Treasury's view on the appropriate conduct of policy were far from destroyed. Its role as co-ordinator of the Civil Service, and the day-to-day powers that involved, continued to be enhanced. However, its role was reduced under the Liberals from 1906. Unlike in 1902/3 it could not exploit divisions within the government to pursue its point of view. It was unhappy with the public expenditure implications of the Liberal reforms, but could do little to resist them in the political climate of the period. In this 'period of intricate, radical innovations which placed a premium on imagination and initiative the Treasury was momentarily eclipsed' (Roseveare 1969, p. 233). But in the long view the emphasis should be on the 'momentarily'; the circumstances of the war and post-war period were to make the Treasury the dominant institution in economic policy-making, which position it has retained ever since.

The Board of Trade

The Board of Trade never attained a role anywhere near equivalent to the Bank of England or the Treasury in this period. But it should not be neglected in a discussion of the agencies of policy for two reasons. First, and most simply, its role did expand substantially from the 1880s. Second, this expansion and the reasons for it relate to important reorientations of public policy that were taking place at this time.

The mid-nineteenth-century triumph of free trade, and the consequent displacement of duties for protection by duties for revenue, substantially reduced the Board of Trade's importance, and enhanced that of the Treasury (Llewellyn-Smith 1928, p. 57). The Board of Trade was left with a rag-bag of largely commercial and industrial responsibilities, which gave it no claim on a central place in policy-making in the hey day of *laissez-faire*.

However from the 1880s the growing concern with 'the labour problem' and unemployment (see below, sections on Doctrine and Politics and Policy) opened a space for a revival of the Board of Trade's activities. From the 1860s there were pressures for the collection and publication of statistics on labour issues. In the 1880s these pressures culminated in the Board of Trade taking on responsibility for such data, including statistics on wages and unemployment. This new responsibility devolved on the Board of Trade not because it fell within the Board's administrative responsibility (the Home Office had a stronger claim, as the Ministry responsible for the Factory and Mines Inspectorate), but because of its statistical expertise. Partly as a legacy from the era of protection, the Board produced most of the very limited economic statistics then available (Davidson 1972, pp. 229–32).

This role, expanded by the creation of a Labour Department at the Board in 1893, was resisted not only by the Home Office, but also by the Treasury. In part the Treasury's view was simply part of its general opposition to an expansion of public expenditure. But it also foresaw the danger that the production of statistics would lead to pressures for 'something to be done' with much more serious implications for the state's role. The Treasury's view of the Board was that it was 'taking advantage of public interest in the topics with which it dealt in order to make exorbitant demands upon the exchequer' (Davidson 1985*b*, p. 724).

The Treasury pressed its views by trying to confine the Board of Trade's role in labour affairs to a purely statistical one, and having a conservative statistician, Robert Giffen, put in charge. Many in the Board of Trade saw the collection of labour statistics as a way of refuting the claims of the Left about current conditions (Davidson 1985*a*, pp. 264–7). But the Treasury was probably right to foresee that such statistics would escape their conditions of emergence, and be used to support reformist programmes.

By the turn of the century it could be said that in so far as the state took any role in industrial relations, most of that role was played no longer by the Home Office, as for most of the nineteenth century, but by the Board of Trade. This was greatly reinforced by its responsibility for the administration of the Industrial Conciliation Act of 1896.

In the new century this role was enhanced by the addition of responsibilities for the Trade Boards and Labour Exchanges in 1909. Both of these were pressed as the logical extension of the Board's statistical role, especially in the face of the failure of any other Ministry (notably the Local Government Board, responsible for the Poor Law) to provide adequate data on labour issues. Also important were the civil servants and politicians who, because of the Board's 'expert' status, were able to build it up into a key ministry in the period of the Liberal reforms after 1906.

Whilst the concern with labour and unemployment certainly did not originate with the Board of Trade, it did have a major impact on the form and implications of that concern. As Davidson (1972, pp. 260–1) argues, the Board of Trade's statistical role had three, largely unintended, consequences. It focused public attention, in the way a Royal Commission would. It defined some of the issues for public debate. And it provided feedback on the impact of policy.

Although its role in the area of labour was greatly enhanced, largely accounting for the 595 per cent increase in expenditure between 1900 and 1914, the Board's other concerns stagnated. Whilst there was growing concern in this period over the balance of payments position and the competitiveness of the British economy, little officially was done to translate these concerns into statistics or action. No official balance of payments (as opposed to trade) statistics were collected. On the production side, a Census of Production was inaugurated in 1907 but yielded no clear message, and was in any event of little significance in an age before government dreamt of taking on responsibility for either individual industries or the progress of industry in general.

Doctrine

The impact of economic theory on public policy towards the economy was minimal before 1914. The reasons were both intellectual and institutional.

Intellectually, the predominant concern of the small but growing number of professional economists in British at this time was with working out the implications of the 'marginalist revolution' of the late nineteenth century, which had displaced much of the classical orthodoxy, especially of course in the theory of value and price (Blaug 1985). Hutchison (1953, p. 344) notes a 'striking' absence of concern with crises and trade cycles in Britain economics in the 1890–1920 period. Most of the dominant neo-classical school saw trade cycle theory as the 'last chapter' of the book of economic theory, to be arrived at only when the much more important implications of 'maximizing' analysis and self-equilibrating dynamics had been worked through. The trade cycle was receiving increased study 'very much as a special problem of abnormality, or "pathology" to be tackled after the "normal" laws are discovered' (Hutchison 1953, p. 409, also pp. 374–5).

This approach to the trade cycle was similar to the approach to unemployment—it was increasingly talked about by economists, but as an issue which was *theoretically* not that problematic. Economists were not by any means simple-minded advocates of 'market forces' as a solution to unemployment, but they did not see any fundamental challenge to existing economic theory in the existence of pools of unused labour power.

Economists were also concerned with monetary theory, but this was largely in a separate compartment from discussions of the trade cycle, and was concerned with problems and elaborations of the quantity theory of money, such as bimetallism (Morgan 1943, p. 228). Only right on the eve of the First World War did Hawtrey's *Good and Bad Trade* attempt an integration of monetary and trade-cycle theory, the intellectual basis for much of the later development of macroeconomics.

Hence the economists did not have very much to say on many of the issues which dominated public policy on the economy in this period. (For one exception, see below.) In any event, even if the economists' concerns had been more closely attuned to the policy-makers, their impact would probably have been limited. For whilst one can outline the main concerns of contemporary economists, at this time they had not built themselves up into a body of professional experts that would be called on as a matter of course in economic policy discussions.

The number of professional economists was very small, and only in 1890 had they begun to publish the Economic Journal as an organ of professional opinion. No economists were employed as professionals by the Civil Service. Although individual economists were consulted by Ministries (e.g. the Treasury consulted both Marshall and Jevons in the late nineteenth century), there was no systematic channels of influence available for economics to shape policy formation.

When economic expertise was perceived as necessary, for example by the Treasury in its budget making, it usually called on other than the professional economists. Typically this would involve people from the City, ex-Chancellors of the Exchequer, non-economist civil servants in other Ministries (Coats 1968, pp. 184–5). Similarly the Bank of England could draw upon a body of 'doctrine' in analysing its role, but this was much more a set of practical dicta than a recognizable theory of monetary policy (Morgan 1943, pp. 242–4; Checkland 1957).

Individual economists did play a considerable advisory role during the Tariff Reform controversy of the early 1900s (Coats 1964, 1968). Most of the neo-classicals supported the free-trade position, albeit with a substantial degree of theoretical qualification for the pure free-trade case. Both Pigou's and Marshall's critique of Tariff Reform was indeed notable for its argument that whilst economically a case could be made for tariffs under certain circumstances, such a course should be avoided because of the political dangers it raised (Pigou 1904; Marshall 1926; Winch 1972, ch. 3). On the other side of the argument were ranged most of the economic historians and the non-neo-classicals.

In August 1903 fourteen professional economists wrote a joint letter to *The Times* attacking Tariff Reform. The response to this indicated the low esteem attached to academic economists, an esteem not helped by the evident differences of view amongst them. Whilst much of the debate focused on economic issues (though often with little empirical basis for debating the issues), it cannot be said that economics was central to the outcome of the Tariff Reform debate. The preponderant calculations were in political, diplomatic, and strategic terms. Economic issues were not yet the predominant concern of politicians, nor were the discipline's professionals yet established as taken-for-granted sources of advice for government.

Politics and Policies

Policy issues are ultimately settled in political arenas. Yet whilst politicians make policy choices they don't make them in circumstances of their own choosing. And in making those choices highly variable forms of calculation are set in play—political and economic, diplomatic and strategic—and these calculations will all be articulated in particular forms of argument, particular ideologies which politicians will deploy with variable degrees of cynicism and conviction. Yet even the most self-interested and cynical will not be able to escape calculating where self-interest lies through some form of argument as to the path of possible future events.

This general point is perhaps especially important in looking at the main issues which defined public policy and the economy in this period. For in broad terms this can be seen as a period when the two main political parties tried in different ways to come to term with shifts in the dominant domestic political issues, a shift towards a predominance of concern with social reform and social welfare. The fact of the growth in such a concern is perhaps uncontentious—unlike the reasons for it (Hay 1975; Thane 1978). These reasons may be seen in terms of 'high politics'—as mainly a matter of personal political calculation by prominent members of the political parties (e.g. Bentley 1985). Alternatively emphasis may be placed on the shift in the ideologies of the parties (Semmel 1960; Freeden 1978), or on the long-term political calculation that social reform was the way to capture the newly enfranchised masses (Gilbert 1966).

From the point of view of public policy on the economy the most important consequence of this shift in concern was to put public finance at the centre of the political agenda in the Edwardian period (Emy 1972; Murray 1980). Both of the major domestic political controversies of this era—Tariff Reform in 1903–5 and the 'People's Budget' 1909–10—were about social issues, but crucially about the way in which new public expenditure on welfare was to be financed.

In the case of Tariff Reform we have already noted some of the cross-currents of concern which made up this issue. For Chamberlain an important component was a concern to turn the White Empire into an economic unit, thus turning the issue from one of protecting British markets to one of privileging Empire goods in Britain, and British goods in Empire markets. This imperial enthusiasm had its own dynamic in the Edwardian period, but was not a separate issue from that of social reform. For Chamberlain the imposition of a preferential tariff would fund programmes of welfare reform, and at the same time bind the working-class electorate to the Conservative cause. And by financing reform in this way it would dispose of the need to tax the rich:

Political historians have long debated how this high-risk strategy came to capture the Conservative Party (Green 1985). The judgement that it was high-risk is not just retrospective. Already in 1903 it was apparent it would face two insurmountable obstacles— the opposition of the self-governing colonies and the lack of enthusiasm of the organized working class. The first of these was founded on the desire of such colonies to protect themselves against British manufactures in order to build up domestic industry. The second was founded on a continuing and powerful wage-earner attachment to cheap food, as well as in many cases opposition to the ideological trappings of Chamberlain's imperialism (Coats 1968, pp. 199–200; Semmel 1960, p. 107).

However problematic the political calculation which underlay the Tariff Reform agitation it formed a coherent strategy of response to combine what were perceived as the imperatives of democratic politics with a defence of existing norms of tax distribution. It was a strategy for getting the workers to fund their own welfare.

The Liberal strategy may also be seen as responding to the same imperative. But the mixture here was different. The Liberals were divided over imperialism, and the issue could never focus their policies as it did the Chamberlainites. Given their commitment to social reform but hostility to tariffs the only way of squaring the circle was progressive taxation. In its wake this brought a battle with the Lords and severe political crisis, but it was at root an issue of public finance.

For the Liberals the key problem of their strategy was to finance social reform from enhanced direct taxes without alienating too much of their traditional middle-class support. In fact the 'People's Budget' of 1909 was nicely judged to achieve this result, most of its imposts falling not on the middle-class salary earner but on landed wealth and the unearned income of the rich (Murray 1980, pp. 9–

10). The budget raised the income tax from 1s. (5p) to 1s. 2d. (5.8p) in the pound, and introduced a super-tax to be paid by those with an income of over £5,000 per annum. What raised particular fury was the valuation of land with a view to future taxation on profits from increases in land values (in the event a tax which yielded very little revenue).

In the longer view the striking feature of public finance in the Edwardian period is that, even after the 'People's Budget' the tax base remained extremely narrow (only about 900,000 income-tax payers) and still regressive in incidence, given the continued importance of indirect taxation on working-class consumption. Lloyd George's budget strategy nibbled only a little at both middle-class incomes and landed wealth.

The issue of public finance emerged from the need to pay for welfare expenditure, which in turn followed from the striking concern with the 'Condition of England' question which so dominated late Victorian and Edwardian politics. One index of its role is that, between 1880–4 and 1905–9, memoranda on 'social issues' presented to Cabinet quadrupled (Bentley 1985, p. 262). For the first time politicians offered 'social programmes' and 'social policies' to the electorate. How far this concern with welfare is to be related to a concern to capture the votes of the newly enfranchised is a moot point. Undoubtedly this was part of the calculation of both Liberals and Conservatives, but it would be unhelpful to reduce it purely to that. How far the working-class electorate responded to such claims is also disputable (e.g. Thane 1984). Another aspect of this concern which is of great long-term significance is that it rested on a concept of poverty which was newly refined and for the first time systematically measured in this period (Williams 1979; Davidson 1985a).

A concern with poverty has no one ideological or political implication, and this indeed is why it could be deployed as easily as the Conservatives in arguing for their vision of reform as by the Liberals for theirs. There is, however, one particular aspect of that debate over poverty which is of substantial importance in looking at the evolution of public policy and the economy in this period— its links to unemployment.

The beginnings of the modern concern with unemployment may be dated to the 1880s after half a century in which 'unemployment as a serious theoretical and practical question was virtually ignored by English economic theorists and social reformers' (Harris 1971, p. 1; also Stedman Jones 1971). It was the social reformers who mattered, for it was largely through the concerns of social reformers that unemployment was established on the political agenda.

The concerns were attached to poverty in a diverse and changing series of linkages. In the 1880s the common elements were crime, vagrancy, and prostitution. In later decades before the First World War these perceived consequences were expanded into racial degeneration and military unfitness. Policy stances on unemployment could then be as various as those on poverty itself— repressive or reformative, individualist or 'social', charitable or state-interventionist. But all of these existed within a problematic of social administration, or relief and mitigation of the effects of unemployment rather than 'economic' prevention or cure (Harris 1972).

The section of the unemployed who fitted most readily into this definition of the problem were casual workers—those in intermittent unemployment who swamped most urban labour markets.[3] Most of the reforms addressed to the unemployment problem before World War One saw the nub of that problem as dealing with the casuals, or preventing the skilled workers from slipping from temporary interruption of employment into a chronic state of casuality.[4]

This is apparent in the Royal Commission on the Poor Laws (1905–9), where casual labour is seen as the major cause of pauperism, itself the central concern of the Commission (Cd. 4499). In certain respects the Fabian-inspired Minority Report of that Commission does break new ground in respect to employment policy. Accepting the common hostility to local relief workers as tainted by association with the Poor Law, the Report proposed counter-cyclical variations in work contracted by central government

[3] The classic sector of casual labour was the docks, on which see Phillips and Whiteside (1985), chs. 1–3.

[4] The point made here is that contemporaries *perceived* the unemployment problem as largely concerned with casual labour. This is not to say whether that was the 'real' problem. The cyclical unemployment recorded in Table 2.3 was very uneven in its regional incidence, and that spatial pattern was similar to that with which we are familiar after the First World War, i.e. where unemployment was highest in the areas of the major exporting regions in North and West Britain (Southall 1988). However it is important not to confuse the retrospective significance of this pattern with the actual concerns of policy-makers at the time.

departments, with labour engaged in the normal way for standard wages. In addition the Report raised the issue of financing such works from borrowings from 'underemployed' capital during the depression, to be repaid in the boom. But overall even this 'progressive' position remained dominated by the traditional concern with poverty and its prevention, and by the notion of non-casual unemployment as essentially cyclical in character.

Also important to unemployment discussion in the Edwardian period is Beveridge's *Unemployment: A Problem of Industry* (1909). Here unemployment was posed as an economic problem—in the sense of a problem of matching supply and demand in the labour market. Beveridge's aim was to improve the workings of the labour market, 'making reality correspond with the assumptions of economic theory' (p. 231). But again the approach was dominated by a concern for casuality and its effects, and was even further than the Webbs from relating unemployment to the workings of the economy as a whole. The possibility of a general excess supply of labour was vehemently denied (Williams and Williams 1987, ch. 4).

The work of the Poor Law Minority and Beveridge provided the main intellectual underpinnings of the Liberal Government's policies on unemployment. These involved three major strands. Labour Exchanges to improve, including to decasualize, the labour market. Secondly, national insurance for those in cyclical trades, to redistribute worker incomes over the trade cycle. (For evidence on cyclical unemployment, see Table 2.3). Finally, a policy of 'Development Works' combining the encouragement of works of 'national utility', mainly roads and agriculture, with a possible counter-cyclical timing (Harris 1972, ch. 6).

These policies represent a culmination of thirty years of fluctuating but generally growing concern with unemployment. Unemployment was on the agenda mainly because of its perceived relationship to poverty. It was also seen as an issue on which the Left might mobilize to challenge the existing order, though such efforts had relatively little impact in or out of Parliament before 1914 (Brown 1971). It was not yet an issue which was generally seen as linked to the functioning of the economy as a whole, nor to the management of that economy.

Table 2.3   *Recorded[1] Unemployment, 1900–1913*

	Numbers (000)	Percentage of Working Population
1900	450	2.5
1901	600	3.3
1902	730	4.0
1903	870	4.7
1904	1,130	6.0
1905	950	5.0
1906	690	3.6
1907	710	3.7
1908	1,520	7.8
1909	1,510	7.7
1910	930	4.7
1911	600	3.0
1912	670	3.3
1913	430	2.1

[1] Based on TU records of unemployment, the only source before the creation of unemployment insurance in 1912. For a discussion of this data source and its helpfulness as a general indicator of the labour market, see Garside (1980), ch. 1. Broadly, the figures emphasize the incidence of cyclical unemployment in skilled trades, but do not reflect the scale of casual unemployment.

Source: Feinstein (1972), Table 57, p. T125–6.

Conclusions

Public policy on the economy at the end of the Victorian era was limited to a narrow range of objectives and instruments. The major objectives were threefold. To maintain the gold standard and with it the free flow of capital, the value of money, and the stability and strength of the financial system. To maintain free trade in Britain and as far as possible in the Empire. Finally, to keep the budget small and in balance.

By 1914 the first of these objectives remained in place and largely unchallenged. The second had survived despite robust challenge. The third had proved less resistant. Government spending had risen sharply and with it the range of state responsibilities—especially central state responsibilities (Hicks 1958). But public finance was still essentially a matter of finding the tax revenue for current spending—the budget in peacetime yielded a surplus, and was not used as an instrument of other public policies.

Redistributive taxation can be regarded as a new instrument of policy, its foundations firmly in place by 1914, though its impact as yet minimal. In other respects the limited means available to the government were consonant with its limited objectives.

These objectives most notably lacked any concern with the stability and growth of the economy. The scale of enmeshment with the international economy, and the lack of perception of unemployment as an economic problem together meant that the idea of a national economy, which could be subject to management, had not even reached its infancy. Equally government had accepted no responsibility for the growth of the economy, and whilst there were widespread perceptions that the economy was performing less well than others, notably the German and American economies, this did not lead to significant new policy initiatives (Newton and Porter 1988, ch. 1). For all the changes and challenges of the Edwardian era, the shape of public policy on the economy on the eve of the war was not sharply dissimilar from that at the end of Victoria's reign.

Further Reading

Davidson, R. (1985): *Whitehall and the Labour Problem in Late Victorian and Edwardian Britain*, London.

Eichengreen, B., ed. (1985): *The Gold Standard in Theory and History*, London.

Harris, J. (1972): *Unemployment and Politics*, Oxford.

Hicks, U. K. (1958): *British Public Finances 1880–1952*, Oxford.

Hutchinson, T. W. (1953): *A Review of Economic Doctrines 1870–1929*, Oxford.

Murray, B. K. (1980): *The People's Budget 1909/10*, Oxford.

Roseveare, H. (1969): *The Treasury*, London.

Sayers, R. S. (1936): *The Bank of England 1891–1944*, vol. i, Cambridge.

—— (1976): *Bank of England Operations 1890–1914*, London.

Sutherland, S., ed. (1972): *Studies in the Growth of Nineteenth-Century Government*, London.

Winch, D. (1972): *Economics and Policy*, London.

3

1914–1925: 'A World Shattered—and Rebuilt'?

IF, politically, the First World War can be seen as a culmination of trends already apparent before 1914, in the field of the economy it (eventually) marked a major break in trend. At its most general, this break combined a revolution in the way Britain related to the world economy, and domestically a vast extension of the role of the state. These consequences only gradually became apparent as the war progressed from 'business as usual' to a 'nation in arms' to 'total war' (French 1982). But whilst many foresaw—and some hoped—that this break, especially in its second aspect, would be permanent, by the early 1920s the thrust of economic policy was an attempt to re-establish British links to the world economy at their pre-1914 basis, and to rein back the state's role. Policy looked back to a golden age and tried to restore it, just as post-revolutionary conservatives in France attempted to undo the French revolution, and in the long run just as unsuccessfully.[1]

Institutions

The Gold Standard

The history of the gold standard gives to 1914–25 a significant unity. During the war years the gold standard was effectively suspended, to be formally abandoned in 1919, and then restored in 1925. But throughout the early post-war years policy was aimed at restoring gold, and this is the most obvious and most significant sign of the desire to restore pre-war conditions.

Much ink has been expended on debating the effects of the 1925 decision, and we will return to this in Chapter 4. But separate and

---

[1] Boyce (1987) provides a thorough account and persuasive explanation of the 'internationalist' orientation of British policy after the First World War.

prior to any question of effects is the question of why gold restoration was the overarching aim of policy in those early post-war years.

The Interim Cunliffe Report of 1918 is the classic source of the case for going back to gold, although in fact its deliberations *assumed* a restoration and focused on how this was to be done (Moggridge 1972, pp. 17–22). But along the way it outlined the three considerations which were crucial to that assumption. First, that the gold standard was anti-inflationary—any excessive domestic credit creation would be immediately counteracted by gold loss. Second, that the standard was an automatic one. Third, that stability of the exchanges was vital to Britain's role in the world economy.

The idea of the gold standard as a defence against inflation gained from the war and post-war experience. Prices rose more or less continuously during the war, and then exploded at war's end, to reach 150 per cent above their 1913 level by 1920. In addition, rapid and hyperinflations in much of post-war Europe were associated with social and political upheavals, an association which many saw as a causal connection, and drew the conclusion that only gold could stand in the way of social unrest and political chaos.

The fear of inflation, and the belief in gold as a bulwark against it, linked to the idea of the gold standard as an automatic mechanism. Inflation was seen as the consequence of the role of politicians in credit policy, a role perhaps inescapable in wartime, but to be contained and preferably eliminated in peace. The best constraint was seen as the mechanisms of gold, which were perceived as abstracted from any institutional context, as a purely mechanical arrangement ideally suited to keep politicians on the straight and narrow path of financial responsibility.

Finally, the third leg in the defence of gold was a belief that Britain's role in the world economy, and especially its role as financier, depended upon stability of the exchanges. Restoring gold was seen as above all about restoring such stability. This meant the focus was *not* on the level of the exchange rate; that level was not an instrument of policy as it became to later generations, but largely a datum. To return to gold meant implicitly to return at the pre-war parity of $4.86 (Hume 1970, p. 126; Moggridge 1972, pp. 84–5).

These Cunliffe assumptions about the gold standard did not go unchallenged. But to give them the predominance accorded here seems appropriate because of their pervasiveness. Perhaps the most striking feature of the gold-standard discussions of the post-war years was the weakness of opposition to the policy; the hegemony of the gold-standard idea was not complete, but covered much of the political spectrum and was not consistently opposed by any one major interest group. This can be seen if we look in more detail at the evolution of policy on the gold standard from 1914 to 1925.

After the initial disturbance, the impact of the war was fundamentally to undermine Britain's gold-standard position. Above all this arose from the dollar deficit, as Britain, and through her many of the Allies, increasing came to depend on American supplies, but decreasingly were able to finance these from exports. This position was only sustainable by gold sales, sales of securities, private borrowing, and ultimately most important, US-government dollar loans. With some difficulty Britain persuaded the USA that some part of these dollar resources should be deployed to defend the exchange rate of $4.76, where it was pegged from 1915. Keynes, amongst others, persuaded the Americans that a fall in the sterling rate would fatally undermine confidence in the *Entente*, and would place the whole of the burden of financing the Allied war effort on the USA (Burk 1979*a*, 1979*b*, 1981). So despite the disturbances of war, a façade of normality was maintained with other Allied countries also pegging their exchange rates close to pre-war levels. But it was well recognized that, at the end of the war, adjustments of some form would have to be made to bring into line economic and financial conditions and the survival of a gold regime.

Out of this problem arose the Cunliffe Committee. Its presumption in favour of gold ran into little opposition, certainly as a principle. There was to be much debate over timing and over the deflation that accompanied the return, but this was within, and constrained by, a framework which took the desirability of gold as given (Hume 1970, pp. 125–6).

Despite the initial favourable response to Cunliffe's objectives, the government was unwilling to will the means, which meant high interest rates and deflation at a time of reconversion of the economy and demobilization. In a straightforwardly political decision the government instead allowed the pound to float down from April 1919. 'External monetary considerations were for the present subordinate to domestic peace' (Morgan 1979, p. 58).

But this was a short-term political calculation which was changed by the sharp shift in economic conditions in the year after leaving gold. In 1919–20 Britain partook of one of the fiercest booms in recorded history, as world-wide restocking unleashed a torrent of demand. This 'natural' consequence of the war was initially intensified by monetary policy, where again Lloyd George's political considerations outweighed calls for financial prudence. However, fiscal policy was less accommodating from the beginning (Table 3.1), and in autumn 1919 monetary policy was also tightened (Howson 1975, ch. 2).

Table 3.1   *The Budget 1913/14–1924/5* (£m.)

	Expenditure	Revenue	Surplus/Deficit
1913/14	189.9	196.6	+6.7
1914/15	487.0	225.4	−261.6
1915/16	1,228.9	333.9	−895.0
1916/17	1,638.5	564.7	−1,073.8
1917/18	2,189.4	659.6	−1,529.8
1918/19	2,368.1	844.6	−1,523.5
1919/20	1,202.0	1,311.9	+109.9
1920/21	1,116.8	1,393.6	+276.8
1921/22	1,007.5	1,194.3	+186.8
1922/23	764.2	901.1	+136.8
1923/24	723.6	830.4	+106.8
1924/25	715.7	786.3	+70.6

Source: Morgan (1952), Table 9, p. 104.

The key turning-point for policy and the economy was spring, 1920. Just as the restocking boom was running out of steam, Bank Rate was raised sharply to 7 per cent—a crisis rate—and held there for almost a year. This was a crucial decision. The move was unambiguously directed at producing a domestic deflation of prices, ultimately with the aim of securing the return to gold. For the first time Bank Rate was used for a wholly domestic purpose (having been used almost entirely to regulate gold flows before the First World War—see Chapter 2). This policy was widely supported, including by Keynes, above all because of the fear of inflation. He indeed became the most articulate purveyor of that fear: 'A continuance of inflationism and high prices will not only depress the exchanges, but by their effect on prices will strike at the whole basis of contract, of security, and of the capitalist system generally.' (Howson 1973, p. 459.)

When contemporaries advocated a policy of deflation they saw this as a policy affecting prices but not output. Thus the slump which ensued, the worst of the twentieth century, worse even than 1929–32 or 1979–81, was not anticipated. As the depression developed the Bank Rate did come down, but only slowly, and did not reach 3 per cent until July 1922. But whilst GDP fell 6 per cent, unemployment rose to over 11 per cent (Table 3.2), and wholesale prices fell by 35 per cent from 1920 to 1922 (Table 3.3), the exchange rate recovered. At its low point in February 1920 it had touched $3.40, but by the end of 1922 it was over $4.60. (Morgan (1952, pp. 345–55) has a monthly series for the exchange rate in this period.) From this time until 1925 the policy discussion was largely a tactical one—how and when to manage the final appreciation of the exchange back to the pre-war parity finally achieved in April 1925 (Moggridge 1972, ch. 3).

Table 3.2   *Unemployment 1914–1925*

	Numbers (000)	Civilian working population (%)
1914	660	3.3
1915	200	1.1
1916	70	0.4
1917	100	0.6
1918	140	0.8
1919	660	3.4
1920	420	2.0
1921	2,212	11.3
1922	1,909	9.8
1923	1,567	8.1
1924	1,404	7.2
1925	1,559	7.9

Source: Feinstein (1972), Table 57, p. T126.

Table 3.3   *Price Indices 1913–1925* (1913 = 100)

	GDP Deflator	Consumer Price Index
1913	100	100
1914	100.7	99.7
1915	111.6	112.3
1916	127.4	132.5
1917	161.1	166.0
1918	191.1	202.5
1919	225.1	222.9
1920	270.8	257.2
1921	242.3	235.0
1922	203.4	202.2
1923	187.1	190.0
1924	184.5	188.5
1925	185.0	189.2

Source: Feinstein (1972), Table 61, pp. T132–3.

Why was this decision taken? A number of positions on this are available in the literature. Keynes initiated a highly characteristic version which emphasized the nature of the advice given to Churchill, the Chancellor of the Exchequer in 1925—Keynes originally called part of his abbreviated version of the 'Economic Consequences of Mr Churchill', 'The Misleading of Mr Churchill' (Keynes 1972, ch. 5). Churchill in this view was persuaded by the orthodox economists and financiers to take a decision which a more rational set of experts would have rejected.

Pollard, on the other hand, sees the role of the City, acting through the Bank of England, as crucial. In his view the decision was based on the capacity of the City to impose its interests on policy-making, against the interests of both industry and workers: the City's 'interests, their priorities and their aims were totally different from those of . . . the large majority of the British population' (Pollard 1970, p. 12).

Tomlinson (1981a, ch. 6) has criticized these two approaches, and argued that neither is satisfactory. The Keynesian view puts too much emphasis on the role of 'ideas' in policy-making, as opposed to institutional and political aspects, such as the Treasury and Bank of England view, shared by many politicians, that the only alternative to gold was the dangerous one of a managed monetary system. On the other hand, Pollard's approach may be criticized for exaggerating the role of the City in the decision and in doing so overstating the scale and coherence of opposition to the decision—which related much more to timing than to the principle of return.

Moggridge's summary of the reasons for returning in 1925 (1972, pp. 94–7) gives full weight to the political calculation of the impossibility of doing anything else, given the near unanimity of support, the position of the Treasury and Bank of England, and the fact of a rate for the pound which was only 'slightly' below that of $4.86.

Moggridge (1972, p. 97) also emphasizes that the decision was not one based on what today would pass in academic circles as an acceptable analysis of the issues involved. Rather, it was the consequence of certain deep-seated 'attitudes towards gold, debt repayment, and good faith, which were essentially moral, and in a deep faith in the apparent mechanisms of the pre-war gold standard'. This seems a fair point to make, but it leaves open the question of why no alternative 'faith' came to be widely articulated in this period. Such an alternative was essayed; there was a small but growing volume of advocacy of 'managed' money, of which the most famous example is Keynes *Tract on Monetary Reform* (Keynes 1971). But such advocacy had limited impact. First, its proponents' fear of inflation made them not always readily distingishable from gold advocates. Second, the key institutions of economic policy-making, i.e. the Treasury and Bank of England, saw managed money as a weak barrier against inflation, whilst the gold standard was 'knave-proof' (Bradbury, cited in Moggridge 1972, p. 86; for 'knave' read 'politician'). Finally faith in gold went largely unchallenged by the political forces claiming to represent those most harassed by its effects—the workers and the unemployed. This political failure is returned to below, in the section on Policies and Politics.

Free Trade

The war posed no such immediate threat to free trade as it did to the gold standard—the balance of payments difficulty was based on incapacity to finance an inescapable level of imports, for which any general protection could only be a minor solution. Consequently, the breaches in the edifice of free trade during the war period were small. In 1915 the 'McKenna duties' (after the Chancellor of that year) were imposed, consisting of an *ad valorem* duty of 33⅓ per cent on a small range of luxury goods. The ostensible purpose was the saving of foreign exchange and shipping space, but they continued after the war (except, briefly, under the 1924 Labour Government) and were extended slightly in 1926. Their main impact was to aid the growth of motor manufacturing (Pollard 1983, p. 119; also Capie 1983, pp. 40–1).

Also it was considered that the war had revealed a strategically unwise import-dependence on certain commodities; these were subjected to licences along with others considered reducible in war conditions. These commodities and a few others continued to be protected by 'key industries' legislation in 1920 and 1921, and this allowed a narrow range of industries protection, expanded slightly in 1925. All this was very *ad hoc* and the motives muddled—it did not constitute a coherent protectionist policy, though advocates of such a policy hoped it would lead to one, and their enemies feared it would. By 1930 only 17 per cent of imports by value were subject to duty, but protection covered no more than about 3 per cent of all imports.

As before the war, the issue of protection was inextricably linked to the question of Empire. In 1917 the British government, at the behest of the (white) Empire agreed to a policy of Empire settlement and Imperial Preference. But the results of both were meagre. In the case of preferential duties, Britain, with so little protection to start with, had little to give away, and indeed granted only a one-sixth reduction on safeguarding duties to Empire goods (one-third on the McKenna duties) (Drummond 1974, pp. 25–7; see also Drummond 1972).

In 1923, to most people's surprise, Baldwin went to the country, and lost, on the issue of free trade. But this event gives a misleading perspective on economic controversies in those years; perhaps surprisingly, whilst the Conservative party was a protectionist party, such a policy did not figure strongly in economic discussions at this time, even with the collapse of the post-war boom. The Imperial visionaries, like Amery and Hewens, pursued their old dreams, but the main linkage of Empire to unemployment was by the encouragement of emigration, not the discouragement of non-Empire imports. Indeed, in the international economic sphere 'The *laissez-faire* free traders may be said to have dominated the monetary reconstruction of the period, a reconstruction whose goal was to restore the good years before the war. With respect to any more innovative policy in Empire development or protection, they were primarily obstructive' (Drummond 1972, p. 35).

In sum, the principle of free trade and non-discrimination had been breached before the blizzard of 1931, but it is only in retrospect that these breaches can be seen as auguries of a fundamental break in Britain's orientation to the world economy.

The Budgetary Framework

The most unambiguous change in the domestic economic environment brought about by the war was the expansion of the government budget. Whilst such expansion was hardly surprising as the direct accompaniment to war on the scale of 1914–18, in fact post-war expenditure never fell back to its pre-war level. From approximately 12.5 per cent of GNP before the war, state expenditure rose to over 50 per cent, falling back to around 25 per cent in the 1920s (Peacock and Wiseman 1967, p. 166). In the broadest terms public expenditure was 'displaced' on to a new level by the effects of the war. Peacock and Wiseman emphasize this effect as arising from a shift upwards in the perception of the tolerable burden of taxation. On the other side of the accounts, the war shifted the perception of the state's responsibilities, and hence what constituted a reasonable level of state expenditure— though both tax and expenditure were the subject of political battles in the eary 1920s (see below, Politics and Policies).

In the short run even more striking than the growth in the scale of government expenditure was the growth of the debt. The pre-war precept that war could be financed out of taxes and borrowing from current savings was quickly seen to be impracticable. But Chancellors were very slow to come to to terms with the situation by increasing taxation or, indeed, by imaginative forms of borrowing. The slow growth of tax revenue meant that larger and larger deficits accumulated through the war—rising from £261.6m.

in 1914/15 to a peak of £1529.8m. in 1917/18, equivalent to approximately 40 per cent of national income in the latter year (Morgan 1952, pp. 104–5). Why did taxes rise so slowly? Morgan (p. 94) suggests three reasons. First, the technical difficulties of expanding tax revenues, especially the income tax, whose imposition on the working class had been explicitly rejected by Lloyd George in 1913. Second, the common perception that as long as money could be raised by borrowing then war finance was not a problem. Third, a lack of understanding of the principles of war finance by Ministers and their advisers.

The first of these is evident in the slow growth of direct taxation, which only rose from 43 to 51 per cent of total tax revenue. The second was a common but not universal perception (Mallet and George 1929), but the minority voices made little impact until the results of accumulated borrowings became evident at the end of the war (see below). The key aspect of this 'lack of understanding' was the lack of realization that the war required a massive transfer of *real* (not just financial) resources to the government and hence a major reduction in civilian expenditure. In the absence of such a policy the result was not just a mountain of debt but rapid inflation as government and civilians competed for resources.

By the end of the fiscal year 1918/19 the internal debt had risen to £6142m., involving debt charges of £224m. at an average interest rate of 4.65 per cent. In 1913 the debt had been £754m., costing £24.5m. at 3¼ per cent (Morgan 1952, ch. 4). Not only was there a debt of unprecedented size, but a substantial proportion was in the form of floating, i.e. short-term, debt which posed monetary problems in that it added enormously to the liquidity of the economy and hence the capacity to spend. This proportion had risen especially after 1917, when the government found long-term interest rates hardening against it, and therefore shortened the age of its borrowings to try and prevent an extended burden of high rates.

The scale and structure of this debt are a key element in the economic policy-making of the early 1920s. The key institutions of economic policy-making, the Bank of England and the Treasury, saw reduction and changes in the composition of the debt as key objectives. Debt funding (i.e. reduction in its length) was pursued with vigour, with funding operations in every year from 1919 to 1924 which resulted in a gross reduction of floating debt of £530m.

in total. (For net figures see Howson 1975, Table 1). This was coupled with a sharp reversal of fiscal policy to ensure that the debt was not added to by current budget deficits. The deficit was slashed in the fiscal year 1919/20, and the budget was in surplus by the end of the calendar year 1919. Thereafter surpluses allowed debt redemption in excess of £150m. by the end of 1924/5 (Howson 1975, Table 4B).

This turn-round in the budgetary position was accomplished primarily by cuts in expenditure, although taxes were increased in 1920. But the growth of public expenditure since 1913 included many items of civilian expenditure which could not be readily reversed. Once the post-war boom broke in the summer of 1920, there was sustained pressure to cut expenditure, epitomized by the famous 'Geddes Axe' of 1922 and heralding a recurrent theme of economic debate for the next 60 years. Whilst politically the Geddes cuts in social welfare expenditure were of most importance, the largest cuts were in defence, amounting to 40 per cent 1921/22 to 1922/23. Social expenditure over the same years fell by 11½ per cent and then remained stable on trend through the 1920s (Peden 1985, pp. 76, 78).

As already noted, the share of government expenditure in national income remained at roughly twice the pre-war level. This shift was by no means linked to a clear shift in the dominant views of public expenditure—business, governmental, and official opinion seems to have been wedded to the old 'Gladstonian' truths (Roseveare 1969, p. 258), but the increases of spending in such areas as housing and unemployment insurance could not be reversed in post-war political conditions. Hicks (1970, pp. 20, 38) suggests that social welfare expenditure increased approximately three times between 1913 and 1920, and continued its upward trend thereafter. (Though the biggest proportionate increase was expenditure on servicing the Debt.)

On the tax side the war increased the burden without radically altering the structure. The balance had slightly shifted towards direct taxation, but the income tax remained a tax which fell on few members of the working class. The old idea that the workers should pay indirect taxes and the better-off direct taxes was sustained through the 1920s, and not, for example, challenged by the wide-ranging Colwyn Commission on Debt and Taxation (Colwyn 1927, paras. 686–8).

Agencies

The Bank of England

The war was traumatic for the Bank of England. Its central concern, the gold standard, was suspended for the duration. In addition, war saw it forced into all kinds of uncongenial policies—blocking gold exports; discriminating between different borrowers in interest rates; witnessing an inflation aided, if not fundamentally propelled, by the expansion of the currency notes and the expansion of the floating debt (Sayers 1976, pp. 98–9). Its loss of ground to the Treasury was symbolized by the issue of Treasury notes and the displacement of Bank Rate by the Treasury Bill rate as the key interest rate. But the Bank was far from functioning less in the war period, and in particular it found a new role in managing Britain's foreign exchange resources.

All this was clearly viewed by the Bank as a temporary interlude, before the restoration of pre-war norms of policy. Its views were those of Cunliffe (an ex-Governor of the Bank), above all a restoration of the gold standard, made possible by monetary restriction, involving the ending of Currency Notes (i.e. notes issued by the Treasury without gold backing), a reduction in the floating debt, and dear money. Such deflation was urged on the government from before the war's end and right through the boom, but only began to be taken up from late 1919, and not in full force until the spring of 1920 (Howson 1975, pp. 14–23).

The Bank's problem was not only the political objections to deflation, but the weakening of its control over monetary forces brought about by the liquidity of the banks and loss of control over the note issue. The clear problem from the Bank's point of view was that the monetary contraction was dependent upon a change in government fiscal policy—and so it was drawn into urging 'fierce' budgets in 1919 to 1921, a policy area outside its traditional domain of responsibility (Sayers 1976, p. 114).

Central to the Bank's posture from 1918 to 1925 was gold restoration. But this traditional goal led to non-traditional approaches, especially as it became apparent that such a policy required a long-term strategy. It led to a focus on international co-operation which had never figured prominently before the war, when London had normally been strong enough to orchestrate the world economy on its own. But in the conditions of the 1920s the Governor of the Bank, Norman, developed a 'missionary zeal for financial reconstruction in Europe' (Sayers 1976, p. 120). This was a logical corollary of the Bank's view that Britain's prosperity depended upon re-stabilizing the international economy, to which end financial stability was crucial.

Above all, the conditions of the 1920s required that the focus of the Bank's attention be on the United States and the dollar. America had emerged from the war radically strengthened as a financial power, a creditor nation, and the major supplier of new capital in international markets. This change in the balances of financial power had been forcibly brought home to British officials by wartime discussions over Britain's dollar borrowings. Slowly the USA realized how their changed financial position offered them leverage over British policy. By 1918 Keynes was lamenting about the USA that 'it almost looks as if they took a satisfaction in reducing us to a position of complete financial helplessness and dependence' (cited in Burk 1979*b*, p. 416; see also Burk 1979*a*).

This leverage was deployed more emphatically after the war, with the USA as the new 'top dog' pursuing a policy of *laissez-faire* in international financial matters, i.e. an unregulated gold standard. Whilst the British in general, and the Bank in particular, wanted the standard, they put forward a variety of schemes for managing such a restoration, which the USA would not support (Costigliola 1977). The return to gold in 1925 was in part a response to this American predominance. Norman argued that if Britain failed to go back 'the world centre would shift permanently and completely from London to New York' (Moggridge 1972, p. 69). Banking relations with the USA in this period were close and amiable, but this should not hide the fact that Britain was now a subordinate centre, a subordination nicely symbolized by the actual return in 1925 being passed in part as a gamble on rising price trends in the USA (Moggridge 1972, p. 90).

The focus of the Bank's attention was overwhelmingly external. Not only was it absolutely sure of the rightness and importance of restoring gold, but it was also 'sceptical of its power to make much impact directly on internal economic conditions' (Sayers 1976, p. 110). It was perhaps growing in sensitivity, but this had little or no impact on the actual policies pursued. However in one area the Bank was drawn willy-nilly into a new area of domestic responsibility. This resulted from the collapse of the post-war boom and the effects of that collapse on the financial position of one of the Bank's few private industrial customers, and on the position of commercial banks which had lent to firms on an extravagant scale in the boom. In this way, unwittingly, but willingly, Norman and the Bank were led into major schemes of industrial reorganization for key staple industries, though much of this did not develop far until the end of the 1920s (Sayers 1976, ch. 14; below, ch. 4).

The restoration of gold symbolized the restoration of the Bank's traditional role, struggled for through the early 1920s. But the post-war condition of the British economy made playing that role exceedingly more complex and difficult than before 1914, as well as drawing the Bank into unaccustomed interventions in industry which were oddly at variance with the lack of domestic consider-ations in its conduct of monetary policy.

The Treasury

The Treasury role in economic policy was up-ended by the war. On the one hand, its concerns for limitation of public expenditure and good house-keeping were blown away by the scale of the war effort. On the other hand, finance played a key role in the war effort, and drew the Treasury into new modes of intervention in the economy. Monetary policy became important to it via the role of note issues (Treasury Notes were issued from 1914), and because of the key role of the Treasury Bill Rate in domestic interest rates as this form of finance expanded. It was also drawn into control of the capital market via control of new issues. Also of great importance were the negotiations in the USA over dollar finance. This led to conflict with the Bank, especially over the control of exchange-rate policy, a battle the Treasury won and which therefore symbolized its gain in power relative to the Bank in the war years (Burk 1982, pp. 84–96).

But perhaps the most significant effect of the war on the Treasury was not its new roles (several of which it lost after the war) but the substantial enhancement of its traditional and interrelated roles as overseer of government spending and of the civil service. Calls for a reorganization of the Treasury to play such an enhanced role pre-date the war. A Royal Commission Report of early 1914 called for a special Treasury division to supervise and control the Civil Service, but this was prevented by the war. During the war a whole series of Ministries was created, from Food to Munitions, which underwent rapid and largely unregulated growth (Burk 1982, pp. 96–102).

Wartime fears about this mushroom growth were echoed in the Report of the Haldane Committee on the Machinery of Government in 1919. This Report was very critical of the traditional manner of Treasury Control as unreasonably negative, and called for 'control to be exercised in a sympathetic spirit and with an adequate knowledge of the circumstances and difficulties of other departments'. To do this task the Committee called, amongst other reforms, for greater expert knowledge to be available in the Treasury, so that the principle of 'investigation and thought as a preliminary to action' could be realized (Roseveare 1969, pp. 244–5).

The Treasury was reorganized after the war, but the relation of these changes to the Haldane Report was ambiguous. This ambiguity arose from the context of a 'perception of runaway expenditure as a fundamental threat to society and the state [which] was one shared by the Treasury, the House of Commons and a wide section of the informed public' (Burk 1982, pp. 99–100). This allowed the enhancement of Treasury powers, but evidently without the reform to make these powers operate in the positive manner envisaged by Haldane (see below on Ministry of Labour). Overall the war left the Treasury greatly strengthened, and on this basis remained by far the most important Ministry for economic policy through the inter-war period.

Whilst the Treasury had wartime differences of view with the Bank of England, both bodies shared a view on the major priorities of post-war policy (Boyce 1987, chs. 1, 2). This centred on the restoration of the gold standard as a guarantee of a non-inflationary future, and carried with it a number of corollaries concerned with debt-funding, high interest rates and cuts in public expenditure to secure a budgetary surplus. Within this strategy the Bank and the Treasury might occasionally disagree over tactics, but the general thrust of policy went almost unquestioned without these two bodies. One element in this agreement which perhaps cannot be overstressed was the hostility to economic management it embodied. The wartime inflations and post-war hyperinflations seemed to many people at this time convincing proof of the dangers of 'managed money'. Keynes, one of the advocates of such management, recognized that 'It is natural, after what we have experienced, that prudent people should desiderate a standard of value which is independent of finance ministers and state Banks' (1971, p. 135). Niemeyer, Controller of Finance at the Treasury in the years prior to 1925 tended to treat management as synonymous with inflation. Overall, as Moggridge (1972, p. 86) argues, 'the managed money alternative was, in the conditions of 1924–5, a non-starter which received little consideration outside academic circles'.

As in the Bank, the Treasury decision to return to gold in 1925 was not based on what later generations would regard as sophisticated economic analysis. For example, calculations of the purchasing-power parity of the pound relative to the dollar (based on the idea that the exchange rate in equilibrium would reflect its buying power in the two countries) were done on the basis of wholesale prices, which were not independent variables, because they themselves were strongly dependent on the exchange rate. This is only one indication of the economic amateurishness which was the other side of basing economic policy-making on essentially political judgements, political judgements which were widely shared at the time and therefore did not come under much scrutiny. (On the problem of assessing the appropriate exchange rate see below, ch. 4.)

The Ministry of Labour

The war period saw a multiplication of Ministries, some with a purely temporary remit, like Food and Munitions, others suggesting a change in the perception of the role of government in the economy which might be more permanent. Of these, the most important was the Ministry of Labour, created in 1916.

The origin of the Ministry lay in the Lloyd George Coalition's desire to be conciliatory towards organized labour, given the recognition of how crucial labour acquiescence in government policy was to be for the war effort. Initially the Ministry was supposed to take over the labour functions of the Ministry of Munitions, but it did not, and this was characteristic of the failure of the Ministry to find a clear role in the war period. In each of the three aspects of its operations—industrial relations, manpower planning, and demobilization—it shared responsibility with other agencies (Lowe 1982, pp. 108–19).

The Ministry's relationships with labour were never straightforward, but in the period at the end of the war it did operate to press for reformist policies such as the minimum wage. This policy was accepted by the Cabinet in 1919, but its failure to be implemented is symptomatic of the Ministry's weakness. First of all, the Ministry pursued a policy of 'home rule for industry' which meant encouraging voluntary collective bargaining and a 'non-interventionist' stance, clearly in contradiction to a wage regulation policy. Secondly, the Ministry did not have the expertise and drive to work through all the implications of a minimum wage policy and thus help make it stick. Thirdly, the Ministry suffered from Treasury hostility from its beginnings, based on that agency's enthusiasm for wage flexibility and the need to prune public expenditure. Finally, the Ministry suffered like all others from the change in political climate in 1920, as fears of unrest and Bolshevism gave way to fears of inflation and the public sector getting out of control (Lowe 1978*a*, also 1978*b*).

The drive for decontrol and cuts in public expenditure after 1920 almost saw the abolition of the Ministry—a course advocated by the Geddes Committee. Its survival was not the result of any political calculation as to the importance of a Ministry to deal with 'labour' in a newly democratic polity, but of its administrative role. This role was partly as pre-war, that of supplying statistical expertise, but most importantly that of responsibility for employment exchanges—newly important in the post-war world of mass unemployment.

The Ministry remained a political backwater under the 1924 Labour Government as well as those that preceded it. Though the Treasury could not force its abolition, it cribbed and confined the new Ministry at every turn—for example in its resistance to realistic state contributions as part of the three-element (state/employee/employer) finance of unemployment insurance. The Treasury 'culture' in relation to the Ministry was one of negativism, hostility to expertise and to outside contacts, and of using its administrative role for political ends. No wonder Treasury civil servants were known in the Ministry as 'abominable no-men', and that the historian of the Ministry can make a powerful case for finding the Treasury guilty of 'narrow minded arrogance' (Lowe 1986, especially chs. 2, 3).

One final element of this disabling Treasury role, and the failure of a Ministry like Labour to exert itself against the Treasury, was that it prevented the emergence of a Ministry with clear responsibility for unemployment. With the Treasury essentially a financial rather than an economic Ministry, the Board of Trade with no unified role, and the Ministry of Labour lacking political clout and hemmed in by Treasury restrictions, the emergence of unemployment as a policy problem in this period was unmatched by the emergence of one body charged with its reduction or even amelioration (Lowe 1980).

Doctrine

The wartime incursion of state bodies into regulation of the economy could be viewed through the lens of a number of ideologies. One of great importance was the ideology of scientific expertise, of the expert who could be consulted and used to guide the state in its new areas of responsibility. During the war a small number of economists and statisticians were drawn into a few Ministries—notably the Treasury and the Board of Trade. Within the last agency a General Economic Development Department was established, and this supported the desirability of an 'economic general staff', with which the Haldane Committee also agreed. This idea, like much else, rose and fell with the rise and fall of the reconstruction movement. Once the movement receded, the General Economic Development Department was felled by the Geddes Axe, leaving only Llewellyn Smith of the Board of Trade as Chief Economic Adviser. Even then, the CEA seems to have played no substantial policy-making role, his concerns largely falling outside the main policy areas (Howson and Winch 1977, pp. 5–7).

In consequence of all this there were no clear and established channels of economic advice into the main agencies of economic decision-making. In the case of the gold-standard decision, as already noted, it is clear that economic expertise played little role in the policy. Economists were present on important committees—

Pigou was on both the Cunliffe and later (Treasury) Bradbury–Chamberlain Committees on gold—but in the words of Moggridge (1972, p. 97), 'merely played a priestly role, justifying decisions taken for more deep-seated reasons'. He summarizes the role of economics: 'Economic analysis, as such, played a minimal role in the decision. Public as well as official economic discussion was profoundly anti-empirical' (p. 96). Economists, most obviously Keynes and Hawtrey from different theoretical viewpoints, were talking more and more about managed money in this period—but, as already noted, this idea was never a runner in the policy stakes.

As regards the emerging concern with unemployment, the role of economists was also minimal. Here, unlike the gold standard, little was actually done (see below, Politics and Policies). But in any event economists had little to contribute. Predominantly unemployment was regarded as a temporary maladjustment problem, automatically eliminated in the long term by the play of market forces, if these were allowed to operate. In the period considered here there was no fundamental challenge to that view. Plainly the war had been highly destabilizing, and there was no compelling reason initially in the early 1920s to disbelieve the view that restabilization of the world economy would eliminate unemployment (Hancock 1970).

Belief in long-term full employment equilibrium was logically compatible with a belief in the desirability of ameliorative measures—notably relief public works—to tide over the difficult years until stability returned. Such works were widely, though not unanimously, accepted by economists at this time, especially if they could be organized in a manner unlikely to cut across other accepted objectives of policy, like tight control on public expenditure. Thus as Winch (1972, pp. 113–14) points out, small-scale relief works, partly funded by local authorities on a decentralized basis, were commensurate with a general sympathy for the Treasury economy campaign.

In the period before 1925 attitudes on unemployment had not crystallized in the way in which they did in the late 1920s. The Treasury, whilst pro-economy, had not yet articulated the full 'Treasury View' which charged that public expenditure crowded private expenditure out completely, and therefore no gain in employment could be had from public works. On the other hand,

Keynes had not yet launched a theoretical attack on what he perceived as the theoretical foundations of economic policy. Although Keynes felt himself powerless to affect policy in this period, it is not at all clear that this resulted from the opposition of other economists to his views, rather than from the lack of impact of economists in general on economic policy.

This issue of the role of economists and economics in policy-making becomes a controversial one from the inter-war years. Whilst it is important not to caricature positions, there seems no doubt that there is a strong body of mainly Keynesian opinion which does see in the evolution of economic theory a key determinant of the evolution of economic policy. A classic example of this is Howson (1975). The approach is quite explicitly spelt out: 'one of the most interesting developments in economic policy-making in the inter-war years is the change in the theories on which policy was based' (p. 1). We will return to this general view in later chapters, but one example is pertinent here. This concerns inflation. Howson argues that the Treasury's and Bank of England's fear of inflation from 1919 onwards was largely conditioned by economic theory. 'Fear of inflation was a logical consequence of holding the classical economic theory, whereby the volume of output and employment are determined by real factors, inflation being a purely monetary phenomenon' (p. 29). Whilst this concept of inflation may have reduced a little the authorites' worries over the consequences of their deflationary policies, it is difficult to see the fear of inflation as grounded in any helpful sense in 'theory'. Fear of inflation was based on the belief that fluctuating prices undermined political and social stability, in the ways so graphically outlined by Keynes (1971, ch. 1). Such a view, accurate or not, was based on no necessary concept of the economy. Indeed it is striking how much exactly the same fears surfaced in the great scare over inflation in the mid-1970s, despite the very different intellectual climate of that period.

Overall the war and its aftermath did not mark any fundamental shifts in economic theory, nor did they see economics playing a substantially increased role in economic policy-making. Economists played some role in public debate—as they always have done—but it is difficult to see any distinctive 'economics' approach having an impact on policy.

Politics and Policies

Measured by the state's share of GNP, the scope of government
regulation, or the proliferation of new Ministries, the war
massively enhanced the role of the state in the economy. This had
not happened in response to any plan—rather it had taken the
form of a long-drawn-out realization of, and response to, the fact
that the pre-war strategic notions of the shape of the likely war
were entirely mistaken. Rather than a predominantly naval
struggle, with Britain using its navy to blockade Germany and
support allied armies, the war became a struggle between mass
armies which could only be sustained by systematic regulation of
the economy, and not least of labour. This expansion of the state's
role had to overcome not so much ingrained *laissez-faire* ideas, but
a military and hence economic strategy which was simply
irrelevant (French 1982).

Ideologically this expansion had no clear foundation. It was
predominantly justified on a purely pragmatic basis—as a condition
for winning the war, during which normality must be suspended. It
was introduced by a Liberal (or at least Liberal-led) government,
and promoted a profound crisis for liberalism. But it also opened
up the possibility of using the state as much pre-war New
Liberalism had advocated, as an agency of amelioration of the
conditions of labour and the poor. The case for such amelioration
was made more compelling by the need to propitiate labour—
improved in its bargaining position and on occasions unsure in its
commitment to the war effort.

Thus under Lloyd George not only was the state deployed the
better to prosecute the war effort, but also to devise a programme
of post-war reconstruction, to deliver the land fit for heroes that
motivating the workers in the factories and the soldiers at the front
was seen to require. (Also to improve the health and conditions of
the vast numbers of the urban working class who were unfit to
fight.)

The devising of this reconstruction programme was pursued
with energy and vigour. Plans were drawn up for major reforms
across a broad front from education to pensions, from wage
regulation to housing (Johnson 1968). Little of this effort came to
fruition. Perhaps the most significant programme which did lead

somewhere was housing, where central government money was deployed to some effect, especially in the spring of 1921 (Swenarton 1981). Education was also reformed, and a start made on compulsory secondary education. But most areas were 'patched' rather than systematically reformed, basically because of the hostility to government spending which developed at the beginning of the 1920s (Morgan 1979).

This gap between promise and performance can be read as a straightforward political ploy to gain support, abandoned once conditions changed to make this seem safe strategy for the government (Wrigley 1976). Certainly the government was able to take advantage of the slump after 1920 to renege on previous promises, and to 'roll back the state' both as a provider of welfare and as a regulator of industry (Armitage 1969). As noted above, social expenditure remained well above pre-war levels, but fell far short of what was envisaged by the reconstruction plans.

This enhancement of the state's role during the First World War had an important ideological outcome, beyond that of destroying liberalism as a political force. It acted to crystallize the left–right political divide as substantially synonymous with differing views as to the efficacy and desirability of state action. Politically, pre-war Labour had not been far removed from important strands of radical liberalism in distrusting the state, and had not been readily enticed into changing its views by the more positive state role pursued by New Liberalism. Of course 'labour' was not homogeneous, and Fabianism in particular had usually been a keen supporter of state action. But on the eve of the first war anti-state syndicalism was a powerful force within labour generally, and at the parliamentary level, the Labour Party claimed only a minimal role for state intervention.

In 1918 the Labour Party constitution was rewritten, and included Clause IV, which committed the Party to 'common ownership', which clearly meant state ownership, albeit in a form yet to be decided. This change was very much based on a perception that wartime regulation had demonstrated the efficacy of state action, and that this should be maintained in peacetime (Tawney 1943). Thus was a central feature of British twentieth-century politics—argument over the extent of the state's role—established in the wake of the war.

Not only was the expansion of the state a potent force changing labour's ideology, but that expansion can be seen as a response to the enhanced role of 'labour' in society.

Before 1914 parliamentary Labour had been weak, and had largely functioned as an 'advanced' wing of liberalism. When historians speak of the 'challenge of labour' in this period they normally refer not to the Labour Party, but to the militant trade-unionism of the period, the strikes that resulted from this, and the explicitly anti-parliamentary ideology, syndicalism, which many of its leaders espoused. As already noted in Chapter 2, how far the reforms of the pre-war period can be seen as simply a response to 'the challenge of labour' is much debated. Alternative explanations stress the autonomous weight of ideologies such as New Liberalism in generating reform (e.g. Freeden 1978). Others again, looking at 'high politics', 'argue that 'labour' was not the predominant concern of pre-war politicians—rather they focused above all on the Irish question (Stubbs 1975).

In any event the war undoubtedly shifted labour in all its forms to the centre of the political agenda (Cowling 1971). At the parliamentary level the first Labour ministers entered government, and a Ministry of Labour was created. More significantly, at least in the short run, trade unions were given a new status, directly bargained with by a government concerned to maintain their consent for the changes in labour practices that wartime demands for manpower and production were perceived to require. Implicitly or explicitly these changes were bargained not for better wages, but for reforms by the government—rent controls, food rationing, excess profit duties could all be seen in this light (Pollard 1983, pp. 38–47).

As already noted, concessions were made to the 'challenge of labour' both by the initial movement towards social reconstruction and in the decision of 1919 to go off gold in order to avoid the deflationary consequences of any immediate restoration of the pre-war parity. But in 1920 macroeconomic policy sharply altered course. At the same time there was a sharp adverse movement in world economic conditions, and this confirmed the government in its already weakening commitment to social reform. The Cabinet records for 1920 'show a marked change of tone. Ministers more and more shared a feeling that in financial terms they were doing too much and reaping no advantage thereby' (Johnson 1968, p.4 91). Conciliatory government was replaced by a more aggressive, negative stance as the slump progressed, culminating in the Geddes Axe of 1922.

This period can be seen as government standing up to labour and winning. Certainly labour's fortunes slumped with the economy as unemployment mounted, wages (eventually) fell sharply, and union membership fell. However one interpretation, despite these post-war events, sees a sea-change in relations between the state and labour occurring in the war period. This is the work of Middlemas (1979).

Middlemas sets out to explain the comparative political stability of twentieth-century Britain, arguing that this is best interpreted as the consequence of British governments from 1911 onwards deliberately fostering employees' and employer's organizations. This encouragement transformed these bodies from pressure groups into 'governing institutions' which in turn acted to control dissent in their own ranks, reduce the power of parliament, and enhance the role of the civil service in the ensuing stalemate.

This 'corporate bias' thesis is generally unpersuasive. Whilst it is certainly right to stress the state's role in encouraging both employees' and employers' organization during the First World War, this hardly establishes the thesis. First, and most generally, Britain has been characterized by the weakness of its 'peak associations' of employees and especially employers—these have normally lacked the capacity either to 'deliver' their members for policies or to discipline the recalcitrants (e.g. Zeitlin 1987).

Second, the peak associations in inter-war Britain, the TUC and the National Confederation of Employers Organizations, may have been consulted by governments, but in a manner parallel to other pressure groups, not as key 'social partners'. Their main impact was on the details of legislation, and rather than forming a harmonious tripartism, these bodies were quite often locked in serious conflict with government. Finally, there is no clear evidence of a loss of parliamentary capacity in their favour; parliamentary scrutiny of the executive may, as always, have been patchy, but it was not lost to these bodies (Lowe 1980; 1986, pp. 245–67). This debate is important if only in the negative sense of bringing out Britain's failure to develop forms of corporatist policy-making which in other countries (most obviously Sweden) have brought such notable success in economic management in more recent times.

The other facet of the post-war rise of labour was the growing electoral strength of the Labour Party. As noted already this had, in 1918, acquired its socialist constitution and thus set the parameters of its ideology for the next seventy years. Probably this ideological sharpening played only a minor role in the electoral strengthening of Labour, which propelled it into government, albeit without a majority, in 1924.

This socialist ideology and electoral advance was accompanied by a profound conservatism in economic and financial policy, which greatly inhibited the Labour Party from providing plausible proposals for dealing with the mass unemployment which emerged from 1921. Labour's leading economic and financial spokesman (and Chancellor of the Exchequer in 1924) was Philip Snowden. In 1920 he published a book entitled *Labour and National Finance*. The first sentence of this book summed up a whole world view which was to be central to Labour's outlook up to 1931: 'Sound finance is the basis of national and commercial prosperity.' The book went on to berate the wartime government for borrowing to fight the war, rather than following the Gladstonian view that wars should be fought from current tax revenue. It called for a programme of public expenditure cuts and stressed the absolute priority of reducing the National Debt.

This acceptance of financial orthodoxy included acceptance of the need to return to gold. Thus whilst Labour certainly regarded unemployment as a major issue in the early 1920s, its proposed remedies were markedly similar to those of the Liberals and Conservatives. These remedies focused on reviving the international economy, especially through an end to reparations and war debts, and a stabilization of trading relations with Germany and Russia (Morgan 1979, p. 224).

This profoundly conservative stance was accompanied by a commitment to counter-cyclical public works, financed by loans—though Snowden himself never seems to have accepted this form of finance. For the party leadership such works were seen as at best a temporary, stop-gap measure pending the reconstruction of the international economy. Whilst the Independent Labour Party, at this time a major force within the Labour Party, developed a more ambitious programme of domestic reflation, it did not have a clear position on Britain's relation to the international economy and how such domestic policies could be made compatible with the balance of payments constraint (Booth and Pack 1985, pp. 17–26; on the ILP see also Garside 1985).

Overall, therefore, we cannot see the early 1920s as a period when a growing labour movement fought against prevailing economic orthodoxies. As Booth and Pack suggest 'In spite of its reconstruction pledges, there is every reason to suspect that even a Labour Cabinet would have been swayed by orthodox financial pressures into defending the exchange rate at the cost of higher domestic unemployment' (Booth and Pack 1985, p. 11). It should be emphasized that this stance of the Labour Party was not just a consequence of the capture of its leaders by the ideology of sound finance. It also reflected the lack of intellectual resources available to the Party to draw upon in the area of economic policy. Even the best work in the Labour Party (mainly from the ILP) tended to be overly concerned with such issues as bank nationalization, whose relation to economic policy was extremely unclear. But beyond this, it also needs to be noted that financial orthodoxy was a deliberate strategic choice by the Labour leadership. For the overall strategy of the party at this time was one of demonstrating its 'fitness to govern'. This was clearly the case when Labour eventually came to power in 1924. In this period as Prime Minister, MacDonald's objective 'was to achieve such advances as were open to him within the framework of conventional politics and to convince anyone whose might wish to know that Socialism meant men of business pursuing the half measures constitutive of radical progress as England knew it' (Cowling 1971, p. 360).

The Labour government of 1924 saw no interruption to the long-term programme of gold restoration. On the unemployment front also Labour departed remarkably little from existing policies. This meant essentially policies of public works, and relief via the 'dole'. As noted above, the early post-war governments had pursued a modest programme of relief works (and that cut back by Geddes), organized by the Unemployment Grants Committee; but it was heavily dependent on local initiative, and trivial in impact compared with the scale of the unemployment problem (Hancock 1970, pp. 107–11). Labour was committed to a large-scale expansion of this programme—but also to financial orthodoxy. This contra-diction led only to frustration and impotence on the part of those charged with developing unemployment policy, given Snowden's and the Treasury's policy-making weight (Booth and Pack 1985, pp. 19–21).

Most of Labour's energy in relation to unemployment went to changing the conditions of relief. The 1911 Insurance Act had envisaged a self-financing unemployment benefit scheme amongst a narrow range of industries. But under wartime pressures this scheme had been expanded to cover around 60 per cent of the workforce. With demobilization followed by the slump the insurance base of the scheme had dissolved; large numbers of workers could not meet the contribution conditions to claim benefit. In the face of this from 1919 onwards various 'out-of-work donations' and 'uncovenanted benefits' were deployed to maintain unemployed incomes and prevent massive recourse to the Poor Law.

As a corollary to these changes a 'genuinely-seeking-work' test was imposed on claimants, and a means test. Much of the political debate of the 1920s focused on this collapse of insurance and the various tinkerings with which the government attempted to patch up the system. Labour in office widened the scope of the genuinely-seeking-work test but dropped the means test. It did not initiate any fundamental reform of the system (Deacon 1976, 1977; more generally on social policy, Crowther 1988).

From the point of view of the Conservative Party and the governing classes generally the Labour government of 1924 was a calculated risk. In the event their faith in the conservatism of Labour's leaders was largely justified; some small reforms were enacted, but the main thrust of economic and social policy was unchanged.

Across the political spectrum, with few exceptions, financial conservatism dominated economic policy from 1920 to 1925. The main opposition to political conservatism was now Labour, but the Labour leadership lacked the capacity to translate widespread concern with unemployment into a challenge to that financial orthodoxy. Whilst serious policy discussion went on, notably within the ILP, the Labour leadership often only managed to combine windy socialist rhetoric with 'unbending Gladstonian' financial policies (Beloff 1975, p. 217).

Conclusions

The First World War had a profound impact on many aspects of British life (Marwick 1965; Milward 1985). It destroyed the basis for the international hegemony enjoyed before 1913. But at the level of policy its impact was strikingly limited. The state rolled forward, but to a substantial extent was then rolled back. Above all the commitment to an unmanaged national economy, in which adjustment to international conditions could be seen as a necessary constraint on domestic extravagance, remained largely unchallenged. In retrospect the desire to return to 1913, when the conditions of 1913 had gone forever, may appear nostalgically naïve. But to the key agencies of policy-making a gold standard would appear to offer the best chance of a stable, non-inflationary world in which the traditional limited role of the state could be maintained against domestic political pressure. Policy had not yet 'adjusted to democracy' (Lowe 1986, ch. 1).

Further Reading

Armitage, S. (1969): *The Politics of Decontrol of Industry: Britain and the USA*, London.

Booth, A., and Pack, M. (1985): *Employment, Capital, and Economic Policy*, Oxford.

Burk, K., ed. (1982): *War and the State*, London.

French, D. (1982): *British Economic and Strategic Planning 1905–1915*, London.

Howson, S. (1975): *Domestic Monetary Management in Britain 1919–1939*, Cambridge, chs. 1,2.

Lowe, R. (1986): *Adjusting to Democracy*, Oxford.

Marwick, A. (1965): *The Deluge: British Society and the First World War*, London.

Milward, A. (1985): *The Economic Effects of the World War on Britain*, 2nd edn., London.

Moggridge, D. (1972): *British Monetary Policy 1924–1931*, Cambridge, chs. 1–3.

Pollard, S., ed. (1970): *The Gold Standard and Employment Policies Between the Wars*, London.

Winch, D. (1972): *Economics and Policy*, London, chs. 4–6.

4

1925–1931: The Old World Restored and Found Wanting

IN 1925 the central economic policy objective of the previous five years was achieved, and Britain returned to gold. This restoration of the old framework of policy was ill-matched to the new conditions of both the British and the world economy. The hope that the restoration of gold would restore pre-war normality was urealized, and with the onset of the world slump from 1929 the policy became increasingly fragile. In 1931 Britain was forced off gold, never to return.

This chapter is concerned with the evolution of public policy under the restored gold standard, and the conditions which led to the ultimate demise of that standard, and with it many elements of public policy on the economy which previously had been taken for granted.

Institutions

The Gold Standard

The new gold standard was in place for six years, but its history can be helpfully sub-divided into two: the period from 1925 to 1928, and that from 1928 to 1931.

From 1925 to 1928 the gold standard existed in the context of an upswing in the cycle of economic activity which covered most of the world (Aldcroft 1977, ch. 8). For most of the period this upsurge was accompanied by greater stability in exchange rates and a general renewal of economic stability, in marked contrast to the early 1920s.

This context undoubtedly made Britain's attachment to the gold standard easier than otherwise would have been the case—but it was by no means easy in any other sense. The ideal of the gold standard, as we have seen, was that it should be an automatic mechanism, but in the conditions of the late 1920s Britain's position on the gold standard had in fact to be continually managed (Sayers 1976, vol. i, chs. 9, 15; Williamson 1984).

Some part of this difficulty arose from the overvaluation of sterling. The debate over this overvaluation is one of the most persistent in the history of British economic policy. Few now would take the view of Johnson (1972, p. 110) that all Britain's problems of the late 1920s derived from the overvaluation. There has always been an alternative view which disputes the existence of any overvaluation—most recently expressed by Matthews (1986). Much writing now takes the view that whilst sterling was overvalued at $4.86, this was only one factor contributing to Britain's difficulties in the late 1920s (e.g. Dimsdale 1981, Wright 1981).

This debate arises from the difficulty of specifying an equilibrium exchange rate. The standard method of approach involves the use of purchasing-power parity calculations. These calculations mean deciding on a base year in which the exchange rate can be held to have been in equilibrium, looking at the divergence of price trends between countries from that base to the year under consideration, and seeing how far those price divergences are reflected in the exchange rate. Thus if over the period since the base year country *A*'s prices have doubled, and those of country *B* have risen by 50 per cent, the exchange rate between *A* and *B* should have fallen by half to maintain equilibrium.

In practice such calculations are extremely complicated. First, there is the choice of appropriate base year; then of the appropriate price index. This latter is especially problematic, as what is needed is an index which as far as possible only reflects changes in domestic costs—and no price index does this entirely satisfactorily. In addition, even if a good index of purchasing power is obtained, this will not reflect the myriad of other factors relevant to a country's capacity to compete—changes in tastes, technology, movements of tariffs for example. Most such calculations for the pound in relation to the dollar in the mid-1920s show some overvaluation, ranging up to 10 per cent (Moggridge 1972, pp. 101–4).

Another important way of looking at the consequences of the gold standard is to look at the balance of payments. At the given exchange rate, was Britain able to pay her way in the world? Britain's balance of payments in the years 1926–8 show a current account surplus, allowing for the impact of the general strike of 1926. But this was accompanied by a persistently high level of unemployment, which would have substantially improved the current balance by reducing imports far more than it reduced exports. Hence we can conclude that most evidence suggests that the pound was overvalued at \$4.86, and this provided a constraining influence on many aspects of British policy in the late 1920s.

The presumption here is that the traditional view of the 1925 decision as a policy error is correct. However this view does not by any means imply that a lower exchange rate for the pound would have been either easily attained or a solution to all of Britain's economic problems. On the ease of attainment, it should be noted that several other countries returned to gold after Britain, and at devalued rates of exchange, so that a lower value for the pound might have led to an even lower parity for these currencies especially the French and Belgian francs (Sayers 1970). Also, many Empire countries pegged their exchange rate against the pound, so an effective devaluation against such currencies might not have been easily attained (Tomlinson 1978). On the other hand, even if attained, a 10 per cent lower value for the pound is likely to have eased rather than solved the problems of the staple exporting industries. Whilst Moggridge's elasticity calculations for the effects of a lower exchange rate are plausible (1972, app. 1), they do not rest on detailed industry-by-industry studies which might throw some doubt on how responsive markets were likely to be to relatively small price changes (always assuming the devaluation was passed on to consumers in lower prices, and not taken in the form of increased profits).

It would be mistaken to believe that, for the authorities at the time, the gold standard was seen largely as a problem of trade competitiveness. Rather, the gold standard in the 1920s, as before World War One, led to a focus on the gold reserves. The state of these reserves was the central index of pressure on gold adherence. The state of the reserves in turn reflected the underlying features of the British payments position. These features may be crudely summarized in most years in the late 1920s as consisting of a current account surplus coupled with an even larger outflow on long-term capital account. This required that London attract a continuing inflow of short-term capital to bridge the gap and finance this capital outflow (Moggridge 1972, pp. 126–9, 199).

Between 1925 and 1928 this was achieved, with effort. A number of weapons, traditional and new, were deployed in this effort (see below on Bank of England). But it is important to note that Bank Rate was *not* used as the key element in defence of the pound in this period. In fact whilst Bank Rate was, by previous standards, a little high, it was not altered at all frequently (Sayers 1976, vol. i, pp. 216–17). Policy did not consist of a full-blooded deflation (in comparison with 1920–1, or 1979–81) but an unhappy medium of a little deflation and a little overvaluation, which exacerbated Britain's short-term problems without attempting any long-term solutions.

As discussed in Chapter 3, the economic basis for restoration of gold was extremely vague, and the conditions of success of such restoration not clearly spelt out. But three elements in particular seem to have been assumed to operate under the new gold regime, none of which materialized. First, it was thought that American prices would rise to restore the old pound–dollar ratio, but this failed to occur. The US 'central bank' (i.e. the Federal Reserve Bank of New York) co-operated with the Bank of England, but not to the extent of inflating to help the pound. Second, it had been assumed that money wages in Britain would prove flexible, so that 'deflation' would be a matter of price and wage adjustment, not adjustment of output. Especially after the general strike, the costs of such attempts at wage reduction were too apparent to encourage any repetition. Finally, it had been assumed that under gold, capital flows would be equilibrating i.e. would aid balance of payments adjustment. But this was not the case. Funds were now more mobile, more likely to respond to changes in expectations, more difficult to counter with orthodox financial weapons.

Overall the search for a gold-based normality proved a chimera. By 1927 Norman accepted that the 1925 restoration had been a mistake; 'the more fundamental aspect of this mistake had not been a miscalculation on exchange rates but his supposition that the return to gold meant the restoration of a tolerably smooth system of international and domestic monetary adjustment' (Sayers 1976, vol. i, p. 334).

Up to 1928 the consequences of this mistake were manageable, at least from the Bank of England's point of view, but from that year, even before the slump, the costs of adherence began to increase. The cause of this was the boom on Wall Street.

The growing role of the New York financial markets and the general strength of the dollar meant that. it was the relative attraction of New York and London that dominated London's capacity to attract short-term funds in this period. The boom on Wall Street acted as a magnet to 'footloose' funds, and this led to a rising trend in Bank Rate from mid-1928, which went along with a general upward movement of short-term rates until late 1929 (Moggridge 1972, pp. 153–8).

The initial effect of the Wall Street collapse of October 1929 was relief for London, and short-term rates fell back. This relief, however, was set against a background of deterioration in the balance of payments position. The current balance, after peaking at £124m. in 1928, fell back progressively to a deficit in excess of £100m. by 1931. This deterioration exacerbated London's reliance on short-term inflows, and the mismatch between these liabilities and the Bank's gold and foreign exchange resources.

When London came under pressure in the summer of 1931 with the crises of the Austrian and German banking systems it was thus already in a very vulnerable position. But this vulnerability was translated into an inevitable collapse of the gold standard by the loss of confidence that developed in the same period. This loss was based partly on a realization that the $4.86 parity was excessive, and that little had been or perhaps could be done to fully correct this. More prominent was the linking of confidence in the pound to the budget. The growing deficit on the budget was the key symbol of the British government's financial lack of probity. The failure of the Labour government to act swiftly to reduce this deficit, including cuts in unemployment benefit, was treated in financial circles as an index of irresponsibility and a reason for offering no further aid to London (Sayers 1976, vol. ii, ch. 17; Kunz 1987; and see below, Politics and Policies).

Even the demise of the Labour government was insufficient to rescue the pound, and on 21 September Britain 'went off'. The world did not tumble around the Bank of England's ears, but a new era was opened in which the old rules did not apply.

Free Trade

The war had opened up the issue of Britain's continued adherence to free trade as never before, but despite the limited incursions into protection recorded in the previous chapter, this principle remained dominant in policy. However the conversion of many in the Conservative party to protectionism meant that the issue was never off the agenda, even after the Tories' election defeat on the issue in 1923.

The pressure for protectionism in the late 1920s had no one source. In part it was a 'natural' response to the growth and persistence of unemployment. But most people perceived that Britain's problems were predominantly ones of export collapse, to which simple protection was no answer. However, it could be made relevant if an offer of protection were used as a lever to encourage the staple industries to reform themselves, to increase their efficiency by amalgamation and closure of less efficient capacity. In the late 1920s, with the realization that the problems of the staples were not going to go away, there was growing concern with such industrial change, commonly called 'rationaliz-ation' (Kirby 1987, pp. 131–5). However, governments were unwilling to concern themselves directly with industry, and by and large sought to encourage industry to put its own house in order, with perhaps the offer of protection as an inducement, where relevant.

One industry where such an approach had relevance was iron and steel, which faced significant import competition. But in the event nothing came of the idea. Partly this was because the industry itself never formed a coherent pressure group single-mindedly pursuing protection. Equally the government was wary of granting protection *before* rationalization, fearful that it would only serve to reinforce inefficiency (Tolliday 1984, pp. 52–5).

The other theme in discussion of free trade versus protection was that of the Empire. The pre-war Conservative agitation had, of course, been one in favour of Imperial Preference, and this idea of a closer economic union within the Empire had been reinforced for many by the political and military co-operation of the war period. Much of the pressure of the 1920s within British politics, mainly but not exclusively in the Conservative party, came from those who linked Imperial Preference to unemployment by suggesting that such a system would protect British industry against non-Empire competition, at the same time boosting Empire demand for British exports.

In fact the 'Imperial Visionaries' tried to link Britain's economic difficulties to imperial solutions by two other strands. First, they wanted to encourage migration from Britain to the Empire, to decrease unemployment and people the underpopulated Dominions. Second, they wanted to encourage British investment in the Empire both to develop Empire self-sufficiency and expand the demand for British exports (Drummond 1972, ch. 2; 1974, chs. 1–3).

It was unemployment which gave the Imperial Visionaries some success in the 1920s. Empire settlement was encouraged by an Act of 1922, and encouragement was given to the British financing of Empire public utilities, culminating in the Colonial Development Act of 1929, thus imperial preferences were built into the protective measures of these years. The scale of these efforts was reduced by Treasury parsimony and advocacy of consumer interests. But in any event the likely impact on the British economy of such measures was grotesquely disproportionate to the rhetoric of the Visionaries. The British desire for cheap food and the White Dominion interest in developing their own manufacturing fundamentally militated against any idea of the Empire as an economic unit. Whilst a broadly open international economy continued in being, these objections were decisive (Howson and Winch 1977, pp. 37–9).

Budgetary Orthodoxy

As noted in Chapter 3, the early 1920s had seen a reassertion of the traditional verities in budgetary policy, of low expenditure, and a surplus sufficient for debt redemption, symbolized by the Geddes Axe of 1922. At the same time the war period had driven government expenditure to a new plateau above its pre-war level. In the late 1920s government expenditure moved slowly upwards, fuelled by such measures as the Contributory Pensions Act of 1925, the rising expenditure on unemployment insurance as well as military expenditure. It also included a substantial expenditure arising from the de-rating legislation, which reduced the rates paid to local authorities and replaced the revenue by increased subventions from central government (Hicks 1970, pp. 7–11).

Churchill, the Conservative Chancellor from 1925 to 1929 presided, therefore, over a relative profligacy in public expenditure which contrasted with Snowden, his immediate predecessor and also successor at the Treasury. It also contrasted with the constraints supposedly imposed on financial policy by adherence to gold. Churchill became notorious to the fiscal-minded for financing his increases in expenditure out of all manner of devices—'raids' on the Road Fund, i.e. taxes earmarked for road building; using capital assets to balance current revenue; anticipating future revenue by altering the due dates for tax.

Under Snowden between 1929 and 1931 expenditure continued to grow, most notably because of expenditure on unemployment. Most of this went on relief, this cost to the Exchequer rising from £98.4m. in 1929 to a peak of £164m. in 1931, whereas expenditure on all kinds of relief works never exceeded £20m. in their peak year, 1930 (Hicks 1970, p. 194). Unlike Churchill, Snowden's commitment to financial probity allowed less scope for window-dressing, so the necessary consequence of increased expenditure was increased taxation, falling in the 1930 budget mainly on the higher-income groups.

Increasing taxes to prevent a budget deficit in a depression is like walking up a down escalator; the decline in economic activity automatically reduces revenue and raises expenditure. Hence despite Snowden's best efforts the gap between receipts and expenditure widened from 1929/30 onwards. However, if one separates out the effects of rising unemployment on the budget from budgetary policy, it is clear that fiscal policy was sharply deflationary. This is shown in Table 4.1 where the budgetary balance for a constant level of unemployment is calculated, showing how on this basis governments were achieving larger and larger surpluses, rising to 3 per cent of GNP by 1932/3.

Initially this deflationary stance was the consequence of increased taxation. But in 1931 the growing agitation against the burden of government expenditure reached its peak with the publication of the May Committee Report (Cmd. 3920), calling for expenditure cuts of £97m., including unemployment benefit cuts of 20 per cent, to counteract a prospective deficit of £120m. in 1932/33. The Minority Report of the Committee did not contest the basic stance, but called for greater equality of sacrifice in the cuts (Skidelsky 1970, pp. 379–88; Middleton 1985, pp. 109–13).

This Report exacerbated the unravelling crisis of confidence in sterling. The Labour government's response was to search for some kind of compromise, but one which embodied at least some cut in unemployment pay, which had become the symbol of financial responsibility. This was a route which a small majority of the Cabinet were willing to follow, but they faced the hostility of the rest of the Cabinet, the TUC and most Labour opinion. On this issue the Labour government fell in August 1931 (see below, Politics and Policies).

Table 4.1   *Budgetary Policy 1929/30–1932/3*

	Nominal Budgetary Stance		Constant Employment Budget	
	£m.	*% GDP*	*£m.*	*% GDP*
1929/30	+17.4	+0.4	+17.4	+0.4
1930/31	−24.2	−0.6	+47.1	+1.1
1931/32	−45.7	−1.2	+106.7	+2.5
1932/33	−50.2	−1.3	+124.5	+3.0

Note: The nominal figures are not those calculated at the time, but are based on the elimination of window-dressing devices aimed at maintaining confidence in fiscal policy.
Source: Middleton 1985, p. 135.

In the event the economy package imposed by the 'National' Government in September 1931 was only marginally more severe than that agreed by the Labour Cabinet. Two features of this package stand out. First, it focused to an almost unparalleled extent on cutting current expenditure—almost all other twentieth-century cuts packages have focused on politically less transparent cuts in capital expenditure. Second, whilst it achieved its immediate aim of making more loans available from American bankers, the budget was insufficient to maintain the gold standard, departure from which followed within days. 'At the moment of its greatest triumph orthodoxy failed in its object' (Winch 1972, p. 145; also Middleton 1985, pp. 99–101).

Agencies

The Bank of England

The restoration of gold was also the restoration of the role of the Bank of England. Between 1925 and 1931 the bank reasserted its traditional prerogative as the non-political custodian of the monetary system, and its immunity from governmental pressure. But whilst these positions were almost unanimously accepted in public, in private the Bank's freedom of manœuvre was reduced. The Bank's relations with government were one more constraint on its difficult role of managing the gold standard in these years.

As noted in Chapter 3, the central strategy embodied in gold restoration was restabilization of the world financial system. This required an active role by the Bank of England in aiding other countries to restore and maintain the conditions of gold adherence. The orientation of the Bank in these years was primarily external. The most important area of activity was in Europe, where financial instability was greatest and most threatening to British interests. These efforts were crowned with some success, though this was most apparent in the relatively quiet years of 1925–8 (Sayers 1976, vol. i, pp. 183–201; Clarke 1967, ch. 8).

The most successful international co-operation by the Bank was with the USA, i.e. with Benjamin Strong, the Governor of the Federal Reserve in New York. But Strong died in 1928 on the eve of the renewed pressures brought about by the Wall Street boom and its subsequent collapse. The attraction of funds to New York by the boom, and hence the reduction of the Bank's reserves, posed a very serious threat to the gold standard through much of 1928 and 1929. Bank Rate was raised in February 1929, but apart from domestic considerations (see below) the Bank no longer believed in the pre-1913 magical ability of Rate changes to attract gold (Sayers 1976, vol. i, pp. 223–34).

The collapse of the Wall Street boom in October 1929 brought some immediate relief, but interest rates continued high into 1930. As the depression worsened it became apparent that the threat was no longer primarily one of gold loss to the USA, but illiquidity brought about by the collapse of foreign banking systems and the effects of this on London's position as a short-term debtor, with outstanding debts much greater than gold and foreign currency reserves.

Against this tide central bank co-operation was insufficient. In June 1931 the Bank helped the Reichsbank, and this was followed by help to Austria and Hungary. When the pressure turned on London the Federal Reserve and the Bank of France initially helped, but the growing focus on the budgetary position led to further aid being made conditional on government action in that area. The Bank was thus unable on its own to save the gold standard, though it continued to press the government for action which would achieve that goal (Sayers 1976, vol. ii, ch. 17; Williamson 1984; Kunz 1987, chs. 3–5).

It bears repeating that the primary focus of the Bank's activities in these years was external, and this was especially so if the attention is on monetary policy. At the same time, policy was not one of wholehearted deflation of the domestic economy in order to maintain the reserves. Fundamentally the reason seems to have been a belief within the bank that the reserves could be defended without recourse to actions which added substantially to domestic unemployment.

Traditionally the primary weapon of defence of gold was the Bank Rate. But for much of the late 1920s this weapon was largely in abeyance. There were two reasons for this. First, despite formal acceptance of the Bank's independence, it was subjected to substantial informal pressure to hold down Bank Rate to mitigate unemployment. The Treasury under Churchill made its view of the undesirability of increases in the Rate clearly known, and whilst there was an element of the rate being 'ratcheted up', the Bank's decision-making was sensitive to these pressures (Moggridge 1972, ch. 7). How far the Bank accepted the adverse effects of high Bank Rates on domestic activity is unclear. Under pressure before the Macmillan Committee Norman admitted that there would have been less unemployment if interest rates had been 2 per cent lower (Macmillan 1931*b*, Qs. 3492–3), but this was in 1931 and it is not clear if, in his view, the point applied before 1928/29. Norman's attitude to unemployment, it has been argued, was not one of indifference, 'but he did not regard it as falling within his field of responsibility or power of control' (Clay 1957, p. 167).

At an earlier stage of this evidence to the Macmillan Committee,

Norman was also asked about the effect of Bank Rate decisions on industry, and in his reply he stressed that 'the main consideration in connection with movements of the Bank Rate is the international consideration' (Q. 3319). But the international consideration could be addressed in many other ways. Apart from international central bank co-operation, it included the resurrection of the gold 'devices' of pre-1913—operating directly in the gold market to reduce gold losses without recourse to Bank Rate charges. More innovatory were operations in the foreign exchange market (Moggridge 1972, ch. 8).

A more reluctant deviation from pre-1913 norms was control over foreign investment. This had been instituted originally in 1914 to protect the exchanges. Initially it was operated on a statutory basis by the Treasury, but passed to the Bank to operate informally in 1919. In the early post-war period the main object of the controls was to ease the government's financing position in the London capital market. But from November 1924 it received renewed statutory backing to support the pound prior to and just after gold restoration. The government was unwilling to make the controls permanent in peacetime, partly in the belief of a close relation between foreign lending and British exports, partly because in the absence of foreign exchange controls it was impossible to prevent sterling holders buying foreign issues in foreign financial centres. However the Bank continued with a policy of 'informal blackmail' through the 1920s and this may have helped solve short-term exchange problems (Atkin 1970; Moggridge 1972, ch. 9).

It is worth noting in this context that controls on foreign lending were never used in this period to help domestic industrial investment. The reasons seem to have been threefold. The major staple industries were not in a position to borrow, so were not perceived as short of funds. Secondly, they did not for the most part bring forward rationalization plans requiring major funding. Finally, they were 80 per cent dependent on ploughed-back profits for investment, so, as for most of the twentieth century, external credit was unimportant (Atkin 1970, p. 332; but see Best and Humphries 1986).

By these various means the Bank was able to maintain gold adherence without very high Bank Rates for most of the period

1925–31. In other words, the precarious adherence of Britain on gold could be maintained by policies which to some extent insulated the domestic economy from external pressure.

Thus, up to the end of 1928, the effects of the gold movements and general monetary policy on the domestic economy were relatively limited, at best creating slight restraining pressures on an expansion originating elsewhere. Interest rates were relatively high in historical terms, but the availability of bank finance at these high rates does not appear to have been greatly impaired. (Moggridge 1972, pp. 154–5).

In 1929 Bank Rate rose, and even when it fell back in 1930 and 1931 credit remained tight, and long-term rates especially remained high. By 1931 the conflict between domestic and international considerations made continued gold adherence impossible, and with the end of gold ended the centrality of the Bank as an institution in economic policy. It was never to regain quite such a role again.

Whilst gold was the foundation of the Bank's role in monetary and general economic policy, in the late 1920s it was drawn into a rather different and almost startling role as an organizer of intervention in industry.

The Bank's role in this area can be viewed from two angles. Negatively, it reflected the lack of any other agency active in this field. As regards government, the First World War had seen a number of significant but piecemeal interventions in the conduct of industrial firms, most notably in the management of munitions firms where the state's interest was most obvious. Also, in 1915 the Department of Scientific and Industrial Research was founded to encourage what today would be called Research and Development (Mowery 1986). After the war other measures followed, for example the beginnings of Export Credit Guarantees in 1919. *Ad hoc* assistance was also given to particular industries, for example dyestuffs and coal.

In 1918 the Board of Trade got a special department to deal with industries, and this reflected what was undoubtedly a new concern with the state of British industry. But this concern led to no coherent policy, and was restricted in its development by retrenchment after 1922. The Balfour Committee on Industry and Trade (1924–9) reflected this concern, but its conclusions also reflected the dominant non-interventionist view, neatly summarized in the sentence 'The promotion of manufacturing industry by means of direct financial subsidies is no part of the policy of this country' (Balfour 1929, Survey, Part I, p. 384; see also Tolliday 1986, pp. 100–4; Tolliday 1984, pp. 50–63; Kirby 1987).

Within government circles the dominant view by the late 1920s was that 'industrial policy', that is rationalization was best left to industry itself with some pressure from banks (Lowe 1986, pp. 210–14). But of course British banks had never played a strategic role in British industry, and their involvement mainly arose from having become unwittingly enmeshed in industry's affairs by overlending in the 1919/20 boom. The one agency seemingly able to take up a more strategic role was the Bank of England.

The Bank's role in industry was initially a matter of unintended consequences. These arose from the problems of firms to which it had itself lent, and from the problem of some clearing banks whose overall viability was threatened by bad debts to staple industries. From initial *ad hoc* responses to these problems, the Bank developed a strategic role aimed at rationalizing whole sectors, notably cotton and shipbuilding.

The Bank's activities in this area fitted well into the politics of this time. The government was generally anxious 'to do something' but unwilling to get directly involved, for example, in the shipbuilding case; the Bank for its part was anxious to keep government out of industrial matters. In addition, the clearing banks proved incapable of rising to the needs of 'rationalization', for example in the case of cotton where they were most seriously enmeshed.

To manage these interventions the Bank created first, in 1929, the Securities Management Trust as an advisory body and channel for Bank funds. Second, a Bankers' Industrial Development Corporation, in 1930, in partnership with other financial institutions, which responded to, and in appropriate cases helped finance, schemes of reconstruction put to it. Norman played a very active role in this area, formally as Chairman of BID (Sayers 1976), vol. i, ch. 14; Clay 1957, ch. 8).

The impact of all this can be measured in two ways. First, it was successful in keeping government at arm's length from industry— this was especially important to the Bank in 1929–31, when Norman perceived a threat of enhanced intervention from the

Labour government. He quite explicitly threatened the Bank's withdrawal against any suggestion of nationalization.

Second, as to the overall impact on the structure and efficiency of British industry, some scepticism seems appropriate. The Bank certainly had the strategic vision that was necessary, but it was a long way from this vision to effective action: 'Norman was almost obsessed with grand schemes, but where they proved not to be feasible, he and BID lacked the sort of managerial capabilities and industrial expertise to devise and pursue more flexible strategies. Once the industrial strategist was scratched, the orthodox banker lurked not very far below the surface' (Tolliday 1986, p. 98).

It is a curious commentary on public policy on the economy in this period that the only even partially coherent approach to industrial reconstruction which emerged came from a body traditionally so divorced from industry, and ultimately so poorly equipped to deal with those entirely novel problems.

The Treasury

The Treasury was in full agreement with the Bank of England in seeing the return and maintenance of the gold standard as the keystone of economic policy in this period. The Treasury agreed that the primary aim of policy was to restore pre-war financial conditions—stable exchange rates internationally and sound money and sound budgets at home. It was concerned with unemployment, but saw the long-run solution to this problem as happily coinciding with these traditional goals.

The Treasury then became a bulwark against any adventurousness in policy which involved increased expenditure of public money—from proposals for the Ministry of Labour to extend its role in the labour market, to the Empire Visionaries' schemes for subsidized emigration and Colonial Development grants. But above all, and especially from 1925 onwards, the Treasury outlook became symbolized by its hostility to public works as a solution to the unemployment problem.

Related to the focus on the restoration of international financial stability was the belief that post-war unemployment was transient in character—due to a normal cycle, exacerbated by the consequences of war. In such circumstances the Treasury could support temporary relief works as a palliative measure (Hancock

1970). In the early 1920s these were organized by the Unemployment Grants Committee. This Committee represented an early
case of an important inter-war theme—an attempt to take
contentious issues 'out of politics'. It stood between central and
local government, and provided a façade of independence from
political control (Lowe 1986, p. 204). Its activities embodied an
important truth about public works in Britain—that public
investment was largely in the hands of local authorities, which had
to be encouraged, coerced, or bypassed if large-scale public works
was to get anywhere (Middleton 1983).

The effects of the UGC financed schemes was very limited
(Hicks 1970, pp. 198–203; Howson 1981, pp. 279–83). The Treasury
provided only 30 per cent of the funds, and hence total
expenditure was constrained by local resources. In the peak year
in the 1920s (1923/24) expenditure reached £24.2m., providing
directly perhaps 62,000 man-years of jobs. If we add the indirect
effects, at the most optimistic this would only raise the level to
180,000. Whilst separate road schemes were also pursued at this
time, it is apparent that even adding these in and giving an upper
limit estimate of the multiplier effects, the impact of public works
on unemployment was limited.

Part of this relative failure of public works in the early 1920s was
the consequence of policy e.g. the limited scope of central finance.
Nevertheless this sense of failure, coupled with the change in
perception of the time-horizon of a cure for unemployment, led to
a hardening of Treasury attitudes to public works. The return to
gold coincided with—and no doubt reinforced—this hardening:
'By 1925 the stabilization of European relations was within reach,
but the return to prosperity in Britain seemed more remote than
ever' (Hancock 1970, p. 101). From December 1925 the UGC was
reined back, and the numbers employed on such schemes became
minimal.

Treasury opposition to public works came to be described as the
'Treasury View'. The View can be summarized by two quotes. In
his budget speech of 1929 Churchill argued, 'It is orthodox
Treasury dogma, steadfastly held, that whatever might be the
political or social advantages, very little additional employment
can, and as a general rule will, be created by State borrowing and
expenditure.' This was because 'the supply of capital in this
country being limited, it was undesirable to divert any appreciable

proportion of this supply from normal trade channels' (cited Winch 1972, pp. 118, 115).

In more modern jargon, this view can be seen as arguing for 100 per cent crowding out of private by public expenditure. We return to the theoretical basis of this below (see Doctrine) but a key issue for the understanding of public policy in this period is how far the Treasury View is to be seen as gaining its impact on policy from its theoretical cogency, and lack of a theoretically grounded alternative, and how far from an administrative and political logic, for which the theory provided a rhetorical cover.

Traditional interpretations (e.g. Winch 1972, Howson and Winch 1977) have emphasized the theoretical grounding of the Treasury View, and the only very slow development of a (Keynesian) alternative. More recent work (Tomlinson 1981*a*; Middleton 1983; Peden 1984) has tended to emphasize the constraints on Treasury policy imposed by administrative and political conditions and economic problems beyond those arising from the theoretical allegiance of Treasury officials.

This disagreement is best analysed by looking at the dispute which surrounded the Liberals' proposal for a large-scale public works programme at the time of the 1929 General Election, the document *We Can Conquer Unemployment*. This proposed a programme of public works over two years, at a cost of £250m. and offering jobs to 600,000 workers. The focus was on a crash programme, financed from a combination of increased borrowing and from savings on expenditure and unemployment relief, whilst the long-term policy remained a very traditional one of international co-operation, freer trade, cheap money, greater industrial efficiency, and labour mobility.

The government document produced in response to this[1] was co-ordinated by the Ministry of Labour and in fact most of the paper focuses on other than financial issues (Cmd. 3331). These other issues were essentially that public works take time to be planned and executed because of the role of local authorities and the legal complexities of land purchase; that such unskilled manual work as the works offered would be unsuitable for many of the

---

[1] Peter Clarke (1988 ch. 3) has analysed the development of the Treasury View, stressing the stimulation given to its development not only by Keynes's pronouncements, but by the proposals of the Home Secretary, Sir William Joynson-Hicks, for a public works programme.

unemployed (the skilled and women) and at the same time draw some labour not from the unemployed but from poorly paid agricultural workers; that much of the need for new roads was in prosperous areas whereas most of the unemployed were elsewhere (Tomlinson 1981*a*, ch. 5).

The point made was not that these problems made public works impossible, and indeed between 1925 and 1929 Parliament had voted £254m. for such works without Ministerial opposition. Rather the objection was one of scale and timing given the political circumstances. Of course these circumstances were to a degree malleable, for example much greater control of central over local authorities was not inconceivable. The point in the current context is that, given the assumptions of the government and civil servants, the stated objectives were not just a blind, a cover for 'theoretical' objections. The same point applies to the Treasury section of the 1929 document. It reiterated a version of the Treasury View, but it also stressed fears that increased borrowing to finance such schemes would threaten financial confidence and hence the gold standard. As the Liberals were also concerned to maintain gold, and given the difficulties of the authorities in its maintenance by this time, this point does not appear absurd (Peden 1984, pp. 171–6).

A similar set of concerns informed the Treasury's evidence to the Macmillan Committee. The vagueness of the Treasury's theoretical views is apparent from this evidence, but so also is the grounding of those views on the kind of political, administrative, and economic issues raised in the government document of 1929 (Cmd. 3331). Hopkins, on behalf of the Treasury, emphasized that 'the scale of the capital expenditure is therefore not a question of principle but of degree' and that 'it is from a political aspect that the difficulties of the scheme seem to me to emerge' (Macmillan 1931*b*, Q. 5565). Keynes seems to have recognized that he was not just dealing with a mistaken economic dogma when he noted that 'the Treasury View has been gravely misjudged' (Q. 5689).

The issue here is certainly not to defend the Baldwin government against the Liberal attack. The Conservatives' policies were clearly inadequate to the task, and this in part stemmed from the fact that they did not regard the problem of unemployment as the economically central, and consequently had not thought through plausible solutions to it which anyway would have almost certainly involved a politically unpalatable extension of the state's role in the economy. (It was Mosley who attempted to grasp *this* nettle: see below on Politics and Policies.) But equally the Liberals' proposals were naïve, combining a striking conservatism on most issues of policy with a Utopian approach to the impact of public works. Most recent research has suggested that even if fully pursued the Liberals' proposals would not have made much impact on total unemployment (Howson 1981, pp. 279–83).

More generally the important thesis illustrated by the Liberal proposals and the response to them is that economic theory is not the key to economic policy. The view that policy is closely linked to theory is expressed (in a nuanced form) by Winch, when he writes that the 'real difficulty' preventing the Treasury from accepting Keynesian style proposals for public works 'arose on an intellectual level', in that Keynes's arguments were novel and 'required the use of unfamiliar theory' (1972, p. 121; but compare his comments on the divergent political priorities underlying economic policy decisions, p. 122). This rationalist view of economic policy follows Keynes's classic statement on the importance of theory for policy (1973, p. 383),[2] but is unhelpful in understanding the determinates of policy-making in this period. This is not to say that economic theory was used by the Treasury in a purely cynical manner to cover reasons which it wished to hide. Rather the priorities of the Treasury—adherence to gold, reduced debt and public expenditure, and a limited state role in the economy—were manifest, but had to be defended in a number of arenas. One of these arenas was that of economic theory, and here they unsurprisingly deployed theories which fitted with their overall policy stance. These theories were the truth as they saw it

---

[2] 'The ideas of economists and political philosophers, both when they are right and when they are wrong, are more powerful than is commonly understood. Indeed the world is ruled by little else. Practical men, who believe themselves to be quite exempt from any intellectual influences, are usually the slave of some defunct economist. Madmen in authority, who hear voices in the air, are distilling their frenzy from some academic scribbler of a few years back. I am sure that the power of vested interests is vastly exaggerated compared with the gradual encroachment of ideas. Not, indeed, immediately but after a certain interval; for in the field of economic and political philosophy there are not many who are influenced by new theories after they are twenty-five or thirty years of age, so that the ideas which civil servants and politicans and even agitators apply to current events are not likely to be the newest. But soon or late, it is ideas, not vested interests, which are dangerous for good or evil.'

and formed one part of their world view, but they were not what made the Treasury View such a bulwark of orthodox policy-making in this period.

Doctrine

Economic theory underwent no immediate major shifts as a result of the mass unemployment of the 1920s. Most economists continued to adhere to the view that in the long run a properly operating labour market would deliver full employment of labour. This meant that unemployment which did exist must either be cyclical or transient in character, or if persistent then due to some maladjustment in the labour market (Hancock 1960; Casson 1983, chs. 3, 7). Thus in famous articles in the late 1920s, Pigou (1927) and Clay (1929) attributed the continuation of unemployment, to, respectively, the enhanced role of trade unions, and the enhanced role of the state and collective bargaining in preventing wages falling to their equilibrium level. (Interestingly, neither suggested a direct attack on real wages as the appropriate policy response; Pigou looked to rising productivity to raise the equilibrium real wage, Clay to some form of non-sectoral wage bargaining.)

The predominant doctrinal view of public works was more complex (Hancock 1960). As is clear from the UGC episode, support for public works could be fully compatible with an orthodox view as to the long-run causes and solutions for unemployment, and this introduced an ambiguity into doctrine as to when special circumstances warranted such short-run remedies. Hawtrey, for example, a favoured Treasury expert in the 1920s, argued as a general principle that public works were in most cases an irrelevance as, if monetary conditions were favourable enough, credit would be taken up by private-sector investors. However he conceded that there would be a case for public works if low interest rates did not bring forth such a private-sector response (Peden 1984, p. 172).

Even more centrally related to the public works issue was the issue of 'crowding out'. The full-blown Treasury View suggested 100 per cent displacement of private by public investment, which in turn required that there be no idle capital to be employed. Hopkins before the Macmillan Committee explicitly denied holding such a view, agreeing that all the capital available was not in use. Rather, the Treasury took the view that idle balances could only be drawn into use by higher interest rates which, allowing for continued adherence to gold, the Treasury wanted to see lowered to reduce the cost of government debt and to stimulate economic recovery (Macmillan 1931*b*, Q. 5622).

Keynes' attacks on Treasury orthodoxy had not, before 1931, challenged the theories they adhered to in a fundamental way, but rather their applicability to the circumstances of the time. Henderson's and Keynes's (1929) endorsement of the Liberal Party's *We Can Conquer Unemployment*, like that document itself, rested not on new theoretical principles but on a belief that more could and should be done using already existing techniques in a more adventurous spirit.

It has already been suggested that the Treasury View drew much of its strength from sources other than the theoretical. Equally the Bank of England's policies and activities drew remarkably little on theoretical economics. Indeed, it is one of the most striking features of the Bank's operations at this time how much they explicitly rested on 'feel' and on 'experience' rather than any clear doctrine (Sayers 1976, vol. i, esp. pp. 369–71).

The overall failure of connection between economic theory and economic policy in this period rested on an institutional severance. Economists were called in as occasional experts to advise on policy, but had no systematic role in policy decisions. This started to erode from 1930 with the appointment of the Economic Advisory Council. This followed from the Labour government's concern to have both a representative and an expert source of economic policy advice. These two modes were somewhat uneasily combined in the Council's early period, but the EAC was inserted at the highest level of policy-making in Downing Street, and from its beginning issued a series of powerfully argued reports. But the impact of these was far outweighed by the pressing demands of world trade and financial collapse in the events of 1930 to 1931, and it cannot be said that the policy response to these events was substantially shaped by the Council (Howson and Winch 1977).

Politics and Policies

The Conservatives were in power from the restoration of gold until
almost the beginning of the slump. Their policies in this period
were firmly set within the framework of the gold standard and,
allowing for Churchill's creative accounting, orthodox finance.
Within these parameters there was substantial debate about the
adequacy of the response to unemployment. Imperial Visionaries
within the Conservative Party pressed for their policies to be given
priority, whilst Baldwin felt that the electoral defeat of 1923
prevented him from embracing full-scale protection, if not some
extension of safeguarding duties.

Baldwin's approach to policy was within his perception of a
country that had seen a radical extension of the franchise and
therefore needed time for the new electorate to be educated to the
requirements of (capitalist) democracy. For him the key was
education, conciliation, and co-operation, especially in the industrial
relations field, where class conflict most threatened the established
order. His approach to the General Strike was broadly within this
framework, presenting the issue as one of constitutionalism versus
anarchy, rather than a fundamental clash of interests. In the wake
of the strike he seems to have resisted too savage a right-wing
backlash, despite the passing of the Trade Disputes Act of 1927
which restricted union powers and the political levy paid to the
Labour Party (Williamson 1982).

Despite the Trade Disputes Act the Conservative government
still tried to encourage industrial co-operation. Their first effort
was rebuffed because of union hostility to that act, but eventually
the TUC met with a large group of employers selected by Alfred
Mond of ICI (the Mond–Turner Talks). A Joint Interim Report
was agreed, accepted by the TUC but decisively rejected by the
employers' organizations, the FBI and NCEO. Further tentative
talks were held by the three bodies, but employer resistance
prevented any substantial progress. The deterioration in the
economic situation, the weakness of the central organizations
(especially on the employers' side), and the absence of a spirit of
compromise required to make progress, meant that although
discussion staggered on until 1933, there was little suggestion of a

'corporatist' approach to Britain's economic problems in these years (McDonald and Gospel 1973; Dintenfass 1984).

Much of Conservative Party hostility in the late 1920s was directed at the Liberals, seen as 'rackety' and dangerous under the leadership of Lloyd George. The political aim was to crush the Liberals and have Labour as the 'natural party of opposition'. The approach to policy was to contrast the dangerous radicalism of the Liberals (and less often Labour) with the 'safety first' measures of the Conservatives. Williamson (1982) argues that this was not just a vague and cautious approach to policy, but a planned strategy aimed above all at discrediting Lloyd George.

Such an approach was hardly likely to produce major policy initiatives. Given the resistance to Empire Preference and the desire to avoid any direct role in industrial rationalization, the Conservatives major ideas on dealing with unemployment were limited to industrial transference and de-rating.

Both of these policies accepted that the staple industries were in a state of chronic decline which was unlikely to be corrected by the gold standard policy focusing on financial stability. Industrial transference involved subsidizing the movement of workers from the hard-hit staple export regions to the more prosperous 'Inner Britain' of the Midlands and the South East. The Industrial Transference Act of 1928 created a Board which aided the movement of just over 100,000 individuals between August 1928 and December 1930, in what seems to have been a humane and well-administered scheme. Whether this was a sensible response to structural/regional unemployment is a controversial issue. It was certainly not a solution to unemployment, and migration of this sort tended to deprive the depressed areas of their younger and possibly more dynamic elements. On the other hand migration was occurring anyway and the Board may mainly have helped towards a better organization of that 'natural' process (Ward 1988, pp. 145–53). It also represented the fact that one Ministry (Labour) was willing to take a more activist role to try and do something to combat unemployment within a general climate of inertia (Lowe 1986, pp. 207–9).

The other policy of some significance was de-rating. This too flowed from eventual acceptance of the idea that unemployment was not a transient phenomenon, and this led to a focus on reducing industrial costs. Under the de-rating provisions of the

1928 Act 'productive industry' was relieved of 75 per cent of its rate liability, the loss of rate revenue to local authorities being made up from central funds. The focus on 'productive industry' was intended to cover the heavy industries where unemployment was concentrated, and was undoubtedly seen as an employment measure. The impact never seems to have been measured, but was unlikely to have been large, given the small proportion of rates to total costs and the staple industries' problems on the demand side (Hicks 1970, pp. 77–81).

If the Conservatives had political power but few ideas what to do with it, the Liberals were the exact opposite. Their political decline continued, but they were the most productive of new ideas of all the parties—if not quite such radical ideas as has sometimes been suggested.

The two most famous products of this ferment of ideas were *Britain's Industrial Future* (the Yellow Book) of 1928, and *We Can Conquer Unemployment*, the Manifesto for the 1929 General Election. Whilst the former was a major effort and superior to most of mainstream Conservative or Labour thought at the time, a recent overall judgement seems fair: 'The Yellow Book was a flawed document: an expansionist limb grafted on to a body of deep economic orthodoxy, combining perceptive economic analysis with ill-judged hankering for a world free of class conflict. The economic analysis was undermined by the political requirements of a centre party which lacked a secure foothold in class politics' (Booth and Pack 1985; pp. 47–8).

The 'perceptive economic analysis' referred to the proto-Keynesian proposals for public works which were extracted from the Yellow Book and presented in more detail in *We Can Conquer Unemployment*. Undoubtedly this again represented a call to a more active role for government to combat unemployment which was urgently needed in 1929. However, as suggested above, the proposals were ill-matched to the practical problems of a rapidly implemented large-scale public works programme, and spatchcocked into a highly orthodox framework of economic analysis and long-term policy proposals. Overall it is hard not to agree with Booth and Pack (p. 34) that the Liberals' efforts have been given rather exaggerated praise, presumably because of the lustre of their association with Keynes and their edging towards new economic theory which many have traditionally seen as decisive for policy changes.

Somewhat to everyone's surprise it was the Labour Party which emerged victorious from the 1929 General Election, benefiting from the three-way split of votes in many constituencies. Like the Conservative and Liberal leaderships, that of the Labour Party was broadly in agreement with the policy of the gold standard and financial orthodoxy, but given its constituency of support was unsurprisingly more concerned to do something on the unemployment front than were the Conservatives.

It was an unfortunate time for Labour to come to power; the depression was about to envelop the economy, yet the traditional institutions of policy, the gold standard and free trade, remained in place. Any government would have found it difficult to cope with the conflicting pressures this situation created, but especially a party which was grounded in a class who had suffered most from unemployment and who saw the Labour Party predominantly as an agency of defence, if only the defence of the standards of living of the unemployed.

Debate has raged over the alternatives available to Labour. McKibbin (1975) stoutly defends the 1929–31 government, explicitly attacking Skidelsky's (1970) view that alternative policies were available, and could have been successful as in other countries. He rightly points out that it was very difficult for any government to escape from orthodox policies whilst the gold standard remained (the Swedish Social Democrats for example were fortunate to come to power *after* departure from gold), and that expansionary policies tried in other countries still on gold had to be reversed (for example in Australia).

Almost certainly any successful policy would have required an earlier, deliberate departure from gold. This never appeared likely. Even the most radical analysts stopped short of proposing departure from the standard; Bevin and Keynes in their Addendum to the Macmillan Report, hesitated to propose this, in the face of fear of international financial disintegration (Macmillan 1931*a*, pp. 190–209). Such a policy would have required a major extension of controls over capital and foreign exchange markets and other major extensions of the state's role. This would have required above all a major political challenge to the governing classes, which Labour never looked like mounting, and which was perhaps made less likely both by the lack of collapse of the domestic financial system (compare the USA) and by the dole offering some relief to the unemployment as an alternative to schemes which created work (McKibbin 1975, pp. 104–6).

On the other hand, Skidelsky is surely right to emphasize the intellectual conservatism of Labour in this period. It did lack programmes (except to some degree in the ILP) other than financial orthodoxy, tempered by ameliorative measures (unemployment relief and public works) and windy socialist rhetoric. But Skidelsky overstates the case when he suggests that this problem could have been overcome by embracing Mosley's proposals (Skidelsky 1970, ch. 8; Booth and Pack 1985, ch. 1).

Mosley's Memorandum of 1930 built on earlier work within the Independent Labour Party (then still a part of the Labour Party), especially a document, *Revolution by Reason*, produced by Mosley in 1925. This called for the nationalization of the banking system and, through it, the issue of consumer credits to the unemployed and producer credits to manufacturers to stimulate demand. The Memorandum was different from much contemporary ILP work in not focusing on redistribution of income to correct underconsumption, and highly innovative in calling for a floating exchange rate and a reorientation away from the world economy. At that time Mosley's proposals fell between the socialism of the ILP (despite bank nationalization, it accepted a mixed economy) and the financial orthodoxy of Snowden and the Labour leadership.

Five years later, as a junior member of the Labour government, Mosley circulated another document which followed something of the same expansionist lines, but dropped bank nationalization in favour of loan-financed public works, and retreated on the issue of abandonment of the gold standard. Its only new element was a call for a substantial centralizing of administrative power, to provide the ability to put through a major public works programme (Booth and Pack 1985, pp. 23–4, 30–1).

This document was rejected above all because it broke with financial orthodoxy (Mosley was at his most rhetorical on this issue—Skidelsky 1970, p. 204). This orthodoxy was not just a matter of choice of economic strategy, but of the fundamental stance of Labour as trying to demonstrate its fitness to govern, by not breaking with the major thrust of orthodox assumptions about state and society.

Conclusions

Labour was unfortunate in coming to office just before the world slump began. It was continuously on the defensive as the world economy plunged into recession and domestic unemployment rose. Whilst these events were in no way the consequence of Labour policies, they cruelly exposed its weaknesses as a party of government in a capitalist economy. A central aspect of this weakness was the Party's dual role as a socialist party, with a rhetoric of fundamentally transforming the social order, and its short-term role as defender of working-class interests.

The Labour Party had to function as a pressure group for labour and the trade unions, and this meant, for example, not attempting to break with the export orientation of British industry (as Mosley proposed) on which much union strength had been built. More positively, this role meant defending the living standards of the unemployed as an absolute priority, as a minimum without which a Labour government would be pointless. But this defence itself tended to reduce the pressure for policies to actually bring down unemployment; until its 'burden' became intolerable the dole was a politically easier option than the radical reorientation of policy cuts in unemployment would have required.

It is perhaps not surprising then that the Labour Party lacked both the political and intellectual resources to break out of the dilemmas it was faced with in the first years of the slump. In the end it was broken between its commitment to financial orthodoxy and its function as a defence union for the unemployed. This point can be given a number of nuances, but barring the 'only' in the final clause, Clay's (1957, p. 393) summary of the collapse of Labour seems fair: 'The cause of the split in the Cabinet was a fundamental conflict between Snowden's policy . . . which was actuated by a deep-seated fear of inflation, consciousness of the weakness of the country's external economic position, and knowledge of the dangers of the political situation in Europe, and a policy which looked only to domestic needs and aspirations.'

Labour was succeeded by Conservative governments which progressively accepted the need to give priority to these 'domestic needs and aspirations'. Despite its immediate appearance, the fall of the Labour government was a major defeat for the subordination of those needs and aspirations to the traditional cosmopolitanism of English radicalism and its Labour progeny.

Further Reading

Booth, A., and Pack, M. (1985): *Employment, Capital, and Economic Policy*, Oxford.

Clarke, P. (1988): *The Keynesian Revolution in the Making, 1924–1936*, Oxford.

Hicks, U. K. (1970): *The Finance of British Government 1920–1936*, 2nd edn., Oxford.

Howson, S. (1981): 'Slump and Unemployment', in R. Floud and D. McCloskey (eds.), *The Economic History of Britain since 1700* ii. *From 1860 to the 1970s*, Cambridge, pp. 265–85.

Keynes, J. M. (1972): *Essays in Persuasion. Collected Writings* vol. ix, Parts 2, 3, London.

Moggridge, D. E. (1972): *British Monetary Policy 1924–1931: The Norman Conquest of* $4.86, Cambridge.

Pollard, S., ed. (1970): *The Gold Standard and Employment Policies Between the Wars*, London.

Sayers, R. S. (1976): *The Bank of England 1891–1944*, vol. i, chs. 9, 14, 15; vol. ii, ch. 17.

Skidelsky, R. (1970): *Politicians and the Slump*, Harmondsworth.

5

1931–1939: The Rise of Economic Management?

In the 1930s all three pillars of the Victorian economic policy regime—the gold standard, free trade, low and balanced budgets—came under enormous pressure. Gold and free trade succumbed, but the status of the budget remained ambiguous. Expenditure was initially cut and then rose rapidly by peacetime standards, but budget balance, with its implications for fiscal policy, survived largely intact. At the same time, government moved falteringly into greater regulation of major sectors of the economy, notably coal, iron and steel, and agriculture. Undoubtedly the British economy in the 1930s became more managed—but the scope, coherence, and significance of that management remain highly controversial, as indeed does much of the economic history of the 1930s.

Institutions

The Exchange Rate Regime

Britain was forced off gold, and the authorities expected this departure to open the way to a downward plunge of the exchange rate, coupled to rapid domestic inflation (Howson 1975, pp. 79–80). In the event, the dollar/pound rate initially fell sharply from the $4.86 gold standard parity, hitting a trough at $3.14 in December 1932. But this heralded no financial panic nor hyper-inflation. Indeed, whilst the fall in prices (mainly the consequence of falling world commodity prices) slowed, it continued until the winter of 1932–3 (Table 5.1).

Philip Snowden, Chancellor under Labour and one of the defectors to the 'National' government, argued that this refutation of previous fears related to budgetary policy.

Table 5.1 *Main Economic Indicators 1929–1939*

	Output (£m.)[a]		Prices[b]	Balance of payments[c]	Unemployment	
	Current prices	1938 prices			Numbers (000)	%
1929	4,214	4,216	161	96	1,503	8.0
1930	4,185	4,210	155	36	2,379	12.3
1931	3,843	3,980	145	−103	3,252	16.4
1932	3,746	4,008	141	−51	3,400	17.0
1933	3,776	4,046	137	−8	3,087	15.4
1934	4,016	4,334	138	−22	2,609	12.9
1935	4,197	4,496	140	23	2,437	12.0
1936	4,389	4,633	144	−27	2,100	10.2
1937	4,708	4,834	152	−47	1,776	8.5
1938	4,959	4,985	153	−55	2,164	10.1
1939	5,225	5,190	158	−150	1,340	5.8

[a] GDP at factor cost.
[b] Consumer prices 1913 = 100.
[c] Current account.

Source: Feinstein (1972), Tables 4, 5, 65, 15, 58, pp. T13, T16, T140, T39, T128.

It is one thing to go off the Gold Standard with an unbalanced Budget and uncontrollable inflation, but it is far less serious to take this measure, not because of internal financial difficulties, but because of excessive withdrawal of borrowed money. We have balanced our Budget, and therefore removed the danger of having to print paper, which leads to uncontrolled inflation (cited Winch 1972, p. 215).

Whilst there was a fair amount of political mendacity in this statement, it brings out how far the consequences of departure from gold were very much conditioned by the particular circumstances, economic and political, which accompanied it. For most of the 1930s, after the initial shock, capital flowed *into* London, so that the pound, until the imminent threat of war, was a relatively attractive currency to hold in this depressed and politically turbulent decade. The actual path of the exchange rate has been the source of some dispute. Table 5.2 shows that against the dollar the pound quickly exceeded its old parity once the USA left the gold standard in 1933. Against the French franc the rate reflects the much longer attachment of that currency to gold, the franc only falling against the pound from 1937. However, these nominal rates may mislead, because what matters is the exchange rate against all the major countries Britain traded with. The Real Exchange Rate in Table 5.2 is one calculation of this. Redmond (1980) and Broadberry (1987) have alternative measures which differ from Dimsdale's. Despite these divergences, they all show

Table 5.2   *Sterling Exchange Rates in the 1930s* (1929 = 100)

	£/$	£/French franc	Real Exchange rate
1929	100	100	100
1930	100.1	99.1	98.5
1931	93.3	93.2	94.2
1932	72.1	68.2	81.4
1933	86.8	62.0	82.8
1934	103.8	62.0	81.7
1935	100.9	59.9	81.8
1936	102.3	66.9	86.1
1937	101.8	100.5	91.9
1938	100.7	137.6	91.8

Source: Dimsdale (1981), Tables 3, 9, pp. 317, 333.

that after the sharp initial fall of the rate after departure from gold, it remained somewhat below the 1929 level, at least until 1937.

This path of the exchange rate reflected deliberate management by the British authorities, though the exact contribution of that management in comparison with underlying economic forces is open to dispute (Broadberry 1987).[1] Certainly it was symbolically and politically important that the idea of 'automatic' exchange rate determination was formally given up, however threadbare such an idea had become by 1931.

Deliberate management of the exchange rate had not been envisaged immediately on the departure from gold (e.g. Keynes 1982, pp. 1–2). Its adoption reflected the realization that the heavens had not fallen without gold, and that substantial advantages could accrue from a lower value for the pound. These advantages were the low interest rates ('cheap money') that the absence of the need to defend the pound allowed, and the hope that a lower value of the pound would cause prices to rise. (We return to both these points below.) These calculations led to the establishment of the Exchange Equalization Account in the Finance Act of 1932 with the stated aim of 'checking undue fluctuations in the exchange value of sterling' (Howson 1980*a*, p. 1).

Under the EEA, controlled by the Bank of England with the advice and consent of the Treasury, the pound was managed. The objectives of this management were never simple, but apart from the formal objective of preventing speculative movements of the currency away from some notion of its equilibrium value, the predominant objective was domestic i.e. to maintain cheap money. Thus, whilst in the 1920s the level of interest rates was subordinated to the exchange-rate target, in the 1930s this was reversed. For most of the 1930s, up until 1938, low interest rates were compatible with upward pressure on the pound, as capital flowed into London. Thus the EEA acted to hold the pound down, and in doing so accumulated reserves, which in itself was seen as a desirable outcome because of the low ratio of such reserves to

[1] By 'underlying economic forces' is meant purchasing power parity. This theorem argues that in the long run the relative value of a currency will reflect changes in relative prices between countries and hence the purchasing power of that currency in terms of what it can buy in other currencies. Thus if prices in Britain rise 10% faster than in all other relevant countries, the exchange rate of the pound should fall 10%, so that both British citizens' and foreigners' real capacity to buy goods is left unchanged by the change in prices.

mobile funds deposited in London. 'Domestic economic objectives remained the dominant influence on exchange rate targets for the rest of the 1930s, although the determination with which the authorities pursued their targets was relaxed under pressure of events' (Howson 1980*b*, p. 55).

This domestic focus of exchange-rate policy could not mean a complete neglect of the wider context of international monetary relations. In the 1930s this context particularly involved two themes—the development of the Sterling Area, and relations with the USA.

The basis of the Sterling Area had partly been laid before the demise of gold. Even under that standard, many countries had chosen to hold substantial portions of their reserves in pounds, given the importance of that currency in international trade and finance, and its ready availability through British commodity imports and capital exports. After September 1931 this feature was added to by the pegging of many countries' exchange rates to the pound. This included most Empire countries (the main exception being US-oriented Canada), Scandinavia, Argentina, Japan, and, in 1938, even France (Drummond 1987, p. 42).

The reasons for this varied. India and the colonies had no choice. For Australia and New Zealand Britain was the chief market and chief competitor. Scandinavia had similar close economic links, whilst Portugal's decision was affected by a desire to avoid capital losses on its balances in London. The establishment of this area was originally unintended, and never a central concern of British policy, but it was aided in a small way by Britain, for example by credits to Denmark, Finland, Australia, and New Zealand (Drummond 1981, pp. 5–10).

The motives behind this encouragement were spelt out by a senior Treasury Official (Hopkins):

One of the leading objectives that we ought to have in mind as soon as we can keep sterling steady at a reasonable level, is to make it easy for as many as possible of the unstable currencies to base themselves on sterling so that we may became the leaders of a sterling block which, pending our restoration of gold, would have the best opportunities of mutual trade and would give sterling a new force in the world (cited Drummond 1981, p. 10).

One obvious implication of this widespread pegging of exchange rates to the pound was that against many currencies there was no sterling devaluation, and this is reflected in the limited overall depreciation of the currency (Table 5.2). The significance of departure from gold was not that it gave Britain a competitive advantage in many markets, but rather that it removed a constraint on domestic policy. Because this was true of other 'early leavers' from gold, British trade expanded more with such countries than with those whose attachment was prolonged.

In domestic policy-making the sterling area probably served to reinforce fiscal conservatism. The willingness of participants to hold sterling was perceived in London as conditional upon confidence, founded above all on fiscal rectitude in Britain (Drummond 1981, pp. 15, 22). At the same time the Treasury was worried that the other members of the Sterling Area would 'gang up' to impose public works and other expansionary schemes on Britain, a course advocated by Keynes. This fear led to resistance to any Sterling Area or Empire discussions of monetary policy. At the Ottawa Conference of 1932, and subsequently, London successfully limited its commitment in this area to cheap money, and resisted pressure for 'rash' schemes favoured by some Empire countries (Drummond 1981, pp. 23–7; also pp. 177–9).[2]

Overall in this period the Sterling Area worked because many countries desired a stable exchange rate, had strong economic links with Britain and were happy to accept the 'cheap money' consequences of adhering to the pound. Britain welcomed this reassertion of monetary leadership, albeit in a restricted sphere, though was worried by implications of the sterling balances, especially given the evidence from 1931 of their footloose nature. This worry provided an impetus to both fiscal conservatism and reserve accumulation.

If Britain fairly easily asserted its hegemony within the sterling area, its capacities in the wider world were much more restricted, especially in relation to the US dollar. The dollar was kept on gold until 1933, but then devalued to over $5.00/pound for the period 1934–38. This was a much weaker dollar than Britain would have preferred, but it was accepted on the basis that any attempt to peg the pound at a higher rate would be seen by Roosevelt as 'a

---

[2] At the World Economic Conference of 1933, Chamberlain attacked Empire proposals for public works as 'so extravagent that they might almost have emerged from conversations with Mr Lloyd George and Mr Keynes' (cited Drummond 1981, p. 178).

declaration of war' (Howson 1980*a*, p. 22). In any case Britain's main concern, given cheap money, was not so much the level as stability in the exchange rate, and this was in fact achieved against the dollar once the initial gyrations following the US departure from gold were over.

Stability was seen as important to encourage the remaining gold countries to reduce tariffs and quotas. But Britain wanted this stability to be grounded in stabilized world monetary conditions, for fear that otherwise deflation would be forced on the authorities (Drummond 1981, chs. 7, 8). Existing stability was seen mainly as the result of the failure of other countries to adhere to the 'rules of the game' of the gold standard. This meant above all the gold-accumulating activities of France and the USA via trade restrictions, and the failure to settle war debts with their psychologically damaging consequences for exchange stability.

This outlook meant that for much of the 1930s the USA was seen by Britain as the central problem for international financial stability. Co-operation was difficult in the face of lack of clarity and changes in US policy. The World Economic Conference of 1933 had originally had proposed by the USA to address issues on tariff policy and the world monetary system. In the event discussions were dominated by the question of currency stabilization, but these were wrecked when Rosevelt made it clear that he was unwilling to commit the USA to any such course, his concerns being overwhelmingly domestic (Kindleberger 1973, ch. 9; Drummond 1981, chs. 6, 7).

In 1936 an informal agreement was reached between Britain, the USA, and France which may appear to suggest a more co-operative trend. However recent research has tended to emphasize the severe limits to this arrangement (Drummond 1981, chs. 9, 10; Drummond 1987, pp. 50–2). Whilst each government declared its willingness to collaborate and consult on currency values, the main initial impact was to allow France to devalue without retaliation, in return for French reductions in tariffs and quotas. This paved the way for the dissolution of the 'gold bloc', the group of countries that had stubbornly maintained adherence to gold. But French policy was extremely erratic after 1936, and was dominated by unstable domestic politics and 'consultation was spasmodic, incomplete and absent-minded' (Drummond 1987, p. 51).

In the 1930s Britain had lost the capacity to dominate the world financial system, and to a substantial extent lost the will to try. The USA did not play a role which helped stabilize the system; despite a current account surplus it had high tariffs and deliberately depreciated its exchange rate. In short the world monetary system lacked a 'hegemon', able to enforce and encourage good behaviour on others and act as guarantor and support of the system—a view emphasized by Kindleberger (1973, ch. 14) and supported by recent work (Eichengreen 1987*a*; see also Rowland 1976). On the other hand, the disorderly nature of the regime has perhaps been exaggerated in the past. As Drummond (1981, p. 254) argues, 'the decade was no more disorderly than the 1920s—and a great deal less disorderly than the 1970s'. Equally it was not characterized by widespread competitive devaluation, the US being the main culprit in this regard.

British policy was domestically oriented, and for most of the period the EEA was holding the pound down and accumulating reserves. However this cannot be seen in quite the same light as US policy, as Britain had an almost continuous current account deficit in these years (Howson 1980*a*, ch. 5; see Table 5.1 for data). What kept the pound strong was not the competitiveness of its traded goods but the repayment of old loans, plus an inflow of new short-term money. When these funds began to leave as war loomed in 1938, the British authorities had little choice but to allow the pound to depreciate. In 1939 the rate was supported at substantial cost in reserves to appease the Americans (Parker 1983), but in the last months before peace ended there was further pressure and the rate fell to $4.03 where it was then pegged until 1949.

The Trade Regime

The collapse of the gold standard was quickly followed by general protection. This had been seriously discussed as an option at Cabinet level under the Labour government, as an alternative to cuts in expenditure as a means of balancing the budget and helping the balance of payments. In a notable shift of line, Keynes had come out in favour of a tariff, arguing that as long as the gold standard continued it was the best way to provide some relief for the balance for payments and to raise prices relative to wages (Keynes 1982, pp. 297–301; 488–528; Winch 1972, pp. 160–1;

Eichengreen 1984). However the Chancellor, Snowden, was as vehemently opposed to protection as he was to unbalanced budgets, and tariffs made no headway under Labour.

In November 1931 however (the month after the General Election) the National government introduced the Abnormal Importations Act, which was a prelude to the Import Duties Act of 1932. This imposed a 10 per cent tariff on all goods except those specifically exempted, which were mostly primary produce from the Empire and food and raw materials generally (details in Capie 1983, ch. 3).

The reasons for this introduction are complex. Capie (1983, chs. 4, 5) emphasizes both the long-term pressure which had been building up for protection within the Conservative Party, and the origins of much of this pressure in industry. Eichengreen (1981, p. 38) stresses that it reflected the National government's view that the depreciation of the pound threatened to be both cumulative and unsuccessful in curing the balance of payments difficulties. In that context the government 'supported the imposition of the general tariff in order to guard against the dangers of hyper-inflation and unbound exchange rate depreciation, and they made this choice knowing that the tariff might exacerbate the problem of domestic unemployment. This possibility, however, was the price to be paid for the exchange rate and price stability'.

The tariff also represented a victory of sorts for the Empire Visionaries within the Conservative Party, who had long seen a tariff as the basis for a system of Imperial Preference. Neville Chamberlain in his speech introducing the tariff described his proposals as the 'direct and legitimate descendent' of those of his father, Joseph. But it would be hard to argue that Imperial sentiment was more than marginal to the decision, which can probably best be seen as the Conservative Party taking advantage of the crisis and its electoral consequences to introduce a long-favoured policy.

The macroeconomic results of this policy are difficult to disentangle from those of the fall in the exchange rate, which in analytical terms is a very similar policy, that is, it acts to shift domestic expenditure away from imported goods and on to domestic output. (There will also be interactions between the policies: other things equal, protection will improve the trade balance and raise the exchange rate). The debate over the effects is surveyed most recently by Broadberry (1986, ch. 13, especially pp. 135–6). He argues that

the effects of the exchange rate depreciation in 1931–2 represent the total effect of external sector policies, since the effect of the tariff was to appreciate the exchange rate from 1932. Thus it is invalid to suggest that the tariff gave an *additional* boost to output and employment. It is simply that some of the relative price effects were transmitted through the tariff rather than the nominal exchange rate, which began to appreciate.

The microeconomic effects, effects on particular sectors, are more controversial. Capie (1983, ch. 8) has stressed that it is not nominal but effective rates of protection that matter, i.e. not the 10 per cent *ad valorem* tariff, but the extent to which domestic value added is protected. The importance of this point is that if a producer's inputs as well as outputs are subject to tariff, then the effective protection will clearly be less than if only the final product is protected. Capie uses this approach to show that whilst in most industries effective protection was higher than nominal (because value added is about 50 per cent of final value, and most inputs were unprotected in the 1930s), there were important exceptions. Housing had *negative* effective protection, because inputs were taxed but not the final product. A similar result applies to shipbuilding. Perhaps most interestingly, Capie suggests that iron and steel had a low rate of effective protection because of tariffs on many of its inputs. Capie's results have been challenged (Foreman-Peck 1981) on the grounds that they assume imports and domestic products to be perfect substitutes, with imports in perfectly elastic supply and the home product in less than perfectly elastic supply, conditions that were not met in inter-war Britain. His alternative calculation suggests that iron and steel in particular did benefit substantially from protection.

It is arguable, therefore, that the importance of protection in the 1930s was more important as a sign of reorientation of British policy to domestic objectives than as a substantive cause of such a reorientation in its own right. But any such conclusion must take into account indirect effects of the tariff, most noticeably its use to try and persuade domestic producers to rationalize their activities in return for protection. Such a deal was struck in iron and steel, where a British Iron and Steel Federation was sponsored by the government to organize rationalization. But the BISF members agreed on little except the desirability of a tariff to maintain prices, and there was little change in the industry in the 1930s, and the authorities were reluctant to interfere on any greater scale in the industry. The BISF 'became an organization effectively geared to defending the interests of its existing membership rather than promoting change in the industry . . . the body that the government had established in the 1930s to promote restructuring, became the guarantor of long-term organisational inertia' (Tolliday 1986, p. 103).

One of the long-standing arguments against tariffs, apart from the directly economic, was that they would corrupt the political process, leading to the creation of powerful vested interests whose influence would be insidious and difficult to resist (see Marshall and Pigou's views noted in Chapter 2 above). The government in the 1930s addressed this problem by creating an Import Duties Advisory Committee. This was an independent body that publicized applications for protection and held hearings where objections were raised. Capie (1983, ch. 6) argues that this mechanism successfully reduced the traditional political clout of concentrated industries in claiming protection, the granting of protection being correlated with smallness of scale (and level of regional concentration).

For domestic industry, protection was probably not of major importance in the 1930s, though this conclusion would not apply to agriculture. As Pollard (1983, p. 84) argues, 'In 1931 the Government abandoned free trade. Agriculture was turned into a highly protected, organised and subsidised sector of the economy,' mainly by the Wheat Act of 1932, the Import Duties Act of 1932, and the Agricultural Marketing Acts of 1931 and 1933. The first of these provided 'deficiency payments' whereby wheat was freely imported, but domestic producers were subsidized by payments to make up the difference between the world price and an agreed norm. The Agricultural Marketing Acts allowed price and output control by the producers, and such schemes were established for potatoes and milk, less successfully for bacon and pigs.

Direct controls on agricultural imports were limited, initially granted only to horticultural products, later extended to oats and barley. The problem with greater import controls in this area was that it would cut across preferences granted to Empire producers, who were substantial producers of many of Britain's traditional agricultural (and raw material) imports. In the Import Duties Act of 1932 preferences (free entry) were granted to Empire goods, but for the Dominions as opposed to the dependent Empire these were temporary (Drummond 1972, p. 92). The whole issue was to be settled at the Ottawa Conference in 1932, already scheduled at the previous such conference in 1930 (Drummond 1974, chs. 5–8).

The combination of British tariffs and an Imperial Conference raised the hopes of the Imperial Visionaries that the old-pre First-World War dreams could at last be realized. But this is a misleading context in which to view Ottawa; the reality was one of hard bargaining between separate states, not a fraternal meeting of minds governed by imperial sentiment. This is easy to understand if we remember both the traditional issues that had prevented substantial Imperial Preference in the past, and the economic circumstances of the early 1930s.

On the first issue, the problem was basically that the more radical versions of Imperial economic unity envisaged a fixed division of labour in which the Dominions provided food and raw materials to a manufacturing Britain. But this was clearly against the grain of Dominion development of their own manufacturing capacity. Before the First World War this problem had been coupled with the attachment of Britain to free imports of foodstuffs, with their implications for the working-class cost of living (Drummond 1974, introduction).

In the 1920s this impasse, especially after the election defeat for protection in 1923, led to the Visionaries emphasizing migration and investment rather than trade. In the 1930s the rise in unemployment renewed interest in the possibilities of protection for employment creation. But unemployment reinforced the desire of Dominion producers to protect their domestic manu-facturing. At the same time Britain was willing to move away from free imports of foodstuffs, but mainly as a way of protecting domestic agriculture, not Imperial producers.

In this light the Ottawa negotiations and agreements of 1932 can best be understood; 'The British leaders had not come to the conference table as missionaries of Empire. They had been driven to it by an unprecedented economic and financial crisis which had shattered Britain's established fiscal system and created nearly 3m. unemployed' (Amery 1969, p. 1015). The result was a muddled conference, with no clear objectives, but dominated by hard bargaining over a rather narrow range of products. The main results were the stabilization and small increase in the already existing preferences—but mainly by increasing barriers against non-Empire producers, rather than reducing those on inter-Imperial trade.

In aggregate the effects of the Ottawa Agreement were small beer. They probably reduced the rate of decline of the share of Empire imports drawn from the UK. They also probably increased slightly the share of UK imports coming from the Empire. But these changes in trends may have partly been at the expense of trade outside the Empire i.e. simply trade diversion rather than trade creation. Even ignoring this, the total value of any changes was small in relation to either UK or Empire trade and employment (Drummond 1974, pp. 284–9). As so often with Empire economic policy, the volume of rhetoric and discussion was out of all proportion to the concrete results.

As Aldcroft (1986, p. 76) rightly stresses, British protection in the 1930s does not account for the falling share of trade in total output. This trend was already apparent by 1931, when imports were 20.8 per cent of national income compared with 31.3 per cent in 1913, exports 12.1 per cent compared with 28 per cent. In 1938 the figures were very little lower than in 1931. The British economy was becoming more 'home-oriented' long before the tariff, and if one sees the sources of such recovery as there was in the 1930s lying in the growth of domestic markets, this growth probably owed little to protection, especially if one accepts Capie's (1983) estimates of effective protection rates. The most that can be said is that protection might have aided business expectations in the 1930s, especially in staple industries particularly hard hit by low-price imports.

The Budget

Public expenditure as a share of national output fell between 1931 and 1934, then stabilized, to rise sharply from 1937 onwards. Without rearmament public expenditure measured in this way would have fallen, instead of ending the decade at around 27 per cent of output, roughly where it began (Middleton 1985, pp. 37–47). Within this total, expenditure on goods and services showed a persistent growth, as did capital formation, offset by falls in debt interest and transfer payments (p. 38). The former was caused by the lower interest rates prevailing in the 1930s, the second by the (eventual) fall in unemployment and hence unemployment benefits.

Within this overall total, and against the long-term trend, a growing share of expenditure was by local authorities rather than central government. This shift on the expenditure side was in some ways misleading, because an increasing proportion of local expenditure (over 30 per cent by the late 1930s) was financed by central taxation rather than local rates. But it was none the less important because it reflected the dominance by local authorities of public capital expenditure, which was six to eight times higher than such central expenditure until rearmament shifted the balance towards the latter (Middleton 1985, p. 46). Local autonomy thus raised difficulties for any centralized initiatives on public investment (see below, section on the Treasury).

Government expenditure in the 1930s, and prior to rearmament, lacked the upward trend of most of the 1920s. Despite this, it should be noted that direct expenditure by government, i.e. excluding transfers, *was* growing. Thus even in a period of Conservative government, strongly committed to limiting the public sector's growth, direct public use of resources was not successfully held back. We may plausibly link this to two features—unemployment with the political pressures it created for expenditure, and the political context of universal suffrage and two-party competition. (A similar combination of a rhetoric of budgetary orthodoxy, expenditure growth, and mass unemployment was to recur in the early 1980s—see Chapter 11 below).

Much more central to the public policy debate, then and since, was the overall balance of the budget. Here again the rhetoric of Chancellors of the Exchequer in the 1930s was strongly hostile to unbalanced budgets—this issue had of course been at the centre of the great political crisis of 1931. Britain was certainly more orthodox in this regard than almost any other European country (Middleton 1985, pp. 111–12; Dalton 1934).[3] But on the other hand there was a degree of sleight-of-hand in this orthodoxy. The announced Budgetary balance in the 1930s was substantially affected by fiscal window-dressing, i.e. the inclusion of revenues and exclusion of expenditures which on a strict definition of

---

[3] Chamberlain, in his 1933 budget speech, used this fact to 'explain' the relative mildness of the depression in Britain in comparison with such benighted countries (Sabine 1970, p. 16).

budgetary orthodoxy would not have been allowed. The reasons for such devices are plain enough, and clearly summarized by Middleton (1985, p. 83):

> In the circumstances of the 1930s where the existence of mass unemployment made it politically difficult to achieve the tightening required to balance the budget in the face of autonomous fluctuations in activity, fiscal window-dressing and related practices served the essential function of allowing the Treasury apparently to adhere to orthodox financial principles, whilst simultaneously limiting the extent of fiscal tightening required in a depression to maintain a balanced budget.

Elimination of fiscal window-dressing simply redefines the public budget to conform with contemporary norms of good practice. More radical (and controversial) are attempts to redefine budget balance to separate out the impact upon it of policy changes from those brought about 'exogenously' i.e. by fluctuations in output and employment with obvious feed back on to tax revenues and expenditure. Such approaches are standard in Keynesian analyses of budgetary policy especially in periods of major fluctuations in output, and have notably been used in discussion of the early 1980s (see Chapter 11). For the 1930s Middleton (1985, ch. 7) has carried out such calculations (Table 5.3). They show a very substantial tightening of fiscal stance in the 1930s.

In Keynesian terms, therefore, actual policy was much worse, more deflationary, than the conventional figures for the budget suggest.[4] This was not, of course, how the government at the time saw the issue. For them, budgetary balance was a positive, indeed crucial, aspect of policy, designed to allow low interest rates, prevent inflation and maintain private-sector confidence. But these issues are best discussed in the context of the Treasury's overall posture.

---

[4] For another broadly Keynesian assessment see Broadberry (1984). His approach takes into account the differential impact of different types of expenditure and revenue on national income, as well as allowing for the effects of price changes. His conclusion is that 1930s' budgets were broadly neutral.

Table 5.3 *Fiscal Stance in the 1930s*

	Notional Balance (% GDP)	Constant Employment Balance
1930/31	−0.6	+1.1
1931/32	0.0	+2.5
1932/33	−0.9	+3.0
1933/34	+0.8	+4.2
1934/35	+0.2	+3.2
1935/36	+0.1	+2.0
1936/37	−0.1	+0.8
1937/38	+0.6	0.0
1938/39	−0.3	−1.6

Source: Middleton 1985, p. 135.

Agencies

The Treasury

The end of the gold standard reduced the role of the Bank of England and thereby heightened the predominance of the Treasury as the crucial agency in economic policy-making. However the primary functions of the Treasury were still the traditional ones of budgetary control and debt management. Its strictly economic role expanded under the pressure of events throughout the inter-war period, but remained secondary to these financial aspects. To put the point more specifically: unemployment was a growing concern within the Treasury, but its reduction was never the central objective in the 1930s (Middleton 1987, pp. 110–11).

Much of the historiography of the Treasury in the 1930s is dominated by its resistance to proposals for expansionary macroeconomic policies, especially public works (for a survey, see Peden 1988). This was a continuation of the posture adopted in the mid-1920s, and famously expanded against the Liberals' proposals in the 1929 election (Chapter 4). Understanding this resistance has been a major source of controversy, and raises wide issues about how we understand the nature of, and changes in, economic policy-making.

Traditional Keynesian historiography (Winch 1972; Howson 1975; Howson and Winch 1977) has focused upon the impact of Keynesian ideas on the Treasury (and other agencies) in the 1930s. This, as noted in Chapter 4, led to seeing the Treasury View of hostility to public works, as grounded upon an attachment to certain theoretical positions concerning the workings of the economy. This kind of analysis has been extended into the 1930s, and led to attempts to assess how far, by the outbreak of war, Treasury thinking had been permeated by Keynesian 'new economics'.

Hutchison (1978, pp. 155–6) argues that even before the publication of Keynes's General Theory in 1936 the Treasury (and the Bank of England) were largely converted to Keynesian policies. Howson (1975, p. 143) is more circumspect but sees a clear growth of acceptance of Keynesian principles, laying the foundations of post-war economic management. A similar analysis is apparent in Howson and Winch (1977, pp. 158–65). However, Peden (1980, 1983) and Booth (1983) argue that the public records suggest that Treasury scepticism about public works remained largely unabated up until the war.

This debate largely takes it as read that what matters to the evolution of policy are the economic ideas adhered to by individuals in the Treasury. But such a focus can be challenged. Tomlinson (1981*a*) and, in much more detail, Middleton (1985, 1987) have attempted to locate the Treasury in a broader framework where the focus is on the economic, political, and administrative constraints faced, rather than seeing it largely as a battleground of economic ideas.

This approach has already been discussed in Chapter 4. Applied to the 1930s it suggests that whilst the Treasury had increasingly to respond to the arguments of the advocates of public works, it saw these arguments not so much as theoretically 'wrong' but inappropriate to the broad circumstances of Britain in the 1930s.

In 1933 Keynes published the *Means to Prosperity*, advocating a substantial public works programme (Keynes 1972). The Treasury certainly had theoretical objections to this programme, focusing on the problem of monetary conditions necessary to prevent the initial rise in expenditure from raising interest rates before the new higher level of savings from higher demand, and hence incomes, came into being (Middleton 1985, pp. 167–8). But what was at stake in the debate was far wider than this theoretical issue. For the Treasury, large public-works programmes in the 1930s threatened the low interest rates and financial confidence which it perceived as both the beneficial consequences of previous budgetary orthodoxy and the basis for recovery.

Such an approach did not rule out public works entirely. They could be countenanced on a small scale as an *accompaniment* to cheap money as long as they did not threaten confidence. Thus in 1937, with the approach of a recession, substantial pressure was put on the Treasury to push forward such works. In response the Treasury conceded the case for a small programme, but wanted to lay stress upon

the need to avoid adding to the already excessive demands upon labour in the building and allied trades and not upon the need to have something in store for the 'slump'. Experience shows how easily business sentiment is influenced and if anything is said that leads to the feeling that the Government agree with those economists who see an imminent slump, many people may shift their plans accordingly and bring about the very thing we all want to avoid (cited Middleton 1985, p. 170).

The Treasury's concession on public works was indeed very limited. It accepted the case for rephasing public-works expenditure over the cycle, but saw this as affecting only 10 per cent of such expenditure. It was also to be financed by local authorities, not, as advocates of such a programme argued, by a central government loan.

Following this, in May 1938 the Treasury issued a circular to local authorities requesting them to compile five-year forward investment plans. However, this was not so much a precursor of later attempts to get local authorities to build up a 'shelf' of projects against a future slump, but rather an attempt to get information to limit local authority investment in order to facilitate rearmament (Middleton 1985, p. 169).

Rearmament is of broader significance in our understanding of the Treasury's stance. From 1935 the Treasury accepted to need to borrow on a growing scale for rearmament. Contrary to what has often been claimed by military historians, the Treasury seems to have had little reluctance to launch itself on this path (Peden 1979, pp. 71–9). As every schoolgirl knows, this rearmament programme made a substantial contribution to reducing unemployment in the immediate pre-war years. This of course was not the purpose of the programme, but the attainment of full employment did allow the Treasury to borrow more (as savings rose) and to tax more (to prevent inflation and reassure financial markets). In this way the Treasury was drawn for the first time into managing demand. This did not mean the abandonment of old concerns. There was still the desire not to allow borrowing for defence to become a licence for borrowing for other purposes; the desire to maintain confidence by attempting to reconcile actual policy with budgetary orthodoxy. Treasury policy did shift in the late 1930s. But the significance of this should not be exaggerated. War had always been a legitimate reason for borrowing, and rearmament can be seen to fall under that heading. On the other hand borrowing in the late 1930s was integrated with a much more sophisticated and more broadly based management of the economy than had ever been previously envisaged or attempted.

This debate over 'how Keynesian was the Treasury?' and 'why wasn't it more so?' reflects the dominance of what we may call 'Keynesian issues' in the historiography of 1930s. This debate predominantly covers public works and budgetary issues but it can be extended to others. Howson (1975), for example, focuses on interest-rate policy, and it is possible to argue that cheap money, undoubtedly a major concern of the Treasury in the 1930s, was partly accepted as a result of Keynes's emphasis on this issue in the 1920s. Equally one can assert that Treasury emphasis on cheap money was only possible once Britain was forced off gold. Once it became apparent that this departure did not threaten civilization as the Treasury knew it, cheap money offered the possibility of cheapened debt payments (after the big Debt conversion of 1932) as well as a means of encouraging recovery.

Booth (1987*a*) has attempted not only to challenge Keynesian historiography of the 1930s, but also the issues it brings to the foreground. He argues that there was a more coherent and less negative Treasury policy in the 1930s than previous writers have suggested. This focused upon a combination of the (well-known) budgetary orthodoxy 'and the competitive power of British industry and . . . measures which improved profitability' (p. 503). Improving profitability meant, above all, encouraging prices to rise, with the hope that wages would not follow suit, that investment, output, and employment would thereby be encouraged, and the budgetary position relieved.

Such an emphasis led to the position (noted above) of seeing the fall in the exchange rate after 1931 as a source of international price increases, refusing to stabilize the pound until such increases were secured, and using the EEA to hold the pound down. On the home front, Booth argues, it was a persistent theme in the Treasury of the 1930s that prices needed to be higher, which was in effect a 'code' for saying profits needed to be higher to encourage investment. The emphasis was on a controlled rise in prices, not a rapid inflation, and this may be seen as reinforcing the concern for fiscal orthodoxy with its alleged anti-inflationary consequences.

Booth's argument may be summarized as saying that the Treasury had a coherent view of the way out of the depression— price increases to raise profits. Direct attempts to cut wages it saw as politically impossible. Cheap money and industrial policy at home and exchange rate management externally were then the only means to achieve this end. The Treasury may have been committed to a long-term return to *laissez-faire*, but the 1930s are not best seen as a clash between such a principle and insurgent Keynesianism.

Aspects of Booth's argument are returned to in the discussion of doctrine and industrial policy below. But one way of viewing its general thrust is as a reassertion of an old truth; that if you want successfully to manage a capitalist economy you must have regard to profit levels. Of course, such a point can be deployed in a highly reductionist way, to reduce all policy to pursuit of 'capitalists' interests'. But used more subtly (as Booth does), and combined with Middleton's emphasis on the maintenance of financial confidence, it re-emphasizes the constraints imposed upon an agency such as the Treasury by the broader social relations within which it must pursue its objectives.

The Bank of England and Other Agencies

'One of the most important consequences of the abandonment of the gold standard had been a shift of power from the Bank to the Treasury', (Howson 1975, p. 95). The Treasury had no rivals for its place at the centre of economic policy-making in the 1930s, as management of the gold standard, which had been so important in the 1920s, disappeared.

Of course what replaced management of gold was management of sterling by the Exchange Equalization Account. This was operated by the Bank under the guidance of the Treasury. It seems clearly to have been the case that whilst the Bank was allowed some discretion in this role, the main lines of policy were set by the Treasury. The same point would broadly apply to other aspects of policy in this period.

Like the Treasury, the Bank was initially concerned that the departure from gold heralded an inflationary explosion and limitless depreciation of the pound. Like the Treasury this fear in the Bank soon abated. But the Bank always hankered after the 'norm' of the gold standard throughout the 1930s (Howson 1975, pp. 94–5; Sayers 1976, pp. 455, 472). In this context the EEA was looked upon as a temporary expedient for steadying the exchanges until gold could be restored (Sayers, p. 486).

Like the Treasury, the Bank looked to higher prices to relieve the depression. This led to the approach publicly proclaimed at the Ottawa Conference and at the World Economic Conference—to postpone any question of restabilization of exchange rates until this price rise had taken place, and in the interim to focus on improving the environment in which a gold standard might be made to work—by reducing tariffs and reducing international indebtedness (Sayers 1976, pp. 449–59). Within this broad consensual framework, the Bank, at least initially, was much less enthusiastic about the cheap money policy. The Bank was concerned by the loss of traditional constraints exercised by adherence to gold. Norman, the Governor, 'was alarmed by the increased scope given to political exigencies by the increased influence in the money market of the Treasury. He felt the loss of the compulsion exercised by the adverse movement of the exchanges on the gold standard, and missed the traditional warning signals which then operated' (Howson 1975, p. 95).

The reason for these doubts was the fear of excessive expansion of the money supply via increased bank credit. One result of this was persistent pressure from the Bank for funding (i.e. lengthening the term) of the debt, which to some extent worked against cheap money by pushing up long-term interest rates. Howson (1975, pp. 99–103, 130–1) places a lot of emphasis on this conflict, though it did not prevent cheap money continuing throughout the 1930s.

Domestic monetary policy does not seem to have been very clearly conceived or operated in the 1930s. This was not the traditional strength of the Bank or its governor, so in a strong sense departure from gold left the Bank somewhat adrift, without a clear focus of policy to replace managing the gold position (Sayers 1976, p. 499). However the Bank was able to rectify its long-term concern about the weakness of the exchange reserves, a concern strengthened by the growth of hot-money flows in the 1930s. It also became an adept at exchange-rate management via the EEA, initially (1931–5) building up reserves to offset flights from the pound, then successfully stabilizing the rate (1935–8) before war's approach heralded new downward pressures. Finally, whilst international collaboration was at a low ebb in comparison with the 1920s, the Bank was successful in getting some co-operation, with the French after 1933 and with the USA after 1936 (Sayers 1976, pp. 468–81).

As suggested above, whilst the Treasury's economic role expanded in this period, it remained primarily concerned with finance. The other side of this coin was the absence of an employment Ministry, an absence symbolic of the fact that unemployment was not the central issue of economic policy. This did not, of course, mean a complete absence of concern with either unemployment or the labour market more generally. In this area of concern a major agency was the Ministry of Labour.

Much more parliamentary and legislative time in the 1930s (as in the 1920s) was devoted to the relief of unemployment than to its reduction. The central issue in the organization of relief was what to do about the incapacity of unemployment insurance to cope with unemployment of the scale or longevity of the period, and the compelling political need to keep the mass of the unemployed out of the grip of the Poor Law. This nettle had not been grasped in the 1920s, when all sorts of temporary expedients had been tried in rapid succession. In 1934, however, the National Government reorganized the system under the Unemployment Insurance Statutory Commission, and the vast bulk of those ineligible for insurance benefits were able to claim from local bodies under the Unemployment Assistance Board (Booth 1978). The UAB was made the responsibility of the Ministry of Labour, to signify the departure from the Poor Law, which had been supervised by the Ministry of Health. The Ministry was also responsible for substantial amendment to the arrangements originally proposed by the Treasury (Lowe 1986, pp. 154–90).

Much less was done on the creation of employment. The Ministry of Labour helped the development of a slightly less hostile attitude to public works (Lowe 1986, pp. 217–22) but this was well contained within the Treasury's overall policy thrust (as above). More significant was the growth of regional policy, partly stimulated by the Ministry. This growth was in part a continuation of the 1928 Industrial Transference Act policy of taking workers to the work, under which a gross flow of 183,000 workers was organized between 1932 and 1938 (Lowe 1986, p. 223). More innovative was the Special Areas Act of 1937, which for the first time permitted governments, through the Special Areas Commissioners (first appointed in 1934) to give direct financial aid to profit-making concerns in certain regional unemployment blackspots. However only in principle would this approach seem to have much radical about it; its direct contribution to relieving unemployment in the 1930s was trivial (Lowe 1986, p. 231; see also Heim 1983).

In retrospect these policies may be seen as laying the groundwork for the strong regional policies developed in the Board of Trade during the Second World War and applied thereafter (see Chapter 8), though Booth (1982) puts much more emphasis on the war period in generating post-1945 policies. Equally, they may be seen as marginalizing the unemployment problem, by designating it a problem of limited geographical impact, requiring no shift in overall policy (Parsons 1986, chs. 1, 2).

Lowe (1986, p. 216) summarizes the position in the 1930s in these words: 'Official faith in a balanced budget and an unmanaged economy remained unshaken. Within the confines of orthodoxy, however, there was undoubtedly increased opportunities for political and administrative experiment.' This summary rightly emphasizes 'official' and not just 'Treasury' faith, for it would be certainly wrong in general to picture an orthodox Treasury resisting the blandishments of unorthodox subordinate Ministries. Rather the Treasury's search for, and usually achievement of, departmental consensus (within which it was *primus inter pares*) meant that 'administrative workability' was central to policy discussion. 'The danger inherent in the process, indeed in any process in which a large number of interests and considerations have to be taken into account, is that the ideal course of action may be completely lost sight of in the discussion of departmental difficulties and objections.' (Cited Middleton 1985, p. 36.) At the official as well as the political level, the search for consensus led to cautious policies incapable of grappling with mass unemployment.

Doctrine

Historians of economic thought would probably all agree that the most important event of the 1930s was the publication of Keynes's *General Theory*, though it was far from the only significant departure in economic theory in this decade (Shackle 1967). However the significance of Keynes's book for economic thought has generated an enormous literature which shows no sign of abating—a recent *selection* of articles on this work ran to four volumes (Wood 1983). It would be inappropriate in any event to try and summarize this literature in a book on economic policy.[5] However a number of issues relating to the significance of this work for economic policy need to be discussed.

First, Keynes wrote the General Theory because of his view about how economic policy is made. This was basically a 'rationalistic' view, that in the long run economic theory was crucial to economic policy, a view summarized in well-known sentences near the end of the General Theory:

the ideas of economists and political philosophers, both when they are right and when they are wrong, are more powerful than is commonly understood. Indeed the world is ruled by little else. Practical men, who believe themselves to be quite exempt from any intellectual influences, are usually the slave of some defunct economist . . . I am sure that the power of vested interests is vastly exaggerated compared with the gradual encroachment of ideas . . . soon or late, it is ideas, not vested interests, which are dangerous for good or evil. (Keynes 1971, p. 383.)

This view in part explains a seeming paradox about the General Theory: it was fundamentally concerned to change economic

[5] For discussion of Keynes's General Theory, in ascending order of difficulty, see Moggridge (1976, ch. 5); Stewart (3rd edn., 1986, chs. 4, 5); Bleaney (1985, ch. 1); Blaug (1985, ch. 16); Shackle (1967, chs. 11–15); Chick (1983).

policy, but says remarkably little about such policy. Keynes believed that his failure to convince the authorities on his policy proposals was fundamentally an intellectual failure.[6] The General Theory was designed to remedy that failure by providing a theoretical rationale for policies that he had long advocated.

In the General Theory Keynes attacked the 'classical' doctrines of economists like Pigou as a counterpoint to his own theories. Pigou was, in fact, a supporter of Keynes on the issue of public works, and signed a famous letter to *The Times* to that effect in 1932 (Keynes 1982, pp. 125–7, 137–40). Indeed probably a majority of economists accepted the case for such works (Hutchison 1968, Appendix; Dimand 1988, chs. 3, 4). Keynes's argument was that this disparity between practical proposals and theoretical foundations fatally injured the case for such proposals. But this seems unpersuasive in accounting for the Treasury's obduracy on public works and other expansionary proposals. Whilst at times the Treasury attacked the theories behind public-works policies, most of its attention was on the administrative issues, above all how to persuade/subsidize local authorities to pursue such policies; or the broad practicalities, such as the likely effects of such policies on confidence; the danger to control of public expenditure of any allowing of deficits; the threat to cheap money likely from a major expansion of government borrowing (see further below, Politics and Policies).

The other notable aspect of this debate is the extent to which even in the General Theory Keynes did actually depart from the economic assumptions of the Treasury. This, of course, relates to the whole debate about the significance of Keynes's work. But one issue may be discussed, both for its inherent importance and as an example of the complexities of the relation between doctrine and policy. This issue is one of wages and employment.

Booth (1987a), as noted above, has divined a central strand of argument in Treasury policies which emphasizes the need to raise prices as a means of depressing real wages, raising profits and thereby investment and output. How did Keynes stand on this

---

[6] Some of the policy proposals were very much 'throw-away lines'—for example his advocacy of a 'comprehensive socialization of investment' seems to provide the basis for many exam questions, but its meaning remains extremely obscure. For a view which plays down Keynes's rationalistic approach to economic policy, see Clarke (1988), pp. 15–16, 191–2, 308–10.

issue? Up to and including the General Theory the answer would seem to be that he agreed that labour had a diminishing marginal productivity, and hence for more workers to be employed the wage would have to fall, in accordance with the simple rules of supply and demand. Indeed, as Garside (1987) has emphasized, Keynes and Pigou were in accord in the early 1930s in arguing both that real wages needed to fall to raise employment, and that the best way to do this was to raise prices. As Pigou wrote in 1933: 'Either money costs must fall or money prices must rise. The practical difficulties in the way of the former solution have proved so serious and the friction to be overcome so great that the main body of informed opinion was turned towards the latter' (cited Garside 1987, p. 78; see also Howson and Winch 1977, pp. 64–5). The 'practical difficulties' were, of course, the General Strike which symbolized resistance to any policies of wage cuts.

As of 1936 Keynes did not consistently dissent from this view.[7] Only in 1939 did he move towards today's 'radical Keynesianism', which argues that under conditions of unused capacity there could be increasing returns to scale if output were stimulated, the marginal product of labour could rise, and therefore demand increases could increase employment without a fall in the real wage (Keynes 1939; compare Chick 1983, pp. 7–10, 72–5).

Booth (1987*a*) rightly emphasizes the Treasury's attachment to the idea of raising prices to cut real wages and raise profits. However raising prices could be seen in a rather different light, as concerned with the stability of the financial system, where price falls undermine the value of securities held as loan collateral but raise the value of debt. In that context price rises may be a necessary condition for stability in the financial system (e.g. Keynes 1982, pp. 51–2). The point once again is that advocacy of a particular course of action (raising prices) cannot be seen as simply the consequence of allegiance to a particular economic theory. It

---

[7] The whole question of how far Keynes saw wage reductions as a means to increase employment is extremely complex and controversial. One popular version, noted already, is that the whole of Keynes's analysis was based on the idea of 'sticky wages' which didn't contradict the theoretical case for wage cuts, but only their practicality. Another version would be that Keynes's whole notion of the instability of capitalism related to investors' expectations, and that wage reductions might add to the uncertainty of these expectations, especially because of their potential impact on the future demand for output. Hence wage cuts might boost investment only when they had clearly come to a halt. On this issue, apart from those works cited in n. 5, see Dimand 1988 and (more difficult) Drobny 1988.

was not the case in the 1930s that on one side the Treasury and allies lined up behind one theory and its policy consequences against, on the other side, Keynes, his theory, and its policy consequences.

One area where policies actually pursued seem to reflect more success for the ideas of Keynes was in the area of monetary policy. Cheap and managed money had been advocated by Keynes in the 1920s, and were adopted by the Treasury in the 1930s. The issue is how far these can be seen as cause and effect. The Treasury's adoption of 'managed money' was initially of course because the alternative, the gold standard, proved untenable. Cheap money subsequently emerged when it was realized that low interest rates were compatible with the absence of rapid inflation, and with stability in the exchange rate, and not only cheapened the debt service but perhaps provided a means of raising prices and getting the economy going again. Realistically, therefore, whilst Keynes's advocacy of such a policy no doubt helped, from 1931/2 it was no longer going against the grain of official thought—unlike public-works policy.

Official policy-making in the 1930s was dominated by non-economists. The Treasury remained overwhelmingly an agency staffed by generalists. But the channels of economists' debates into policy-making were expanded, mainly through the Committee on Economic Information. This had its origins under the Labour government as the Economic Advisory Council, with ambitious aims to embody both representative and expert opinion on economic affairs, and use these to have a major impact on the formulation of policy. These hopes were not realized, but under the National Government the body was reformed and *de facto* replaced by the CEI. The committee consisted mainly of economists, along with two senior representatives of the Treasury. Keynes and his advocacy of cheap money, public works, and international monetary measures to help debtors dominated the Commitee's work (Howson and Winch 1977, pp. 106–8).

Howson and Winch argue that the CEI had a major significance in pushing Treasury thinking towards macroeconomic management. The dispute on this point has been outlined above. Less contentiously, the Committee certainly aided the acceptance of the cheap money policy, albeit, as suggested above, this was in line with the Treasury's perception of the changed constraints and opportunities opened up by departure from gold (Howson and Winch 1977, pp. 109–14).

Whilst the direct impact of the CEI on policy remains contentious, the long-term significance of its establishment is clear. It was 'the first attempt in Britain to recruit economists into government service on a full-time basis, and to create a mechanism whereby the government could call upon a wide range of outside experts for advice on a regular and formal basis' (Howson and Winch 1977, p. 1). Economists, for good or ill, were never to lose this privileged place in the government machine thereafter.

Politics and Policies

Unemployment

To commentators in the 1950s and 1960s it seemed obvious that with three million unemployed the issue of unemployment must have been at the centre of economic policy in the 1930s. Looking back from the end of the 1980s we know that this assumption is naïve; mass unemployment can be tolerated by governments, without dominating their agenda.

After 1920, conditions seemed ripe for unemployment to become an even more highly charged political issue; the franchise had been extended to cover many more working-class voters; unemployment must have directly affected between 5 and 6 million voters each year; and there was intense three-party competition for votes from 1922 until 1931. However, unemployment assumed top priority in the inter-war political debate only very rarely. In only one of seven inter-war general elections was unemployment policy the main issue, and, paradoxically, this was in 1929 when unemployment was at its lowest point between 1921 and 1939 (Booth 1987*b*, p. 43).

To ask why unemployment figured so little is perhaps itself tendentious; it assumes that in the natural course of things mass unemployment would dominate politics. But of course unemployment, whilst widespread, directly affected only a minority. This minority tended to be concentrated in the regions, and mainly lived in constituencies which were non-marginal (strongly Labour) and therefore were not crucial to the Conservatives, who were in government throughout the 1930s. Also those in employment in the 1930s enjoyed quite substantial gains in their living standards for most of the period. And the unemployed, whilst harshly treated by such mechanisms as the Means Test, were not treated ungenerously, in terms of benefit levels, in comparison with other periods of unemployment (including the 1980s). Finally as Jahoda (1982) emphasized in her classic study, unemployment generates adaptation and apathy, reinforced by the cutting of ties to channels of political involvement, the workplace, and the trade union, which unemployment brings in train (Middlemas 1981). Under these conditions, the political attention of the unemployed was rarely aroused, and when it was, it usually focused on short-term issues in the *relief* of unemployment, not its reduction (Deacon 1987).

At the level of governmental policies 1930–40 was a Conservative decade. Whilst the débâcle of 1931 was far more one of seats than of votes, it may be seen as a verdict on Labour's failure to deal with the unemployment problem—the issue on which it had been elected in 1929. Labour consequently had difficulties in claiming any policies for solving unemployment, and slipped into the role of being a defender of the unemployed, this being acceptable to its warring factions, as few other positions were. Whilst it was unambiguously the second party in the 1930s, with the decline of Liberalism, Labour's intellectual effort was not primarily concerned with immediate issues of solving unemployment, but with broader issues of economic and social reform (Durbin 1985). On current issues it was still Liberals—notably Keynes and Lloyd George—who acted as the most intellectually threatening of the government's critics. Yet only Labour had the electoral support to be a plausible alternative government to the Conservatives. Finally, paradoxically, Labour was opposed for most of the 1930s to the one policy which would have quickly reduced unemployment—rearmament. Overall the Conservatives' 'safety first' approach struck a chord with the electorate, especially given the presentation of the 1929–32 slump as externally caused, and the gradual but unambiguous recovery from 1933. Minor concessions on unemployment relief usually defused political opposition to the Conservatives' policies (Miller 1976).

If a government more committed to the reduction of unemployment had been in office, what policies could it have pursued to deal successfully with the problem? Until the mid-1970s the dominant view of the literature was that there was a clear and potentially workable alternative, a Keynesian-style reflation using public works. But such a view is now highly contentious.

Two types of criticism of the relevance of the Keynesian solution may be divined. On the one hand there is work that takes a Keynesian framework for analysing the macro-economy as given, and then attempts to assess how far, in the 1930s, an expansionary fiscal policy would have solved unemployment. The results, from a Keynesian point of view, have generally been disappointing. The alternative strand of criticism (so far much thinner) has been that derived from a wholesale rejection of Keynesian notions of aggregate demand, and a return to pre-Keynesian notions about the workings of the economy.

The pioneer of the first type of analysis was Thomas (1981). He built a relatively straightforward Keynesian model of the British economy between the wars, and estimated the effects on the economy of the 1929 *We Can Conquer Unemployment* package of public works. His conclusion is that this programme would have made only a rather small dent in the unemployment problem, and that a package large enough to have made a substantial impact would have involved a very large deficit on the current account of the balance of payments, leaving aside any impact on the capital account. These broad conclusions have been endorsed by other investigators (Glynn and Howells 1980; Broadberry 1986, ch. 15). Others have argued that these views are too pessimistic about the size of the multiplier, and that a Keynesian programme would have made a not inconsiderable dent in unemployment (Hatton 1985; Garside and Hatton 1985). However, even the strongest supporter of a Keynesian policy has to acknowledge the serious current account of the balance of payments consequences of such a policy, and that to eradicate rather than just reduce unemployment would have required a public works programme on a scale 'not seriously contemplated by contemporaries or by historians' (Hatton 1987, p. 89).

In addition to the balance of payments problem, most recent writers have accepted that there was a substantial regional/ structural problem in the inter-war economy (Glynn and Booth 1983; Garside and Hatton 1985; Glynn and Booth 1985). Raising aggregate demand might have helped this, in the sense that movement between sectors and regions is likely to be encouraged if the economy is generally being run at a high level of demand. A clearer picture would depend on a distinct separation of regional and cyclical unemployment, which is in principle easy but quantitatively difficult (Howson 1981; also Jones 1985). On the other hand, it raises the question of how far wages would have responded to any such policy and thereby posed difficulties for structural change, an issue on which little work seems to have been done (Hatton 1987, p. 93).

Most recent commentators have played down the relevance of Keynesian policies to Britain's inter-war unemployment problem. For example, Middleton (1985, p. 180) argues that 'without a willingness to allow major economic and political changes, the obstacles to large-scale public works appear insuperable'. Lowe (1986, p. 235) argues that 'Keynesian public works proposals in 1929 and again in 1935 were—as has been seen—theoretically unsound, administratively impractical, and culturally unacceptable'.

Two points can be made about this seeming consensus on the limits of Keynesian policy. First, it may in part be seen as a reaction to the clearly exaggerated claims of Keynesians of an earlier period that demand management would be a complete solution, rather than *part* of the solution. The plausibility of the stimulation of aggregate demand depends in part on the precise timing. As Peden argues (1988, p. 32) the Keynesian case is stronger for periods of high cyclical unemployment like 1930–4 when prices were falling than for periods of cyclical recovery like 1936–7 when prices were rising. In the latter period at least a successful Keynesian policy would have required a much more active policy to concentrate demand regionally coupled with labour-market policies to improve labour supply.

Second, this consensus is clearly based on the view that the obstacles to Keynesian policies were not purely economic. They also included administrative problems such as the lack of central government control over local authority expenditure, the administrative conservatism of the Treasury and Whitehall, the political infelicities of the proponents of public works, to the whole political culture of 'safety first' (Middleton 1985, pp. 180–2; Skidelsky 1975).

Another line of attack on Keynesian proposals for the inter-war period has come from the revival of neo-classical economics in the 1970s and 1980s. These writers have doubted the relevance of Keynesian solutions, and instead have revived some of the 'orthodox' views of the 1920s and 1930s. One strand has been the reassertion of the view that real wages were too high, and that this led to the failure of the labour market to clear (Beenstock *et al.* 1984; Capie 1987). The other, that much of the unemployment was voluntary, induced by the level of unemployment benefits (Benjamin and Kochin 1979).

The first argument is extremely contentious (Dimsdale 1984; Garside 1987) and seems strongest for the initial post-World-War-One period than for the 1930s (Broadberry 1986, ch. 8). For most of the inter-war period movements in the real wage were small, and the elasticity of employment with respect to the real wage was quite low (Dimsdale 1984). The view that most of the fluctuations in employment were due to fluctuations in international and national demand appears robust.

Even less plausible is the view that a substantial proportion of the inter-war unemployment was benefit-induced. The original Benjamin and Kochin thesis has been attacked on a number of grounds. Ormerod and Worswick (1982) have shown how the results are highly sensitive to the period chosen, Jones (1985) has argued that their model cannot account for regional variations, Hatton (1986) and Crafts (1987) have thrown serious doubt on their cross-sectional evidence. Most recently, Eichengreen (1987*b*) has studied survey data on the adult male unemployed in London in the 1930s, and found that whilst the benefit/wage ratio had some small effect on non-heads of households, it had practically no effect on heads of households.

In sum, the conclusions of most recent discussions of the 1930s unemployment problem is that a shortage of demand was an important component of the problem, but that at best demand-boosting methods would have had to be accompanied by a range of other policy instruments to get unemployment down substantially.

Recognition of the multiple economic problems of the 1930s is the starting point of Booth and Pack (1985). They are concerned to assess whether any of the inter-war proponents of policies alternative to those actually pursued had a good case. This requires them to establish a standard of assessment which consists of three elements:

1. To find ways of defending the balance of payments at high levels of economic activity either within existing institutional arrangements or under a modified system;

2. to evolve policies which would absorb at least some of the unemployed but which would not prejudice the search for higher efficiency and lower unit costs in both sides of a dual economy; and

3. accelerate the pace of structural adjustment, either with the support of private investors and businessmen or by fulfilling their functions in alternative ways without inhibiting the expansionary potential of the home market sector.

These are extremely high standards of assessments to which, unsurprisingly, none of the inter-war programmes quite match up. Nevertheless they do provide a very useful summary of the problems of the British inter-war economy. It need hardly be said that the actual policies pursued did not come near to matching these standards.

Industrial Policy

Neither public debate nor public policy on the economy in the 1930s was dominated by macroeconomic issues. Public policy was increasingly concerned with the efficiency of particular industrial sectors, but this did not lead to a coherent industrial policy. Rather, the picture seems to be one of ill-co-ordinated, *ad hoc* interventions at different levels (Roberts 1984; Kirby 1987; Booth 1987*a*, pp. 510–12, 514–15).

As already noted, the government in the 1930s attempted unsuccessfully to use the tariff to persuade the iron and steel industry to rationalize itself. The Bank of England did play some part in establishing new steel plants, but these interventions did not provide a coherent policy for the industry (Sayers 1976, pp. 546–51; Tolliday 1986, pp. 94–100). By and large the efforts of the controllers of the industry went towards defensive cartelization and price maintenance, rather than rationalization.

A similar failure may be recorded in the coal industry, where official support for rationalization was frustrated by the resistance of both owners and workers to the provisions for compulsory amalgamation under the 1930 Coal Mines Act (Kirby 1977, pp. 108–68). Eventually more successful was the rationalization of the cotton industry under the Cotton Spinning (Reorganization) Act of 1936. This is an interesting example where the legislation came at the end of a long process of informal 'industrial diplomacy', which resulted in a consensus within the industry. On the other hand the government had strong ideological objections to any formal tripartite, 'corporatist' arrangements which in Britain have always run up against the strength of the rhetoric of limitless parliamentary sovereignty (Roberts 1984).

In sum, industrial policy in the 1930s did not move much beyond the propaganda and hectoring for rationalization which emerged in the late 1920s. Booth (1987*a*, p. 512) has raised the question of how far those few interventions that did take place can be seen as part of a coherent strategy to raise profitability. The difficulty, as he accepts, is that almost *any* industrial policy would presumably have this object somewhere in view, and we lack the relevant research to know whether this idea was the core of government policy. Available evidence suggests that policy lacked any such rational kernel.

Industrial policy in the 1930s cannot sensibly be described as *laissez-faire*, however much government rhetoric may have wanted to present its activities as temporary deviations from that norm. Those deviations in some regards were quite substantial, not only in the sense of positive policy interventions, but a general willingness to allow cartelization and restrictive practices, anathema to any free market policy. Indeed the most obvious legacy of 1930s' industrial policy may be seen in the reaction to it, leading to substantial emphasis on anti-monopoly policy in much wartime and post-war economic discussion (Chapters 6, 8).

Conclusions

Departure from gold in 1931 opened the way for a much more managed economy. It increased the autonomy of domestic economic policy; it also undercut the rhetoric of automaticity in the economy, so important in the debates of the 1920s.

The clearest shift towards management was on the external account. The exchange rate was managed, tariffs (albeit for a variety of reasons) regulated the current account, capital outflows were restricted for much of the period. Yet in crucial respects this management reinforced Conservative policies on the domestic front. If the exchange rate was to be successfully managed then confidence had to be maintained, and this required an orthodox fiscal policy—a point for which the events of 1931 could always be deployed in evidence. The dominant view was therefore that monetary policy (cheap money) was in conflict with an activist fiscal policy.

The issue of confidence remains a bugbear of discussions of economic policy. There is clearly an element of circular reasoning when governments argue that policy X is impossible because it will undermine confidence: they themselves partly determine which policies are and are not deserving of confidence. Nevertheless, if we make the elementary point that in a capitalist economy the controllers of capital have always to be persuaded rather than coerced to certain courses of action, then confidence can never be ignored. What of course we cannot know is how far a different government in the 1930s might have been able to persuade those controllers that different policies were also deserving of confidence.

The confidence issue remains vital to the debate about the possibility of more expansionary macroeconomic policies in the 1930s. So also does the issue of the 'fiscal constitution' (Buchanan and Wagner 1977; Middleton 1985, pp. 84–5). Hostility to a more activist fiscal policy was grounded broadly on a fundamental distrust of democratic politics, and the view that a balanced budget was a necessary safeguard against the desire of vote-gathering politicians to spend without taxing. Such activist fiscal policy also required radical reform of the administrative apparatus to make possible the actual delivery of such expenditure in a sufficient quantity to make a significant impact. The total volume of that expenditure was also small relative to later periods, and it took the rise in expenditure during the war to make small variations in expenditure significant for the whole economy.

All these points illustrate how far the obstacles to 'Keynesianism' policies were not just those of economic theory. But important as this understanding is in regard to much of the literature of the 1930s, it should not obscure the point that to a degree the whole debate concerning the relevance of a Keynesian solution to the problems of the 1930s misleads us as to what policy discussions were about in this period. As Drummond (1974, p. 426) usefully reminds us, 'the Cabinet spent more time worrying about Imperial economic policy than about any other aspect of economic affairs'. Neither unemployment nor proposed macroeconomic solutions dominate the economic policy debates of the 1930s. Indeed the departure from gold in combination with mass unemployment seems to have opened up a Pandora's Box of ideas about 'managing' the economy, where that term is used to cover everything from planned emigration to the Empire to the nationalization of the banks to secure industrial investment.[8] In the political circumstances of the 1930s much of this could be, and was, dismissed or ignored. But in the longer term we may see the 1930s as the period when economic management got decisively on to the political agenda, albeit in a form which had little coherence, and for many in government the idea represented short-term necessity rather than long-term commitment.

Further Reading

Booth, A. (1987*a*): 'Britain in the 1930s: A Managed Economy?', *Economic History Review* 40, pp. 499–522.

—— and Pack, M. (1985): *Employment, Capital, and Economic Policy*, Oxford.

Drummond, I. (1981): *The Floating Pound and the Sterling Area, 1931–1939*, Cambridge, chs. 1, 6–11.

Floud, R., and McCloskey, D., eds. (1981): *The Economic History of Britain since 1700* vol. ii. *1860 to the 1970s*, Cambridge, chs. 10–14.

Glynn, S., and Booth, A., eds. (1987): *The Road to Full Employment*, London.

Keynes, J. M. (1982): *Activities 1931–1939: World Crises and Policies in Britain and America, Collected Writings* vol. xxi, London, chs. 1–3, 6.

Middleton, R. (1985): *Towards the Managed Economy: Keynes, the Treasury, and the Fiscal Policy Debate of the 1930s*, London.

O'Brien, P. K. (1987): 'Britain's Economy Between the Wars: A Survey of a Counter-Revolution in Economic History' *Past and Present* 115, pp. 107–30.

Peden, G. (1988): *Keynes, the Treasury and British Economic Policy*. London.

Winch, D. (1972): *Economics and Policy*, London.

---

[8] On various strands of economic argument in the 1930s see Marwick (1964); Booth and Pack (1985); Durbin (1985).

6

1939–1945: Planning the War and Plans for Peace

SLOWLY at first, but with gathering speed from 1940, the peace-time economy was transformed into a 'war economy'. By the peak period of the war effort (1943/4) the military were using the output of 55 per cent of all manufacturing manpower, civilian consumption was about one-fifth below 1939 levels, and government was spending half the national income. In comparison with most belligerents, and especially the major Axis powers, this was an unparalleled level of devotion of resources to the war effort (Milward 1987, ch. 3). It necessarily involved a radical recasting of the instruments of economic policy, which, albeit to a contestable degree, left a permanent mark on the relations between the state and the economy. Parallel to this planning of the economy for war purposes was an increasing concern for planning the peace; and whilst much of this was only to reach fruition after 1945, it is in many ways as much a part of the history of the war as is the planning for war. Whilst the first half of this chapter deals with wartime planning, the second half outlines this planning for peace and its significance.

Institutions

Exchange Controls and the Exchange Rate

In retrospect it may seem obvious that a total war can only be fought with the utmost economy in foreign exchange by means which include rigorous control over international transactions. But at the beginning of the 1939 war the movement to such controls in Britain was initially reluctant and half-hearted. Plans had been prepared in the last days of peace, the Bank of England pressing the need on a reluctant Treasury. But the example of such devices in Germany was mainly seen as a warning of the bureaucratic nightmare such controls might involve rather than a model to be followed. Equally, there was an awareness of the threat such controls posed for the international role of the pound, especially in the context of the sterling area and the pounds its members had accumulated (Sayers 1956, pp. 226–32).

When war broke out controls were initially exerted only over resident holders of sterling, so non-resident holders of sterling balances were free to convert them. Holdings of hard currencies (notably dollars) had to be surrendered, and the Treasury was given a legal monopoly of all transactions in gold and foreign currencies. The scale of exemption from these controls was the cause of much criticism (e.g. Balogh 1940), and, as in so many other areas, a decisive change came with the German conquest of France and the arrival of the Churchill coalition in the summer of 1940. In July 1940 'the view that sterling must remain a free currency was finally put aside as a peace-time luxury, and the control at last became strict enough to prevent any appreciable leakage of the proceeds of exports' (Sayers 1956, p. 251). Non-resident as well as resident holders of sterling were now subjected to strict licensing of foreign exchange transactions.

In effect Britain moved a long way down the German road to bilateralism, i.e. where purchases in one currency had to be matched by receipts in the same currency. An important feature of the control system was that it was around the sterling area, not Britain alone. Payments in sterling were unrestricted within that area, with exchange controls operated by all members of the area, who also pooled their gold and foreign currency reserves. This gave a formal status to this previously informal grouping, helping to make possible both the short-term benefits and long-term dangers of the massive accumulation of sterling balances (see below).

This system of rigorous exchange control made possible stabilization of the exchange rate. In the last few weeks before the outbreak of war the rate had been allowed to fall from $4.68 to $4. In the period of weak exchange control the free rate for sterling fell as low as $3.44, but at the stage when stringent exchange control was imposed the rate was stabilized at $4.03. 'It was thought best to fix something just wide of the round figure because it would look less committal and be less difficult to adjust if experience showed that adjustment was necessary' (Sayers 1956, p. 461). In the event this level was to be maintained through the thick and thin of the war years.

This defence of the parity seems to have had two major objectives. On one side was the lingering concern with the status of the pound as an international currency: 'There was always, even in the grimmest days, some concern for the post-war prestige of sterling as an international currency, and some struggle to maintain its wartime value untarnished was worthwhile on this account alone' (Sayers 1956, p. 239). On the other side, the scale of British exports in wartime was largely determined not by their price competitiveness but by the availability of supplies. In this context a high exchange rate gathered as much foreign exchange as possible from limited exports, as well as keeping imports relatively cheap.

Trade Controls and the Balance of Payments

The single most striking summary of Britain's wartime economic position is given by the balance of payments figures (Table 6.1). Only 40 per cent of imports were financed by current receipts, the rest coming mainly from Lend Lease (grants from the USA), the accumulation of sterling balances in sterling area countries, and sale of investments.

Table 6.1   *Britain's Cumulative Balance of Payments 1939–1945* (£m.)

Imports	
(including all munitions)	16,900
Exports	
(including reciprocal aid and foreign government expenditure in UK)	6,900
Current Account Deficit	−10,000
Sources of Financing	
(Net) grants from USA	5,400
Sale of investments	1,100
Requisitioning of gold and dollars	100
Accumulation of liabilities (in pounds and dollars)	3,500
Fall in reserves	−100
Total	+10,000

Source: Sayers 1956, p. 499.

A deterioration in the balance of payments was an anticipated consequence of the war, but not on the scale which eventually occurred. Initially, in the phoney-war phase down to spring 1940, the focus of concern was on preserving gold and dollar reserves by concentrating import demand on the Empire and the sterling area. Purchases from the USA had to be made on a normal commercial basis (up until November 1939 these purchases could not include munitions because of the US Neutrality Act). Initially planning for the war was geared to this financial constraint. Including the foreign exchange requisitioned at the outbreak of war, Britain's gold and dollar reserves stood at £525m. This limited sum could be augmented by sales of investments in the USA, and this policy was pursued down to the summer of 1940. Also early in 1940 substantial effort was devoted to export promotion, until Hitler's blitzkrieg in the West ended this curious hangover of the 'business as usual' mentality.

By this time the notion of husbanding financial resources had given way to a policy of throwing caution to the wind in the face of impending military disaster. By July 1940 Britain was spending more in the USA than she could afford on any time-scale but the very shortest. Asset sales continued; gold was secured from wherever possible (e.g. the exiled Belgian government's reserves). The basic thrust of policy was to use every expedient until the re-election of Roosevelt in the November 1940 Presidential election made possible putting Anglo-US economic relations on a new footing (Sayers 1956, ch. 12; Hancock and Gowing 1949, ch. 4).

This new footing for Anglo-US economic relations was Lend-Lease. Under this arrangement the US supplied (with small reciprocation by the UK) munitions, food, and materials which were unpaid for, but were 'leased' to Britain to pursue the war effort. The figures in Table 6.1 make it unambiguously clear how dependent Britain's external position was on the lend-lease arrangements. On the other hand, lend-lease was shot through with political difficulty. Once the USA entered the war, the British view was that the war was a common effort which should be reflected in a pooling of financial resources, not any kind of client–lender relationship. In the USA on the other hand the view was common that lend-lease was a loan, albeit for political purposes, which at a minimum required some 'consideration' from the borrower (Sayers 1956, ch. 12; Hancock and Gowing 1949, ch. 9; Hall and Wrigley 1956, chs. 8–11).

One significant consequence of this US view of lend-lease was the pressure put on Britain to make sure that lend-lease goods were used solely for war purposes, and in particular that they were not embodied in British exports sold in competition with US producers. This was especially sensitive in the American continent, where Britain's need for export receipts was greatest, but so also was US sensitivity to British competition. Britain was happy to accept the principle of not re-exporting lend-lease goods, but turning this acceptance into practice proved difficult. Britain leant over backwards to appease American sentiment, publishing a White Paper (Cmd. 6311) in 1941 in which she gave all that the USA wanted, probably with substantial damage to UK exports, especially in South America (Hargreaves and Gowing 1952, pp. 145–65; Sayers 1956, pp. 398–405).

Lend-lease affected British economic policy in two other ways. Perhaps most importantly in the long run, the commitment to trade liberalization given as a 'consideration' was a major ingredient in the debates over the reconstruction of the post-war world economy (see Chapter 7). Also of importance was the US view of Britain's reserves. Britain had traditionally operated on low reserves relative to outstanding liabilities. In the 1930s this had been ameliorated by the accumulations consequent on the Exchange Equalization Account's policy of holding sterling down. But in the early months of the war these reserves were soon spent, and fell to around £40m. in July 1941, when the authorities thought £150m. close to the acceptable minimum. To the US providers of lend-lease, reserves looked like a resource on which Britain should call first. To Britain a sufficiency of reserves seemed like a necessary condition for both the short-term conduct of policy without periodic scares of insolvency, and in the longer term the only hope of London playing a full part in an open post-war international economy, especially as sterling liabilities were growing fast. There was no real resolution of this difference, but by 1944 the USA had come to accept a rather more generous level of reserves as necessary for Britain than had often been the case earlier in the war. After the low point of mid-1941 Britain did accumulate reserves to total over £600m. by the war's end. This, of course, was only a fraction of the liabilities accumulated at the same time (Sayers 1956, pp. 427–36, 468–74, 496).

Lend-lease was crucial to maintaining a level of imports otherwise unfinanceable. Imports were also cut back directly by controls. In principle exchange control could be used to control import volumes, and in Germany the two had indeed been closely integrated from the late 1930s. But in Britain, as noted above, exchange control was only slowly made watertight, and in any case its operations were decentralized on to the clearing banks. Therefore the government adopted measures to scrutinize and regulate import levels directly. But, like the exchange control, these were initially lacking in both comprehensiveness and vigour of implementation. It was the shortage of shipping rather than foreign exchange which eventually stimulated a more effective control. The control worked mainly through the development of responsibility by major government departments for the great bulk of overseas supplies. But it was a long time before it became based on a clear national programme of priorities. Most important to this was the shipping crisis brought about by the North Atlantic U-Boat campaign (Hancock and Gowing 1949, pp. 113–14, 124–35, 264–8, 422–37). The eventual impact of this policy on the volume of imports is evident from Table 6.2, though of course it was nothing like enough to compensate for the fall in exports.

Table 6.2   *Imports and Exports 1938–1945*

	Imports		Exports	
	Value (£m.)	Volume	Value (£m.)	Volume
1938	858	100	471	100
1939	840	97	440	94
1940	1126	94	411	72
1941	1132	82	365	56
1942	992	70	271	36
1943	1228	77	234	29
1944	1294	80	266	31
1945	1053	62	399	46

Source: Sayers 1956, p. 495

The Budget

In the sphere of Britain's external transactions the war brought
unprecedentedly severe restrictions on the norms of an open,
'liberal' economy. On the home front equally momentous changes
came about in budgetary policy, though in this case the long-run
significance of these changes has been much debated.

Perhaps in no area of the conduct of war were memories of the
First World War so evident as in the area of budgetary policy.
Both inside and outside the Treasury the belief was pre-eminent
that *this* time there should not be the legacy of debt left at the
war's end, with all its destabilizing and inflationary consequences
(Hancock and Gowing 1949, pp. 3–13). The initial emphasis of
wartime budgetary policy (in the budget of September 1939 and
two budgets of 1940) was to tax 'as much as possible' to finance
government war expenditure, with the aim of containing the
necessarily inflationary consequences of the rapid rise in government
demands on the economy. (For the revenue and expenditure
position in wartime see Table 6.3.)

Table 6.3   *Budgets 1939–1945* (£m.)

	Revenue (less debt interest)	Expenditure*
1939	771	1,198
1940	1,158	3,100
1941	1,905	4,239
1942	2,314	4,715
1943	2,759	5,054
1944	2,897	5,076
1945	2,806	4,217

* On National Income basis i.e. 'Public Authorities' expenditure on goods and
services'.

Source: Sayers 1956, pp. 491, 493.

Debates over these first three budgets were dominated by the
adequacy of the volume of government expenditure in the
prosecution of the war, and the balance of financing between
borrowing and taxation. That of July 1940 came under especial

attack as not being ambitious enough in terms of total war expenditure, and not doing enough to widen the scope of taxation and so make possible less borrowing (Sabine 1970, ch. 8; Sayers 1956, ch. 2).

The following budget, that of 1941, has commonly been seen as a watershed. As always, such turning-points can be over-dramatized. Even before 1941 the government was groping towards the view that the budget was not just about financing expenditure, but about the whole problem of the balance between expenditure on one side and the sum of taxation and money borrowed by ordinary methods on the other. This 'gap' was always important to the Treasury because it was the source of the demand inflation so much feared. In the early budgets of the war this approach was not clearly delineated from traditional financing concerns, although both led to the general conclusion of the need for as rapid a rise as possible in total taxation (Sayers 1956, pp. 23–5, 67–8).

The year 1941 put the matter on a new footing by integrating the budget with the arithmetic of overall resource availability in the economy. The budget was not just to be about the balance between taxation and borrowing, and the way in which that taxation would fall, but about maintaining the balance between total demand and total supply in the economy. Maintaining this balance was a key task because of the belief that the only alternative was inflation, and that apart from its intrinsically undesirable features, inflation would not do the job it had done during the First World War of reducing civilian consumption, and providing material resources for the war effort. The belief was that such an inflation would only set off a wage–price spiral, which would be strongly dysfunctional for the social solidarity required by the war effort.

This new approach to the budget is usually thereby closely linked to Keynes's newspaper articles, and later a pamphlet *How to Pay for the War* (Keynes 1978, ch. 2; see also ch. 4). In the pamphlet, published in February 1940, Keynes started from the presumption that the basic problem of war finance is higher working-class incomes which people cannot be allowed to spend. The problem is then one of containing working-class expenditure. Rationing is seen as a pseudo-solution in the context of a general excess of purchasing power, and therefore it is unavoidable that taxation must bear much more heavily on working-class incomes. This should be made more palatable by making some part of this taxation into deferred savings, to be released post-war when the context is one of inadequate rather than excess demand. Keynes thus proposed a combination of much higher taxation of working-class incomes and compulsory saving, to supplement existing voluntary savings and taxes largely upon middle-class incomes and working-class expenditure. Also part of the package was the subsidization of key commodities to keep down the cost-of-living index[1], and so try to prevent cost inflation by discouraging wage increases granted on a cost-of-living basis.

Keynes's campaign for his proposals was highly and explicitly political. It was aimed predominantly at making his measures palatable to working-class/Labour Party opinion. The central argument was that, willy-nilly, working-class consumption would have to be squeezed to allow for resources to be devoted to the war, so the only issue was the equity with which this squeeze was accomplished. His proposals were argued to be the best way of spreading the burden, and avoiding an inflation which would benefit no one (Keynes 1978, pp. 82, 86–91, 97–104).

How to Pay for the War also depended upon developing estimates of the National Income, in order to calculate the components of national expenditure and link these to the sources of expenditure to be restrained by the budget. Apart from one effort by the Inland Revenue in 1929 (Stone 1977), practically nothing official had been done on estimating the National Income. As part of the preparation of *How to Pay for the War* Keynes, together with Erwin Rothbarth, had developed estimates of National Income based on private work by Colin Clark (Clark 1937; also Cuyvers 1983). By the time of the 1941 budget these efforts had been pushed much further on by Richard Stone and James Meade, working in the nucleus of the Central Statistical Office.[2] This made possible the accompaniment of the 1941 budget

---

[1] The 1941 budget included a commitment to stabilize the Ministry of Labour Cost of Living Index at 25–30% above 1939 levels, a policy continued throughout the war. This index was based on 1914 'weights' of expenditure and was highly unrepresentative of wartime patterns. Nevertheless its stabilization was of substantial symbolic and political significance (Hargreaves and Gowing 1952, pp. 552–5).

[2] The CSO along with the Economic Section was formed in December 1940 by splitting the Central Economic Information Service.

by an official paper on *An Analysis of the Sources of War Finance and an Estimate of the National Income and Expenditure in 1938 and 1940* (Stone 1951).

Many of the detailed proposals of Keynes's pamphlet were not enacted, in particular compulsory saving (Post-War Credits) never had the prominence in overall financial policy Keynes had hoped for, partly because of political opposition, partly because of Treasury fears about the impact on voluntary saving. More generally, the focus of budgetary policy on eliminating excess demand did not remove the need for rationing. Even if overall balance had been achieved, there was still the need to secure equity in distribution (see below on Rationing). In the event, there was continuing inflationary pressure in the economy, and it is very difficult to see financial policy being so finely tuned as to prevent such pressure altogether (Sayers 1956, pp. 90–3).

Budgetary policy for the remainder of the war followed the precedent set in 1941. The logic of encompassing working-class incomes in the direct tax net led to PAYE in 1943. The political importance of avoiding any appearance of profiteering led to a 100 per cent Excess Profits Tax. Subsidies on items of consumer expenditure grew in scale to reach over £300m. by 1945. All these developments followed from the logic of the 1941 approach, with its focus on securing working-class consent to the war, holding back inflation, and making the budget the crucial instrument for overall management of the economy (Sayers 1956, ch. 4).

The long-term significance of the 1941 budget has been the source of disagreement. It is common ground that it marked a new departure by its integration of the budgetary arithmetic with the national income estimates, making possible the use of the budget as an instrument of demand management, of management of the national economy in an unprecedented way. 'What was new in 1941 was the universal acceptance of the Keynesian formulation and the existence of Keynesian arithmetic as one weighty element—but only one element—in the emergence of the decisive "hunches" ' (Sayers 1956, p. 69). In this way Sayers suggests 1941 as a crucial year for the 'Keynesian Revolution' in economic policy.

Sceptics of this weight of significance given to the budget of 1941 have noted the specific conditions of that year. It was of course a year of war, which had always licensed *temporary* deviation from financial norms. This was the way Keynes presented his proposals, and how they were widely interpreted (Booth 1983, p. 107; Sabine 1970, pp. 187–8). It was also, of course, in the name of preventing inflation that the approach was readily embraced by the Treasury—a hardy traditional aim of Treasury policy. Treasury endorsement of Keynesianism in the name of anti-inflation did not imply endorsement for employment-creating purposes (see Post-War Plans below). In short, wartime Keynesianism involved no break with traditional concerns of sound finance, however much it may have revolutionized the role of the budget in the management of the economy.

Agencies

The Treasury

Up until the arrival of the Churchill Coalition in May 1940 the constraints of finance remained important in guiding the war effort. The availability of foreign exchange externally, and the concept of 'acceptable' tax levels internally, limited the war effort. But by the time of Churchill's arrival 'the political atmosphere was definitely antagonistic to the Treasury. There was a strong feeling that finance should be put in a less dominant position . . .' (Chester 1951, p. 6). As already noted, external financial caution was thrown to the wind in the summer of 1940. Internally, financial prudence was maintained by imposing unprecedently high tax levels, but the role of finance declined. Its central function was to contain inflation, and this was successfully done by the Keynesian budgetary approach from 1941 onwards. Hence the relative importance of the Treasury, as the agency of financial policy, was bound to diminish. What Chester (1951, pp. 5–6) calls the 'Treasury period' in the management of the war economy (September 1939 to May 1940) was followed by the 'period of committees' and then by the dominance of one Committee, the Lord President's, from January 1941. The eclipse of the Treasury from its primacy in economic policy-making was symbolized by the exclusion of the Chancellor of the Exchequer from the War Cabinet for much of the war.

The basic force leading to the relative fall in importance of the Treasury was the growth in importance of 'physical' methods of economic management in comparison with financial methods.

'Given that the new planning priorities began with manpower, continued with production, and ended with finance, it was natural that the Treasury should lose its peace-time primacy' (Middlemas 1986, p. 28.) In retrospect we know this was only an interregnum in the Treasury's dominance of economic policy—a dominance unambiguously restored by 1947. But even in this interregnum the loss of place for the Treasury can perhaps be exaggerated. Its bureaucratic role at the centre of the government machinery was not by any means fully displaced. In particular, from the beginning the Treasury was at the centre of post-war economic planning (Middlemas 1986, pp. 28–9, 32).

The Bank of England's position was perhaps similar only more so. Its direct role in the organization of the war economy was very small, but it was fully involved in plans for the post-war future. It was important in the initial organization of exchange control and its extension to the Sterling Area, and in pressing financial institutions to finance government borrowing in the early months of the war. 'Although the Bank kept to its own sphere thereafter, unrepresented on only one of the production or manpower organizations, it took a continuing interest in labour supply, industrial investment, and the export–import balance, so that when reconstruction came, its collective opinion carried weight far beyond that of former individual Governors' (Middlemas 1986, p. 27).

The Ministry of Labour

The Ministry of Labour enjoyed a rapid rise to ascendancy in the war years, after being largely a backwater in the inter-war years. This was consequent upon two inter-related features of the war. On the one hand, the successful handling of labour was a primary political objective in the war period, with memories of the labour unrest of the First War still very strong. Secondly, labour eventually emerged as the key constraint on the war effort. Initially foreign exchange was the problem, to be replaced from the time of lend-lease by a combination of manpower and shipping, but from 1943 it was unambiguously the case that manpower resources were the ultimate limit on the capacity to fight the war (Gowing 1972, p. 148).

This elevation of the Ministry was not an immediate consequence of the outbreak of war. Before the crisis of early summer 1940

'Trade unions were cautious, employers conservative, and the Ministry of Labour timorous; the Minister of Labour, Ernest Brown, was a weakling in a feeble government' (Gowing 1972, p. 149). Conscription had been immediately introduced at the outbreak of war, and a schedule of reserved occupations used to prevent industry losing its skilled labour. In this regard the lessons of the First World War had been well learnt. But little or no movement had been made to foresee and plan future manpower requirements in a systematic way. In late 1939 one enquiry (the Wolfe Committee) produced highly impressionistic estimates of future labour demand, and more such, albeit slightly more firmly based, were produced by the Stamp Survey in May 1940. But these forecasts, with their implication of sharp increases in demand for skilled workers as the war effort strengthened, led to little action (Parker 1957, ch. 4; Bullock 1967, pp. 6–9; Hancock and Gowing 1949, ch. 5).

The Ministry of Labour under Brown, knowing the hostility of unions to industrial conscription, was relying on market forces to bring about the necessary re-allocation of labour. But although a million still remained unemployed at the Battle of Britain, shortages of skilled labour began emerging even before this date. Consciousness of the need for action on the manpower front coincided with the fall of the Chamberlain government, and the replacement of Brown by Bevin as Minister of Labour. So ended months of 'indecision and procrastination' (Parker 1957, p. 474).

Bevin's appointment elevated a labour leader to a key role in wartime economic planning. Politically it must be regarded as perhaps the most astute ministerial appointment of the Churchill coalition. More than most labour leaders, Bevin could represent himself to the mass of the working class and trade unionists as 'one of you', and he played a big part in securing Labour's consent to the war in a manner strikingly at variance with the experience of the First World War.

As Minister of Labour Bevin was endowed with Draconian powers. The Emergency Powers Act of May 1940

armed the Minister of Labour with power undreamed of in the philosophy of any previous British Minister. He might direct through his National Service Officers any person in the United Kingdom to perform any service required in any place. He might prescribe the remuneration and conditions of such services and the hours of work. He might require persons to register particulars of themselves; he might order employers to keep and produce any records and books. Into his hands has been given the unrestricted powers of industrial conscription (Hancock and Gowing 1949, p. 298).

But these powers were used very sparingly, especially initially. Bevin's view was that persuasion was superior to compulsion, and would in the long run yield better results in terms of productivity (Hancock and Gowing 1949, pp. 310–14; Bullock 1967, pp. 64–70). Also for the first year or so of his period in office, the Ministry simply did not have the administrative capacity for a centralized, full-blooded allocation of labour. Even before the toughening of policy in Autumn 1941 Bevin had taken powers under the Essential Work Order to schedule factories or enterprises, which meant that workers could neither leave nor be dismissed except with the consent of an officer of the Ministry. However this departure from voluntarism was sweetened by the issuing of such Orders conditional on adequate pay and conditions, including welfare and training provision.

A similar conciliatory approach to labour's worries was taken in respect of 'dilution'—the replacement of skilled workers by unskilled. As in the First War, this was an inescapable policy to provide sufficient supplies of skilled manpower, especially in engineering. It was equally inescapably contentious, especially for those skilled workers accustomed to long spells of unemployment in the 1920s and 1930s. Bevin had also to fight against firms and their sponsoring Ministries anxious to hang on to 'their' skilled labour. The acceptance of dilution was never complete, but in most industries it was slowly achieved by patient negotiation. A similar verdict may be recorded on the Ministry's efforts to increase training provision, focused initially on government Training Centres and technical colleges, later on successfully encouraging firms themselves to expand provision as the labour shortage started to bite (Bullock 1967, pp. 26–9, 59–63; Gowing 1972, pp. 157–8; Parker 1957, ch. 22; Inman 1957, chs. 2, 3).

In late 1941 the long-predicted general manpower shortage had clearly arrived. Coupled with the shift in public opinion related to the battles on the Eastern Front, and the growth in administrative capacity of the Ministry of Labour, the way was open to a much greater degree of state regulation of the labour market, 'a greater degree of compulsion in directing people to the work they should do had become by the autumn of 1941, necessary, acceptable, and practicable' (Bullock 1967, p. 141). Reservation by occupation was replaced by individual reservation and made much more selective. All men and women between 18 and 60 were placed under statutory obligation to do some kind of national service. Women were to be called up by age groups for compulsory service in the Auxiliary Forces (Bullock 1967, pp. 137–45).

These measures were partly in response to a manpower survey of 1941, which foresaw an additional demand for over 2 million men and women for the armed forces and munitions industries by the middle of 1942. This survey begins the real period of manpower budgeting:

Investigation was no longer a speculative exercise; it was the immediate prelude to action. The famine of men and women was not an unpleasant possibility which would emerge if and when the scarcities of machine tools and raw materials were overcome. An acute shortage of manpower was part of the present, painfully afflicting every department which had any dealings with any industry or service (Hancock and Gowing 1949, p. 294).

Henceforth the Ministry of Labour had a definite plan and worked out for twelve months in advance the measures necessary to achieve the manpower aims set by the War Cabinet after they had considered the surveys. Mobilization became a planned operation rather than a series of disconnected steps. Strategic objectives were now set in interaction with manpower availability, and manpower became the key planning number which gave the War Cabinet control of the overall allocation of resources leading notably to a crucial restriction on the numbers available as ground troops (Hancock and Gowing 1949, ch. 11; Gowing 1972; Bullock 1967, chs. 5, 6).

This centrality of manpower planning had important political implications which will be discussed further below. But at a lower level of generality its scope and methods had a number of features of note. First the scale of labour shifts involved was immense: 4½ million people, about 14 per cent of the population of working age moved into the forces, munitions production, or war-related industries. But this was by no means all closely planned from the centre. Total directions of labour probably amounted to under half a million—for many others the traditional mechanisms, of job availability and wage differentials, continued to operate (Gowing

1972, pp. 152, 159). Indeed, a striking feature of the war period is thus the absence of state regulation of wages. From the beginning Bevin was committed to voluntarism, to the continuation of normal collective bargaining with only 'fall-back' powers of compulsory arbitration. As in the area of manpower direction, Bevin was attacked for his unwillingness to be more *dirigiste*, but he stuck to the view that state regulation of wages would be a political and administrative nightmare (Bullock 1967, pp. 86–92).

Finally, the mobilization of 'man' power drew or pulled an unprecedented number of women into the workforce. About 2¼ million women were added to the working population between September 1939 and the peak of mobilization in mid-1943 (Gowing 1972, p. 159; Parker 1957, ch. 13). Yet for all the short-term significance of this phenomenon,[3] its long-term impact was probably small. For most people this seems to have been registered as a temporary aberration rather than a permanent transformation of women's social role. If women left the labour force more slowly after the Second World War than after the First, this owed much more to the tight labour market in the late 1940s than any substantial shift in either opinion or policy (Smith 1984; Summerfield 1984).

Other Agencies

No single Ministry dominated production during the war period. The three services each had their own supply Ministry—the Ministry of Aircraft Production, the Admiralty, and the Ministry of Supply. A Minister of Production was appointed in 1942, but his function was not as 'overlord' of production, but mainly as the London end of the US War Production Board i.e. to co-ordinate attempts to make a rational division of war output between Britain and the USA. Churchill seems to have been determined not to have a single dominant agency in the supply area, and indeed many decisions were made by Churchill himself or in the War Cabinet (Lee 1980, p. 83; Postan 1952, ch. 4). The Ministry of Labour in many ways functioned as the crucial 'allocative' Ministry, though the Supply Ministries did not readily accept this

---

[3] This author owes his existence to the mobilization of women during World War Two. Skilled male engineering workers setting up lathes for women dilutees apparently also found it possible to set up marriages, despite the constraints of a twelve-hour working day.

role—there was a notable clash between Bevin and Beaverbrook whilst the latter was Minister of Aircraft Production (Bullock 1967, pp. 33–4). Eventually Bevin so strongly resisted giving Beaverbrook an overlord role as Minister of Production that the latter resigned, and the Ministry of Production's role was much less than some of its advocates hoped (Bullock 1967, pp. 114–17, ch. 6; Postan 1952, pp. 248–74).

Apart from the War Cabinet itself, the closest to a co-ordinating Ministry for the non-military aspects of the war effort was the Lord President's Committee. Under Sir John Anderson, and later Attlee, this came to have such a central role that Churchill referred to it as 'almost a parallel Cabinet concerned with home affairs' (Chester 1951, p. 9; see also Robbins 1971, pp. 173–6). Many important decisions were made by the Minister of Labour in collaboration with the Lord President, albeit with ultimate War Cabinet approval. Finally the Board of Trade essentially functioned as a Ministry for Civil Industry and Trade, important but unsurprisingly overshadowed by those more directly concerned with the war effort and the allocation of resources to it.

Doctrine

A short but 'total' war is not the context in which profound reflection on economic theory is conducted. Nevertheless the war could be said to have helped forge a new doctrinal consensus amongst economists, partly because it involved a radical shift in the role of economists in government policy-making.

We can look to the war years for the beginnings of what later came to be called the 'neo-classical synthesis' in economic doctrine. This involved an acceptance of the possibility of a Keynesian under-employment equilibrium, and hence the need for Keynesian policies to regulate aggregate demand. But this was coupled to a continued commitment to orthodox microeconomics, with its implicit but strongly normative element of treatment of market relations as the starting point for analysis, however much overlaid by welfare economics to deal with 'exceptions' to this 'normal' state of affairs.

This package of doctrine was never as neat as this outline suggests, nevertheless it does represent the dominant consensual view of post-war mainstream economics (see Doctrine in Chapter 9 below). Like the Treasury, many previously hostile economists came to accept the Keynesian component of this package during the war, as its usefulness to achieve shared goals emerged. Thus Robbins, a major opponent of Keynes in the 1930s, recanted his previous hostility to aggregate demand analysis, partly as a consequence of seeing its use in fighting wartime inflation, always an obsession with such 'orthodox' economists (Robbins 1971, pp. 88–9).

Hayek, another opponent of Keynesianism in the 1930s, congratulated Keynes on *How to Pay for the War*, saying 'It is reassuring to know that we agree so completely on the economics of scarcity even if we differ on when it applies' (Keynes 1978, p. 106). This shows how Keynes could be converted into a component of more conservative versions of the neo-classical synthesis—as an analyst of a 'special case' of under-employment, but who agreed that in the 'normal' case of full employment of resources traditional neo-classical analysis would come into its own. This was what Keynes himself had strongly averred in the General Theory.

In terms of underlying theory Robbins (head of the Economic Section 1942–5) was not so far apart from more radical economists, like Meade (head of the Economic Section 1945–7). Meade might have put much more emphasis on income redistribution and market failure than did Robbins, but their underlying theoretical positions at this time were not very divergent (Meade 1988 chs. 14–17; Booth 1986).

This doctrinal convergence was forged in circumstances where almost all major economists were directly involved in policy-making as temporary civil servants. The starting point for much of this insertion of economists into Whitehall was the Stamp Survey of Economic and Financial Plans carried out at the very beginning of the war. Out of this Survey developed the Central Economic Information Service, itself bifurcated into the Economic Section and the Central Statistical Office. The Economic Section then emerged as the dominant, but by no means only, source of economic advice to government (Booth 1986*b*; Cairncross 1984; Coats 1981).

The Economic Section was attached to the Cabinet Secretariat, but crucially fed into the Lord President's Committee, contributing to the premier role of that body. It was thus kept outside direct departmental responsibilities (including those of the Treasury). From this position the Economic Section provided briefs ranging over economic aspects of all the major war policies. A high degree of success seems to have been achieved by the Section, partly because it worked very hard to adapt to the norms of civil service existence, rather than being a caste apart (Coats 1981, p. 44; Robbins 1971, p. 184).

It was not only in the Economic Section that 'between 1939 and 1945 qualified economists and statisticians enjoyed unprecedented opportunities for government employment' (Coats 1981, p. 30). Other departments also employed economists in influential positions. One of the most important and interesting examples of the consequences of such employment was in the field of rationing. Here economists, especially those in the Board of Trade, but supported by the Economic Section, made a major impact: 'it was one of the outstanding examples of the influence of economists on wartime economic policy' (Booth 1985*b*, p. 298).

Rationing was a politically unavoidable consequence of the shortage of consumer goods which necessarily followed from the growth of working-class earnings (even after heavy taxation) coupled with the diversion of resources to the war effort. Rationing therefore aimed to provide a 'system to secure orderly distribution and a certain degree of equity . . . a more acceptable pattern of distribution than would emerge from the alternative "system" of queues, favoured customers, shop-crawling, and the like' (Reddaway 1951, p. 183; see also Hargreaves and Gowing 1952, ch. 14).

The system devised, points rationing, allocated a points value to the rationed items and aimed to maximize consumer choice of articles within a set of rationed goods. It was a classic economists' device, effectively creating a new type of money, allowing maximum choice to consumers within a budget constraint. Its proponents were successful, Booth (1985*b*, pp. 313–7) argues, because of their academic excellence, and the professional utility they exhibited in this area, as well as having the support of powerful Ministers. More generally we may note that this was an area where technical expertise was likely to be decisive—because it operated in a context of consensual political objectives, concerning the need for equitable distribution of products in short supply.

The war undoubtedly marked a decisive stage in the evolution of the role of economists in government policy-making. However this role was not the grandiose one implied by 'Economic General Staff', a term coined by Beveridge and mentioned in the 1944 White Paper on Employment Policy. Rather the major role during the war—as an advisory Section reporting to a co-ordinating body—was to be continued, until absorption into the Treasury, with its re-emergence as that co-ordinating body, eventually followed (in 1953). Outside the Economic Section the number of economists in government departments contracted after the war, and initially at least, the emergence of macroeconomic management was not matched by the increase of government economists that might be expected (Booth and Coats 1980).

Politics and Policies

The Politics of War

From the fall of the Chamberlain government and the beginnings of the Churchill Coalition in May the Second World War might reasonably be called a People's War (Calder 1971). Not that everyone in Britain was a single-minded enthusiast for the war effort, but there was a general consensus about the necessity of war, a consensus notably absent in the First War. This consensual character of the war is symbolized by the Coalition government, the only genuine all-party coalition in twentieth-century Britain. This coalition held together throughout the war, and the main disruptions to its unity came not over its policies for conducting the war, but its plans for the peace.

This consensus was not taken for granted by the Coalition. Apart from the general expenditure of effort on war propaganda on a substantial scale (Calder 1971, pp. 579–87), a major concern was to maintain the consent, and preferably support, of labour. This is symbolized, above all, by Bevin's place as one of the Big Three of the wartime coalition along with Churchill and Anderson. Conciliation of labour arose from the early recognition that labour unrest on the scale of that of the First World War was the most likely source of breakdown of the war effort. Equally, labour soon emerged as the ultimate limiting factor on the scale of the war effort. The fact that the war was planned in manpower terms symbolized the transformation of labour from a factor in excess supply to one in excess demand, and much, politically, flowed from that shift.

Beer (1982, pp. 214–16) has argued that 1940 marked a crucial change in the balance of class forces in British society: 'it was initially not by their votes, but by their control over instrumentalities necessary to carrying out vital national purposes that the organised working class raised themselves from their old position of exclusion and inferiority' (p. 215). Union leaders like Bevin and Citrine (General Secretary of the TUC) had pursued a strategy of influencing government via consultation in the 1930s—but until the war years little came of this. In 1931–2 unions sat on one government committee, in 1939 on 12, by 1948–9 on 60 (Beer 1982, pp. 212–13).

Middlemas (1986) has pursued a similar theme, arguing that World War Two produced 'an unprecedented extension in the power of organised labour, almost to the point of equivalence with management, and an integration of both into the wartime state, through their central and regional organisations' (p. 7). He stresses the build-up of tripartite bodies like the Joint Consultative Committee (on industrial relations issues) and the National Production Advisory Committee on Industry (on production issues). Similar consultative bodies existed at the regional level, and 'bi-partite' union/management bodies—Joint Production Committees and the like—at factory level.[4] Middlemas's designation of this structure as 'corporatist' may be controversial, but the general emphasis on the war's effects in transforming labour's position in the political economy of Britain seems incontrovertible. In this context, the 1945 General Election may be seen as a manifestation of a pre-existing shift in the power of labour brought about by the nature of 'total war'. Equally, the emphasis on full employment in plans for the post-war period must be related to the new place of labour in British society after 1940.

Fighting the War

The aims of the Second World War can be easily stated—to beat the Axis powers by mobilizing as many resources as possible compatible with the maintenance of the physical health and

---

[4] For the story of wartime JPCs see ILO (1944) and Inman (1957), pp. 371–91.

morale of the civilian population. But such a bland statement conceals, of course, the contentious issues both about the scale of resource mobilization possible, and the means to be used to this end.

Once the external constraint was lifted by lend-lease, the crucial constraint was manpower availability. But this then led to the question both of the minimum amount of labour to be left producing civilian goods (and exports)[5] and the balance of the rest between production of munitions and actual fighting. On the first issue there was much wartime debate about how far civilian consumption could be reduced without morale cracking (Robbins 1971, pp. 179–80). Consumption standards in the UK seem to have been forced down certainly more than those in the USA (where they rose), and more controversially, below those in Germany (Harrison 1988; Milward 1987, ch. 3).

The question of the balance between production of arms and men to use them partly depended on the kind of war to be fought. In the German case of Blitzkrieg, the assumption was that rapid military successes would obviate the need to accumulate vast supplies of munitions. For Britain, no such choice was available— rearmament had to be 'deep' and this necessitated clear limits on the number of men to be put into the field (Postan 1952, pp. 120–1). Nevertheless by 1943 Britain had more than one in five of its workforce in the armed forces, only slightly fewer than in the 'war-related' industries (Harrison 1988, p. 186).

Overall, the war effort of Britain, measured by intensity of resource use, may be said to have fallen only a little below that of Germany and the USSR, and to have been greater than that of the USA (Harrison 1988). The lower intensity of the US effort partly reflected high productivity in US industry—in other words, the USA needed fewer workers in munitions to equip a given quantity of fighting troops. This raises the whole issue of the efficiency (as opposed to intensity) of the British war effort. On this one can say little, except that no one so far seems to have dissented from Postan's (1952) 'official' view that the production effort was efficient—a view endorsed by, for example, Barnett (1986, p. 61).

If the British war effort was efficient (and this seems most plausible in comparison with the German effort e.g. Milward 1965,

---

[5] For export policy see Hargreaves and Gowing (1952), chs. 7–9.

Carroll 1968; Overy 1982), what were the instruments of this efficiency? A striking feature of the organization of the war effort was that it was 'war by committee' (Harrison 1988, p. 179). As already noted, co-ordination of British production was handled mainly by the Lord President's Committee, with very little resort to the pattern of political leadership over personal fiefdoms so characteristic of the German economy. The one important exception to this was Beaverbrook's efforts at the Ministry of Aircraft Production and at the Ministry of Supply, but even here the success of his method of producing aircraft and tanks is controversial (Postan 1952, p. 118), leaving aside the issue of how far such success was bought at the price of a more rational overall allocation of resources to the war effort. Without idealizing bureaucratic procedures, those procedures with their clear chains of command, lack of competing hierarchies, and intelligent co-ordination seem to have delivered an effective war effort[6] (Chester 1951).

Controls

The wartime economy was both managed and controlled. The main instrument of management was fiscal; monetary policy was restricted to making possible cheap borrowing—a 'Three Per Cent War'—in order to reduce the debt burden at the war's end (Sayers 1956, pp. 159–62, ch. 7).

Controls existed over most parts of the economy. There was (eventually) rigorous foreign exchange control. Labour allocation, if not wages, was controlled by the Ministry of Labour. Imports came to be mainly purchased by the Supply ministries (including the Ministry of Food), and allocated to the industries within their orbit. Consumption of food, clothing, furniture, and furnishings was subject to rationing, and of other goods to price control (Hargreaves and Gowing 1952, ch. 4).

Ultimately all these variegated control mechanisms were concerned to facilitate the maximizing of war production. Of course this process involved deciding which kinds of war production should be produced in what proportions. At the first crisis of the war—the Battle of Britain—overriding priority was given to

---

[6] For some criticisms of Britain's economic decision-making in the war period see Robinson (1951).

aircraft production. This was successful, but only at the cost of disrupting long-term mobilization plans. Such a system of priorities, however unavoidable in time of crisis, was wholly unsuitable as a means of long-term resource-allocation decisions, because it involved no assessment of the forgone production of other goods, perhaps only slightly less important. In 1941 priorities were increasingly replaced by an allocation system of raw materials, factory space, and labour (Postan 1952, pp. 92–3, 159–63). Of course this was no magic wand. Disputes over allocation were inescapable, failures to co-ordinate allocations of different factors of production an inevitable consequence of the scope of the administrative exercise involved. But this system, with labour allocations usually determinate, dominated 'higher level' resource allocation for the rest of the war.

At the lower level, of turning allocations into actual programmes of output, similarly complex procedures evolved. A vivid account of such programming is given by Devons (1951), who emphasizes the range of skills involved for successes in this area, and the importance of informal alongside formal procedures. Again the crucial problem was to know what quantum of goods X, Y, and Z would have to be sacrificed to produce more of good a, b, or c, and to make such decisions in a world of necessarily incomplete information.

Government's control over the structure of industrial production derived from its role as chief customer (of the war industries) the chief supplier of raw materials, components, and capital, plus its role in the allocation of labour. Direct ownership of productive capacity was extremely limited. Royal Ordnance Factories were the most important element in such capacity, producing 20 per cent of Army supplies. Much more extensive were 'agency' factories where the state provided plant, machinery, and buildings, but where management was on a private fee basis. Direct government intervention inside the factories was very limited, though the Supply Ministries tended to follow the Ministry of Labour in encouraging welfare provision for workers as the labour market got tighter, and similarly with the establishment of Joint Production Committees (Postan 1952, ch. 9; n. 4 above).

The war effort obviously had a significant impact on the structure of output of British industry, some industries contracting sharply, others enjoying a renaissance (Pollard 1983, pp. 200–10).

But in terms of the organization of industry, the impact was rather limited. Postan (1952, ch. 8) argues that in the war industries and existing structure of lots of small firms and many general engineering firms was reinforced by the procurement policies of war years, with their need to use all industrial capacity and to maintain flexibility through variations and fluctuations in demand.

In the civilian sector there was a deliberate government policy of concentration of industry, to secure the lowest level of costs for reduced output and to free capacity for war uses. The government attempted to pursue this in a 'hands-off' manner by leaving the firms themselves to devise plans for sanctioning by the Board of Trade. Some laggard industries were the subject of compulsory schemes, and in others industry-wide measures did reduce the number of establishments in operation substantially—in cotton, for example, by about 3,500. But whatever the wartime effects, these policies were explicitly 'for the duration', so the long-term consequences were limited (Allen 1951; Hargreaves and Gowing 1952, ch. 10).

Far more long-lasting in their implications were the relations established in the war period between government and private-sector owners and managers. The myriad of control schemes operated by the government were largely staffed by the existing owners/managers of the industries concerned, or members of the industry's trade associations (Middlemas 1986, p. 23). This may well have been unavoidable—no one else had the competence for such a task—but it meant that when Labour came to power in 1945 it inherited not only the controls but also this insertion of private-sector businessmen into control mechanisms. This was to be a major constraint on Labour's attempts to construct a feasible policy for the private sector (Chapter 8 below).

The Objectives of Wartime Economic Policy

War, it can be plausibly argued, immensely simplifies economic policy by limiting the range of objectives that it seeks to achieve (Robbins 1971, p. 177). Those objectives can certainly be readily summarized as (*a*) maximize resources devoted to the war effort, and (*b*) meet essential civilian needs and distribute available goods fairly to maintain efficiency and morale. The first of these has been dealt with in the previous part of this chapter, but some comments on (*b*) can serve both as a conclusion to the first part of this chapter and a bridge to the second part.

This was the first war in which, from the beginning, the welfare of the civilian population was a crucial policy consideration (though it was emerging at the end of the First World War). Because of the significance of economic output for the prosecution of the war, as well as the fear of labour unrest, 'keeping the working class sweet' became a primary objective of domestic policy. This could not, however, be done by improvements in working-class consumption standards; whilst total output rose in the war years, unlike in the USA and Canada this was not sufficient to provide for the war. In Britain more guns meant less butter.

Pre-tax earnings of the working class rose during the war, though real wages stagnated. (Between 1938 and 1945 consumer prices rose about 55 per cent, wage rates about 50 per cent, earnings about 75 per cent (Cairncross, 1985, p. 12)). For many working-class people these were prosperous years, especially in comparison with the 1930s, even if at the cost of very long hours of work. Hence, as Keynes emphasized in *How to Pay for the War*, the crucial purpose of financial policy was to make restrictions on working-class consumption as palatable as possible. Keynes himself saw the solution primarily through deferred savings. In the event rationing played a much greater role, but both deferred savings and rationing may be seen as attempts to 'sell' the idea that the unavoidable sacrifices of the war would be equally shared.

A closely related concern was that of inflation. The avoidance of rapid inflation was a central objective of economic policy in 1940/1. Sayers (1956, p. 23) has noted of the war period that 'the story of budget policy is a story of struggle against inflation'. Equally the impetus to rationing was very much related to the fear of inflation if demand exceeded the supply of consumer goods (Booth 1985*a*). Whilst the authorities had always opposed inflation, this had a special urgency in wartime when there was so much fear of working-class discontent and how this might be sparked off by price increases. Suppression of inflation and conciliation of working-class opinion were thus intertwined objectives of wartime policy.

Both objectives were largely achieved. The unrepresentative official consumer price index rose by only 30 per cent between

1938 and 1945, whilst a more accurate index rose by about 55 per cent. Most of this inflation took place in the early months of the war and was more or less inescapable with sharply rising import prices. From 1941 to 1945 the official cost of living index was held stable, whilst wholesale prices rose by just over 10 per cent. 'During the Second World War price questions did not become, as in the later stages of the 1914–18 war, a storm centre of economic stress, social discontent and political controversy' (Hancock and Gowing 1949, p. 152).

Working-class discontent, though less easily measured, was also much less than in the previous war. One obvious (though imperfect) index is strike levels. In the First World War the yearly average of days lost through strikes was 4.23 million; in the Second War (1940 to July 1945) 1.8 million. Unrest was not absent during the 'People's War' but it never threatened the political consensus nor the actual conduct of the war as it had in the later stages of the First World War (Bullock 1967, pp. 265–70; Parker 1957, ch. 25).

Plans for the Post-War World

The Importance of Reconstruction

The change in the internal balance of power in the Second World War meant that the war, unlike that of 1914–18, could never be pursued on the basis of an anticipated return to the pre-war status quo. Hence 'reconstruction was a coherent process, an intrinsic consequence of the changes of 1940–1; it was not an afterthought or a sop to raise public morale as in World War One' (Middlemas 1986, p. 46).

Reconstruction had a number of facets, and for the dominant élite of economic policy-makers the agenda for such reconstruction was dominated by the need to restore Britain's economic position in the world, and that meant attention to the balance of payments and the role of sterling as the overarching priorities. Hence the importance to Britain of the terms on which reconstruction of the world economy was to take place, a topic which deserves a separate chapter (Chapter 7).

Domestically, wartime plans for reconstruction were dominated, at least as far as public discussion was concerned, by what can be called plans for social amelioration—above all plans for the welfare state and for full employment. The question of whether there might have been an alternative agenda is returned to in the last section of this chapter, but first it is necessary to look at the actual agenda, the reasons for its emergence, and its precise content.

In a famous discussion of the Second World War, Titmuss (1976, pp. 506–17) argued that a policy concern with social welfare emerged as an unintended consequence of the war effort. He argued that the changes in welfare policy arose from a combination of factors:

Some were pressed forward because of the needs of the war machine for more men and more work. Some took place almost by accident. Some were the result of a recognition of needs hitherto hidden by ignorance of social conditions. Some came about because war exposed weaknesses ruthlessly and brutally . . . which called for revolutionary changes in the economic and social life of the country (p. 507).

This kind of argument has been generalized by Andrzejewski (1954) to propound that there is an inherent link between the growth of total war, the extension of civilian involvement in war, and the development of welfare policy. When all are exposed to the risks of war, all expect to have their conditions of life improved. Marwick (e.g. 1965) has produced a similar emphasis on the impact of war, albeit as an accelerator rather than an initiator of trends (compare Jeffreys 1987).

One of the difficulties of Titmuss's thesis is that the actual reforms he points to arising within his framework are rather limited, restricted to the provision of school meals, milk, and vitamins for children (pp. 509–13). Whilst he does note other reforms (p. 514) these are not linked to his analysis and in any case do not include major features in the welfare state's development like National Insurance and the NHS.

This rather narrow focus of Titmuss's work is related to its apolitical character. In his account it is war *per se* that produces changes, and the political conditions under which the war was fought, or reform programmes produced, are not discussed at any length. War may produce changes in this way, for example the Second World War produced full employment without this being politically willed, and this was important. It facilitated the shift in concern within welfare policy from unemployment to poverty. It facilitated a belief that unemployment could and therefore should be fought by state action. But equally Titmuss's emphasis on *unintended* consequence is partial in leaving out the importance of the political element in wartime reform programmes.

The politics of wartime reform plans were complex. As early as December 1939 Anthony Eden was arguing that 'The war will bring about changes which may be fundamental and revolutionary in the economic and social life of the country. On that we are all agreed' (cited Tomlinson 1985, p. 20). However, most Conservatives, and notably Chamberlain and Churchill, were reluctant to see such changes as a necessary condition for the successful prosecution of the war, which was the view propounded by Attlee and many at the centre and left of British politics. Also in December 1939, Attlee recalled the belief in the First War that unemployment would not be tolerated by returning soldiers, and argued that this time round it would indeed not be tolerated. From this he drew the further implication that 'peace aims and reconstruction cannot be postponed till the end of the war' (cited Tomlinson 1985, p. 21). Reconstruction would not just have to deliver the goods to prevent post-war unrest, but in some (especially socialist) eyes it would be crucial to wartime morale. Cromwell's famous phrase was quoted in support of this: 'we can only fight well if we know what we fight for and love what we know' (Wintringham 1942, p. 89).

The linking of wartime morale and post-war plans became a commonplace in the war. In 1940 a War Aims Committee was established, and from the beginning such aims were agreed to include full employment and social amelioration post-war (Addison 1977, ch. 6). Churchill in particular was sceptical of the resources deployed in drawing up plans of this kind, but the Labour Party Ministers who dominated the 'home front' took a different view '. . . the Labour team could applaud and encourage the work of Butler, Beveridge, Reith, Keynes, and others. Thus they obeyed the rules of Coalition punctiliously, while gratifying their appetite for amelioration' (Addison 1977, p. 182).

Thus the Labour Party both gained from and encouraged the linking of the war effort to post-war reform. Ultimately, in 1945, the party was to be the political legatee of the wartime enthusiasm for reform. But its direct role in formulating the wartime programmes was limited, and others played the most prominent parts in forging a new reformist consensus. The two key planks of that consensus were a reconstruction of the welfare system and a commitment to full employment. The Beveridge Report (1942) and the White Paper on Employment Policy (Cmd. 6527 1944) are the two most public emblems of that new consensus.

Beveridge and Social Insurance

The Beveridge Report arose from a piece of political opportunism by Beveridge, but one that worked because despite governmental and bureaucratic hostility, his proposals evoked an enormous degree of popular support.

Beveridge was initially given the job of chairing a civil service committee on piecemeal reforms of the social security system in order to get rid of him from the Ministry of Labour. However, he turned the Report on Social Insurance and Allied Services (SIAS) into a manifesto for a thoroughgoing reconstruction of the whole of the income maintenance system (Harris 1977, ch. 16; 1975; 1981; Addison 1977, ch. 8).

Beveridge's proposals were much more radical for their comprehensive character than the principles they embodied. They were resolutely based on the idea that most problems of poverty were the result of interruption of earnings; that the way to deal with this was by insurance, based on flat-rate contributions and benefits; and that such benefits should provide a subsistence minimum on which 'voluntary action' could build higher incomes. Politically Beveridge's focus on the problem of poverty, very much related to the inter-war poverty survey ideas, led to a clearly limited sphere of state action: 'it focused attention on the issue of a deficiency of income at the bottom end of the range of distribution and it diverted attention from the issue of inequality and the whole distribution of income from top to bottom' (Williams and Williams 1987, p. 45). The interruption-of-earnings framework led Beveridge to the conclusion that in principle (though he didn't advocate this) poverty could be abolished by redistribution of income over the life-span and between members of the working class. The principle of social insurance was seen to avoid both the individual scrutiny and discouragement to thrift involved in Means Testing, and the 'Santa Claus state' of non-contributory benefits (Harris 1977, ch. 16; Williams and Williams 1987, ch. 2).

In sum what Beveridge proposed was a vast extension of the contractual obligation between the citizen and the state. This has recently been dubbed a form of 'liberal collectivism', aimed at maintaining the traditional organization of a capitalist society, whilst relieving poverty in a manner congenial to liberalism (Williams and Williams 1987; Cutler *et al.* 1986, ch. 1).

Beveridge's scheme was very popular with the public at large— the SIAS Report was a best seller, not usually a feature of HMSO reports. Within the government, however, Beveridge was regarded as having grossly over-reached himself in an attempt to obtain publicity. The political popularity of Beveridge's proposals initially led to them being accepted 'in principle' by the Coalition, with the hope that many of them would be whittled away in detailed criticism. The eventual White Paper produced included a fundamental whittling away by abandoning the principle of a subsistence income (Addison 1977, ch. 8; Jeffreys 1987, pp. 129–33). Labour members of the Coalition believed that a key objective was to maintain the Coalition in being so as to prevent Churchill from winning a general election. As a result they did not strongly press Beveridge's proposals, about which some of them, notably Bevin, had doubts anyway (Addison 1977, pp. 224–5; Bullock 1967, pp. 225–34; Harris 1977, pp. 425–6).

Conservative and official opposition to the Beveridge Report was founded not on its principles but on its alleged cost, including the cost of a comprehensive health service and family allowances which Beveridge saw as a corollary to his insurance proposals. Beveridge substantially modified his proposals in response to Treasury-backed criticisms, especially in suggesting a very slow build up (20 years) to full pensions. After substantial discussion one of the Treasury's advisers, Keynes, became a full-hearted supporter of Beveridge's proposals, arguing that it was 'the cheapest alternative open to us' and that 'the suggestion that is being put about in some quarters that there are financial difficulties is quite unfounded' (cited Harris 1977, p. 423; also pp. 407–12; Keynes 1980*a*, ch. 4).

The SIAS Report has often been seen as the foundation stone of the post-war welfare state. This is probably accurate if suitably qualified, as Beveridge's biographer suggests:

Beveridge's plan was acted upon much more quickly and thoroughly than the vast majority of comparative public inquiries. It is true that there were some important deviations from Beveridge's proposals . . . But the main structure and many of the principles of the welfare legislation of 1945–48 were those which Beveridge had laid down in 1942. In devising these principles, Beveridge's role had been mainly that of a synthesiser and publicist rather than that of an innovator and it is difficult to claim that he made any inherently original contribution to subsequent social policy. But, nevertheless, it was Beveridge who interpreted the mainstream of public opinion and who transformed an incoherent mass of popular feeling into a blueprint for social reform (Harris 1977, p. 449).

Whether this was a workable or desirable basis for the welfare state is, of course, another matter (Williams and Williams 1987). What is striking is the extent to which, at the time, it carried all before it—there was no comprehensive alternative put forward. In the face of Beveridge, left and right positions on the welfare state fell away (Harris 1981).

Full Employment

Beveridge saw SIAS as workable only on the basis of three assumptions—family allowances, comprehensive health services, and 'maintenance of employment, that is to say avoidance of mass unemployment' (Cmd. 6404, p. 120). The assumption that post-war full employment was both desirable and possible was one that was widely shared during the Second World War—including by many officials and politicians in policy-making positions.

The genesis of the 1944 White Paper on Employment Policy was in the Economic Section as early as 1941. In that year James Meade produced a Memorandum, *The Prevention of General Unemployment* (Meade 1988, ch. 11), which despite all subsequent vicissitudes of the official debate can be seen as the kernel of the 1944 White Paper. This paper, whilst recognizing the problem of frictional and structural unemployment, emphasized the centrality of unemployment caused by demand deficiency. Thus the paper placed employment policy firmly in an income–expenditure (Keynesian) framework, and its policy proposals, such as public works, expansionary monetary policy, and measures to stimulate consumption, followed this logic (Meade 1988, ch. 1; Tomlinson 1987*a*, ch. 3).

Debate over Meade's proposals was limited until 1943, when a Steering Committee on Post-War Employment was established under the chairmanship of Sir Richard Hopkins, Permanent

Secretary of the Treasury. The Report produced by this committee, which was the basis of the 1944 White Paper, was a compromise between Meade's Keynesian proposals and the opposition of major Treasury figures. In particular, the latter wanted to emphasize the importance of structural unemployment, and the related question of the impact of balance of payments difficulties on the maintenance of employment. They were also hostile to the public finance implications i.e. unbalanced budgets, which seemed to be at least implicit in the Economic Section proposals (Peden 1983; Tomlinson 1987*a*, ch. 3).

The White Paper of 1944 (Cmd. 6527) then can be seen as essentially a compromise between the full-hearted Keynesianism of most of the Economic Section and the traditional objectives of the Treasury. This simplifies the position, but not to the point of distortion.[7] One simplification that should be noted is the exclusion of the role of other departments, notably the Board of Trade. The Board occupied a position which, whilst emphasizing the importance of local and structural unemployment, also involved a ringing endorsement of the Economic Section's stress on adequate aggregate demand as a necessary pre-condition for a solution of these problems (Tomlinson 1987*a*, p. 56; Hall 1982). The White Paper's compromise is most apparent in the treatment of budget deficits, which was highly ambiguous. Para. 74 said, 'None of the main proposals contained in the Paper involves deliberate planning for a deficit in the National Budget in years of sub-normal trade activity.' On the other hand para. 79 said, 'in controlling the situation . . . the Government will have equally in mind the need to maintain the national income, and the need for a policy of budgetary equilibrium'.

This ambiguity reflected not simply a clash between Economic Section fiscal radicalism and fiscal conservatism in the Treasury. The Keynesians themselves were not of one voice in their statements on this key issue. Meade proposed using a separate social security budget as a means of keeping the ordinary budget in balance, an idea endorsed by Keynes but seen as problematic if, as he supposed, consumption habits did not respond readily to income changes (Peden 1983, p. 288). Keynes favoured a capital budget separate from the ordinary budget, which he felt should

---

[7] Henderson (1955) cuts across this distinction.

only be in deficit in extreme circumstances (Keynes 1980*a*, ch. 5; also Wilson 1982). These equivocations by the Keynesians reflected a desire to overcome Treasury objections to budget deficits, whilst maintaining the basic thrust of the demand-deficient analysis.

The 1944 White Paper's ambiguity went beyond the discussion of the budget. As has often been noted (e.g. Winch 1972, pp. 279–83) the one clear declaration of the document is the first sentence, 'The Government accept as one of their primary aims and responsibilities the maintenance of a high and stable level of employment after the war.' This commitment was qualified not only by the ambiguities about the budget, but by reference to other conditions that would have to be fulfilled for the commitment to be fulfilled. Most significantly these included

The principle of price stability means that increases in the general level of wage rates must be related to increased productivity due to increased efficiency and effort (para. 54).

If an expansion of total expenditure were applied to cure unemployment of a type due, not to absence of jobs, but [to] a failure of workers to move to places and occupations where they were needed, the policy of the Government would be frustrated and a dangerous rise in prices might follow (para. 56).

These conditions in the 1944 White Paper have led some commentators, including the Conservative government in 1985, to present that Paper as involving a type of contract whereby government would deliver adequate aggregate demand on condition that workers did not pursue inflationary wage claims and agreed to labour mobility (Cmnd. 9474; also Jewkes 1978, ch. 3; R. Jones 1987, ch. 3). But it is not clear how in any sense a contract could be said to have been entered into. The White Paper was not the subject of any kind of bargaining with employers or the TUC outside government, and at one stage the TUC explicitly repudiated any contractual view of employment policy (R. Jones 1987, p. 30). So even if the writers of the White Paper saw it in contractual terms, it was the most implicit of implicit contracts, or as Middlemas (1986, p. 92) suggests, 'The White Paper proposed, but did not contain, a contract.'

The 1944 White Paper is undoubtedly of great symbolic significance in the reordering of government responsibilities for the economy.[8] However its impact on the instruments of policy was minimal. Investigation of the various techniques it proposed for dealing with unemployment continued well into the post-war years, but they never came into use in the absence of the expected recurrence of unemployment (Tomlinson 1987a, chs. 5, 7, 8).

Reconstruction and its Significance

As already noted, the reasons why the war led to such a substantial output of reform proposals has been disputed by historians. But much more controversial has been the attempt by Barnett (1986) to argue that this reconstruction effort was a fundamental misdirection of effort and resources which should have been deployed in restoring Britain's weak industrial base. In Barnett's view wartime Britain chose a future of 'New Jerusalem' rather than a 'national corporate strategy' of industrial revival. In particular he castigates the Beveridge and full employment plans as products of a sentimental high-mindedness wholly inappropriate to economic survival (ch. 12).

On Beveridge, Barnett's discussion seems fundamentally flawed (1986, pp. 26–31, 42–9, 238–41). He presents him as a Utopian, left-wing collectivist pursuing radical redistributive policies without heed to their cost. In fact Beveridge was concerned to put forward closely specified, costed policies aimed at minimizing the sphere of state action. He was well aware of the economic costs of his proposals, which is why he was so concerned to link his welfare proposals to high employment and increased industrial efficiency— both in SIAS itself, and in what he saw as the logical sequel, *Full Employment in a Free Society* (1944).

Barnett's comments on full employment are equally unpersuasive (pp. 257–63). He treats full employment as a welfare measure, completely ignoring the resource costs of mass unemployment. He implies, but with no evidence, that full employment reduces productivity (p. 262). He ignores the evidence which suggests that it was the mass unemployment of the inter-war period which in wartime inhibited worker acceptance of measures to raise productivity (e.g. in shipbuilding; Bullock 1967, pp. 59–62) or that post-war productivity growth in the full employment period was the fastest in Britain's history.

[8] On which, see Tomlinson (1987a), ch. 4; Williams and Williams (1987), ch. 4.

Overall Barnett's polemical text fails to convince because it does not give a satisfactory account of Britain's undoubted economic weakness, and so fails to show why post-war reconstruction contributed to that weakness. Its one persuasive section is on the education system (ch. 14). As it describes in great detail, the 1944 education reform was extraordinarily dominated by religious issues to the neglect of questions of appropriate competences for school children to acquire. Furthermore the lack of technical and scientific education at school was continued at higher levels. But such weaknesses could at most be a relatively small contributory element in Britain's industrial problems.

One question touched on by Barnett, and discussed in more detail by other historians, is why the legacy of the war for economic policy was so much emphasis on demand management and so little on industrial reorganization. As both Barnett and Middlemas (1986) have made clear the wartime government, notably the Board of Trade, was fully and unprecedentedly well informed about the depths of Britain's industrial shortcomings. The Board of Trade 'had gone far in 1943 towards uncovering the long roots of Britain's historically poor industrial performance' and had proposed a wide range of remedies over the whole gamut of 'supply side' policies from reform of management to schemes for regional boards for particular industries, under an overall Industrial Commission to rationalize production (Middlemas 1986, pp. 54–5, 97–8).

That little came of such proposals for industrial policy even in the wartime reconstruction debate is explained in different ways by different historians. Middlemas explains it in broad terms as the result of the consensual bargaining which he sees as characterizing wartime policy-making. This ruled out government-sponsored radical changes in the private sector, just as it ruled out any challenge to trade unions' attachment to free collective bargaining.

Booth (1986*a*) approaches the issue from the opposite angle. Why did 'simple Keynesianism' i.e. fiscal policy, become so dominant in the economic policy agenda by the end of the war? He notes that up to about 1943 a much wider range of issues was emphasized by Keynesians in general and the Economic Section in particular. But, he argues, the battles with the Treasury over employment policy led to a tactical decision to focus on demand management and fiscal policy, as a counterpoint to the Treasury's excessive emphasis on structural unemployment. He also notes that the Economic Section's theoretical views were dominated by what has been called above the 'neo-classical synthesis' which has little role for industrial policy, believing in competition as the royal road to economic efficiency. Thus Beveridge's *Full Employment in a Free Society*, which was much more interventionist than the White Paper of 1944, was anathematized by the Economic Section.[9]

As Booth rightly points out, the policies of the early years of the Labour government included wage, regional, and industrial policies which found no place in simple Keynesianism (1986*a*, p. 19). But in the longer run the legacy was a powerful one, and dominated policy-making from the late 1940s to the late 1960s. Alongside the welfare state and the full employment commitment, this 'simple Keynesianism' was one of the most important legacies of the wartime reconstruction era.

Further Reading

It should be noted that historiography of the war effort is still overwhelmingly dominated by the volumes of the Civil History of the Second World War, indicated below by an asterisk.

War Planning

Bullock, A. (1967): *The Life and Times of Ernest Bevin* vol. ii. *Minister of Labour 1940–1945*, London.

Chester, D. N., ed. (1951): *Lessons of the British War Economy*, Cambridge.

Gowing, M. (1972): 'The Organisation of Manpower in Britain During the Second World War', *Journal of Contemporary History* 7, pp. 147–67.

*Hancock, W. K., and Gowing, M. (1949): *British War Economy*, London.

*Hargreaves, E. L., and Gowing, M. (1952): *Civil Industry and Trade*, London.

Keynes, J. M. (1978): *Activities 1939–1945: Internal War Finance, Collected Writings,* vol. xxii, London, chs. 2, 4, 5.

*Parker, H. M. D. (1957): *Manpower: A Study of War-Time Policy and Administration*, London.

---

[9] The failure of the post-war Labour government to intervene radically in the private sector is taken up in Chapter 8.

*Postan, M. M. (1952): *British War Production*, London.
*Sayers, R. S. (1956): *Financial Policy 1939–1945*, London.

Reconstruction

Addison, P. (1977): *The Road to 1945*, London.
Barnett, C. (1986): *The Audit of War*, London.
Booth, A. (1986*a*): 'Simple Keynesianism and Whitehall, 1936–1947',
   Economy and Society 15, pp. 1–22.
Harris, J. (1977): *William Beveridge: A Biography*, Oxford, chs. 16, 17.
Keynes, J. M. (1980*a*): *Activities 1940–1946: Shaping the Post-War World:
   Employment and Commodities. Collected Writings,* vol. xxvii, London,
   chs. 4, 5.
*Titmuss, R. M. (1976): *Problems of Social Policy*, (annotated edition;
   1st edition 1950), London.
Tomlinson, J. (1987*a*): *Employment Policy: The Crucial Years 1939–1955*,
   Oxford.
Williams, K., and Williams, J., eds. (1987): *A Beveridge Reader*, London.

7

Reconstructing the World
1941–1958: Economy

THE war and early post-war years saw the most sustained attempt in the twentieth century to reconstruct the international economy. The objectives and instruments, successes and failures of this effort form a vital backdrop to British economic policy in the war and post-war period. But Britain was by no means just a passive observer, but a major architect of this attempt, second only to the USA.

The Second World War accentuated the already apparent predominance of the US economy in the world, its major rivals being forced to commit resources to the war effort and to suffer destruction on a scale which meant that, by the end of the war, the USA was unambiguously the front-rank world economic power. But the role of the USA in reconstructing the world economy was dependent not only on its economic weight, but also on a shift in American foreign policy: a shift from a broadly isolationist stance for most of the inter-war years (save for the brief and unsuccessful internationalism of Wilson at the end of the First World War), to one which accepted that America could and should play a world-wide role.

This role in its most general sense has been subject to a vast and contentious interpretative effort. How far is it to be seen as an assertion of dominance over the world economy, driven by a desire to make the world safe for American capitalism; how far as driven by a concern to sustain and extend democratic institutions by building a base of successful economic activity? Slightly more particularly, is this role best understood in terms of the acceptance by the USA of a hegemonic status in the world economy, previously in the hands of Britain? This framework, as noted in Chapter 5, sees stability in the world economy as predicated upon the existence of a dominant, hegemonic, economic power with both an interest in, and a capacity to sustain, 'liberal' economic institutions in the international economy. In this view the economic institutions created at the end of World War Two can be seen as serving the needs of the American economy for access to new markets and stable trading relations in the world economy, but as a by-product also serving to provide a framework for a period of general, international, and rapid economic growth.

This general framework of analysis, the 'hegemonic stability thesis' cannot be discussed in depth here; for such discussion see, for example, Gilpin (1987, chs. 3, 4), Eichengreen (1987*a*), Ruggie (1982). But it should be borne in mind when looking more specifically at the development of American economic policy, itself a necessary starting point for discussing British policy on the international economy in this period.

American and British Policy

To talk of American policy it is necessary to gloss over the many strands of opinion present not only in different parts of that society, but also, very obviously at times, different parts of its government. Nevertheless without too much violence to the record, the broad thrust of American policy can be outlined. The starting point for this was the belief that much of the political breakdown of the 1930s and eventual outbreak of war should be seen as having economic causes. These causes were economic instability brought about particularly by economic nationalism, expressing itself through trade restrictions and competitive currency depreciations. From this analysis emerged a desire for a regime built on multilateralism in trade and convertibility in currencies, and, secondarily, a regime of more stable exchange rates. 'Multi-lateralism' needs to be defined with some care; whilst its advocacy had much in common with traditional free-trade arguments, such arguments were problematic in a country like the USA, protectionist for most of its existence. Hence the focus was on an absence of discrimination in trade, not on free trade. In a similar manner, 'convertibility' meant not a complete absence of controls of foreign exchange transactions, but that foreign holders of a currency should not be subject to such controls. Finally 'more stable' exchange rates left open the question of what exactly the exchange-rate regime would look like which would bring this stability (Gardner 1969, chs. 1, 2).

Within this framework of ideas Britain was by no means seen as a natural partner for the USA in the reconstruction effort. Britain was seen as a major violator of non-discrimination in her system of Imperial Preference, and generally in her role of an imperial power. The Anglo-American basis for discussion of the post-war world emerged initially more from the exigencies of the war than from a decision in principle by the USA that this collaboration was the way forward.

The concern of the USA to reconstruct the world economy on the lines sketched above is apparent almost from the beginning of the war. But it was not until 1941 that it was first given concrete expression. In that year the US President, Roosevelt, desired to put forward a statement of Allied war aims, which, prior to direct US participation in the war, he saw as important to secure American public support for the war effort. For Britain, Churchill's concern was the immediate need for US help, not the post-war world. Out of a meeting between the two emerged the Atlantic Charter, which dealt in very broad terms with the form of the post-war order, including an endeavour 'to further employment by all peoples of access on equal terms to the trade and to the raw materials which are needed for their economic prosperity', but with a saving clause that this should be done 'with due respect for existing obligations'. This last was inserted by the British, with clear reference to Imperial Preference. Nevertheless, at this stage there seems to have been little worry in Britain that the broad thrust of the Charter was clearly antithetical to such devices as Imperial Preference (Gardner 1969, ch. 3).

Much more specific than the lofty avowals of the Atlantic Charter were the commitments embodied in the Mutual Aid Agreements of 1942. These commitments were given by Britain in return for US lend-lease, basically free gifts of equipment to prosecute the war effort, which were enormously important in making available to Britain the supplies she could no longer afford to buy from the Americans after the summer of 1941. Hence Article VII of those Agreements embodied a British commitment to work towards the abolition of trade discrimination, however the extent to which this was a commitment to the abolition of Imperial Preference was much disputed at the time and subsequently (Gardner 1969, ch. 4; Harrod 1952, ch. 12; Pressnell 1986, ch. 3).

The discussions leading up to British acceptance of Article VII revealed the divergence of emphasis between Britain and the USA in shaping the post-war world. Whilst at the highest level Churchill was reluctant to see much effort put into post-war plans rather than the current war effort, work on a small scale on the shape of the post-war world had begun soon after that in the USA. Much of this effort was informed by worries about the state of the British balance of payments in the post-war years (Pressnell 1986, Appendix 27), in combination with fears about the dangers of an American slump. This latter fear in turn related to a British belief that the USA did not accept the key place of full employment in a desirable post-war world. These doubts were put in characteristically pungent form by Keynes, who at this stage was far from endorsing what he saw as the obsessive attachment of the USA to free trade (Keynes 1979*a*, chs. 4, 6). On the other hand, Britain was as anxious as the USA that lend-lease should not generate a burden of post-war debt which had been so disastrous a feature of the settlement after World War One. In the event in response to British feelings the Agreements included commitments to the 'expansion of production, employment, and the exchange and consumption of goods' and a reference to the proposals being interpreted 'in the light of governing economic conditions' (Gardner 1969, p. 59).

Towards Bretton Woods

That the Atlantic Charter and the Lend-Lease Agreement focused on multilateral trade reflected American priorities. Concern with the international financial regime was at this stage secondary. In this latter area of concern Britain initially made the running, with Keynes drafting his first proposal for a Clearing Union in the summer of 1941 (Keynes 1980*b*, pp. 2–40; subsequent drafts and discussion, pp. 41–144; Pressnell 1986, chs. 4–6).

These various drafts and discussions of post-war financial policy have an explicit political presumption—that Britain would continue to be a great power. 'But, however hard up we may be for the time being, we—on the assumption which underlies all our post-war plans—shall be standing on top of the world, one of the two or three masters of the future' (Keynes 1980*b*, pp. 42–3; also pp. 54, 60). Thus it was clear that in Keynes's and the British government's eyes the world was to be remade by an Anglo-American partnership. This presumption served to focus attention on possible differences with the USA.

One of the most obvious areas of potential difference was the treatment of creditor countries in any new system. The predominant British perception was that in the inter-war period the most important creditor countries (especially the USA) had deflated the world economy by accumulating trade surpluses, and not offset them by adequate capital outflows. Hence a more desirable framework would put pressure on creditor as well as debtor countries to return to equilibrium. Whatever the merits of this as a feature of a world financial system, the fact that the USA was likely to be the world's biggest creditor, and Britain one of its major debtors, could hardly be ignored.

This was coupled to Keynes's pivotal proposal, for a 'world central bank', providing automatic credits on a substantial scale to countries in deficit. This, too, was likely to prove contentious for the Americans who were inclined to look less kindly on the plight of such countries.

These two points were to prove the main areas of contention with the USA in the years ahead. On these Keynes's proposals represented a rough consensus in British policy-making circles. Other aspects of his proposals were much more contentious domestically. He accepted the long-term goal of a non-discriminatory international system, albeit with emphasis on the need for a substantial transition period (1980*b*, p. 51). He argued that the option of a Commonwealth or sterling bloc as an alternative to co-operation with the USA was not viable, as only a multilateral not a bilateral system could offer the advantages of banking in London which sustained the sterling area (1980*b*, pp. 82–4, 99). Keynes also accepted the idea that future arrangements should allow little scope for exchange-rate depreciation, both because of the experience of competitive depreciations in the inter-war period, and because wages could be expected to respond rapidly to offset any such currency fall (1980*b*, pp. 106–7).

Keynes's proposals have been highlighted because the Bretton Woods agreement of 1944 emerged largely from discussions about these proposals in combination with those of the American Harry White. White's proposals were for a Stabilization Fund which would be based on subscription by its members (not credit creating, as in Keynes's proposal), and whose resources would be much smaller than those envisaged in the Clearing Union plan. The question of sanctions for creditor countries was dealt with by the 'scarce-currency' clause, whereby a country which piled up excessive credit balances in the Fund could be discriminated against by countries in deficit. This, in principle, represented a very substantial concession to the British point of view, which initially Keynes could not believe would survive to be enacted (1980*b*, pp. 226–7).

From early 1942 through to the Bretton Woods Conference of 1944 these proposals were debated within Britain and America, and between the two countries. On the British side the basic thrust of Keynes's proposals became government policy, and were issued as a White Paper in April 1943 (Cmd. 6437). However the proposals had to be vigorously defended against domestic critics, and Keynes was eager to argue their benefits for Britain. These he listed (1980*b*, p. 137) as: giving an expansionary stimulus to the world economy; enabling credit balances to be used to offset deficits elsewhere; giving a margin of help post-war other than from the USA; allowing rectification of the exchange rate; allowing for the continuation of London as a financial centre of the sterling area.

The first point addressed the predominant political worry that Keynes's proposals would inhibit full domestic employment. The fourth was related; Keynes was concerned to reassure opinion in Britain that his proposal involved the regulation of exchange-rate changes, but not the denial of that possibility to countries whose circumstances justified such a change. The final point aimed to reassure both 'imperial' opinion and those who saw continued benefits from the pound's large role in the world economy.

Anglo-American discussions concentrated on the subscription principle versus Keynes's credit-based system; the scale of the fund; the degree of constraint over a participant country's right to determine the value of its currency. Eventually it was conceded in London that to facilitate US Congressional consent to any such arrangements, White's plan would have to form the basis of the agreement.

In April 1944 a 'Joint Statement by Experts on the Establishment of an International Monetary Fund' was published as a White Paper (Cmd. 6519)[1] This accepted White's subscription plan, and a much more limited fund than the British had hoped, but allowed for a 10 per cent devaluation without reference to the Fund, and also embodied the scarce-currency clause (Gardner 1969, chs. 5, 7).

The publication of this White Paper, under US pressure, did not mean the proposals represented a consensus in Britain. Not only was much public opinion, left and right, moving against such multilateralism, as Gardner emphasizes (1969, pp. 122–9), but within both the government and the civil service opinion was divided. In addition, the Bank of England was hostile (Keynes 1980*a*, pp. 399–448; 1980*c*, pp. 1–40; Pressnell 1986, pp. 137–50). The grounds of such opposition were various. On the left such multilateralism seemed to threaten the goal of full employment, believed to be best secured by bilateral and other trade arrangements, and strict exchange controls. On the right the hostility was grounded mainly on the perceived threat to the Empire as an economic unit. Some civil service opposition was based on the belief that whatever the long-term merits of such a scheme, Britain's post-war plight would require the continuation of restrictions and controls for a substantial period. The Bank of England's opposition was based on an adherence to the idea of the sterling area as a currency bloc. Keynes's view was that the sterling area could only survive as such a bloc *and* be based on currency convertibility if there was some international scheme. An inconvertible sterling area, he argued, would soon shrink to nothing (Keynes 1980*b*, pp. 416–17).

Despite this opposition, the government committed itself to the plan and paved the way for the Bretton Woods Conference of late 1944. Ultimately this seems to have been based on a political calculation which was expressed in the following terms by Keynes (1980*b*, p. 447): 'Anglo-American co-operation is absolutely certain to progress in the long run because, however much one may talk and rave, as soon as one seriously considers any alternative, one sees how hopeless and misguided it would be.'

The main business of the Bretton Woods Conference was to get

---

[1] This White Paper had a preface, by Keynes, setting out the differences between it and the previous Clearing Union proposals (Cmnd. 6437). This is in Keynes (1980*b*), pp. 437–42.

formal acceptance by all forty-four countries represented of the proposals drafted by the Anglo-American experts. Most of the changes made at Bretton Woods, for example on voting powers, was designed to sell the Fund to a sceptical Congress.

These proposals involved a fund of $8.8bn., with an American contribution of $3.175bn. On the question of access to these funds some ambiguity was apparent; at some points free access (the British view) seemed clear, at others qualified access (the US view). Keynes's initial hostility to exchange-rate adjustment was considerably moderated, as he came to accept such an adjustment mechanism as desirable in the absence of the much more expansionary fund he had originally envisaged in his Clearing Union Plan. Freedom of action on this was now accorded to signatories to the IMF provided they suffered from 'fundamental disequilibrium' in their balance of payments, and up to 10 per cent changes were allowed without reference to the Fund. Finally, the scarce-currency clause was embodied in the IMF's clauses, though the precise circumstances in which a currency could be so declared left considerable scope for doubt as to how much leverage this would provide on countries persistently in surplus (Gardner 1969, ch. 7; Harrod 1952, ch. 13; Van Dormael 1978, ch. 16; Pressnell 1986, ch. 7).

Despite the agreement of US and British representatives to the Bretton Woods settlement, the precise nature and implications of what had been argued remained unclear. The scope of this ambiguity is well summarized by Gardner (1969, p. 143):

The British appeared to regard the IMF as an automatic source of credit; the Americans seemed to consider it as a conditional provider of financial aid. The British emphasized their freedom to maintain equilibrium by depreciation and exchange control, placing on creditor countries the main burden of adjustment; the Americans looked forward to the early achievement of free and stable exchanges, specifically rejecting the suggestion of any one-sided responsibility on the United States. Most disquieting of all, the British considered their adherence to multilateral principles contingent upon bold new measures of transitional aid; the Americans claimed that the Bretton Woods institutions would meet Britain's post-war needs and that no additional measures would be required.

The legacy of Bretton Woods was, then, an ambiguous one, and this was to become apparent in subsequent years (see below). But in the short run the central difficulty was the transitional period, the period which had always loomed large in British policy-makers' minds, and which was seen as of more immediate concern than long-term plans, the more so as the end of the war approached.

Those fears might seem to have been addressed by the US proposals for an International Bank for Reconstruction and Development (IBRD), which were also agreed at the Bretton Woods Conference. These proposals had been taken up with enthusiasm by the British delegation at the conference, not because they were seen as crucial to the British problems of reconstruction, but rather because of the perception of them as a necessary condition to make the IMF proposals viable in a destabilized post-war world (Keynes 1980c, pp. 48–55, 72–7; Gardner 1969, pp. 110, 117–18).

After considerable debate the US Congress ratified the proposals for the IMF and IBRD in the summer of 1945. British ratification was delayed until after the war's end. Before this ratification was forthcoming the issue had become entangled with the immediate and compelling crisis arising from the cessation of US aid to Britain via lend-lease. This resulted in a British application for a loan from the US which was made conditional on acceptance of multilateralism, and thus raised the same kind of issues as did adherence to the IMF. However before looking at this issue in more detail another major aspect of post-war multilateralism, commercial policy, must be reviewed.

Commercial Policy

As already noted US policy for the post-war international economy had originally emphasized multilateral (non-discrimina-tory) trade as the centre-piece. In Britain at roughly the same time, though with less political drive, discussions were proceeding on post-war commercial policy. In the summer of 1942 James Meade of the Economic Section circulated a proposal for a post-war Commercial Union, embodying multilateral principles, which received Board of Trade and some Treasury support. However they were vigorously attacked by Hubert Henderson (reprinted in Henderson 1955). Henderson's line was that to commit Britain to a multilateral scheme without knowing the full complexities of

Britain's trading position at the end of the war was foolish, and seemed not to take seriously where Britain's immediate difficulties and interests would lie at that time.

Keynes asserted considerable sympathy with the pragmatic tone of Henderson's arguments. This was coupled to a similar sympathy with quota restrictions on trade, and conversely a scepticism as to the efficacy of exchange-rate changes in restoring balance of payments equilibrium—a position already noted in the earliest proposals for the Clearing Union (Keynes 1980c, pp. 248–313).

Disagreements amongst the economists and the Departments of State were mirrored in political disagreements on how to respond to US desires for discussion on commercial policy. Such discussions reopened the issue of Article VII, and in particular its implications for discriminatory arrangements like Imperial Preference. This was coupled to concerns about the compatibility of full employment and a multilateral trade regime. No easy solution of these issues was possible, so the British were notably tardy in responding to American initiatives in this area. Even when Anglo-American expert negotiations made headway in Washington in 1943 (Gardner 1969, ch. 6; Pressnell 1986, ch. 5), advance was blocked in Britain by the political difficulties.

Keynes hoped in the mid-years of the war that financial and commercial multilateralism could be kept apart in discussions with the USA. The reason for that was partly based on a realization of the political complexities of the commercial policy issues, partly on Keynes's own equivocations about post-war commercial policy. In mid-1944 he was stressing a distinction between currency and commercial multilateralism, and that the former was possible without the latter, or more explicitly that Bretton Woods was compatible with variable degrees of trade discrimination (Keynes 1980c, pp. 25–6, 128–9).

But this separation formed no part of the American view. So in 1945 discussions on commercial policy were renewed, leading eventually to the publication of 'Proposals for Consideration by an International Conference on Trade and Employment'. These proposals reflected the misgivings expressed by Britain about the US focus on multilateralism (non-discrimination). They embodied the idea that 'approximately full employment' was an essential accompaniment to the expansion of international trade. Both the British and the Americans accepted the interdependence of these two objectives, albeit with the British emphasizing the line of causation from high levels of employment to buoyant trade, the Americans the reverse.

The British misgivings about the prohibition on quantitative trade restrictions were recognized by allowing exceptions in the case of balance of payments disequilibrium, though the conditions under which this exception might be granted were left ambiguous. The issue was further complicated by both British and US governments' wartime commitments to agricultural support, which implied quantitative restrictions on agricultural imports.

Also left unclear was the specific issue of trade discrimination. The British position was that discrimination could only be dismantled in the context of a general (including US) and substantial reduction of tariff levels. This issue was resolved only by a clause in the Proposals which coupled the ending of discrimination to substantial tariff cuts which were to be mutually advantageous (Gardner 1969, pp. 145–53; Pressnell 1986, ch. 8).

Such a set of proposals seemed to run against the tide of British opinion in the later years of the war, which was putting increasing store by imperial ties and, more specifically, Imperial Preference. This was related to a growing realization of the likely scale of the post-war balance of payments problems, the revival of pro-Empire sentiment in the context of the Empire's role in the war effort, and finally the fact that the USA was using the Preferences as a bargaining weapon in the granting of financial aid (Gardner 1969, pp. 154–8).

Bargaining over the Loan

The whole question of the terms of US aid to Britain was brought to a crisis in the summer of 1945, and with it the interrelated issue of the structure of the post-war international economic system.

The crisis was triggered by the abrupt cessation of lend-lease following the equally abrupt and unanticipated cessation of the war against Japan. This ending of Britain's life-line to US supplies brought on an immediate exchange crisis. This led to a British application for a loan from the USA, an application considered simultaneously with the final settlement of lend-lease, and the proposals on commercial policy. In addition, the question of ratification of Bretton Woods was bound to be brought into any discussion of such issues as the convertibility of sterling which arose in the discussion of the loan. Thus it was apparent from the beginning that the question of the loan was to be considered as part of the whole issue of Britain's post-war economic policy.

Keynes was personally involved in many of the key issues of British economic policy in the Second World War. But in none was his role more central than at the time of the American loan negotiations, where he was 'the controller of the basic strategy (and of 75 per cent of the tactics)' (Clarke 1982, p. 71). Of course this role was played out in the context of all the constraints of British and American economic and political bargaining positions. Nevertheless to focus initially on Keynes's arguments is to get to the heart of many of the issues.

Whilst the immediacy of the need to negotiate a loan arose from the surprising end of lend-lease, there had been much prior discussion in London of the possible scenarios once the war ended. In March 1945 Keynes drafted a paper entitled 'Overseas Financial Policy in Stage III' which set out three possibilities; Starvation Corner, Justice, and Temptation. Starvation Corner involved a rigorous austerity coupled with strict control over imports and the exchanges in a 'siege economy' and a rejection of multilateralism. Justice involved a US refund of the $3bn. spent by Britain on US war supplies prior to lend-lease, coupled with a very soft loan of $5bn., exercisable at any time during the first ten years after the war, and carrying interest of 1 per cent. Finally Temptation would involve a big loan of $5–8bn. on near-commercial terms, with conditions concerning the convertibility of sterling-area receipts into dollars and British commitments to non-discriminatory trade [Keynes 1979*b*, pp. 256–95; Clarke 1982, pp. 52–9, 61–3).

Crudely put, Keynes anticipated getting Justice but found the Americans succumbing to Temptation. It seems clear that he initially misjudged the vantage point of the American negotiators, themselves responding to the marked conservative and isolationist shift in American public and Congressional opinion apparent even before the war's end, and symbolized by Truman's replacement of Roosevelt on the latter's death in summer 1945. This meant that there were to be few 'hand-outs' for the British (Gardner 1969, pp. 192–4; Pressnell 1986, pp. 281–6).

Whilst the settlement of lend-lease may well be considered generous—amounting to the writing off of all debts except a small fraction for supplies already in Britain at the end of the war—it did involve an enforcement of Article VII. Thus it was made clear that any aid to the British would be linked to commitments on multilateralism.

This aid, it soon became clear, was not to be in the form of a grant, but of a loan. And in return the terms to be exacted were surprisingly stiff, at least in comparison with expectations in Britain, and Keynes's own hopes at the time of his arrival in the USA. Indeed the Americans insisted that prior to any discussion of aid should come the discussion of commercial policy, and that any overall deal must involve a commitment by London to the convertibility of all currently-earned sterling one year after the loan came into effect. The Americans regarded the sterling area, whereby Britain, most members of the Commonwealth, and a number of non-Empire countries pooled their reserves, as an organized attempt to discriminate against the dollar. Hence they emphasized their claims to equal access to sterling-area markets. This in turn linked to the issue of Imperial Preference, which as already noted was a major bugbear in the US drive for multi-lateralism.

It has been convincingly argued that the US position on discrimination by the sterling area was illogical, as 'It was not possible for the area to spend more dollars in dollar countries than it acquired, with or without discrimination' (Cairncross 1985, p. 108). But the arguments on this issue were symptomatic of the distrust of British intentions widely felt in the USA at this time, not helped by the election of the Labour government. In a memorable phrase, Britain was accused of 'too damned much socialism at home and too much damned imperialism abroad' (Gardner 1969, p. 237).

Whilst Keynes may well be criticized for his overly optimistic prognosis before departing for Washington, the belief that anyone else could have done better seems doubtful (Clarke 1982, p. 71; Cairncross 1985, pp. 133–4). The key problem obviously lay with American calculations of what was politically possible. Here the negotiations reflected the prevalent US view that prosperity and peace required multilateralism in economic matters, and that no country which failed to adhere to such principles could reasonably expect US aid. This view was little touched by the British belief that they had expended a disproportionate share of their resources on a joint war effort, and were therefore entitled to be dealt with not as a supplicant but as a trusted partner, temporarily fallen on difficult times.

The final settlement gave Britain a loan of $3.75bn. plus $650m., in final settlement of lend-lease negotiations. The rate of interest was 2 per cent, beginning in 5 years along with repayment which was to stretch over 50 years. Some waiver was allowed on interest payments if Britain's current balance of payments position was below a designated floor.

On convertibility, Britain had to accept a commitment to allow this after one year, instead of the indefinite postponement allowed under Bretton Woods. The tying of Imperial Preference to the loan, however, was successfully resisted, but Britain accepted the proposals on commercial policy previously negotiated.[2] On the sterling balances, Britain had resisted any role for the USA in determining their future, but eventually agreed to some writing off (the USA wanted this to be done to all of them), some funding, and some immediate release. The most significant of Britain's commitments, tied to a strict timetable, was to the convertibility of current sterling earnings within one year of the agreement. In return Britain got a 'line of credit [that] was liberal in its size and terms—but not liberal enough to inspire complete confidence that the multilateral undertakings could be successfully carried out' (Gardner 1969, p. 223; Pressnell 1986, pp. 320–9).

The outcome of the negotiations in the USA found little favour in government or public circles in the UK. The different facets of the proposed deal—the loan, the settlement of lend-lease, Bretton Woods, and the commercial policy proposals—were presented as a package, and practically everyone found something in the package they disliked. There was a general belief that an interest-bearing loan was not a just reward for Britain's role in the Allied victory. The commitment to multilateralism aroused hostility from the right as cutting across imperial commitments, on the left as a

---

[2] As Gardner points out (1969, p. 146), this acceptance was not strictly related to the loan, although the American negotiators wanted to present it this way to appease public opinion, whilst the British government wanted to separate the issues to appease British opinion. That opinion generally remained strongly attached to Imperial Preference, and, at most, willing to give this up only in return for very substantial cuts in American tariffs.

threat to full employment policies. The government was perhaps especially worried by the convertibility condition, which however desirable in the long run, was a grave threat in the time-scale allowed. The arguments in favour of the deal were largely ones of lack of alternative—lack of an alternative to the loan as a way of sustaining the balance of payments, lack of an alternative to the Anglo-American alliance as a foundation of foreign policy. Little was heard of the arguments in principle for multilateralism, except by Keynes in a speech in the House of Lords in defence of the agreement (Keynes 1979*b*, pp. 605–24).

At the end of the day acceptance of the loan agreement was based on the Labour government's political calculations. Its senior members

seemed more concerned by the political implications of breaking off negotiations and so putting Anglo-American co-operation at risk than with the positive advantages to the UK of the Agreements themselves. A loan without conditions was not available and the loan with conditions was indispensable if living standards were to be maintained; the terms of the loan compared favourably with those which France had to accept; and those who looked to the sterling area for help might well find that without the loan it was unable to retain its coherence while of the Commonwealth countries Canada would regard a rejection of the loan as quite unjustifiable (Cairncross 1985, p. 109).

The Short-term Consequences of Multilateralism

For these reasons, and without enthusiasm, Britain was persuaded to commit herself to the American grand design for the post-war world. How significant was this for actual policy in subsequent years?

It was very important for convertibility. In the summer of 1947, in fulfilment of the Agreements, sterling was made convertible, but the flight from the pound was so intense that the policy reversed in six weeks, and full convertibility was not restored *de jure* until 1958, though *de facto* in 1955. (The 1947 episode is dealt with in more detail in Chapter 8.)

The inability to move rapidly to sustainable currency convertibility was almost universal in the late 1940s. It was part of the failure of the whole edifice of Bretton Woods to become effective before the late 1950s, conditioned by the overall conception of Bretton Woods, and its uncomfortable fit with economic conditions in the post-war years. The settlement was explicitly designed to deal with a broadly stable economic environment, in which lending by the fund would deal with temporary balance of payments disequilibria, whilst long-term problems could be dealt with by exchange-rate changes. This was hardly the world of the late 1940s. The process of reconstruction of a dislocated world economy took many years, and in the meantime severe and chronic balance of payments difficulties could not be dealt with by short-term borrowing, nor, more contentiously, by exchange-rate changes in conditions of pervasive excess demand. (On this latter issue in Britain, see Chapter 8.)

The IMF consciously excluded itself from giving loans for reconstruction purposes, and hence gave little in the way of loans at all, depriving itself thereby of leverage over countries policies. It could do little to prevent the extension of the traditional instruments of trade and currency restriction, which was the response of most countries to their external economic problems in this period. By 1949 the Directors of the IMF had to record that 'dependence on bilateral trade and inconvertible currencies is far greater than before the war' (cited Gardner 1969, p. 298). For the foreseeable future Bretton Woods was put on ice.

If the multilateralism in currencies envisaged by Bretton Woods was quickly seen to be implausible in the late 1940s, the fate of multilateralism in trade was both more complex and more ambiguous. As already noted, the American conception of multilateralism in trade centred on non-discrimination. Article 9 of the Loan Agreements had secured that Britain, in whatever regime of control over imports it operated, would not discriminate against those from the USA.

Initially this clause had not been of great practical moment, as the possibility of securing imports from non-dollar sources was severely restricted by the absence of supply from such sources. However, in the wake of the 1947 convertibility crisis, it became apparent both that Britain's balance of payments problem was above all a dollar problem, and that sources of supply outside the western hemisphere were becoming available. Hence, from Britain's point of view, was the logic of focusing import cuts on dollar supplies. This was reluctantly conceded by the US government in late 1947, though the issue was fudged for the consumption of the American public (Gardner 1969, pp. 331–6).

The crisis of 1947 made clear that the route to a stable economic (and political) environment on which the hopes of a multilateral regime rested was to be a long and hard one. Eventually that crisis (or American perceptions of it) was to bring about a sharp reversal of American foreign policy, and with it a substantial reordering of the basis for the attempt to reconstruct the world economy. The central feature of this American reorientation was Marshall Aid, which was itself to have substantial, if ambiguous, consequences for multilateralism. But before this is examined, some brief account of the rather separate track of Anglo-American negotiations arising from the wartime discussions on commercial policy is required. As already noted, these discussions led, in 1945 to 'Proposals for Consideration by an International Conference on Trade and Employment', which had been accepted by Britain at the time of the Loan Agreement.

These proposals had envisaged the creation of an International Trade Organization (ITO) to supervise multilateralism in trade in the way the IMF was intended to supervise it in currencies.

On employment, as noted above, the US view was that whilst low unemployment was doubtless desirable, its achievement by government action was uncertain, and the best that governments could do was to encourage trade as a route to employment stability. In Britain (and Australia and New Zealand) there was a much stronger sense of the priority of full employment, the capacity of government to bring it about, and the possible constraints the international economy might put on its attainment. Fears of a lesser US enthusiasm on this objective were added to by fears of an impending US slump, which persisted into the 1950s.

Such a position led to specific proposals that any agreement on trade should enshrine full employment as a priority objective, and that it be accepted that this objective could not simply be guaranteed by unrestricted trade, but that conversely full employment was a necessary condition for the expansion of international trade. More pointedly, Britain suggested that creditor countries had an especially strong responsibility to stop their balance of payments position from exerting deflationary pressure elsewhere in the world economy. The possibility of a commitment to international measures to combat unemployment was discussed but referred on to the Economic and Social Council (ECOSOC) of the United Nations (Gardner 1969, pp. 269–80).

Alongside, but not entirely separate from, the employment issue was that of quantitative trade restrictions. Simply put, the issue here was how tight the conditions were to be on the use of such restrictions—the US wanting very tight restrictions, the UK somewhat looser ones.

On both these issues forms of words embodying compromises were found. But the debate revealed how divergent were American and British perceptions of priorities. As before, in principle multilateralism was clearly a good thing; but any written commitment on the issue was likely to be either too narrowly drawn to be acceptable, given other policy objectives or constraints, or so broadly drawn as to be little more than a statement of pious hope.

A descent from the high ground of principle of trade multilateralism to that of applications was made in the negotiations around the General Agreement on Tariffs and Trade (GATT) in 1947. This was the result of a bargaining process over tariffs and preferences. On the American side it was dominated by the continuing hostility to Imperial Preference, backed by an offer to reduce US tariffs by 50 per cent. But on the British side sentiment for Imperial economic ties was growing—not only in the Conservative party, but also in the Labour government (Gardner 1969, p. 358). This led to offers of only small reductions in Imperial Preference, not the elimination the US hoped for. On this rather limited basis a deal was struck.

Whilst the GATT of 1947 disappointed the advocates of multilateralism, it may be seen as making much more secure progress on specifics than the ITO had done in dealing with generalities. This judgement is reinforced by the subsequent career of the ITO proposals.

The proposals from the London conference of 1946 were further discussed at Geneva in 1947 and Havana in 1948. At the first of these, and in the light of Britain's crisis in 1947, the British delegates sought to liberalize the restrictions on discriminatory trade practices agreed in London, especially with regard to the length of time over which such practices were to be phased out. Concessions on this matter were squeezed from the Americans.

At the end of the Havana conference a Charter for the ITO was agreed and signed by British and American representatives. But on both sides of the Atlantic the Charter was greeted with less than enthusiasm. In Britain misgivings were based on the traditional arguments about Imperial Preference, and the compelling problems of the balance of payments, increasingly seen as a problem requiring discrimination against the dollar. With all the qualifications it embodied, it was unclear that the ITO Charter would have any immediate impact on preference or discrimination. But the principle of multilateralism was clearly enshrined in it, and many in Britain doubted whether this principle could be applicable at home in the foreseeable future. British ratification was delayed to await the American response.

This response was conditioned by the change in international relations, usually subsumed under the heading of the beginnings of the cold war. The significance of this was that it cut across one of the major planks of American support for multilateralism, the argument that it provided the conditions for a durable world peace. This looked much less plausible in 1949–50 than it had in the early 1940s when many had been looking back to the 1930s. Could the struggle with the Soviets be seen as linked to economic exclusion and restrictionism, in the way, it could plausibly be alleged, Nazism had been in the 1930s?

Secondly, there was substantial hostility in the USA to the emphasis in the ITO Charter on derogations from multilateralism based on an emphasis on full employment and the consequent need for trade regulation. This aroused the ire of the Republican majority in Congress, and of the business groups who had previously supported the multilateralist thrust of US foreign economic policy. In sum, there was no longer a majority amongst the political classes in the USA for such policies as represented by the ITO. The ITO was never ratified by either the USA or Britain; it was still-born (Gardner 1969, ch. 17; Diebold 1952*a*).

Marshall Aid and its Consequences

The shift in US foreign policy with the beginnings of the cold war (which partly underlay the failure of ITO) had, of course, much wider ramifications. But here the concern is with that shift's impact on the framework of international economic relations and on British policy within that context.

At the end of the Second World War US policy had assumed a short transitional period of reconstruction before the new world of multilateralism was established. The USA was seen as having only a limited role in providing funds for relief and reconstruction via the UN Relief Aid Agency and the IBRD, but this position came to be seen as increasingly vulnerable in the political and economic circumstances of 1947. The political change was the growing US perception of a Soviet threat, which extended to fears for the possible creation of Communist governments in Western European countries, especially France and Italy. There was also a strongly held belief in American policy circles that the Western European economies in 1947 were in a state of near collapse, and that such a collapse would provide a breeding ground for Communist politics.

The reality of these threats is disputable. The economic state of Europe in 1947 has been especially keenly disputed, with recent 'revisionism' arguing that Western Europe was suffering only from the pains of too rapid a recovery, not the beginnings of collapse (Milward 1984, chs. 1, 14; for the opposite view, Kindleberger 1987, ch. 14). But the important point here is that perceptions of collapse provided a large part of the context for the Marshall Aid programme of financial aid for Western Europe.[3] The precise mixture of motives for this Aid has also been hotly disputed. Many have emphasized the perceived threat of communism, others have focused on the crucial part played by policy towards Germany (Gimbel 1976), the internal concerns of the US bureaucracy (Arkes 1972), or the impact of the growth of 'corporate neo-capitalism' in the USA (Hogan 1987).[4]

Whatever the reasons, the Marshall Plan emerged as an economic programme with four broad aims for the Western European countries. These were: to increase production, to increase foreign trade, to restore/maintain internal financial stability, and to encourage co-operation between the different Western European states (Wexler 1983, p. 5). In the context of

---

[3] There is, of course, a huge literature on the shift of US policy at this time. For example, see Kolko and Kolko (1972), Davis (1974), and, for a survey, Levering (1982), ch. 1.

[4] For a survey of literature on the Marshall Plan, see Hoffman and Maier (1984), and Hogan (1987), introduction.

this chapter, it is the second and fourth of these which most warrant attention (the question of increased production is returned to in Chapter 8).

Unlike the loan of 1945/6, Marshall Aid was never formally made conditional on British or European acceptance of the Americans' broader plans for multilateralism. However, it was inevitable that the two issues would be linked, if only informally, by policy-makers in Britain. Thus for example in the summer of 1949 Gaitskell, Minister of Fuel and Power and the next Chancellor of the Exchequer, was worried that British refusals to make concessions on convertibility and multilateralism generally would lead to the withdrawal of Marshall Aid (Williams 1983, pp. 115–17; also Bullock 1983, pp. 461–2). But such concessions seem neither to have been demanded strongly by the Americans, nor forthcoming from the British government.

What was expected, however, was much more co-operation on economic and political matters between the Western European states.[5] This was quite explicit from General Marshall's first public proposal of the aid programme in 1947: 'he appeared to impose only one condition. This was that the Aid should be used by the European countries in a co-ordinated way rather than be allocated individually to specific countries for specific purposes . . . The United States did not only intend to reconstruct Western Europe economically, but also politically' (Milward 1984, p. 56). This emphasis on unity emerged from two major considerations, one political and one economic. The political consideration was Germany. It was plain that Western European economic recovery would involve the economic recovery of Germany. The issue was how to make this recovery acceptable to those who feared it might be a basis for the revival of German militarism. The solution was European unity, subjecting the German economy to some kind of supranational supervision (Gimbel 1976; Kindleberger 1987, ch. 1).

Equally compelling in many American minds was the argument that economic integration was a necessary prerequisite for the revival of economic growth. This was based on time-honoured economic precepts like 'the size of the market limits the division of

[5] The initial offer of Marshall Aid was made to the whole of Europe, but in the expectation (and probably hope) that it would be rejected by the Soviet bloc, as it eventually was, at the insistence of the Politburo.

labour' (and hence productivity growth), as well as on the perceived benefits to the US economy of a large integrated market. To a degree, European economic unity was seen as an adoption of the American model (Milward 1984, pp. 57–61; Hogan 1987, ch. 2).

The British response to this drive for European unity varied over time and was never less than somewhat ambiguous. But two themes stand out. On the one hand Britain needed Marshall Aid, it needed the dollars to maintain its import programmes and anything like its overall economic strategy. On the other hand, European political unity was directly at odds with the Labour government's view of Britain's place in the world.[6]

At the centre of this view was the belief that Britain was, or could soon be again, a Great Power. This status was seen as primarily based on Britain's world role via its Empire and the Commonwealth (Bullock 1983, e.g. pp. 64–5, 125–6). However, there was little support in the Labour government for the view that Britain and the Commonwealth could go it alone as an economic and political entity, and a general acceptance that collaboration with the USA was vital. There was somewhat more reluctant acceptance that Britain was part of Western Europe, at least in an economic sense. This triad of links was sometimes rationalized into the notion of Britain as a 'middle kingdom'. 'If the Americans envisioned a bi-polar world, dominated by two hegemonic powers, the British envisioned a world in which the Empire, the Common-wealth, and the Western European states would come together in the middle kingdom' (Hogan 1987, p. 118).

This combination of desire for American aid and co-operation, but hostility to any notion of loss of Britain's world role in schemes for European unity, shaped Britain's response to Marshall Aid and the proposals that accompanied it. Bevin, as Foreign Secretary, responded enthusiastically to Marshall's proposals, but wanted the aid to be distributed on a bilateral basis, with Britain playing a special role in its organization but outside any formal system of European co-operation. But this claim for partnership with the

---

[6] Newton (1984) argues that Labour's policy was based on the belief that the basic problem of the dollar shortage was not low production in Europe but the problems of underdeveloped countries, forcing Europe to turn to US imports. He also emphasizes the extent to which the sterling area provided a defence for Britain against the deflationary consequences of the US trade surplus, by making possible multilateral trade within the Empire.

Americans was rejected, and it was made clear that Marshall Aid would be conditional on co-operative activity by the Western European states (Bullock 1983, pp. 413–17).

This American insistence led to the creation of the Organization for European Economic Co-operation (OEEC) to administer the Marshall Aid programme in Europe. However, the British hostility to European union was reflected in battles over the status and role of the OEEC, with Britain resisting it becoming a supranational, integrative body, rather than a body for negotiation between sovereign states (Hogan 1987, pp. 156–7). More ambiguity was apparent in early discussions of a possible Western European Customs Union. This partly reflected divisions within the British government, where, at least in 1947–8, the Foreign Office tended to look favourably on the idea, whereas the economic Ministries emphasized Britain's economic links outside Europe.

It should be noted that as regards trade, Europe was relatively unimportant to Britain at this time. The countries of Western Europe in the OEEC took less than 25 per cent of British exports in 1948, whilst the sterling area took half, and Canada and the USA together took 15 per cent. The sterling area was more generally perceived as a source of economic strength, and hence to be defended against encroachment by Europeanism (Bullock 1983, pp. 845–6).

The judgement made at this time about where Britain's economic interests lay may be challenged. The sterling area was to prove a more slow-growing market than Western Europe. The absence of exchange controls on intra-sterling area transactions was to lead to a substantial haemorrhage of dollars. Britain's commitment to her Empire was deemed to make it impossible to cancel the sterling balances accumulated by countries like India and Egypt in return for goods supplied to the Allied war effort (Pressnell 1986, pp. 218–23, 362–6). The idea of Britain's unique world role based on the possession of that Empire and the related possession of an international currency obviously militated against full-hearted acceptance of American designs for European integration. The British position was thus one of emphasizing their support of unity—meaning co-operation, not union i.e. surrender of sovereignty (Hogan 1987, p. 318).

In the British view the key West European economic problem was the shortage of dollars. Increased intra-European trade would of itself not aid the resolution of this problem. On the other hand, Britain saw a leading role for herself as the key to the success of OEEC and the Aid programme, and hence in 1949 made proposals for considerable trade liberalization in Europe, and eventually this led to substantial progress, aiding the growth of intra-European trade by approximately 70 per cent between 1948 and 1952. But Britain remained peripheral to this in quantitative terms (Cairncross 1985, pp. 284–7; Milward 1984, ch. 6).

Such trade liberalization raised the question of currency liberalization; most of the initial trade expansion took place under conditions of bilateral bargaining. Eventually the OEEC accepted a proposal for the European Payments Union (EPU).

Under the union, each country's surpluses or deficits with every other OEEC country were set off against one another, leaving it with a single net surplus or deficit with the EPU. Debts less than a certain amount were completely covered by an automatic growth of credit. If the debt exceeded the credit grant, part of it was covered by credits and part by payment of gold or dollars (Diebold 1952*b*, p. 87).

In fact debtors faced a sliding scale, whereby the larger the deficit, the higher the proportion paid in hard currency. Creditors faced incentives also, the smaller the credit the greater the proportion received in hard currency. The system made a net loss, financed by American aid.

Britain was a reluctant participant in this system. This was partly because of the threat it was believed to pose to the sterling area. Also, there were worries about the implications for Britain's desire to retain the right to impose trade controls against European currencies. Eventually Britain joined, aided by a fortuitous improvement in its reserve position in 1950 (Cairncross 1985, pp. 288–94; Hirschman 1951).

But any movement to a more supranational framework for Western European co-operation was decisively rejected by Britain, by the refusal to adhere to the Schuman Plan for a supranational coal and steel community (ECSC) which can reasonably be seen as the beginnings of the Common Market. The plan originated in France, which 'had this time taken a bold step towards creating her own Western Europe without regard to Britain and in the full knowledge that official British policy was opposed to such ideas'

(Milward 1984, p. 400). What British policy would not stomach in the proposal was the surrender of sovereignty that it involved.

How far the refusal to adhere to the Schuman Plan can be seen as a crucial turning-point in Britain's post-war policy is open to dispute. Bullock (1983, pp. 783–6) argues that it was not an irrevocable decision to refuse participation in the growth of European unity leading to the Common Market and later to the European Community. He argues that this line could have been reversed at the time of the negotiations leading to the Treaty of Rome in the late 1950s. Milward (1984, pp. 406–7) suggests that the decision was a symptom of Britain's fearful and defensive posture in the world, and this was where its significance lay.

Certainly the decision must be seen in a political context. Whilst, as noted above, Britain's economic links with Europe were much smaller than they were to become, this should not be over-emphasized in looking at this decision. Predominantly it was based on the political posture of a great power, believing it still had a world role to play, albeit in a 'special relationship' with the USA. In that sense the rejection of Schuman was not only symbolic of the international stance of the Labour government, but of the Conservative governments which were to follow in the 1950s.

In other areas of international economic relations the positions established in the 1940s were continued in the 1950s. The British view of multilateralism continued to be that, whilst desirable, it could only come slowly and in stages. On the trade front the reduction of tariff barriers progressed slowly through periodic rounds of the GATT. This process leapt forward at the end of the fifties when the Treaty of Rome established the Customs Union of the Six, followed in 1959 by the European Free Trade Association (EFTA), covering Britain and most of Western Europe outside the Common Market. Whilst it was not always evident that it would be so, these trade blocs (in combination with GATT) were steps on the road to something close to the American dream of free trade, at least in industrial products, and in the advanced capitalist countries, by the end of the 1950s.

Similarly slow but steady progress towards multilateralism was made in currencies. The EPU effectively integrated Western Europe with the sterling and franc blocs. By the mid-1950s, aided by the weakening of the US balance of payments, sterling was *de facto* convertible into dollars, and in 1958 this was made so *de jure* for both the pound and other Western European currencies. The weakness of sterling contributed to this slow pace, to the fact that it was not until the last day of 1958 that the Bretton Woods Agreement came to fruition (Scammell 1983, pp. 108, 114–16).

Conclusions

Britain shared with the USA parentage of the multilateralism enshrined in Bretton Woods and the GATT (a smaller but more robust offspring than the ITO). Yet, as we have seen, Britain's desire and capacity to participate in such a world was problematic from the beginning, and full participation was delayed for more than a decade after the end of the war.

Two issues emerge from this paradox. First, was there a plausible alternative to the Anglo-American grand design for Britain to adopt at the end of the war? Second, would such an alternative have provided a more favourable environment for British economic policy in the post-war years?

As noted above, the crucial political decision on the British role in the world economy was the acceptance of the Loan Agreement in 1945, and all that went with it. Despite widespread hostility, this decision was made for two fundamental reasons. One was that there was no political alternative to the Alliance with the USA; the second that economically there was no viable alternative.

A detailed treatment of the first issue cannot be given in an account of economic history. Suffice it to say that whilst there were advocates of a 'third way' between American capitalism and Soviet communism in the Labour Party in the 1940s, they had little influence on policy. Partly this was because the leading Labour figures (above all Bevin) had built up relations with the Americans through the war years which, though strained at times, had become habitual. Secondly the 'third way' lacked plausibility because of an absence of allies. Britain was not going to throw her lot in with Europe. The most likely candidate was the Commonwealth, but whilst Imperial enthusiasm was at a highpoint at the war's end, the idea of the Commonwealth as politically independent of the USA was never seriously entertained by the government. These reasons became all the more compelling in the face of the rise of a perception of a Soviet threat, and the transparent incapacity of Europe, let alone Britain on its own, to defend itself if such a threat became reality.[7]

On the economic side the picture is more complex. At the time of the Loan Keynes had posed the alternative of either American help—Temptation or Justice—or Starvation Corner. Given this choice, unsurprisingly Britain rejected the latter, tried for Justice, but put up with Temptation. Yet was the choice really of this threefold character?

As Balogh (1952, pp. 479–80 and Brett *et al*. 1982) have pointed out, American aid under the Loan Agreement was more than offset by overseas military expenditure in this period. This suggests the possibility of another road—a much more rapid reduction of that expenditure, hence avoiding the need for American aid.

It is interesting that in early 1946 Keynes tried to alert the government to the fact that all the American credit and more was being used 'to feed and sustain Allies, liberated territories, and ex-enemies, to maintain our military prestige overseas, and, generally speaking to cut a dash in the world considerably above our means'. Keynes advocated, amongst other things, that this problem be tackled by a halving of British troops outside the Empire: 'We surely cannot afford to make our plans on the basis of being half and half-heartedly ready for war with Russia' (cited Tomlinson 1989, p. 6).

Bullock has disputed whether such a rapid reduction in British commitments would have been possible or desirable. He argues that these commitments were not just a matter of national pride; there was an urgent job to be done in 'restoring order and security' which only the USA, the UK, and the Dominions could do (1983, pp. 125–6, 843–7).

As already noted, Britain's pose as a great power was very much related to the idea that for the head of the Empire and Commonwealth such a pose was realistic and appropriate. Yet this role, via the maintenance of the sterling area, was also extremely expensive in dollars. This was because, in the absence of exchange controls within the area, dollars were effectively flowing out on a scale which approximately equalled the dollar loan. This does not

[7] Bullock (1983) is much the most detailed and authoritative account of Labour's foreign policy, though one which does tend to suggest that what was done was the only possible course.

mean that there was an obvious alternative to the policies actually pursued, and as Cairncross (1984, p. 120) points out, 'A smaller outflow of capital would have checked British exports to sterling area countries but not necessarily done much to promote a diversion of exports to the dollar area.'

At the time the issue of the loan presented itself not as a balance of payments problem but very much as a trade problem, as a problem of financing the current levels of imports from the dollar area. For this immediate problem there seemed little alternative in 1945/6 as there were simply no other sources of supply for such imports, at least not in the short run. Hence Starvation Corner was the only alternative *given the political constraints*, which most accepted as compelling. Balogh, for example, a virulent critic of multilateralism, nevertheless conceded that 'the economic case against these Agreements does not imply that it would have been wise politically to reject them' (1948, p. 84).

Whilst the Loan was accepted, multilateralism did not, of course, immediately follow. Apart from the abortive convertibility of 1947, the question of whether multilateralism was a good thing for Britain can only be sensibly viewed over the long run; it was simply not tried in the short run. The long-term aspects of multilateralism are taken up in Chapter 9. Suffice to say here that multilateralism when eventually pursued was not an unmixed blessing for the British economy. As Matthews *et al.* (1982, p. 531) point out, 'On the one hand, high and rapidly growing demand in the rest of the world was a major plus by comparison with almost all earlier periods; on the other hand, the increase in foreign competition made the resultant benefit less than that derived by other countries, to say the least.'

To make this point is not, of course, to say, as Brett *et al.* (1982) suggest, that because trade and exchange controls were successfully employed in the 1940s they were the best framework for the future. Such an argument ignores the political pressures which would have arisen in the 1950s as the 'excuse' for controls, i.e. post-war reconstruction, was eroded by time. Economically, the point to be emphasized is that the whole post-war boom depended upon sharply rising trade ratios in all the advanced countries, so that unless it is suggested that Britain could have participated in the export expansion, whilst limiting imports, controls would have inhibited one of the most potent sources of expansion in the 'long boom'.

Finally, it should be noted, Britain did not just move at a snail's pace to a multilateral world as circumstances were perceived to permit it. At the same time she pursued a particular policy concerned with trying to maintain the sterling area as a viable entity.

The sterling area evolved out of the sterling bloc, the loose association of sterling users in the 1930s which evolved from the breakdown of the gold standard (Chapter 5 above). During the war this area moved from 'a rather indeterminate and loosely organized currency area . . . into a closely integrated monetary association, almost a union' (Strange 1971, p. 56). This involved a tight system of exchange controls, fixed exchange rates between members, and a pooling of reserves in London. All of this was only made possible by the political exigencies of war, above all the desire of members to obtain the supplies of many goods—from arms to food—effectively controlled by the British and Americans through their shipping and supply organizations.

One consequence of this arrangement was the accumulation of sterling balances by countries such as Egypt and India—balances accumulated by Britain paying these countries for imports in sterling. As noted above, in discussing the Loan Agreement, the USA at that time pressed for these balances to be written off as the sterling-area contribution to the Mutual Aid system of wartime finance. But this was vigorously resisted by the British, who saw any such action as threatening both London's role as an international banker, and its political relations with the holders and with the Commonwealth generally.

Thus, as Strange (1971, pp. 60–1, 232–3) emphasizes, the origin of the sterling balances problem, which was to prove such a headache for Britain's balance of payments in later years, was essentially a political decision, very much linked to the idea of Britain retaining both her great power status via the Commonwealth, and her world economic role via London's position as a financial centre.

This position was slowly revived under the Labour government. Labour was active in promoting the sterling area and the use of sterling as a reserve currency. It also slowly reopened London as an international market place for commodities, which was bound to bring increased demand for financial services in its train. There was a curious indifference in the Labour Party and the Labour government to the possible implications of the role of the pound as an international currency—curious given the events of 1931 (Strange 1971, pp. 232–3). Under the Conservatives from 1951 the emphasis shifted from sterling as part of a defensive club to a general international currency.

The sterling area in the 1940s and 1950s was a bloc for discriminating against the dollar (Sargent 1952). Plainly this was in direct contradiction to the US idea of multilateralism. But in fact the Americans not only accepted, but encouraged and underwrote this system. The reasons were, of course, political. The USA saw that regional arrangements like the Sterling Area were preferable to the autarkic policies which might be the alternative in the short run, but which would generally reduce US political influence (Strange 1971, pp. 62–70).

With American support from without, and little questioning within, the pound thus was re-established as a major international currency within a large part of the world. What also made this arrangement feasible were the outflows of capital from Britain, predominantly to the sterling area, reinforcing it as an economic entity. Secondly, it enabled Britain, with her slender reserves, to draw upon the dollar-earning capacity of the colonial territories, by exchanging these dollars for sterling balances held in London.

By mid-1950 the international economic policies of successive post-war governments had led to two major consequences. A step-by-step approach to multilateralism in trade and payments, coupled with a special role for sterling and London in world financial markets. Both of these, in their different ways, had major implications for the conduct of British economic policy right through the 1950s and 1960s.

In the broader sweep of history this period can be seen to have posed the question of how far an attempt to build a liberal international economy would be compatible with the enhanced domestic role of government and its new-found commitment to economic stability and full employment. Clearly much of the resistance to the Anglo-American design in Britain was based on a belief in the incompatibility of these two, though this was partly based on an underestimate of American sensitivities on this issue (Ruggie 1982, pp. 393–400).

In this context the slow dismantling of controls in the 1950s can be seen as reflecting the determination of most Western European governments to subordinate international economic considerations to the domestic goals of growth and employment. Eventually, in the context of historically high rates of economic growth, it becomes apparent that the international economy posed, not a threat to domestic growth, but an aid. For the time being at least, a liberal international regime was not in conflict with cherished domestic policy objectives.

Further Reading

Cairncross, A. (1985): *The Years of Recovery: British Economic Policy 1945–1951*, London, chs. 4–10.

Gardner, R. (1969): *Sterling–Dollar Diplomacy* (expanded edition), New York.

Harrod, R. F. (1952): *The Life of John Maynard Keynes*, London, chs. 13, 14.

Hogan, M. (1987): *The Marshall Plan: America, Britain, and the Reconstruction of Europe 1947–1952*, Cambridge.

Keynes, J. M. (1979*b*): *Activities 1944–1946: The Transition to Peace, Collected Writings*, vol. xxiv, London, ch. 4

—— (1980*c*): *Activities 1941–1946: Shaping the Post-War World, Bretton Woods and Reparations, Collected Writings*, vol. xxvi, London, chs. 1, 2.

Milward, A. (1984): *The Reconstruction of Western Europe 1945–1951*, London.

Pressnell, L. S. (1986): *External Economic Policy Since the War*, vol. i. *The Post-War Financial Settlement*, London.

Van der Wee, H. (1986): *Prosperity and Upheaval: The World Economy 1945–1980*, London, chs. 1, 9, 11.

8

1945–1951: Domestic Reconstruction: Building a New Jerusalem?

THE first majority Labour government, elected in 1945, presided over six years of radical changes in British economic policy. These changes were partly a consequence of its own reformist initiatives; partly of the inescapable requirement to re-orientate the economy from a wartime to a peacetime basis; partly of an attempt to come to terms with a very different international economic context than that of the 1930s. The result of all these diverse forces was a reconstruction of the economy which laid the basis for much of the economic development of the next two decades, and for much of the pattern of economic policy that prevailed in these years.

Institutions

Controls and Plans

Labour inherited a highly controlled economy. As shown in Chapter 6, by the end of the war period a complex of controls had been built up to ensure supplies for the war effort and, along with fiscal and monetary policy, to prevent excess demand on resources and consequent inflation. These controls covered rationing for consumers, prices, investments, purchase and allocation of raw materials, the engagement of labour, imports and foreign exchange.

Labour's broad attitude to these controls was that they were a desirable legacy, needed to aid the conversion to a peacetime economy, to give an egalitarian distribution of resources, to prevent inflation, and restore the balance of payments. Controls were ideologically congenial to a government committed to a much-enhanced role for the state in the economy. In addition, many of the Labour Ministers had been Ministers in the war period and so were used to operating these elaborate systems of controls.

Initially, the one change in the pattern of controls was concerned with labour. During the war direction of labour had been universal, and Essential Works Orders had been used to prevent workers leaving their jobs. However this set of controls, which impinged most directly on personal liberties, was largely dismantled at the war's end. Some controls on workers leaving a few key industries were retained, and in 1947 more general powers were revived though hardly used, but by and large controls (as opposed to persuasion and propaganda) were not applied to labour in this period (Wilson 1952).

Over the lifetime of the Labour government the scope of controls substantially diminished. Consumer rationing covered about one third of consumer expenditure in 1945, falling to around 10 per cent by 1951. The trend was not without deviations. Bread and potatoes, never rationed in wartime, were newly rationed in 1946 and 1947 respectively, and in those years rationing peaked. Price controls over consumer expenditure were also extensive at the war's end, covering perhaps half of the total. The trend here was also for relaxation over time, but this was interrupted in 1950 by a reintroduction to combat the inflationary pressure from the Korean War. Dow (1965, pp. 167–8) emphasizes how price control was reinforced by, and reinforcing of, informal price controls operated by the trade. Without these, governmental price controls would have been much more difficult to administer and much less successful.

Control of investment operated in a number of ways, in addition to the direct controls over public investment discussed below under budgetary policy. These were by the licensing of building, the allocation of raw materials, especially steel and timber, and by inducing manufacturers to accept export targets for machinery. Up to 1948 building licences were issued in such large numbers as to make this an ineffective control, thereafter their issue was tightened and it began to bite. Allocation of steel and timber was closely related to the control of imports, and was continued until 1950 and 1949 respectively (to be reimposed briefly at the time of the Korean War). Pressure on investment goods producers to maximize exports also acted as a control on investment, though mainly on an informal basis, except where the steel allocations were made on condition of allocation of the finished goods to export (Cairncross 1985, ch. 17).

Purchase and allocation of raw materials and import controls very much overlapped in an economy where most industrial materials were imported. The main exceptions to this were steel and coal. The eventual decontrol of the former has been noted. In the case of coal, supply remained a chronic problem throughout the period of the Labour government and was always subject to central allocation. For other materials, allocation was relaxed as the balance of payments constraints eased, though this trend was interrupted during the Korean War. For imports in general the picture was of a rather slow reduction in the scope of controls, interrupted by the periodic balance of payments crises, and by 1951 particularly focusing on imports from the dollar area and imports of food, most of which was still purchased on government account.

Last in the list of controls was foreign exchange. This was continually controlled throughout these years except for the brief period of convertibility in 1947. This, and the only gradual reduction in controls over imports, reflected the fact that the balance of payments constraint came to dominate economic policy in this period, and hence controls continued to retain their rationale after it was perceived to have been lost in other areas (Dow 1965, ch. 6; Cairncross 1985, ch. 12).

The unambiguous if fluctuating trend towards decontrol reflected the fact that most of the controls were designed to deal with shortages, with a situation of excess demand at controlled prices, and hence as supply expanded their basis was seen to erode. Of course, this situation could have been short-circuited by allowing prices to rise to equate supply and demand, but this was ruled out by the government's commitments both to reducing inflation and containing the rise in the cost of living of lower income groups on egalitarian grounds. The latter led to a policy of subsidies, notably on food, which rose to involve a substantial proportion of public expenditure by 1947.

This view of controls, as an essentially interim mechanism of supply management whilst output expanded, was not one readily accepted by the government. Many Labour Ministers and others on the left in 1945 saw these controls as part and parcel of the economic planning they were committed to; as a permanent addition to the instruments of economic control, rather than temporary weapons soon to be discarded.

As in the First World War, the idea of economic planning had gained great credence from its apparent success in the war period. (Though Henderson (1947, pp. 10–11) argued this was largely a myth, and the key to the success of the war effort was the lack of devotion of resources to investment and exports during the war). The inherited machinery of controls, plus nationalization, were commonly seen to provide the instruments for the continuation of planning in order to 'win the peace'. However, the idea of what economic planning could or should do was never clearly spelt out by Labour Ministers (Cairncross 1985, ch. 11; Devons 1970, ch. 3).

Normally when we speak of economic planning we think of state agencies attempting to determine the composition of output (and hence of investment) according to some strategic goal related to the long-term growth of the economy. This would be broadly so for the 'classic' Soviet five-year plans, French post-war planning, or MITI-led planning in Japan in the post-1945 period. The Labour government was in principle deeply committed to planning. Yet what it did under this heading was clearly not on a par with the examples above. Planning mainly boiled down to the use of (inherited) controls to regulate consumption and the balance of payments, under conditions of excess demand and balance of payments problems. It may be argued that in this sense planning was a success—it provided a breathing space for supply to expand and export markets to be captured. But in this role planning was clearly transitory, its rationale disappearing as shortages diminished.

As Cairncross (1985) has stressed, those given the responsibility to plan had very little data to work on. Nevertheless they did succeed in operating some kind of priority system between sectors (Chick 1986, chs. 2, 3, is very useful on this). But these priorities were not determined by any assessment of long-term growth potential but predominantly by pressing balance of payments considerations. For example, in the case of the car industry, iron and steel were allocated on the condition that 50 per cent of output was exported. Similarly coal, textiles, and agriculture were favoured (especially the latter two) because of their potential for export/import substitution. Coal was more complex. This sector was seen as having a strategic role in Britain's long-term development as well as being crucial in the short run. But this was atypical.

Textiles point up the obvious issue arising from this kind of planning. Retrospectively we know that this was a sector doomed to decline, and we may think that it should have been obvious in the 1940s. But even if it was known (and contemporaries were well aware of the long-term trends in industries like cotton and wool) would that mean favouring textiles was a mistake? The point of course is that given the context of current balance of payments difficulties, the costs of not favouring industries with a high short-term capacity to ease that constraint would be very substantial. In these circumstances planners might well have echoed Keynes: 'in the long run we are all dead'.

A National Investment Bank which had been promised in Labour's 1945 Election Manifesto, *Let us Face the Future*, as the basis for investment planning, did not materialize. The controls continued to be operated largely by trade associations i.e. groupings of the firms in the industry concerned, in co-operation with individual Ministries. Only after the coal crisis of 1947 did a Central Economic Planning Staff (CEPS) emerge, along with a tripartite Economic Planning Board (EPB) to secure industrial co-operation in the process. In their period of existence the CEPS and EPB were mainly concerned with the balance of payments issue, not 'industrial planning' in any grander sense. This is reflected in the time-horizon of most of the planning (or forecasting) exercises which were largely restricted to one year. Robinson (1986, pp. 174–6) has emphasized that a longer view was taken of Britain's economic position, at least in some Ministries, but the emphasis even here was on the balance of payments, rather than on economic growth which was the objective of the 'classic' Soviet, French, or Japanese plans. The question of why this was the case is examined in the conclusions to this chapter.

The International Economic Regime

In Chapter 7 we have discussed in detail the British role in the attempts to reconstruct the international economy on multilateral lines, attempts which proved largely abortive in the late 1940s. Britain's policy stance on this issue had an Augustinian flavour— make me good, Lord, but not yet. This meant that whilst the predominant opinion in Britain accepted the long-term desirability of such a regime, the circumstances of the 1940s were seen as compelling a much more restrictive policy.

On the side of imports, Britain did slowly reduce its controls, especially on goods from within the Western European bloc (including the sterling area) after the creation of the European Payments Union. This accompanied a heightened discrimination against the dollar, which reflected the status of the dollar shortage as the central problem of Britain's balance of payments in this period. As Table 8.1 suggests, the dollar deficit increased sharply in 1947, fell thereafter, especially in the wake of the 1949 devaluation, fell close to balance until once again expanded by the impact of the Korean War.

Controls were probably at their most successful in this area. Imports from the USA and Canada, which rose from 30 per cent of the total in 1938 to 45 per cent in 1945, were reduced to just over 25 per cent in 1950, most of the displacement being on to European sources of supply (Balogh 1952, pp. 491–3). Whilst this partly reflected the reconstruction of the European economies, a substantial part was due to the rigorous control over imports from the USA, especially in the period following the 1947 crisis.

Table 8.1   *British Trade with the Dollar Area 1946–1952* (£m.)

	1946	1947	1948	1949	1950	1951	1952
Exports and re-exports	100	130	196	195	324	393	410
Imports	390	567	406	442	439	742	606
Surplus or deficit on visible trade	−290	−437	−210	−247	−115	−349	−196
Surplus or deficit on invisibles	− 11	−73	−42	−49	27	−87	23
Total surplus or deficit	−301	−510	−252	−296	−88	−436	−173

Source: Cairncross (1985), p. 201.

Import controls were a device both for discriminating against goods from the dollar world, and for reducing the total volume of imports. Scott (1963, pp. 71–2) suggests that controls may have reduced imports by around 15 per cent in the years 1946–9, which would count as a substantial achievement. Indeed, Cairncross (1985, pp. 349–51) has argued that control over imports was the most successful aspect of the regime of controls under Labour.

Unsurprisingly, controls over imports were much more effective than attempts to use them over export levels, where leverage was much less and the British government had, of course, no control over the buyers. British producers were encouraged to export by making material allocations or licences subject to meeting export targets. But even this rather limited policy instrument could not do much to affect the *direction* of exports, for example to raise sales in dollar markets.

The severity of the balance of payments condition of this period compelled the continuation not only of import but also of exchange controls. (For the Balance of Payments see Table 8.2.) The American Loan Agreement had committed Britain to a restoration of convertibility, and this was duly done in 1947. The broad context of this episode can be simply stated: dollar shortage and sterling satiation. Practically every country in the world had a balance of payments deficit with the USA, whilst pounds were accumulated in many countries, from the war period as well as from current transactions.

In this context convertibility was very likely to lead to a rapid conversion of pounds into dollars. But even before convertibility in July, the loss of dollars was accelerating, especially via the sterling area, within which Britain operated no exchange control and whose dollar controls were much less effective than Britain's own. So we should not exaggerate the effects of convertibility *per se*; even in its absence a 'crunch' would have come on the dollar side of the balance of payments within a short period. The demand for dollar goods and the 'leakage' of capital via the sterling area were the underlying problems, convertibility adding a speculative force to these basic difficulties. The dollar drain was mainly reversed by import cuts focusing on dollar goods, not by the decision to reimpose inconvertibility (Cairncross 1985, pp. 144–64).

The 1947 convertibility episode was of great significance to British policy. It brought home clearly to policy-makers the underlying balance of payments difficulty as a dollar problem. In the short run this led to a much more vigorous control of dollar imports, in the long run to the embracing of Marshall Aid and the OEEC (see Chapter 7). It also killed off any lingering thoughts that the IMF agreement could be fully operative in anything but the very long run. Finally, the crisis of 1947 was also the first of the balance of payments crises which were to become the staple feature of British post-war economic policy problems.

The question of exchange-rate flexibility was hotly debated in the Anglo-American attempts to reconstruct the post-war world. Broadly speaking, Britain and the USA shared the desire to avoid the competitive devaluations of the inter-war period, but Britain put a lot of emphasis on the need for this weapon of adjustment to be available in conditions where the existing rate threatened to force deflation of the domestic economy and hence unemployment. A compromise had been written into the IMF agreements allowing depreciation under conditions of 'fundamental disequilibrium' (see Chapter 7).

The chronic dollar shortage of the post-war period raised the question of how far a devaluation of sterling (and other European currencies) *vis-à-vis* the dollar would be the appropriate solution. There had been some discussion of the post-war dollar value of the pound even before the war's end (Clarke 1982, pp. 108–9, 122–5) but the issue was not a live one in policy circles in the early years of the Labour government. There was perhaps both an economic and a political reason for this. On the economic side the relevance of devaluation was doubtful where exports were constrained not mainly by their relative price but by their supply, and where imports were controlled by physical means. Such a context meant that the inflationary effects of devaluation and its effects on the terms of trade (i.e. making imports more expensive relative to exports) were good arguments against such a move (Cairncross and Eichengreen 1983, pp. 112–14).

On the political side, the government found controls ideologically congenial as well as effective in dealing with the current account position. However there seems to have been little of the view, so notorious under the 1960s Labour government, that the value of the pound was a political virility symbol, nor that a devaluation represented an unacceptable reneging on debts to foreign holders of sterling (see Chapter 9).

In 1948/9 the issue of devaluation again became a live one. Partly this reflected the renewed dollar drain in that year, related not just to the upward trend of British imports, but also to the slowdown in economic activity in the USA, with its impact on sterling-area dollar earnings. In the USA there was growing support for the belief that devaluation was the rational alternative to continued US aid and trade controls. In Britain the movement towards *overall* trade balance meant that it became realistic to think of redirecting exports to the USA from other markets.

The discussion over devaluation in 1949 is a good illustration of economic policy-making decisions being made on political grounds but within fairly obvious economic constraints. The major economic constraint was the low foreign exchanges reserves of Britain. These were running down rapidly because of the adverse trade balance, but also increasingly because of flight from the pound resulting from fears of impending devaluation. Ministers therefore had to do something before the reserves ran out.

There were long and complex discussions before the decision was made. But amongst probably the majority of Ministers devaluation was ultimately agreed as an alternative to public expenditure cuts and deflation, which they saw as being urged on them by reactionary officials and Americans. Many economists (and some at the time) would argue this is a false dichotomy: if devaluation is to succeed in expanding export sales and substituting home-produced for imported goods, then resources must be redeployed from elsewhere in the economy, which requires cuts in domestic consumption and/or investment. This suggests a close link between domestic and external policy which did not seem to be generally recognized by the decision-makers at that time. Whatever the economic rationality of the discussion, this hostility to anything that seemed to threaten full domestic employment and cuts in expenditure programmes seems to have been decisive (Cairncross and Eichengreen 1983, ch. 4).

The 1949 decision to devalue the pound was not a coolly calculated strategic choice. Whilst discussion of such a policy pre-dated the payments crisis of 1949, it was only that crisis that compelled action. In that sense it was a repeat of the events of 1947. Both showed a rather hopeful, Micawberish, attitude to the dollar position, especially in its capital account aspects, where the policy issues were unavoidably more complex than those governing the current account position. In all, it cannot be said that the Labour government had a clear notion of interconnected issues of the international role of sterling, the sterling balances, and international capital movements. International economic policy, then as now, was dominated by short-term issues and crises.

The devaluation of 1949 was substantial, from $4.03 to $2.80.

Unlike that of 1967 it was followed by most other non-dollar countries, and can be seen as a world-wide adjustment to the gain in relative strength of the US economy since the 1930s. For Britain, it greatly facilitated the expansion of exports to the USA, so that it can be argued that by 1950, before the Korean War disrupted everything, a rough balance had been achieved not only on the current account in general, but also on the dollar account (Tables 8.1 and 8.2).

Table 8.2   *British Trade and Payments 1946–1952* (£m.)

	1946	1947	1948	1949	1950	1951	1952
Exports and re-exports	960	1,180	1,639	1,863	2,261	2,735	2,769
Imports	1,063	1,541	1,790	2,000	2,312	3,424	3,048
Balance on visible trade	−103	−361	−151	−137	−51	−689	−279
Balance on invisibles	−127	−20	177	136	358	320	442
Balance on current account	−230	−381	26	−1	307	−369	163

Source: Cairncross (1985), p. 201.

The Budgetary Framework

The Labour government inherited a budget within which government spent two-thirds of national income, compared with around 27 per cent on average in the 1930s. This figure was already falling from its peak of around 74 per cent in 1943, and fell to under 40 per cent by 1950 before showing a slight increase during the Korean War. This fall of course reflected that in war-related expenditure, which accounted for more than 55 per cent of all expenditure in 1946 (Peacock and Wiseman 1967, appendix tables A5, A7).

As with the First World War, the Second acted to ratchet up the level of public expenditure; the figure was never again to fall below the high 30s as a percentage of output. But more important than the scale of the budget was its use. The war had not only left a legacy of unprecedented levels of expenditure and taxation, but also of use of the budget to manage the economy in an unprecedented manner. As discussed in Chapter 5, 1941 saw the 'first Keynesian budget', and although this wartime use of the budget was accompanied by widespread direct controls, it opened up the possibility of managing the economy in peacetime by using of the budget to control the level of demand.

The Labour government's relation to this budgetary framework was ambiguous. Many of the leading Labour Party economists had enthusiastically embraced the Keynesian approach to public finance in the 1930s, as a way of eradicating unemployment within a parliamentary democratic framework (Durbin 1985, ch. 7). However in 1945 this outlook was complicated by a strong attachment to the inherited controls as part of a planned economy (as above).

In the early years of the Labour government there was therefore a battle between those who wanted as rapid a movement as possible to the dismantling of controls and towards reliance on macroeconomic management, and those who saw controls as a permanent part of the economic policy regime. The most representative figure urging the former course was James Meade who had been pressing for a Keynesian 'liberal-socialist' approach to economic policy since the mid-1930s (Meade 1988 ch. 4). He did not advocate a precipitate abolition of controls, but strongly argued their transitory character, that they should give way to macro-management as soon as conditions stabilized.

This line of approach was not embraced by the government in 1945 and 1946. Dalton, the Labour Chancellor of the Exchequer in these years, was not hostile to Keynesianism, but he was attached to the use of controls, both as a defence against possible unemployment and as a means of redistribution. Also the relevance of Keynesian doctrine seemed to him limited; like many he saw it as concerned with combating mass unemployment in a slump—not the problems of the late 1940s (Pimlott 1985, ch. 26; Dow 1965, pp. 6–20).

However, the balance of payments crisis of 1947 acutely posed the issue of how active a use of the budget was to be made in managing the economy. Dalton's first budgets had seen a sharp turn round from deficit to surplus. But this reflected more the automatic effects of the sharp fall in defence expenditure, than the aim of a deflationary budget. In 1947 the constraint to use the budget in this way, and to tighten the budgetary squeeze to reduce inflationary pressure, became intense.

Table 8.3   *Budget Surplus or Deficit and Public Sector Savings 1946–1952*
(£m.)

	Realized Surplus*		Public Sector Savings
1945/6	−2,207	1946	−348
1946/7	−586	1947	249
1947/8	636	1948	662
1948/9	831	1949	757
1949/50	549	1950	860
1950/1	549	1951	830
1951/2	380	1952	606

* Realized surplus' was the figure publicly presented in the budget accounts. It accurately shows the trend of the budget, but the public sector savings figures give a better idea of the economic impact of the budget.

Source: Cairncross (1985), p. 421.

As always, the issue of overall budgetary policy could not be separated from particular spending programmes. In this instance there was much emphasis on the food subsidies programme, which 'liberals' saw as both extravagant in public expenditure terms and distorting the workings of the market. Government ministers on the contrary tended to see them as both egalitarian, and as reducing inflationary wage pressure by holding the consumer price index down (Cairncross 1985, ch. 15; Tomlinson 1987*a*, ch. 6).

The exchange rate crisis of 1947 ultimately compelled a further deflationary budget in the autumn of 1947. Dalton seems to have initiated the idea of such a budget to attempt to regain confidence in the pound. Many officials saw the opportunity to press for an acceptance of the anti-inflationary use of the budget. Together these led to the budget, which for the first time in peace placed the macro-management of the economy as the centrepiece of budget-making.

The significance of this event has been disputed. There is no disagreement that the budget was placed in a newly pre-eminent position in economic management. Rather the dispute is over the long-term significance of this change, a dispute which has strong echoes of the debate on the significance of the 1941 budget (Chapter 5). The key issue is how 'revolutionary' is the use of the budget to manage the economy, where the context is one of surpluses to defeat inflation. Booth (1983, 1984, 1985*a*; see also Little 1952), for example, sees the use of the budget *per se* as a crucial change. Others (Tomlinson 1984, 1987*a*; Rollings 1985, 1988) argue that what matters is the asymmetrical character of the budget; surpluses to fight inflation are hardly revolutionary, the whole battle over 'Keynesianism' being about the legitimacy of using deficits to fight unemployment.

Whatever its underlying significance, the budget of November 1947 can certainly be seen as marking a shift within Labour policy from the emphasis on the use of controls to use of the budget to regulate the economy. Controls were thereafter dismantled, symbolized by Harold Wilson's 'bonfire' of controls in 1948. Planning came increasingly to mean national income planning and the use of the budget to manage demand—and in the context of inflationary pressure this meant budget surpluses (Table 8.3).

Agencies

The Treasury

The enhancement of the role of the budget during the Second World War was also an enhancement of the role of the Treasury. Equally as the issue of external finance gained in significance, this traditional responsibility of the Treasury came close to the centre of the economic policy agenda. On the other hand the vast and complex structure of controls was operated outside the Treasury.

This ambiguity in the significance of the Treasury in the new policy regime continued in the immediate post-war period, with the relative role of macro-management (essentially budgetary policy) and physical controls unclear. In those early years notional overseeing of economic policy rested with the Lord President of the Council (Herbert Morrison) but his inclinations and other responsibilities (especially for government business and nationalization) meant that most economic decisions rested either with the Chancellor (Hugh Dalton) or the President of the Board of Trade (Stafford Cripps). The former presided over the Treasury with its traditional role in budgetary policy, the latter over the Ministry most important in the operation of controls.

This rather uneasy structure of responsibilities survived until the crisis of 1947. In that year the lack of co-ordination of economic policy was felt to require a new start, and this led to the apparatus of planning under the CEPS and EPB. This was followed by the creation of a Minister of Economic Affairs, whose function was to act as an economic co-ordinator and 'Minister of Planning'. However this Minister (Cripps) and his Ministry were rapidly absorbed into the Treasury when Cripps became Chancellor in November 1947, and the Treasury became, in effect, the central planning department (Chester 1952, pp. 348–9).

Thus in the later years of the Labour government economic policy was increasingly dominated by the Treasury. This dominance was reinforced by the movement to abolish controls, which left the Treasury's traditional concern—budgetary policy—centre stage. In addition the acceptance that the international constraint was pre-eminent, and that policy on the constraint needed to be integrated with domestic policy, reinforced the Treasury which had retained its role in international finance throughout the 1940s (Cairncross 1985, ch. 3).

The Bank of England

The Treasury had become one Ministry amongst several during the war, but was very much back on top by 1951. The Bank of England also declined in power during the war, but saw no such revival under Labour. Above all this reflected the very limited role given to monetary policy in these years. Cheap money, begun in the 1930s and continued during wartime, was sustained by Labour. This reflected both a powerful pragmatic desire to reduce the burden of war debts, and a more general hostility to monetary policy as symbolic of the 'bad old days' of the 1920s.

As well as denying the significance of the monetary policy, the Labour government registered its distrust of the traditional role of the Bank by nationalizing it in 1946. This was largely a symbolic act. Dalton spoke of the nationalization as merely legitimizing an already existing relationship, and the discussion of the issue assumed on the whole that little of substance would follow from this change in legal status (Chester 1975, p. 16, 28, 879–82).

The nationalization statutes embodied the right of the Governor of the Bank to be consulted, which was fully exercised after 1946, and the Bank continued to make itself felt in policy-making discussions. Dow (1965, p. 69) argued that 'Under the Labour administration, with monetary policy in abeyance, the Bank had played a minor role; since the convertibility debate in 1947, it had indeed hardly been more than the government's agent in the operation of exchange control, and in the issue of government stock.' But more recent accounts of, for example, the debates over devaluation in 1949, suggest the Bank still had a significant role in policy discussion (Cairncross 1985, ch. 7). Certainly supporters of the Labour government still saw the Bank as a conservative institution, advocating deflationary policies. Marris (1954, p. 25) records that in the late 1940s it was a common sardonic comment that 'all government needs to do now is to nationalize the Bank of England'. And Balogh's later attacks on the Bank bear out at least the prevalence of the perception of the Bank as not fundamentally having changed its spots (Balogh 1960*b*). Equally, with tight exchange control and cheap money, the Bank could not play the role it had, or was to aspire to, in the Conservative years after 1951.

Other Agencies

Alongside the Treasury, the most important economic ministry in these years was the Board of Trade. Three aspects of that Ministry's rather miscellaneous responsibilities gave it that importance. First, it was responsible for distribution of industry policy (later called regional policy) i.e. with attempting to prevent unemployment in the regional blackspots of the 1930s. The importance of this policy was written into the 1944 White Paper on Employment Policy, and taken very seriously as part of the full employment policy by Labour ministers. The first Distribution of Industry Act was passed just before the fall of the Coalition government, the second under Labour in 1950, and the related Town and Country Planning Act in 1947. These created a policy framework focused on the provision of factory space in depressed areas and restrictions on building in the booming areas (Jay 1980, ch. 6; Parsons 1986, ch. 4.).

Second, the Board of Trade was important in the export drive. For the government this was seen as a central part of its strategy, and much political energy went into this campaign (Jay 1980, chs. 7–9). By 1951 the level of exports had roughly attained the figure thought necessary at the end of the war, about 75 per cent above the 1938 level. However, this probably reflected more the rapid growth of world trade in these years than any underlying improvement in British competitiveness (Cairncross 1985, pp. 35–6).

Third, the Board of Trade, along with the Ministry of Supply in particular, was central to the operation of the system of controls, excluding those over foreign exchange. However this role withered over time, and even by 1951 the Board had lost some of its significance in consequence.

The Ministry of Labour had become central in the war period because of the emphasis on manpower planning. However, despite expectations to the contrary, this planning soon became little more than a broad survey of labour distribution, and except in key industries, notably coal, labour allocation by the state was effectively dropped. This, coupled with the weak nature of the Minister of Labour (Isaacs), meant that the Ministry became a relatively minor body, focusing mainly on industrial relations and personnel issues, not at all central to managing the economy.

In sum, by the end of the Labour government the Treasury had become by far the most important ministry in economic policy-making. The Economic Section, the main source of economic expertise, remained in the Cabinet Office (until 1953) but this did not act as a powerful independent source of economic advice.

This role for the Treasury may be seen as fortuitous. The historian of that institution has noted the circumstances of the replacement of Dalton by Cripps in 1947, and argued that 'Only in this way, quite fortuitously, did the Treasury gain the essential ingredients of its modern character as a department of economic co-ordination' (Roseveare 1969, p. 279). But whilst the short-term circumstances may have been fortuitous, this re-emphasis on the Treasury's primacy was also related to the evolution of economic policy as a whole.

Above all, this evolution involved a movement, albeit slow and by 1951 incomplete, towards a 'liberal-socialist' policy regime in which the main policy instruments were macroeconomic (over-whelmingly budgetary before 1951), and the main objectives those concerned with economic stability. The contrast might be made here with France, where in this period the emphasis was much more on growth, the instruments of policy much more micro-economic (Kuisel 1981). The implication of this distinctive development in Britain was that the Treasury emerged 'naturally' as the body responsible for the new regime, fitting as it did with its traditional responsibilities for public expenditure and taxation. It was not challenged by a Ministry of Economic Affairs, or by any other body more directly knowledgeable and concerned with the productive apparatus of the country. Not that this apparatus was of little concern at this time; but that the concern never translated itself into a coherent political programme, for a variety of reasons (discussed below under Politics and Policies). Only in the 1960s, with the growing anxiety about lagging economic growth, was the role of the Treasury again to come under challenge.

Doctrine

By the late 1940s Keynesianism had been absorbed into the mainstream of economic doctrine in the UK. Prominent anti-Keynesians of the inter-war period recanted (e.g. Robbins 1947, pp. 67–70) and the discipline was not riven by disputes over macroeconomics as in the 1920s and 1930s.

The focus of most disputes amongst economists in this period was economic planning. This was not dispute along highly theoretical lines as in the debates of the 1930s (e.g. Hayek 1935, Lange 1939), but on much more applied lines, closely related to the current government's policies. For example Robbins (1947), whilst starting with a general defence of the price mechanism as an allocative device, quickly moves on to relate this position to Britain's post-war condition. The broad thrust of his argument is that if excess demand can be reduced the case for controls will disappear, and the market once again come into its own.

A similar line is present in Henderson (1947) and Jewkes (1948), though the latter is much more politically polemical. What is striking about this post-war debate is how little separates the antagonists. The arguments of Robbins, Henderson, and Jewkes from the right differ in tone but not greatly in substance from those of the liberal left, such as Meade (1948) or Lewis (1949). The theoretical framework they deploy consists of a broadly Keynesian macroeconomic position, coupled with a hostility to widespread intervention in the market. They have differing views on the speed with which these interventions should be dismantled, especially on the international front, and on such issues as the desirable scale of income redistribution. But there is an underlying consensus on basic issues—a 'new synthesis' of neo-classical microeconomics and Keynesian macroeconomics.[1]

This view of the world is strongly present in governmental economic policy debates. Whilst the number of economists in government service shrank rapidly at the war's end, the Economic Section remained a small but influential contributor to the debates. Its head (Meade until 1947, Robert Hall afterwards) were both pre-war 'liberal socialists', and this approach increasingly chimed in with government policy after 1947, and perhaps especially from 1950 when Gaitskell became the second professional economist to be Chancellor of the Exchequer.

However the acceptability of such advice to the government was related to its shifting policy concerns. From 1947 these became dominated by inflation and the balance of payments, and on these the Economic Section seemed to offer helpful and relevant advice. Budgetary policy to combat inflation and, later, devaluation to deal with the balance of payments. Equally the political case for controls seemed to be eroded as the economy recovered equilibrium, as no movement emerged for a French-style 'dash for growth' and no coherent doctrine of planning to set against Keynesian liberalism in economic policy. The 'new synthesis' offered to provide the stability of employment which was at the heart of the government's economic programme.

Politics and Policies

Full Employment and the Balance of Payments

The 1945 Labour government was the legatee of the shift in popular opinion in the war period, itself very much a reaction to the perceived failures of the 1930s (see Chapter 6). Its political agenda was dominated by the concern to build a more stable economic environment which would provide jobs and welfare for the working class. The moral widely drawn from the war was 'that our productive resources were used far more fully and effectively during the war than they were previously, and the further moral

[1] One of the few economists to oppose this consensus was Balogh (e.g. 1949, especially Appendix 3).

that we might obtain a more satisfactory return from our exertions in time of peace, if we would apply to our peacetime economy methods of organization resembling those which served us so well in war' (Henderson 1947, p. 10).

It was the full use of resources i.e. full employment, which initially dominated the government's agenda. There was widespread fear that after an initial post-war boom, a slump would come as it had in 1921. Preparations against this slump were made, albeit with decreasing enthusiasm as its date of appearance slipped further and further back (Tomlinson 1987*a*, chs. 5, 7). Expectation of its imminent arrival never entirely disappeared, and notably revived in 1949 (and 1953) when the US economy turned down. But policy-makers quickly accepted that the most immediate and compelling threat to full employment lay in Britain's capacity to finance a full employment level of imports. Thus whilst low-key action on unemployment, e.g. encouraging the USA to commit itself to a full employment target, continued throughout the life of the Labour government, the pre-war and wartime perception that the main threat to full employment would come from demand deficiency faded into the background.

The response to the balance of payments problems of these years was a combination of import restrictions, exchange controls, a drive for exports, and devaluation in 1949. In combination these measures may be said to have broadly righted the balance of payments by 1950 (Tables 8.1 and 8.2). This restrictive policy regime was, at least on the import side, slowly liberalized in line with the commitment, which Labour endorsed, to the creation of an open international economy on the Anglo-American wartime design.

The general question which this area of policy raises is how far the general commitment, and rather limited movement, towards a liberal international regime was appropriate in Britain's economic circumstances. First it has to be said that this was not, of course, a matter of 'free choice'; both the 1945 loan and Marshall Aid were used by the USA to impose conditions on British economic policy. Thus it can be argued that the choice was between US aid with the attached conditions, or an autarkic policy which would have maintained bilateralism abroad and austerity at home. This was the choice posed by Keynes in his advocacy of acceptance of the 1945 loan, notably in his House of Lords speech on the issue (Clarke 1982, p. 83).

However the terms of this choice may be disputed. As Balogh (1952, pp. 479–80; also Brett *et al.*, 1982) pointed out, American aid was more than offset by overseas military expenditure in this period, and so there was a third road, which would have been to slash this expenditure, allowing perhaps for only a small US loan in the immediate period after the cessation of lend-lease in 1945.

Such an argument raises two essentially political imponderables. Could overseas commitments have been reduced very much more rapidly, and would the USA have provided *any* aid if Britain had explicitly repudiated the Atlanticist grand design? On the first many would agree that Britain was very slow to adjust her international posture to her straitened circumstances, and the balance of payments consequences of this were serious. Keynes argued in early 1946 that all of the American credit and more was going to be used to 'feed and sustain Allies, liberated territories and ex-enemies, to maintain our military prestige overseas, and, generally speaking, to cut a dash in the world considerably above our means'. Keynes advocated, amongst other things, that this problem be tackled by a halving of British troops outside the Empire: 'We surely cannot afford to make our plans on the basis of being half and half-heartedly ready for war with Russia' (cited Tomlinson 1989, p. 6). This memo was circulated to the Cabinet by Dalton, but Attlee stressed the political arguments against withdrawal and no action was taken in line with Keynes sense of urgency (Tomlinson 1989, p. 6). Defence was well protected from the austerity measures during the Labour government; in 1947, for example, the cut was 5 per cent rather than the 10 per cent originally suggested by the Chancellor (Chick 1986, p. 32). On the second aspect, some doubts must be essayed on the plausibility of US aid if such an openly neutralist posture had been adopted. Even Balogh, a staunch opponent of multilateralism, noted that 'the *economic* case against these agreements does not imply that it would have been wise *politically* to reject them (1948, p. 84 n.).

Labour's policies in this area must be set in a wider context. Whilst the Labour government undoubtedly put a high priority on domestic reconstruction, it also saw the restoration/continuation of Britain as a great power as perhaps its highest goal. This accounts for the privileged role given to defence, especially overseas defence expenditure. It accounts for the determination to make Britain a nuclear-armed power (Gowing 1974, pp. 184–5).

Perhaps most oddly, given the circumstances of Labour's demise in 1931, it contributed to the startlingly conservative attitude towards the role of London as an international financial centre. Attlee may have said that 'the City in the middle of a socialist state is as anomalous as would be the Pope in Moscow' (Durbin 1985, p. 74), but apart from the largely symbolic nationalization of the Bank of England, such views led to little development of radical attitudes to the City's role (Howson 1988). Whilst sterling's role was attenuated in this period by inconvertibility, Labour was active in promoting the solidarity of the sterling area (and hence sterling's place as a reserve currency). The sterling balances must also be seen in this fundamentally political light. American advocacy of their being written off in 1945 was seen in Britain as threatening the fabric of the Empire; hence the famous problem of these balances in the 1950s was essentially self-imposed for political reasons (Strange 1971, pp. 60–1, 232–3).

Production, Productivity, and Investment

The Labour government emphasized the need to raise production and productivity more than any government before, and probably more than any since. The basis of this was not the 1950s rhetoric of productivity increase as a way of 'doubling the standard of living in 25 years', but rather as a way of solving the balance of payments problem by diverting resources into exports, without sacrificing domestic consumption standards.

In pursuit of this objective the government launched production campaigns and productivity drives and engaged in a massive propaganda exercise (Crofts 1986). This point should be emphasized because as Jay (1980, p. 152) suggests, 'A myth has grown up since then that the Attlee government after 1945 plunged into vast expensive welfare schemes and ignored the hard economic base of production and exports which alone could support them. This is at least the reverse of the truth.' Indeed the historiography of this government, notably Cairncross (1985), has also tended to understate the emphasis on microeconomic issues in the government's policies (Robinson 1986).

This production campaign was backed up by a great deal of wartime research on the sources of industrial weakness, and Middlemas (1986, p. 55) perhaps exaggerates only slightly when he suggests that by 1943 the Board of Trade 'had gone far towards uncovering the long roots of Britain's historically poor industrial performance'. However the translation of this knowledge into what today would be called industrial policy was extremely difficult.

This difficulty partly stemmed from Labour's own orientation to the private, industrial sector of the economy. In *Let us Face the Future* the emphasis is on nationalization as the key to solving industrial problems, and the private sector is treated as largely residual. The only specific commitment in the private sector is on anti-monopoly policy. This rather narrow focus set the scene for the often uneasy relationship between the Labour government and the private sector, which still accounted for 80 per cent of economic activity after the completion of the nationalization programme (Rogow and Shore 1955).

The nature of this relationship is well illustrated by the Anglo-American Council on Productivity (AACP). This was a body created under the aegis of Marshall Aid to allow Britain to learn from the USA about methods to raise productivity, mainly by various visits by 'productivity teams' to the USA.[2] The AACP was an employer–union joint body and this was seen by the government as a way of engaging these two interest groups in the productivity drive. Equally both the employers' organizations and the TUC saw this body as a way of getting the government 'off their back' as regards calls for higher productivity. The direct role of government over productivity-raising was therefore reduced. The employers in particular did not support the AACP with great enthusiasm, especially as many of the reports of the productivity teams made clear that British management, not labour, was responsible for low productivity (Carew 1987; Tomlinson 1987*b*).

Further, a radical attempt to raise productivity would have disrupted the rather cosy relations between industry and government departments, via the various employer-based trade associations. This relationship was grounded on the fact that these associations largely ran the various industrial controls—a legacy of war, which was only slowly dissolved along with the reduction of those controls (Leyland 1952). Though this cosiness was threatened by

---

[2] 66 teams went from Britain to the USA, 3 the other way, which reflected the basic purpose of AACP, though 'reciprocal learning' was trumpeted for public consumption.

the growing employer hostility to further nationalization from 1948 onwards, it is central to the basically consensual approach of the government to the private sector.

Above all, this approach disallowed any attack on the legitimacy of private-sector management—such an attack being suggested by Harold Wilson, whilst President of the Board of Trade, but resisted (Middlemas 1986, pp. 181–2). Indeed, the government proved to be strikingly circumspect in challenging the prerogatives of the private sector (other than by nationalization). Monopoly policy was not pursued with any urgency, despite its important part in Labour Party rhetoric (Hall 1952). The campaign to revive wartime Joint Production Committees, as a way of involving the workers in the drive to increase productivity, partly foundered on the government's unwillingness to make them compulsory (Tomlinson 1987*c*).

Labour, it may be summarized, put a lot of emphasis on trying to improve industrial performance, but did not develop policy instruments in this area very far, nor did it achieve much success. This latter point needs some qualification. Output did expand by 15 per cent between 1946 and 1952 (Table 8.4), a quite healthy rate by historic standards. Productivity increase, too, was above inter-war levels—at around 1.6 per cent for the economy as a whole from 1946 to 1951, but accelerating to perhaps 2.6 per cent from 1948 to 1951. Comparable figures for manufacturing are 2.5 and 3.5 per cent (Cairncross 1985, pp. 18–19).

Britain's performance was only poor relative to what Western European countries were beginning to achieve, although the USA was, like Britain, to be a laggard in the post-war period (Matthews *et al.* 1982, p. 31). Whilst this productivity gap *vis-à-vis* other Western European countries was not apparent to the Labour government, it obviously is important to ask whether that government could have done more to prevent the gap appearing.

Cairncross (1985, pp. 499–500) notes that 'few governments have proclaimed more insistently the need for higher productivity' and suggests that 'it must be very doubtful whether any set of government policies could have done more'. Middlemas (1986, p. 12) implies that more could have been done, but for political reasons was not.

Deep questions were discussed at the end of the Second World War, about endemic weaknesses in management, investment, productivity, or

Table 8.4 *Change in Allocation of Resources 1945–1952 (increase year to year in £m. at constant 1948 market prices)*

	1946	1947	1948	1949	1950	1951	1952	Change 1946–52	
								£m.	%
Consumers' expenditure	(750)	274	−48	145	209	−45	−49	486	5.9
Public authorities' current expenditure	(−2,450)	−816	−12	154	−16	149	219	−322	−12.4
Gross domestic fixed capital formation	(650)	246	126	133	78	6	24	613	57.9
Value of physical increase in stocks and work in progress	(325)	414	−181	−112	−251	588	−395	63	
Export of goods and services	(650)	93	416	238	324	129	−55	1,145	77.3
Total final expenditure	(−75)	211	301	558	344	827	−256	1,985	14.9
Imports of goods and services	—	−144	28	−172	−37	−384	292	417	14.5
Gross domestic product	(−75)	67	329	386	307	443	36	1,568	15.0
Net property income from abroad	—	35	50	−20	115	−105	−50	25	24.5
Gross National Product	(−75)	102	379	366	422	338	−14	1,593	15.3

Source: Cairncross (1985), p. 24.

innovation, but they were soon buried by governments intent on maintaining a high level of public and private consent. Macroeconomic management derived some of its attractiveness from the evasion of precisely such hard and divisive matters.

Whether any government measures would have raised productivity more is perhaps best left an open question. That more was not tried surely did depend on the (often implicit) political calculation suggested by Middlemas. In addition one might add that ideologically Labour had not developed a clear perception of how to deal with the private corporation, either in its wartime policy discussions (Taylor 1978) or over a longer time-span (Tomlinson 1982; Hotten 1988).

Apart from nationalization, one issue over which the government did come into conflict with the private sector was investment. Consistently the private sector resented and resisted the government's holding back of investment, as part of its policy of controlling the level of demand. Indeed investment, its level and allocation, has been a contentious issue, both then and subsequently. Whilst industrialists were chafing at the government's restrictions, most economists at the time were arguing for greater control (e.g. Harrod 1947; Jewkes 1948, ch. 2; Meade 1948, Introduction and ch. 2). These economists saw the government as launching too many big investment projects, especially in the public sector, rather than going much more for a 'patch and mend' policy. In this way government added to the excess demand which caused inflation and spilled over into the balance of payments.

More recent work has tended to suggest under-investment in this period. Chick (1986, ch. 1) has pointed out that the share of the national product going to investment in Britain at this time was substantially less than in France; 9.2 per cent compared with 13.2 per cent in 1946, 13.3 per cent compared with 17.1 per cent in 1952. However it may well be argued that a low level of investment was inherited by the Labour government, and that the increase under that government was *proportionately* greater than in France. Table 8.4 makes the same point in a slightly different way by bringing out how fast investment rose (58 per cent) compared with GDP (15 per cent).

This leads naturally to another issue on investment—how far would a higher level have yielded higher growth? For the post-war period up to 1973 as a whole Matthews *et al.* (1982, pp. 520–2) have expressed some doubts, basically on the grounds that most of the growth was not due to higher investment but to higher Total Factor Productivity. Correlatively, they argue, there were signs of diminishing returns—i.e. rising capital/output ratios and a falling trend in the profit rate. However this argument would seem not to apply in the early post-war years, when many long-term trends were temporarily overridden (see below).

The allocation of investment in this period has also attracted criticism. Barnett (1986, pp. 242–7) argues that too much of this investment went on 'New Jerusalem' house-building, at the expense of industrial investment, and Chick (1986, pp. 38–43) makes the same case in a less polemical and better-supported manner. Table 8.5 shows the breakdown of investment in this

Table 8.5   *Gross Fixed Capital Formation in the United Kingdom 1946–1953*
(£m. at 1958 prices)

	1946*	1947*	1948	1949	1950	1951	1952
Dwellings		(523)	486	476	465	456	546
	(930)						
Other new building and works		(446)	480	588	661	640	650
Plant and machinery	(452)	(626)	765	845	942	1,026	308
Vehicles, ships, etc.	(331)	(404)	404	424	391	347	308
TOTAL	(1,713)	(2,000)	2,135	2,333	2,459	2,469	2,479
Manufacturing and construction			554	626	714	768	732
Gas, water, electricity			206	252	282	284	284
Transport and communication			344	355	334	292	273
Distribution, road haulage, etc.			187	231	251	250	248
Social and public services			123	151	182	201	191
Agriculture, mining, etc.			181	189	179	164	167
TOTAL (including dwellings)			2,135	2,333	2,459	2,469	2,479

*estimates.

Source: Cairncross (1985), p. 456.

period. In terms of *trends* it shows a continual fall both in the absolute amount and the share of investment going to dwellings from 1947 to 1951, with an increase thereafter. The share of GNP going to investment in dwellings under Labour was very similar to the average for the period 1925–37, which was 3.3 per cent (Matthews *et al.* 1982, p. 332), and the relative costs of housing had risen sharply (pp. 413–14).

Of course, size by itself cannot tell us if investment in dwellings crowded out industrial investment. But as Matthews *et al.* (pp. 416–18) argue, this seems implausible for the post-war period. The main argument is that not only did manufacturing investment expand sharply in this period, but that its level can be broadly related to the rates of return on manufacturing investment. One can go further and argue that, given the early post-war expectation of a downturn in demand, housing expenditure especially up to 1947, may have 'crowded in' private investment by making clear the government's commitment to expansion (Milward 1984, p. 484).

This is not to deny private investment was constrained by government policy under Labour, but this was mainly done in the name of increasing exports, where there was direct competition both in capital goods and in intermediate products like iron and steel. But as far as dwellings are concerned, whilst the Labour government did launch a very ambitious housing programme, this was substantially in excess of the housing actually built because resources were not made available for it, and, discounting political circumstances, does not seem to have been out of line with a reasonable allocation of investment resources, especially as housing was a very small user of steel.

Investment behaviour must be put in the context of developments in the economy at this time which in retrospect we can see were temporary rather than permanent. Most important in the current context was the increasing profit share in manufacturing, which with higher investment levels must have meant a rising profit rate, though this is more difficult to show (Matthews *et al.* 1982, pp. 182–92; Barna 1949). Firms were experiencing a demand-led boom and high profits, which largely financed investment at a time when private-sector saving was trivial. This profitability also inhibited any move to radically alter production methods as advocated, for example, by the AACP. There was little incentive to change when current methods were so remunerative.

The Welfare State and Nationalization

Labour's two most lasting institutional legacies were the welfare state and the vastly expanded nationalized sector. The welfare state's most obvious impact on the economy was via its effects on public expenditure. A central reason why post-war public expenditure never fell back to its pre-war levels was spending on welfare provision. Peacock and Wiseman (1967, p. 86) calculate that public expenditure on the 'social services' (welfare state) rose from 11.3 per cent of GNP (38 per cent of expenditure) in 1938 to 18 per cent in 1950 (46 per cent of expenditure). This scale and predominance of welfare-state expenditure within all public spending has continued ever since.

Within the lifetime of the Labour government the contentious area of expenditure was the NHS (Webster 1988, ch. 5; Williams 1983, ch. 4). When the NHS began in 1948 no one could predict its cost, which depended primarily on the level of demand. A large supplementary estimate was needed to cover unexpected expenditure in 1949, and another in 1950. Tight scrutiny of expenditure was established to oversee the NHS budget.

Other welfare-state expenditure rose more gradually, notably pensions, where wartime plans for only a slow rise in the National Insurance pension were kept to. This, however, led to many more claimants for means-tested benefits, a pattern that, against Beveridge's hopes, was to become the norm in the post-war period (Cutler *et al.* 1986, ch. 1).

Another link between the welfare state and the economy discussed at this time was the idea of using variations in National Insurance contributions as a way of managing demand. James Meade has proposed such a scheme as a way of giving automaticity to regulating demand, by linking changes in contributions mechanically to variations in the unemployment rate. However this was resisted by the Treasury, as reducing the Chancellor's discretion in budget-making (Tomlinson 1987a, pp. 97–101).

The dominant themes in the discussion of the welfare state were not economic. The case for it rested primarily on the case for poverty relief and income security. Whatever the merits of such a case it did leave the way open for a rather crude discussion of the economic effects almost wholly in terms of the 'burden' it imposed on taxation and the economy. There was very little discussion at the time about its potentially positive impact on the labour market, or on productivity via a better educated and healthier workforce.

Nationalization was alongside the welfare state at the top of Labour's policy agenda. The motives for nationalization were clearly varied. In different industries there were mixtures of desires for rationalization, for higher investment, for greater employment security and better industrial relations, for controlling the 'commanding heights' of the economy. Added to this were the trade unions' concerns to escape from employment by private employers, and the Labour Party's general perception of nationalization as a crucial part of a socialist programme.[3]

The nationalization programme added about 2 million people to the public sector, embracing, by 1951, airways, the Bank of England, Cable and Wireless, the Electricity and Gas Boards, iron and steel, coal, and much of transport (Chester 1975, pp. 38–9). The significance of this massive transfer of ownership for economic policy was ambiguous.

First, even where the industry was nationalized as a 'commanding height' of the economy, the capacity to use an industry as part of an overall strategy was highly constrained by the autonomy of the nationalized industries' boards. Increasing coal production was one of the government's pressing priorities throughout, but even here the capacity to control the industry was limited and provided a continual headache for Ministers (Williams 1983, ch. 2; Cairncross 1985, ch. 18). In any case, few of the industries nationalized were 'commanding heights' in the sense of being crucial to the development of the economy as a whole, except negatively as in an industry like coal, whose slow expansion of output threatened other industries.

Like National Insurance contributions, the nationalized industries' investment levels were envisaged by some to be useful regulators of demand. But in practice, again, little became of this. Nationalized boards were jealous of their independence, and resisted the subordination of their industry's objectives to macro-

---

[3] For a recent discussion of the complex of motives behind coal nationalization, see Supple (1986).

economic policy (Tomlinson 1987*a*, pp. 88–93; Chester 1975, pp. 981–90).

It is commonly said that Labour came to office with clear commitments to nationalize, but little in the way of detailed plans on how to do this. 'In matters of detail such as organizational structure, the integration of services, finance, pricing, compensation to stockholders, and the relations between the industries acquired and the consumers and employees, very little serious thought had been given' (Aldcroft 1986, p. 208; also Chester 1975, pp. 43–3, 1007–9). However this view needs to be qualified. As Durbin (1985) points out, many of these issues had been much debated amongst leading Labour Party economists such as Evan Durbin, Gaitskell, and Crosland in the 1930s. It remains something of a mystery why so much of the discussion in the 1940s was conducted as if in ignorance of these earlier efforts.

More generally it seems clear, at least in retrospect, that nationalization was from the beginning overloaded with objectives, leading to inevitable disenchantment when some of these could not be realized. Equally it needs to be stressed again that whilst nationalized industries were seen as part of Labour's 'planned economy', that did not mean planning in anything like the French, let alone Soviet, style. Hence the nationalized industries were not called upon to be the centrepiece of a strategy of economic reconstruction master-minded by the state. Rather, as the new 'liberal socialist' consensus of economic policy emerged, they became rather marginal to economic policy-making, though their importance in investment meant they could never be wholly disregarded.

Inflation and the Labour Market

Inflation averaged around 4.5 per cent in the first five years of the Labour government, then accelerated under the impact of the Korean War (Table 8.6). The sharp rise to 11.6 per cent in 1947 propelled inflation to the centre of the policy agenda, where it stayed for the rest of the government's period in office. That acceleration, as noted above, was a major reason for the government taking on board the anti-inflationary fiscal policy pressed upon it by the economists. Food subsidies were also used to hold the price index down, but these were much more controversial as they added to government spending and also, of course, altered relative prices (Booth 1983, pp. 121–2; Cairncross 1985, pp. 418–19).

Even more controversial is the effect of 'cheap money' on inflation. Cairncross (ch. 16) argues that the early post-war inflation reflected the world-wide balance of supply and demand, and inflation fell from the end of 1948 as that balance altered. Dalton's attempts to drive down interest rates further, to lower the debt burden, including the cost of nationalization, did increase the money supply (i.e. because non-bank buyers for government debt were not forthcoming at the lower rates) (Howson 1987). But from 1947 the budget surplus was used to extinguish short-term debt, and from 1947 to 1952 the money supply increased by only 5 per cent. Interest rates drifted up in the last years of Labour—but only to 3 per cent.

Interest in monetary policy only revived with rearmament—but Gaitskell, the new Chancellor, preferred to reply on credit restrictions rather than any rise in Bank Rate.

Criticism of this neglect of monetary policy has focused on its inflationary effect (inflation which was partly suppressed by controls). The actual inflation rate (final output prices) was 47 per cent for the six years 1945–51, with two peaks in the annual rate at 11.6 per cent in 1947 and 12.5 per cent in 1951. The biggest contributor to this was import prices, which rose by 123 per cent. The impact of this on consumer prices was mitigated by subsidies, so consumer prices rose by only 35 per cent. Weekly wage rates rose by 33 per cent, and earnings by 36 per cent, which do not look like figures for a period of 'wage-push' inflation. Only in 1951, with an increase of 7 per cent, was the rise in wages clearly outstripping productivity gains. However the bargaining power of Labour under full employment clearly made it possible for the effects of changes in import prices and deterioration in the terms of trade to be passed on rapidly into prices.

Part of the reason for the relatively slow rise in wages was the voluntary incomes policy between 1948 and 1950 (Jones 1987, ch. 4). This seems clearly to have reduced the rate of wage increases, leading to stationary or falling real wages from spring 1948 to late 1950 (Cairncross 1985, pp. 405–6). However, the policy collapsed as the Korean War began, and wages rose fully to compensate for inflation over the succeeding year.

The general issue which arises from this episode is whether there was the basis for a more long-term 'corporatist' arrangement over the division of the national product which evolved later in some other European countries. Pressure for such a policy did exist at this time, mainly coming from the left, in the name of planning (Panitch 1976).

The one point to be emphasized on this issue is that as the Minister of Labour noted a long-term incomes policy 'would involve a complete recasting of the whole system of industrial relations which has been built up in this country over half a century' (cited Middlemas 1986, p. 156). And in the area of industrial relations the Labour government was strikingly conservative (Flanders 1952). It accepted the concept of voluntary 'good industrial relations' propagated by the Ministry of Labour and strongly supported by most employers and the unions. Almost no industrial relations legislation, apart from the repeal of the 1927 Trade Disputes Act, was passed. Relying a good deal on goodwill, the government was anxious to avoid any reforms which might disturb the close agreement between government and unions apparent in those years.

Conclusions

The main features of the performance of the economy in this period is summarized in Table 8.6.

The broad thrust of the Labour government's macroeconomic policies can be easily summed up by quoting Cairncross (1986, p. 500): 'Few governments . . . have held back consumption more assiduously so as to let the pace be set by exports and investment . . . They were successful in achieving a fast growth in exports, eliminating in turn the external deficit and then the dollar deficit and sustaining a high level of industrial investment in spite of the virtual cessation of personal savings.'

Full employment was maintained, except for a few weeks in the coal crisis of 1947, though this owed more to the buoyant level of demand from export and domestic markets than to any policy of the government. Inflation never threatened to get out of hand, and at its worst in 1951 had much more to do with the world-wide effects of the Korean War than British policy.

Table 8.6 *Main Economic Indicators 1945–1952*

	Unemployment %	Prices (1913 = 100)	Current balance of payments £m.		Terms of trade (1963 = 100, exports/ imports)	GDP (1913 = 100, constant factor cost)
			(a)*	(b)*		
1945	0.5	226	−870	−230	134	148.8
1946	1.9	236	−230	−230	132	142.3
1947	1.4	249	−351	−381	123	140.7
1948	1.3	268	164	26	119	144.7
1949	1.2	275	153	−1	121	150.0
1950	1.3	283	447	307	112	154.9
1951	1.1	311	−326	−369	102	159.5
1952	1.6	338	163	163	111	159.2

Note: (*a*) figures in Feinstein (1972); (*b*) figures from Annual Abstract of Statistics, Annual Supplement (1986).

Source: Tomlinson (1987*a*), p. 41.

In short this was a period of successful macroeconomic management by almost any standards. The form of that management also emerged into that which it was to retain for much of the post-war period—demand management, dominated by budgetary policy. This was not what was envisaged in 1945. As Alan Booth (1983, p. 121) argues, 'Attlee's consensus, therefore, consisted of socialist planning as it had been conceived during the 1930s rather than the techniques of Keynesian management.' Only slowly did this change, mainly under the impact of the crises of 1947 and 1949. These crises exposed the incapacity of existing policy instruments to deliver the economic stability and full employment which were at the heart of Labour's concerns. Planning, i.e. controls, progressively became a politically costly irrelevance given that objective and a world of excess demand.

On industrial policy the picture is one of much more caution. This reflected the fact that ideologically Labour was committed to a highly consensual view of society, which attempted to engender co-operative attitudes and co-operative solutions to economic and other problems (Middlemas 1986, p. 12). This was partly based on the Labour leadership's long-standing idea that it must demonstrate its 'fitness to govern' and its 'responsibility'. In part it also reflected the Second World War mood that post-war Britain should move from the perceived conflictual policies of the 1920s and 1930s to a more harmonious state.

As suggested already, such an attitude inhibited much policy movement in relation to the private sector. Lots of initiatives were forthcoming—the AACP, JPCs, the production drive. But policies which led to direct conflict with the private sector—such as Development Councils for certain sectors of private industry—were not pursued very far (Henderson 1952).

If Labour 'failed' at all, it was in this area, of being unable to devise and pursue industrial policies which would have raised productivity to the levels of Britain's Western European neighbours—a failure paralleled by all post-war governments. It did so not because of a desire to build a 'New Jerusalem' in ignorance of economic reality, but out of a failure to deal with the inherently difficult issue for a reformist government of radically altering the practices of the private sector of the economy. And this in the context of having to deal with all the complex and immediate problems of conversion from a wartime to a peacetime economy unparalleled in scope before or since.

Further Reading

Cairncross, A. (1985): *The Years of Recovery: British Economic Policy 1945–1951*, London.

—— and Eichengreen, B. (1983): *Sterling in Decline*, Oxford, ch. 4.

Chester, D. N. (1975): *The Nationalisation of British Industry 1945–1951*, London, chs. 1, 2, 11.

Cutler, A., Williams, K., and Williams, J. (1986): *Keynes, Beveridge, and Beyond*, London, ch. 1.

Dow, J. C. R. (1965): *The Management of the British Economy 1945–1960*, Cambridge.

Middlemas, J. (1986): *Power, Competition, and the State* i. *Britain in Search of Balance 1940–1961*, London.

Rogow, A. A., and Shore, P. (1955): *The Labour Government and British Industry 1945–1951*, Oxford.

Tomlinson, J. (1987a): *Employment Policy: The Crucial Years 1939–1955*, Oxford, chs. 5, 6, 7.

Worswick, G. D. N., and Ady, P. H., eds. (1952): *The British Economy 1945–1950*, Oxford.

9

1951–1973: The Long Boom

In retrospect the period from the Korean War to the first OPEC crisis appears one of unprecedented success for economic policy. Output and output per head grew at rates previously unattainable, at least for such a sustained period. Unemployment averaged under 2 per cent, inflation under 5 per cent. This rosy picture must however be qualified in a number of ways. Whilst British growth was high by historic standards, it was low by the standards of most advanced capitalist countries (Table 9.1). Unemployment (judged from cyclical low to cyclical low) showed a rising trend, especially from 1968 (Table 9.5). Inflation, too, was clearly rising from the late 1960s (Table 9.6). Indeed, it can be argued that the boom was clearly running out of steam by the late 1960s, and only staggered on to be dealt a death-blow by OPEC 1.

From the contemporary policy-makers' point of view this period did not seem to be one of success. Rather, a progress increasingly seen as inadequate in comparison with European neighbours, was interrupted by frequent balance of payments crises and fears of inflation, aggravated towards the end by deterioration in the unemployment position, readily apparent by 1968. In retrospect

Table 9.1   *British Economic Performance 1950–1973*

	GDP			GDP per hour worked		
	1870–1913	1913–50	1950–73	1870–1913	1913–50	1950–73
Britain	1.9	1.3	3.0	1.2	1.6	3.2
5-country* average	2.2	1.7	5.6	1.6	1.6	5.3

* France, Germany, Japan, Netherlands, UK.

Source: Maddison (1987), Tables 1, 2, p. 650.

even the main indicator of achievement in the economy, historically low unemployment, which governments tended to pride themselves on, has come to be seen by many as due to causes other than economic policy. Overall, this is the period when a clear British perception of relative economic decline appeared, and policy was increasingly both constrained by this decline and addressed to attempting to reverse it.

Institutions

The Exchange Rate

The long boom roughly coincided with the existence of the Bretton Woods system governing the international financial regime. This coincidence was, however, especially approximate in the first part of the period; as already noted in Chapter 7, the grand design of 1944 cannot really be said to have been in place until 1958. Only in the second half of the 1950s did the West European countries, including Britain, find their balance of payments position strong enough to break out of the dollar discrimination of the European Payments Union (which was ended in 1958).

Full operation of the Bretton Woods system for Britain meant fixed exchange rates, and free convertibility of sterling. This had ambiguous implications for the British economy. Probably the Bretton Woods system as a whole facilitated the rapid growth of international trade which was so striking a feature of the long boom, and which probably on balance benefited Britain through export expansion, albeit at the price of mounting import penetration and, eventually, current account difficulties.

On the other hand 'The move to convertibility and the withdrawal of direct controls both increased the vulnerability of the exchange rate to sudden pressure while at the same time the great expansion in privately held liquid funds all over the world (for example, with the development of the Euro-dollar market) increased the chances of such pressure.' (Cairncross 1981, p. 407.) With the scale of sterling holdings overseas, the pound was especially prone to such sudden pressures, a recurrent problem in this period.

The Bretton Woods system itself held the seeds of its own demise. It was essentially a dollar-based system. This had obvious implications. As gold output grew only slowly in this period, the liquidity of the system as a whole depended upon the availability of dollars for countries to hold as reserves.[1] In turn this meant the USA running a balance of payments deficit to enable these dollars to be obtained. This both put pressure on the US economy, and relied upon the dollar continuing to be viewed 'as good as gold'. But the very fact of US deficits increasingly worried both US governments and holders of dollars. This problem is summed up in the changing balance between US gold reserves and dollar reserves held outside the USA; the figures were $22.9b. and $8.95b. respectively in 1951, but $10.9b. and $38.5b. in 1968 (Van der Wee 1987, ch. 11; Scammell 1975, ch. 7).

In addition to the problem of liquidity was the problem of balance of payments adjustment. The compromise which emerged from the Bretton Woods negotiations suggested that the main burden of adjustment in the event of 'fundamental disequilibrium' in the balance of payments would fall on the exchange rate, rather than domestic output and employment levels. But in practice resistance to exchange-rate adjustment proved much greater than anticipated—the level of the exchange rate came increasingly to be seen as a sign of economic policy success, a devaluation as an admission of failure. This inflexibility of exchange rates proved increasingly damaging in the 1960s as economic interdependence increased and balance of payments imbalances grew. 'Without doubt it was the failure of the adjustment process that caused the collapse of the par value system.' (de Vries 1987, p. 94.)

These problems of the Bretton Woods system eventually led to its demise, beginning with the US unilateral decision to end gold convertibility and devalue the dollar in 1971. From then until OPEC 1 there were sustained attempts to keep the system going, but negotiations to that end were finally scuttled by the oil crisis. Generalized floating then emerged not so much as an alternative grand design, but as the only alternative in the absence of any agreement on a new structure (Van der Wee 1987, ch. 12; de Vries 1987, chs. 4, 6).

For Britain the exchange-rate question was particularly highly charged because of its links to the whole issue of the role of sterling as an international currency. The most persuasive account

---

[1] Only small additions were made to reserves by Special Drawing Rights (SDRs) in the IMF, first created in 1968.

of this issue in the long boom period is that of Strange (1971). Her basic theme is the failure of British policy to adjust to the straitened circumstances of the post-war world. In particular, this meant the defence of sterling as a reserve currency, imposing unnecessary costs on the domestic economy in the process.

Borrowing, stop-go, and exchange controls were the three policies designed to encourage and maintain confidence in sterling. A purely national currency would possibly have needed help from some of these if the economy had been in external deficit. But the need for all of them together was greatly increased and intensified by the extra burdens on the balance of payments—the greater expense and the greater instability—arising from the international use of sterling. (Strange 1971, p. 237.)

Such a policy stance meant that no decisive steps to reduce the vulnerability of the pound brought about by outstanding sterling balances were taken until the late 1960s. It meant that the post-1949 parity of the pound at $2.80 was seen by many as inviolable if the status of sterling was not to be fundamentally undermined.

The peculiar problems of the pound were in some ways most apparent in the 1950s when the current account of the balance of payments was healthy, (greatly aided by the shift in the terms of trade in Britain's favour (Ady 1952)) and yet sterling crisis followed crisis with monotonous regularity. The basic problem was the insufficiency of foreign exchange reserves in the face of the speculative overhang of sterling balances, high levels of capital outflow, and high levels of overseas government expenditure. The policy response was not to question the role of sterling but to try and build up an adequate reserve to stave off speculative attacks (Radcliffe 1959, ch. 8; Scott 1962).

In the 1960s the current account position deteriorated. The Balance for official financing (deficit on current account plus capital account) fluctuated violently but averaged £350m. per annum in 1961 to 1967 (Cairncross and Eichengreen 1983, p. 158). However confidence factors were still crucial to the pound's position, and the position was aggravated by the added loss of confidence brought about by the election of a Labour government in 1964, resulting in an almost continuous balance of payments crisis in the mid-1960s. Devaluation of sterling was a live (if publicly suppressed) issue throughout these years, but was resisted by the Labour government for three years until 1967 (Cairncross and Eichengreen 1983, ch. 5).

242   *1951–73: The Long Boom*

Table 9.2   *The Balance of Payments 1952–1973* (£m.)

	Current balance			Investment and other capital flows	Total currency flow*
	Visible	Invisible	Total		
1952	−279	+442	+163	−404	−175
1953	−244	+389	+145	+119	+296
1954	−204	+321	+117	−48	+126
1955	−313	+158	−155	−£85	−229
1956	+53	+155	+208	−409	−159
1957	−29	+262	+233	−300	+13
1958	+29	+315	+344	−121	+290
1959	−117	+269	+152	−108	+18
1960	−406	+151	−255	+286	+325
1961	−152	+158	+6	−316	−339
1962	−102	+244	+122	−3	+192
1963	−80	+204	+124	−99	−58
1964	−519	+137	−382	−301	−695
1965	−237	+188	−49	−326	−353
1966	−73	+157	+84	−578	−591
1967	−557	+224	−313	−600†	−671
1968	−659	+379	−280	−1,007†	−1,410
1969	−143	+592	+449	−109	+743
1970	−9	+716	+707	+459	+1,420
1971	+285	+808	+1,093	+1,853	+3,353
1972	−677	+791	+114	−707	−1,414
1973	−2,375	+1,165	−1,210	+1,071	+210

* Includes balancing item.
† Including Exchange Equalization Account losses in operations in forward exchange market.
Source: UK Balance of Payments (1974).

The motives for this resistance were mixed. Partly they related to Labour's belief that restructuring the economy would solve Britain's problems without deflation or devaluation (see below, Politics and Policies). Partly, there was a belief that another devaluation following that of 1949 would brand Labour as the party of devaluation. In addition $2.80 was 'clung to partly as a matter of preserving the "status of sterling" as an international transactions currency, and also as a reserve currency which would stiffen the wilting bonds of Commonwealth policy' (Strange 1971, p. 337).

It is clear that in the face of conflicting economic advice, the delay in devaluation was for fundamentally political reasons (Cairncross and Eichengreen 1983, ch. 5). These related both to a broad conception of Britain's place in the world as the centre of a bloc, and to a perception of London's financial role as crucial to that place in the world. But these views were shifting even before devaluation. The application to enter the EEC in May 1967 (which itself added to the run on the pound) signalled a reorientation away from the Commonwealth. At the same time it was coming to be realized by the mid-1960s that London's role as a financial centre did not depend on the pound being a reserve currency—and after devaluation it was increasingly realized that the City could work in foreign currencies (especially dollars), and that therefore the value of the pound was almost an irrelevance to the City's success as a financial market-place (Strange 1971, ch. 7).

The devaluation of 1967 can, then, be seen as marking a new, more 'realistic' phase in Britain's foreign economic policy. Commitments and therefore expenditure East of Suez were cut back, and by the Basle agreements of 1968 the sterling balances were stabilized by international guarantees which made them as good as dollars. But Britain still saw policy very much in the context of the Bretton Woods system—she received substantial aid during the mid-1960s crises from other IMF states, who feared the fall of sterling would herald the fall of that system. But once the USA had brought that system to an abrupt halt, the way was open in the early 1970s for Britain, for the first time ever, to regard the value of sterling as entirely secondary to domestic economic objectives. This was the great significance of the decision to float in June 1972, which also signalled the definitive end of the sterling area, as the number of countries tying their currency to sterling fell from 65 to 12, and this was followed by a diversification of reserves out of sterling (Van der Wee 1987, p. 491).

Thus the end of the long boom coincided with a final acceptance by Britain that the pound could no longer be seen as a rival to the dollar as an international currency. Of itself this acceptance did not determine the decision to float. But once the Bretton Woods system broke down, it meant that decisions on the pound could be taken without the encumbrances which had been so constricting over the previous decades.

The Trade Regime

As in the sphere of finance, so in trade, the wartime plans for a liberal international economic order were slow to be realized. But in the 1950s the conditions for such an order became achievable, as the chronic 'dollar shortage' of the major European powers disappeared and the way was open to the lessening of controls. However, in the case of trade this process was much less direct and straightforward than in the case of currencies. The failure of the ITO (Chapter 7) left the major burden of international agreement in this area with the General Agreement of Tariffs and Trade, which in a series of rounds of negotiations from 1947 onwards, widened the scope of non-discrimination and reciprocation in international trade. This process culminated in the Kennedy Round (1963–7) in which agreement was reached for a planned reduction of all tariffs (Van der Wee 1987, pp. 349–51, 382–6).

Also very important to the trading order were the moves towards European integration. The original EEC of the Six was formed in 1957, and in 1960 this was followed by the creation of the European Free Trade Association (EFTA), a much lower-key affair involving free trade in industrial good amongst seven non-members of the EEC including Britain. However, in the context of the GATT and general international movement towards free trade, these agreements did not represent protectionist blocs (except for agricultural products) which undermined the growing liberalization of trade which was still going ahead, albeit haltingly, up to 1973.

Britain's enthusiasm for EFTA followed the 1955 withdrawal from the negotiations which eventually led to the Treaty of Rome. However this self-imposed exclusion from the EEC was reversed in 1962, only for the applications to join to be rebuffed in 1963 and again in 1967. However in 1972 Britain joined the EEC. This decision marked a 'new realism' about where Britain's economic and political future lay. But its impact on trade patterns was much less marked than much discussion would seem to imply; Britain was already reorienting towards Europe and the EEC, and Common Market entry probably only marginally reinforced this.

This is unsurprising if we note the generally low tariff barriers on manufactured goods around the EEC, and the growing emphasis in world trade on the exchange of manufactured goods amongst advanced industrial countries.

Table 9.3   *Geographical Composition of Britain's Trade 1955–1972*

1955		1967		1972		
Imports	Exports	Imports	Exports	Imports	Exports	
39.4	27.4	47.0	30.4	23.3	24.4	Sterling Area
19.5	19.7	11.8	16.5	16.0	16.4	North America
(10.7)	(12.6)	(7.0)	(12.2)	(10.6)	(12.5)	(USA)
6.1	4.5	3.8	3.3	3.0	3.5	Latin America
25.7	36.4	28.1	38.0	43.9	42.9	Western Europe
(12.6)	(19.6)	(14.0)	(19.2)	(24.5)	(22.9)	(EEC: the Six)
2.7	3.9	1.2	3.3	3.5	2.8	Soviet Union and Eastern Europe
6.6	8.1	8.1	8.5	10.1	9.7	Rest of world

Source: Prest and Coppock (1974), p. 106.

The trend towards liberalization was not a live issue in British policy-making in this period. Its general desirability remained unquestioned—part of the consensus between the political parties. A specific reversal of the trend in British policy came only with the 15 per cent import surcharge of 1964 (later cut to 10 per cent), which continued until November 1966. But this was unambiguously a temporary measure, and was not renewed even in the dire circumstances of 1966. It also demonstrated to Britain the strength of international feeling on free trade. Protection was not to be seriously advocated again until the crisis years of the 1970s.

The Budget

The budget was the single most important instrument of economic policy in this period. In the 1950s its use was probably at its peak, as the centrepiece of efforts to stabilize demand, the aim being 'to stimulate demand when it is deficient and to restrain it when excessive' (Hall 1965, p. xv). Whilst monetary policy (i.e. use of the Bank Rate, and later credit and hire purchase controls) revived under the Conservatives, fiscal policy remained pre-eminent. In the 1960s demand management was seen as less central and more problematic in its effects, but nevertheless no other instrument of policy was found to challenge budgetary manipulation, and the period ended with a major fiscal stimulus during the Heath/Barber 'dash for growth' (Dow 1965, chs. 3, 7; Price 1978).

Pre-war and wartime discussions of the use of the budget to regulate demand had focused on variations on the expenditure side of the accounts especially capital expenditure. But most fiscal policy in the 1950s and 1960s revolved around variations in taxation. This reflected the fact that 'long boom' fiscal policy was concerned with short-term stabilization around a buoyant trend, *not* the kind of major slump in demand envisaged in the 1940s. In this context it made much more sense to plan for changes in taxation, operating quickly on consumption levels, than to disrupt expenditure programmes for short-term, cyclical reasons. Cuts in projected or actual public expenditure, especially investment expenditure, were still used in this period, but these were little related to short-term stabilization policy (Dow 1965, ch. 8).

Whilst budgetary policy was extremely active during this period, that activity was always in the context of a budget surplus. In other words, government current account revenues always exceeded expenditure; borrowing took place only to finance that proportion of public investment not covered by the current account surplus (Table 9.4).

Thus through the long boom the public sector borrowing requirement tended to fall—averaging 7.5 per cent of GDP in the 1952–9 period, 6.6 per cent 1960–9 (Tomlinson 1981*b*, p. 390). Whilst the accumulated National Debt rose from £25.9b. in 1950 to £33b. in 1970 in nominal terms, its real value fell sharply, and its ratio to the National Income fell from approximately 3 : 1 to 0.7 : 1 over this period (Reid 1977).

Fiscal policy requires the existence of big government; Gladstone would have been unable to run an effective 'Keynesian' policy with the scale of public expenditure in Victorian Britain. Measurement of public expenditure is complicated and controversial, but for this period (unlike the one that followed)[2] the broad pattern seems

---

[2] This issue is returned to in Chapter 10, where measurement of public expenditure is an important issue in the policy crisis of the mid-1970s.

Table 9.4 *Government Finance 1952–1973* (£m.)

	Budget surplus: current account	Public investment	PSBR
1952	604	1,168	771
1953	507	1,445	591
1954	549	1,232	367
1955	777	1,475	469
1956	743	1,541	564
1957	854	1,667	486
1958	935	1,632	491
1959	874	1,768	571
1960	745	1,863	710
1961	905	2,152	704
1962	1,272	2,222	546
1963	1,079	2,366	842
1964	1,444	2,944	989
1965	1,834	3,296	1,205
1966	2,103	3,621	961
1967	2,148	4,353	1,863
1968	2,891	4,736	1,278
1969	4,214	4,704	−466
1970	5,007	5,216	−17
1971	4,542	5,841	1,372
1972	3,102	5,843	2,047
1973	2,965	7,706	4,168

Source: Buchanan *et al.* (1978), p. 34.

clear—there was very little change in trend, with expenditure on goods and services stable around the 20 per cent of GDP level, expenditure on goods and services plus transfer payments stable around the 40 per cent level (Heald 1983, pp. 22–6). This stability of the long-term trends masks both episodic changes and changes in composition. Expenditure fell through much of the 1950s, reflecting the rundown of defence expenditure in the years following the Korean War. This was offset by gentle growth in the 1960s. This pattern of decline in defence continued in the 1960s, so that over the two decades defence fell from half of all public expenditure on goods and services at the beginning of the 1950s to only a quarter in the early 1970s. This was compensated by the growth of welfare-state expenditure, notably on health and education (Heald 1983, pp. 26–7). Finally, it may be noted that a substantial part of the growth of public expenditure in the 1960s was due to the 'relative price effect' i.e. the tendency of costs in the public sector to rise faster than costs generally. This means the costs of a given output of public-sector services requires an increasing share of national inputs over time (Heald 1983, pp. 114–18, 177–86). This factor was to be very important in the sharp rise in public expenditure in the 1970s, but had only just begun before OPEC 1.[3]

Overall it does not seem that this period supports the view either that democratic government in general, or activist fiscal policy in particular, inevitably result in an expanding public sector (Brittan 1978; Buchanan and Wagner 1977; Buchanan *et al.* 1978; Toye 1976; Tomlinson 1981*b*). As will be argued in Chapter 10, much of the analysis of long-term trends in public spending has been overly coloured by the specific fiscal crisis of the 1970s.

The control of public expenditure on this scale in peacetime was a new and difficult problem in this period and was radically reformed, notably following the Plowden Report of 1961 (Cmd. 1432). This Public Expenditure Survey (PESC) system had four key features:

(*a*) The classification of public expenditure as one entity, with programmes allocated to individual Ministerial responsibility.

(*b*) Collective decisions by Ministers on public expenditure and resource allocation.

(*c*) A longer time horizon of control than the traditional annual cycle.

(*d*) The linking of expenditure to resource availability (Clarke 1978, p. 151; Heclo and Wildavsky 1981, ch. 5).

The system was slowly introduced from 1961/2 onwards. Its most controversial feature was (*d*). This linking was done in real terms i.e. related to expected growth of GNP (rather than, say, tax revenues] over the planning period. The critics alleged that this meant public expenditure was planned in relation to inflated

---

[3] Part of the issue of the RPE arises from the fact that the fast rise in input prices reflects the convention of valuing public-sector output by the value of inputs, and hence ruling out productivity increases by definition. For the significance of the RPE see, in addition to Heald, Beck (1979), and Peacock (1979).

forecasts of national income, imparting an upward bias to expenditure programmes. However, as Clarke (who largely wrote the Plowden Report) notes (1978, pp. 52, 152), this was really only true for the National Plan period (see below, Politics and Policies). Indeed, despite all the controversy over public expenditure and its control in this period, in retrospect the striking feature is how far the level was stable and similar to that in other advanced capitalist countries (Heald 1983, pp. 29–32).

Agencies

The Treasury

The Treasury remained the pre-eminent Ministry concerned with economic policy during the years of the long boom. Whilst much of its organizational effort went into the traditional tasks of managing the public finances, this was now coupled to the task of running the national economy. If the comparison is made with Continental Ministries of Finance, the Treasury may be said to have adapted much more quickly to this economic management role, and in particular to have been much more willing to embrace the new concept of budgetary policy that such a role implied.

Nevertheless from the late 1950s the Treasury was increasingly criticized for failing to match the current requirements of economic policy. This criticism had no one form, but much of it suggested that the Treasury was overly concerned with sterling and the external accounts, and unwilling or unable to give enough emphasis to growth—an attitude often linked to its Oxbridgean amateurism (e.g. Shonfield 1959; Balogh 1960*b*; Brittan 1964; later works on the same tack include Ham (1981), Pollard (1982).

Certainly in the 1950s there was a pre-eminent concern in Britain with the 'defence of sterling', which the Treasury fully shared. In its evidence to the Radcliffe Committee in 1959, the Treasury's attitude was clearly that the problems of sterling reflected inappropriate domestic policy, not 'over-commitment' abroad, and that the policy objective should be to build up exchange reserves, not to change external policy (Radcliffe 1959, para. 643; Radcliffe 1960, paras. 77–125). But these political priorities were by no means the Treasury's alone, rather they reflected the views of all the ruling groups in Britain.

Linked to this kind of criticism of the Treasury was the view that a new kind of economic ministry needed to be created which would not have the same external and financial orientation as the Treasury, but would focus on encouraging economic growth. Such a view was embodied in the creation of the Department of Economic Affairs in 1964. This was seen as the Ministerial counterpart to the National Plan which aimed to raise the rate of growth to 4 per cent a year. (Leruez 1975, chs. 6, 11; the general issue of growth is returned to below in Politics and Policies).

Some saw this attempt to separate economic management from growth as fundamentally misconceived (Brittan 1969, pp. 200–2). Others have argued that the DEA was strangled at birth by the deflationary policies pursued by the government to protect the pound, which prevented the growth strategy from getting off the ground. But to talk of a growth 'strategy' presumes that the DEA had a clear perception of the causes of Britain's industrial inefficiencies and a plausible plan to deal with them. But this seems not to have been the case; the DEA, unlike the Treasury had strong links with senior management in industry, but, arguably, they were as much the problem as the solution.

The creation of the DEA was symbolic of a widespread perception of Treasury inadequacy to increase the rate of growth (Browning 1986, ch. 14). Some have argued that governments can do little in this regard: 'the direct influence of governments on economic growth is relatively modest' (Cairncross 1971*b*, p. 21). But even if this view is too defeatist, it surely is right that the creation of a new Ministerial agency would have been only one small element in any policy to deal with British shortcomings in industrial efficiency.

Overall the importance of the Treasury in Britain's relative economic decline during the long boom years has perhaps been exaggerated. In retrospect, its concern with the strength of sterling in the 1950s and 1960s may appear regrettable, but this posture was not only one which went beyond the Treasury, but also one which reflected previous *political* decisions. These decisions included, most notably, not to fund the sterling balances after the war, which reflected the whole posture of trying to rebuild Britain's role as a great power on the back of a sterling financial bloc.

Even so, within the political consensus in which it operated, the

Treasury usually (but not always) pushed the more conservative policy positions. At the same time it seems to have done little to spell out the economic consequences of the great power illusions, especially in the 1950s. Rather it seems to have taken those illusions as given, and blamed domestic policy when the economy got into trouble in pursuing them. Perhaps this is to say no more than that the Treasury ws not an innovative agency, but a reactive one, adapting to new circumstances, but in ways most congenial to its traditional concerns.

The Bank of England

The perceived deficiencies of economic management in the 1950s led also to criticisms of the Bank of England. These reflected the feeling that the Bank's role had been too little altered by its nationalization, and that its activity as spokesman for the City in government circles dominated its position as the Chancellor's instrument in the City. Indeed, as one commentator suggested, the Bank often seemed to extend its City-mouthpiece role to seeing itself as a 'second chamber, as responsible for deflecting governments from the unwise courses they were inherently bound to pursue' (Hirsch 1965, p. 149).

Traditionally this latter role had been played in relation to governments' perceived tendency to pursue inflationary policies; this continued in this period with the emphasis on the consequences of inflation for the balance of payments (and hence sterling). But in the 1950s and 1960s this role was played particularly in relation to government's prospensity to advocate, or at least raise for discussion, policies—exchange control, devaluation—which cut across the Bank's view of the proper role of sterling in the world economy. This approach led to the Bank having a clear-eyed perception of the incompatibility between sterling's role as an international currency and the scale of overseas government expenditure, and turned the Bank into a critic of that expenditure.

The Radcliffe Report (1959, paras. 760–74) was quite strongly critical of the degree of independence of the Bank and its lack of integration into the Whitehall policy-making process. It strongly asserted that 'the function of the Central Bank is clearly seen to be that of acting as a highly skilled executant in the monetary field of the current economic policy of the central government' (para.

760), and called for a standing committee for co-ordination of monetary policy consisting of Bank, Treasury, and Board of Trade representatives. Whilst this latter recommendation was not followed, there were other steps to make the Bank somewhat less of a separate agency with a separate constituency and interests from those of central government (Brittan 1969, pp. 47–9).

As the role of sterling became gradually disassociated from the activities of the City of London, so the Bank's role as defender of the pound declined. By the beginning of the 1970s the 'strength of sterling' no longer carried the old implications for the interest group represented by the Bank. In one sense, the floating of the pound in 1972 symbolized how far the traditional focus of the Bank of England had shifted by the end of the long boom.

Agencies of Industrial Policy

If the 1950s were the golden age of demand management, the 1960s saw a new concern with what came to be called industrial policy.[4] In the 1950s the main emphasis in this area was a decontrol of industry, a process largely completed by 1954, though there were other significant interventions, both *ad hoc*, e.g. in cotton, and continuing, e.g. iron and steel, and aircraft (Henderson 1962). What gave a new sense to industrial policy in the 1960s was the concern with economic growth and how to increase it. This was never the only objective of industrial policy; most obviously, the old regulatory functions continued and regional policy remained important. But growth gave a prominence to industrial policy which was previously absent.

However, reflecting the lack of clarity about the means (if any) that governments could use to increase economic growth was a diversity of policy instruments and a diversity of agencies of what can best be described as industrial policies rather than a single policy (Grove 1962, ch. 4; Mottershead 1978). Not only were several Ministries involved, but equally important at times were non-Ministerial bodies like the National Economic Development Council and the Industrial Reorganization Corporation.

The NEDO ('Neddy') was created in 1961 in the wake of Conservative enthusiasm for French-style indicative planning. It

---

[4] We ignore agriculture, which was at the beginning and end of this period the biggest recipient of government money of any sector of the economy.

was a tripartite body whose objective was to raise growth to 4 per cent annum (from around 2.7 per cent) by 'concertation' between industry, unions, and government—that is the exchange of information, and exploration of the implications of faster growth, with an underlying belief that if everyone accepted that goal this would be nine-tenths of the way to achieving it (Leruez 1975, pp. 97–8). Neddy's impact very much depended on the Chancellor's willingness to take it seriously—its autonomy had as its other side a lack of statutory capacities, which meant its advice could be easily ignored if the Chancellor so decided. NEDO was dominated by its tripartite structure, and gave no new means of leverage over the economy. This is usually the reason given for its failure to engender the 4 per cent target (Shonfield 1965; Leruez ch. 5). This, of course, assumes that in principle governments have the knowledge and means to increase growth rates, which, as already noted, is hardly to be taken as read.

The accession of Labour in 1964 led to both a new enthusiasm for growth and new agencies for its increase. There was, most importantly, the DEA, as noted above. There was also the Ministry of Technology which fitted with the rhetoric of applying to industry the 'white-heat of technology'. Later the Labour government created the Industrial Reorganization Corporation, whose prime function was to encourage mergers, in the belief that international industrial competition could only be fought with much bigger firms (Hague and Wilkinson 1983).

Alongside these new institutions there continued the Board of Trade (merged with the Ministry of Technology in 1970 to form the Department of Trade and Industry), with its long-standing regulatory and overseas trade roles, but never promoted to a 'Ministry of Industry' in the sense of being a body with widespread powers to pursue a clear industrial strategy. The body which came closest to this was the DTI, after the Conservatives' move to more interventionist policies in 1972, leading to the 1972 Industry Act which gave very wide powers to government. But just as in the 1960s the period of the DEA (1964–9) was overshadowed by an even greater-than-usual dominance of policy-making by the balance of payments, so the newly powerful DTI's existence (and the 'dash for growth' it was supposed to pursue) was rapidly overshadowed by the search for an incomes policy and then by the oil crisis.

Doctrine

In retrospect the years of the long boom appear to be a period of calm in economic theory, between the bitter debates over Keynesianism in the 1930s and monetarism in the 1970s. This has a substantial element of truth, especially if the focus is on macro-economics, but requires some qualification.

Within macroeconomics in Britain there was a consolidation around what may be called a santized or conservative Keynesianism, in which unemployment was a special case (albeit an important one) in an economic system which would 'normally' find a full employment equilibrium. Keynesian macroeconomics were inte-grated into the neo-classical framework, creating a 'neo-classical synthesis'. In this the Keynesian system was represented in the IS/LM framework, which largely rid the system of its radical emphasis on the psychological instability of expectations in determining investment levels (Backhouse 1985, ch. 26; Moggridge 1976, Appendix).

At a more applied level there was a general adherence to the Phillips Curve, which suggested a simple trade-off between higher inflation and higher unemployment, and though based on historical statistics rather than theory, was seen as compatible with Keynesian demand-based theories of inflation. There was general but not unanimous resistance to any attempt to focus attention on the money supply as an important concern. This issue was debated with a considerable vigour in and around the Radcliffe Committee of 1959, whose conclusions embodied the famous argument that monetary policy should aim to affect the structure of interest rates by controlling the liquidity of the whole economy, rather than the supply of money (1959, paras. 980–4).

By the late 1960s the consensual Keynesian view was being challenged from at least two angles. On the one hand Clower (1965) and Leijonhufvud (1968) were reassessing Keynes from a broadly sympathetic viewpoint, arguing that his work had been too readily assimilated to the equilibrium framework of neo-classical economics, and arguing that Keynes basic thrust was an analysis of an economy where markets do not necessarily clear (Backhouse 1985, ch. 5). Roughly at the same time Friedman's long-standing attempts to revive and restate the quantity theory of money were added to by his own (1968) and Phelps (1967) work on the Phillips Curve. Broadly, this latter work argued that the traditional Phillips Curve mis-stated the long-run relation between inflation and unemployment; that in the long run the level of unemployment would be determined by real factors (notably the real wage); and that any inflation/unemployment trade-off could only be short-run and based on incorrect expectations of the inflation rate, and hence on incorrect perceptions of real wages.

These latter arguments obviously gained some credence from the rise in inflation and unemployment in the late 1960s, but in the long boom period their impact on economic theory (or policy) in Britain was very limited. Similarly, though for different reasons, economists' discussions of growth had little impact in that area which so concerned policy-makers in the 1960s. Whilst growth theory was a live issue in the 1950s and 1960s it was one of the most abstract areas of economics, where the gap between theory and policy was enormous.

There has thus been no shortage of ideas on the causes and remedies of low productivity growth. It has, however, been an area in which economic theory has provided little assistance, not least because it raises so many issues that are difficult to quantify; attitudes of entrepreneurs and workers, the effects of restrictive practices, the nature of the education system and so on. Most of the literature on growth theory, showing how an economy can converge towards a balanced growth path with an exogenously given rate of technical progress, has been of no assistance whatsoever (Backhouse 1985, p. 405).

This general picture of (qualified) theoretical consensus in Britain should not be taken to mean a consensus amongst economists on policy issues. On issues like the appropriate way to deal with inflation, the desirability of devaluation or entry into the Common Market, economists lived up to their disputatious reputation, as sardonically chronicled by Hutchison (1968; 1977, Appendix). On the other hand there was an apparent underlying policy consensus, that the primary aim of economic policy should be economic stability, above all full employment, which underlies much of the economists' discussion in this period (Cairncross 1971*b*, ch. 2).

Until the Labour government of 1964 the number of economists employed in government service was very small—less than 100 economists and statisticians all told in 1960, 'many fewer in relation to the size of the government service and its economic responsibilities than is thought proper in most Western countries' (Grove 1962, p. 113). Most of the economists were employed in the Economic Section, which was merged into the Treasury in 1953. The logic of this merger was that economists should be in the Department which by that date had clearly regained its dominance in the economic policy-making field. On the other hand it did mean there was no alternative source of economic advice to the Cabinet to that of the Treasury.

In a perhaps rather paradoxical way the number of economists in government multiplied in the 1960s, when the objective (or at least rhetoric) of policy focused on growth, on which topic economists had rather little to offer. This accession of economists was part of the Wilsonian drive to bring expertise and science to bear on problems, and followed the criticism of economic amateurism common amongst radicals in the 1950s. But the increase, however significant in the long run, was accompanied in the short run by substantial confusion. Until 1964 the Treasury's principal economic adviser was the only Government economist of any seniority (R. Hall from 1947 to 1961; A. Cairncross from 1961),[5] but after 1964 he was joined by a number of 'irregular' advisers at the highest advice-giving level. These came and went with great frequency, but the idea of political appointee economic advisers was firmly established (Brittan 1969, pp. 55–6; Coats 1981).

Perhaps the main impact of the rise in the number of economists (from about 20 in 1964 to nearly 400 by 1979) was less at the highest level of policy-making and more at the lower level of day-to-day discussion of economic issues in government departments, which in the 1950s was notable for extraordinary crudity (e.g. Henderson 1962). Certainly the increase in economic advice at the centre had not by 1973 achieved the dramatic improvements in economic performance that some of its rather more enthusiastic proponents naïvely hoped for.

---

[5] Both of these have written on the role of economic advisers. See Hall (1955, 1959); Cairncross (1971*a*), ch. 10.

Politics and Policies

Stop-Go

The picture of consensus on fundamentals amongst economists in the 1950s and 1960s may be also applied to the politicians, again with qualifications. In the early 1950s the term 'Butskellism' was coined to reflect the convergence of approaches between Gaitskell (Labour Chancellor 1950–1) and Butler (Tory Chancellor 1951–5).[6] Butler himself (1971, p. 160) wrote that 'Both of us, it is true, spoke the language of Keynesianism. But we spoke it with different accents and with differing emphasis.' This seems a fair judgement—agreement on fundamentals, disagreement on emphases.

The fundamentals may be described in the 1950s as consisting of an acceptance of the welfare state, of the boundaries between the public and private sectors (barring steel denationalization), of the importance of consensual approaches to economic management, and above all of the primacy of stability and full employment as policy objectives. Labour also broadly supported the attempt to re-establish the pound as a major international currency, though by the late 1950s it was writers on the centre-left who were usually the first to question this priority (e.g. Shonfield 1959).

The centre-piece of policy in the 1950s was demand management, and on this both parties accepted the central place of fiscal policy. The Conservatives did revive the use of monetary policy (Bank Rate), but in a minor, supporting role. They did not follow those on the right who urged a much more stringent use of monetary policy to deflate the economy. The monetary weapon was not allowed to compromise the basic commitment to a full-employment policy (Dow 1965, pp. 66–70).

The dual commitment to full employment and the strength of the pound meant that in the 1950s policy acquired what came to be called its 'stop–go' character. Stops came when the reserves fell to 'unacceptable' levels, goes followed when the deflation raised unemployment to an unacceptable level. (The threshold of 'unacceptable' tended to rise over time—Mosley 1984, pp. 93–

[6] *The Economist*, which coined the word, used it initially to argue that both men would use the same policies in the event of a slump (13 Feb. 1954, pp. 440–1).

Table 9.5   *Unemployment in Great Britain 1951–1973 (seasonally adjusted)*

Year	%	Year	%
1951	1.2	1963	2.5
1952	2.0	1964	1.6
1953	1.6	1965	1.4
1954	1.3	1966	1.5
1955	1.1	1967	2.4 (0.5m.)
1956	1.2	1968	2.4
1957	1.4	1969	2.5
1958	2.1	1970	2.5
1959	2.2	1971	3.3
1960	1.6	1972	3.7 (0.8m.)
1961	1.5	1973	2.6
1962	2.0		

Note: These figures are on the definition used prior to 1982, i.e. all those registering as unemployed, regardless of whether eligible for benefit.

Source: Department of Employment Gazette.

106). Thus the economy was 'fine-tuned' within fairly narrow limits, with policy being very active. Bank Rate was altered 24 times between 1951 and 1964, changes in hire purchase regulations came in most years, as did requests to banks to limit advances (Dow 1965, ch. 9; Kareken 1968). Fiscal changes were not confined to the annual budget, but were supplemented by mini-budgets, and in the 1960s by use of the regulator, which allowed variation of indirect taxes and national insurance contributions outside the annual budget (Dow 1965, ch. 7; Musgrave and Musgrave 1968).

Politically, this pattern of policy implied a close tie between the management of the national economy and the popularity of government. This opened up the possibility of government regulating the level of economic activity in order to gain political advantage. This was a possibility unlikely to be forsworn by parties involved in a close two-party competition, and in fact the 1950s offer the most unambiguous cases of expansionary pre-election budgets followed by post-election slow-downs; in the 1960s such stratagems were more difficult because of the tightening constraint of the balance of payments (Mosley 1984, pp. 183–90).

By the early 1960s stop-go was anathematized by both parties.

Fine-tuning was seen as clumsy and leading to exaggerated lurches in policy; it was also argued that it militated against a higher growth-rate by creating uncertainty amongst companies deciding an investment.

Dow, in the conclusion to his influential book, argued that: 'so far from counteracting such basic causes of instability [i.e. in exports and stocks] the influence of policy seems rather to have exaggerated their effects' (1965, pp. 391–2). This he ascribed to problems of measuring the potential output of the economy, the delay and complexities in the impact of policy, and the inadequacy of forecasting methods. Dow's conclusions did not go unchallenged; Bristow (1968) suggested policy over 1955–65 was slightly stabilizing, whilst Artis (1972) supported the Dow view of minor destabilization by policy for 1958–70 and 1965–70; Price (1978, p. 210) suggests that 'Despite the methodological and other misgivings attached to all tests of demand management there remains a consensus against a positive contribution to stability from budgetary policy.' However, as he also points out, the most striking characteristic of the discussion 'was the smallness of the effects either way (as well, indeed, as the smallness of the fluctuations to be offset)'.

The smallness of effects of policy means that the attacks on stop-go were in many ways 'much ado about nothing'. Even if policy worsened cyclical fluctuations, these fluctuations in Britain were small in historical context and rather less than those in other advanced countries at the time (Whiting 1976). This suggests it is difficult to argue that stop-go made a substantial contribution to Britain's poor growth-rate, however much particular features of those policies, perhaps especially hire purchase conditions, may have borne hard on some industries, notably consumer durables (Matthews 1971, pp. 25–35).

The fact that policy was aimed to offset small fluctuations in autonomous activity raises a profound question about the whole long-boom period. Was its character as a period of full employment much to do with policy at all? Many writers have ascribed the sharp contrast between the mass unemployment of the 1920s and 1930s and the full employment of the 1950s and 1960s to Keynesian-inspired policy. Stewart for example (1972, p. 188) argued that 'Britain and other Western countries have had full employment since the war because governments have been committed to full employment, and knew how to secure it.'

However such a view is, to say the least, contentious. In 1968 Matthews posed the question 'Why has Britain had Full Employment since the War?' and explicitly analysed the view that it was fiscal policy that had made the difference. He argued that such a view was implausible; fiscal stance was deflationary in this period, fiscal policy being changes in the size of the surplus (see Table 9.4). He argued that the reason post-war Britain had much higher employment than pre-war was largely due to a shift in the level of investment, probably little related to government policy. Whilst his article was not free from challenge (Stafford 1970), its general thrust on the limited importance of fiscal policy seems not to have been widely challenged (but see Schott 1982). As Cairncross (1981, p. 374) sums up the position: 'government never had to handle a situation in which full employment was in serious jeopardy . . . The techniques of demand management were shot through with Keynesian views; but demand management itself operated on buoyant market forces and even then only within narrow limits'.

Matthews' method was to use Keynesian analysis to provide a rather non-Keynesian answer to his initial question. His answer to that question in terms of a shift in investment levels is clearly central, but there are still further questions left about why investment was so high. Cairncross (1981, p. 373–4) has suggested that the Keynesian policy of cheap money may have helped spark off the initial post-war boom in investment, and this may have been partly sustained by government commitments to full employment. Matthews himself lays considerable emphasis on the technological possibilities opened up by the war, and the great backlog of investment in Britain, with low domestic investment since before 1914 (see also Matthews and Bowen 1989).

Non-Keynesian explanations of the full employment of this period have not been much in evidence. Real wage explanations look unpromising, given that the product wage rose considerably more than productivity across the war (Matthews *et al.* 1982, p. 171). Also the trend in the benefit-to-wage ratio would seem to run counter to making that a major explanation of the contrast between pre- and post-war unemployment (Metcalf *et al.* 1982; Benjamin and Kochin 1982).

The fact that domestic policy seems to have had rather little direct impact on full employment doesn't mean, of course, that policy was irrelevant. Policy after all could have substantially worsened the position (as it arguably did in the 1930s) if the periodic deflations to aid the balance of payments had not been reversed for unemployment reasons. More broadly, the commitment to, and (slow) movement towards, an open international economy helped Britain share in the dynamism of other economies, and in the 1950s and 1960s at least this openness probably had a net favourable outcome for British output and employment.

Growth

The 1960s were not characterized by stop-go to anything like the same degree as the 1950s—except before the election of 1963, 'stop' was much more in evidence than 'go'. This resulted from the long struggle first against devaluation and then to make it work, which lasted almost the whole of the Labour government's period in office. But this government, like the Conservatives in the early 1960s, had renounced stop-go, a renunciation mainly based on a new-found adherence to growth as a policy objective.

The idea of maximizing growth emerged strongly into public discussion in the mid-1950s, when Butler talked of doubling the standard of living in twenty or twenty-five years. This new policy concern may partly be seen as a natural follow-on to the success in creating full employment—growth was the logical next step to increase welfare. It was also stimulated by competition with the Soviet bloc; by the idea that it would reduce contention over distribution; and, more prosaically, by being seen as the way to solve the balance of payments problems (Arndt 1978; Tomlinson 1985, ch. 4).

Whilst the political commitment to raising growth was apparent from the mid-fifties, little was done to change policy in favour of it in that decade. In the 1956 White Paper on the *Economic Implications of Full Employment* (Cmd. 9725), for example, the emphasis was very much on reducing the obstacles to market forces raising the growth rate, rather than government being seen as having a positive role.

But from 1960/61 the government stance changed under the impact of a number of stimuli (Meadows 1978). International comparisons of growth showing Britain's poor relative performance were first widely published in the late 1950s. The Federation of British Industry adopted a much more pro-growth stance, and this was linked to a general belief that French-style indicative planning could help raise British growth, as it had (allegedly) helped the French rate. Planning lost some of its 1940s association with controls and restrictions, and became seen in a more positive light, as in the contemporary desire to plan public expenditure over a longer time-period (Cmd. 1432, 1961).

Thus it was that it was a Conservative government which first embraced the new rhetoric of planning. The main policy consequence of this was the creation of NEDC, whose rather limited role has already been noted. (A parallel creation was the National Incomes Commission—see below, section on Incomes Policy.) As Hare (1985, p. 33) has noted, it is not clear 'whether this represented a fundamental shift in views about the power of the government to influence the growth rate, or merely the need to be seen to act on an issue that was assuming political prominence'.

One of the most obvious weaknesses of the planning exercise by NEDC was that its projection of a growth rate of 4 per cent per annum for 1961–6 required a growth in exports of 5 per cent per annum, with no good reason to suggest why such an acceleration should take place. As Mitchell (1966, p. 133) suggests, this was typical of the plan, in that the figure was simply a working through of the quantitative implications of the initial 4 per cent 'target'. The central problem with this plan was that it did not identify the difficulties and constraints which prevented the growth rate being higher: 'It outlined a possible future without making clear what steps were required to ensure that we arrived there'. (Hare 1985, p. 35.)

The Labour Party, initially surprised by the Conservative planning initiative, soon made the running on the growth issue, making a plausible claim to be much more the natural party of planning than the Conservatives. The creation of the DEA followed, though NEDC was retained, especially because of its tripartite basis. Like the plan produced by NEDC, that from the DEA envisaged a rise in the growth rate (to 3.8 per cent per annum) without specifying the bottlenecks that such a rate of expansion was likely to create. Like the previous plan, that from the DEA relied predominantly on the idea that if investor confidence could be boosted by everyone agreeing on a faster rate of growth, that increase would be a kind of self-fulfilling prophecy. There was neither compulsion nor incentives for firms to do as the plan projected, so the parallel with French planning was fatally flawed. Finally, the plan, like that of 1961, had to project a wholly implausible rate of growth of exports in order to be coherent. It was this problem which was the immediate cause of its demise; the foreign exchange crisis of summer 1966 leading to deflation and the effective abandonment of the plan.

As Hare (1985, pp. 39–40) summarizes,

Thus the plan was sacrificed to the exigencies of short-term macroeconomic policy, though even if it had not been it contained so little provision for implementation that it is hard to believe it could have had much impact on the economy . . . The National Plan hardly began the task of changing the real constraints facing the economy, and its rapid failure, following a period of quite unjustified optimism, left planning in Britain discredited for many years.

The 'stop' which preceded the devaluation of 1967 was intensified after that year in order to 'make room' for the export capacity required for devaluation to succeed. The 1968 budget was the most deflationary since the war, resulting in a negative PSBR for two years, and aiding a radical turn-round in the balance of payments (Blackaby 1978, pp. 44–52). Thus the decade which had begun with so much talk of the need to shift from short-term concern with the balance of payments to the long-term problem of growth, ended with the sharpest turn to financial orthodoxy for over 30 years. In its own terms this policy was a success, but it was little related to any attempt to make the economy grow faster.

The Conservative government of 1970, like its predecessor, was strongly committed to raising the growth-rate. But the means this time were not to be planning, but economic freedom and administrative reform. This meant a repudiation of the dirigistic policies of Labour, including a withdrawal from industrial intervention and a repudiation of incomes policy. However, the initial period of Conservative government saw a sharp rise in both inflation and unemployment. The response to this was a substantial change of tack by the government which may be summed up as a 'dash for growth' (to reduce unemployment) and an incomes policy (to reduce inflation), coupled with allowing the pound to float to prevent the dash being halted by balance of payments problems. The main weapon used to bring this growth about was budgetary policy—this was intended to be a traditional 'go' policy, but one not to be deflected by balance of payments considerations.

As far as growth and employment is concerned this 'dash' was a success. Growth of 5 per cent to the middle of 1973 was accompanied by a fall in unemployment to half a million. But the anti-inflationary aspect of the policy was a complete failure. Negotiations on a voluntary incomes policy quickly broke down, and in November 1972 a statutory policy was imposed. In the autumn of 1973 the breakdown of this policy and confrontation with the miners coincided with the sharp rise in oil prices, and the end of the long boom. The government fell in February 1974 (Blackaby 1978, pp. 67–76).

The dash for growth in 1972–4 had a substantial impact on economic policy discussion in Britain. For many Conservatives it was seen to have proved the incapacity of Keynesian policies to generate sustainable non-inflationary real growth (Pringle 1977; Joseph 1975). On the other hand, the failure of the policy may be ascribed to its excessive rapidity, which was bound to lead to inflationary pressure (Blackaby 1979*a*). Whatever the case, the Conservative government of 1979 was to cite this period as a failure of the Keynesian consensus, demonstrating the need for its new departure in economic policy.

Industrial Policy

The fifties in Britain were not characterized by the rhetoric or reality of a strategic industrial policy. Government was not innocent of intervention in industry, but most of those interventions were *ad hoc* rather than strategically oriented, and had a low priority in economic policy.

After 1952 de-control was pursued vigorously—most raw material allocations, building controls, and price restrictions were abolished by 1954, along with consumer rationing. In this the Conservatives followed the pattern set by Labour, until interrupted by the Korean War. The Suez crisis likewise saw minor reversals of the trend, notably in oil, but the underlying movement was unambiguous. Development Councils, of which so much had initially been hoped under Labour, were abolished in the face of employer resistance, except that in cotton. Regional Policy, as embodied in the Distribution of Industry Act of 1945 and the Town and Country Planning Act of 1947, was very much reduced in effect in the mid-1950s. By then Industrial Development

Certificates, used to control industrial building in the prosperous areas, became a formality; from 1956 no new factories in development areas were to be built with subsidy. This change in one of the basic commitments of the full employment policies of 1944 reflected the fact that localized unemployment almost disappeared in the mid-fifties. When that unemployment re-emerged in 1958 regional policy too revived, and a new Employment Act was passed in 1960 (Parson 1986, ch. 5).

This general trend towards disengagement should not be exaggerated, but it is right to say that most industrial intervention in this period was 'miscellaneous' and specific. This description would cover decisions like those to build two new steel strip mills in Wales and Scotland (a highly politicized decision), and, in the face of growing Commonwealth imports, to aid the rationalization of the cotton industry by the Cotton Industry Act of 1959. The government also acted to rationalize the aircraft industry into a small number of airframe and engine producers (Henderson 1962, pp. 347–69).

These interventions were in the private sector of industry. But of course the Conservative government inherited a very substantial nationalized sector, which it did not attempt to shift back to private hands except for part of road haulage and iron and steel. In iron and steel a curious situation arose whereby the government was committed to private ownership, but vested much of the control of the industry in an Iron and Steel Board of public appointees, with little role for the Ministries (Henderson 1962, pp. 355–60).

In the public sector it would be difficult to argue that a clear pattern of policy emerged in the 1950s. The Conservatives applied a general bias towards competition and decentralization, but to some degree this was cut across by periodic reorganization of the industries as recommended by various committees of enquiry. Certain priorities were pursued—notably to increase coal production. Other industries suffered sharp reversals of fate—notably the railways where net disinvestment until the mid-1950s was followed by a grandiose modernization plan.

The nationalized industries were affected by stop-go policies in which variations (usually cuts) in public-sector investment played a small but not insignificant role. Equally, macroeconomic considerations led to the holding down of prices below those likely to have been set on purely commercial grounds. As one (critical) account of government policy in this period argued, events in the 1950s 'show the difficulty of maintaining long-term investment and output plans for the nationalized sector, when government decisions are changed from month to month on the basis of short-term reappraisals of the current situation, which are almost as volatile as stock exchange prices' (Munby 1962, p. 389).

In sum, government policy on the nationalized industries in the 1950s was characterized by plenty of activity but little sense of system or strategy. In several cases the monopolistic character of the industries was being undermined by changing consumption patterns, but the industries were neither allowed to respond on a purely commercial basis, nor given clear responsibilities beyond the commercial. Whilst the quality of debate improved with the establishment of the Select Committee on Nationalized Industries in 1956, by and large policy was '*ad hoc* and amateurish' (Munby 1962, p. 428).

Much of industrial policy in the 1960s followed from the commitment to growth and the institutions that commitment spawned, as already discussed. Some of this new effort raised possible conflicts with existing policies. For example, the IRC, with its explicit remit to rationalize, raised the question of compatibility of such a policy with monopoly policy. This latter policy was in fact extended in the 1965 Monopolies and Mergers Act to cover not only mergers which created monopoly, but mergers *per se* if they were large enough. In the ten years prior to that Act only seven reports were produced, and the new Act was supposed to bring a toughening of policy. But what followed was vacillation as fears about market power competed with the 'big is best' approach of the IRC. Clear lines of policy did not emerge: 'while it is not necessarily inconsistent to favour some mergers whilst forbidding others, reasonably explicit criteria are needed to distinguish them' (Mottershead 1978).

Regional policy was substantially expanded in the 1960s. Cash grants were introduced in 1963 on both plant and machinery and buildings, in addition to 100 per cent initial allowances for the former. Differential grants to high unemployment areas were offered when investment grants were later generalized to the whole country. In 1970 there was a switch to tax allowances, but in 1972 cash grants were reintroduced to make sure efficient but not very profitable firms benefited from regional aid (Brown 1972). The impact of these policies was considerable, though they failed to eliminate regional disparities in unemployment, which have remained significant and with substantially the same pattern as developed in the 1930s (Moore and Rhodes 1973).

Whilst the DEA, Mintech, and the IRC were intended to encourage economic success and growth, industrial policy also had to deal with the sufferers from industrial change and competition, which increased in the 1960s with the growth of world trade and import penetration. This was apparent in industries like shipbuilding and cotton, where crisis interventions were substantial. Shipbuilding received £153m. in subsidies between 1960 and 1974, textile £32m.[7] (Mottershead 1978, p. 478). In these years government's desire to grow faster and the political costs of industrial decline drew governments deeper into the industrial field. This was strikingly so with the 1970 Conservative government, which came to power abjuring such interventionism, but felt compelled to engage in big rescue operations like Rolls Royce and Upper Clyde Shipbuilders, and, after the U-turn of 1972, passed an Industry Act with striking power of intervention, aimed at renewing British industry's vigour. Many commentators have been sceptical of the benefits of such interventions, but as Mottershead (1978, p. 478) suggests, there is a compelling political logic: 'governments have found it progressively harder to refuse appeals for help, because of the growing tendency for the short-comings of industry to be seen as failure of government policy'.

Policy on nationalized industries in the 1960s showed much more sense of direction than in the 1950s. Governments in the 1950s had added little to the initial injunctions of the nationalization statutes for the industries to pay their way over a period of years. In the 1960s two White Papers promulgated much clearer guidelines.

The 1961 White Paper focused on the financial objectives of the industries, and said that they should each have financial targets which would involve earning sufficient revenue to cover current costs, depreciation, and at least some contribution to capital expansion. Social objectives should be clarified and properly costed. The proposals were largely implemented in the next few years, but the financial position of the industries, which had

---

[7] Though these sums were dwarfed by the £758m. spent on aerospace over the same period.

sparked off the White Paper, showed little improvement (Jones 1978, pp. 491–3).

By the time of the 1967 White Paper it was widely accepted that the 1961 focus on financial objectives had been too narrow. The new framework paid most attention to investment criteria and pricing policy. On the first it proposed discounted cash-flow techniques, with a test rate of discount to determine whether a project should proceed. On prices, it proposed long-term marginal cost pricing and that cross-subsidization should be minimized. Efficiency improvement was also emphasized as a crucial objective. The basic aim of the policy remained that of improving the financial performance of nationalized industries in order to reduce the level of exchequer financing.

The 1967 approach did achieve some success in increasing the industries' self-financing in the late 1960s, but this trend was reversed in the early 1970s (Jones 1978, p. 506). The main reason for the failure of the policy was the continuing subordination of the industries to macroeconomic policy—above all holding down their prices, as part of anti-inflationary policy. Between 1971 and 1974 such restraints may have deprived the industries of £450m. in revenue (p. 511).

Financial performance is not the same as efficiency. The efficiency record of the nationalized industries in this period was quite good in comparison with other industries (Pryke 1971), albeit substantially because of the rather paradoxical 'success' of the coal and railway industries in shedding vast amounts of labour. But government policy was centrally concerned with finance not efficiency, and here policy was fundamentally contradictory. The industries were encouraged to act 'commercially' but were in the front line in government's attempts to regulate the macroeconomy. In sum, policy on the nationalized industries in the 1960s and early 1970s 'achieved only a limited success in its objectives; the main reasons are lack of clarity in the aims, limitations in the instruments of control and conflicts with other objectives of government policy' (Jones 1978, p. 513).

Inflation and Incomes Policy

Inflation was of growing significance as a policy concern almost throughout the long boom. Britain's record on this front was no

Table 9.6 *Inflation in the Long Boom* (average % p.a. increase in consumer prices)

	UK	France	W. Germany	Italy	USA	Japan
1951–73	4.4	5.1	2.7	4.0	2.7	5.3
1951–60	3.5	5.8	1.9	3.0	2.1	4.1
1960–73	4.7	4.5	3.2	4.5	3.1	6.0

Source: Matthews and Bowen (1989).

worse than most OECD countries for the period as a whole, but showed a relative deterioration from the 1960s (Table 9.6).

Throughout this period the predominant view in policy-making circles was that inflation should be discussed largely in relation to the impact of full employment on wage bargaining. Such a view in turn rested on both a political and an economic argument. The political (and most important) point was that full employment should be treated as inviolable, and therefore any attempt to reduce inflation by substantial increases in unemployment was to be rejected. The economic argument was that inflation was basically 'cost-push' rather than 'demand-pull', and therefore policy should focus on controlling wage costs.

As always there were many cross-currents in the arguments surrounding policy, but broadly we can say that Keynesians supported cost-push versions of the causes of inflation—partly because they put such a high priority on maintaining full employment. Those who later came to be called monetarists tended to favour 'demand-pull' explanations of inflation, and saw monetary weapons as the most important policy instrument. For most of this period Keynesians were in the ascendancy, and incomes policy was the usually favoured instrument of inflation control. But this began to be undermined as inflation increased and the level of 'politically tolerable' unemployment was found to be higher than had came to be believed in the 1950s.

The Korean War, with its impact on commodity prices, caused a sharp outbreak of inflation, but a temporary one, and by 1954 the inflation rate was down to 1 per cent. However the pre-1955 General Election boost to demand again brought an upward boost to prices. This stimulated the government to produce a White Paper on *The Economic Implications of Full Employment* (Cmd.

9725) in 1956, which set out the dilemmas for anti-inflationary policy for much of the long boom period:

In order to maintain full employment the Government must ensure that the level of demand for goods and services is high and rises steadily as productive capacity grows. This means a strong demand for labour, and good opportunities to sell goods and services profitably. In these conditions, it is open to employees to insist on large wage increases, and it is possible for employers to grant them and pass the cost to the consumer, so maintaining their profit margin. This is the danger which confronts the country. If the prosperous economic conditions necessary to maintain full employment are exploited . . . price stability and full employment become incompatible (paras. 10–11).

However the White Paper proposed no new instruments of policy to deal with the problem, but looked to self-restraint in wage and profit setting plus greater productivity as the only viable solution. The policy consequence was then largely one of exhortation, aimed primarily at the trade union movement.

The attitude of the trade union movement to incomes policy can only be understood in the context of its commitment to voluntarism in industrial relations and to free collective bargaining. Voluntarism meant a hostility to any legal intervention in industrial relations, an attitude reflecting both a philosophical bent to *laissez faire* (Flanders 1970, p. 101; Currie 1979) and a more pragmatic view of the largely hostile attitudes of the judiciary to the trade union movement. Adherence to free collective bargaining follows on from this voluntarism, plus the beliefs that such bargaining is both a fundamental right in a free society, and the *raison d'être* of trade-unionism (TUC 1967, paras. 90, 174–5).

Thus throughout this period attempts at incomes policies pitched these basic beliefs against the claims by government that incomes policies were the only alternative to even worse policies of deflation and unemployment. Such divergent pressures usually led to support for such policies only on a temporary, crisis-induced basis and under Labour governments, where the unions expected to exchange their bargaining rights for other policy goals.

The tensions between monetary deflation and incomes-policy approaches to inflation surfaced in 1957 when the Conservative government founded the (Cohen) Council on Prices, Productivity, and Incomes (Three Wise Men) to examine the issue. The first Report of this Council supported the deflationary measures introduced by the Chancellor, Thorneycroft, in September of that year (see further below). But this policy was quickly reversed in January 1958 when the Cabinet became worried by rising unemployment, and Thorneycroft and his supporters (Powell and Birch) resigned. The Report of the Cohen Council also provoked enormous hostility from many economists, politicians, and the unions (Jones 1987, pp. 54–6).

These events led the Conservatives, for the rest of their period in office, to focus on trying to moderate pay increases. In 1961 this led to a 'pay pause' for government employees and those covered by wage councils, which was hoped to set the pattern for the private sector—with some such effect, albeit briefly. This was followed by attempts to gain trade-union agreement on such a policy, first through the National Income Commission ('Nicky') and later through Neddy. Whilst some leaders of the TUC were willing to go down this road, the rank-and-file view expressed through the TUC conference refused any co-operation (Jones 1987, pp. 56–65).

The early days of the 1964 Labour government also saw some hope that an agreement between the TUC and government would be possible, within the framework of the newly created National Board for Prices and Incomes. In April 1965 the desire to keep a Labour government in power, the feared alternatives of deflation, and the rather loose framework of the policy persuaded the TUC to agree to a voluntary incomes policy. But this was ineffective, and in 1966 the 'stop' policy was accompanied by a statutory freeze and a period of 'severe restraint', a policy opposed by the TUC. The wage pressure which re-emerged after the freeze pushed the Labour government on to a new tack—the reduction of union powers in the (inappropriately) entitled proposals of *In Place of Strife*. These proposals, which followed the analysis of the Donovan Commission,[8] would have provided the government with the right to call a 28-day cooling-off period when an unofficial strike was called, and to require a ballot before a strike was deemed official. These proposals were not proceeded with in the face of opposition from unions, many Labour MPs, and Cabinet Ministers (Jones 1987, ch. 6).

---

[8] The Donovan Commission focused on the unofficial, plant-level bargaining pattern that had grown up alongside the official, company- and national-level system (Donovan 1968).

A similar attempt to legislate on union powers rather than try for an agreement with them was followed by the Conservative government after 1970. The Industrial Relations Act reached the statute book in 1971, but was largely inoperative in the face of union opposition and employers' unwillingness to provoke trouble by invoking its powers. The 'dash for growth' after 1972 brought another attempt at agreement with unions, followed by a statutory policy. This policy laid the way open to the clash with the mineworkers and the demise of the Heath government (Jones 1987, ch. 7).

Overall the attempts at incomes policy in this period were not successful. Inflation seems to have been slowed for short periods during statutory 'freezes', and this may have helped in a crisis, but there was then a clear catching-up process (Henry and Ormerod 1978). The basic problems were clearly a lack of consistent political commitment to such policies, a very strong commitment to voluntarism and free collective bargaining, a lack of 'peak associations' of unions and employers willing and able to deliver their members' support for such policies. In the absence of these conditions, incomes policies became largely just another part of the 'stop' of the stop-go pattern of policy,[9] to be used in a crisis and then given up.

Attempts to deflate to reduce inflation ran up against the fundamental commitment to full employment. Deflation was of course pursued—the 'stop' part of the cycle—but quickly reversed as unemployment mounted. Most 'stops' were directly in response to balance of payments difficulties, though under a fixed exchange-rate system, excessive inflation shows itself in balance of payments difficulties. The 'stop' phase of the policy cycle was of course composed of both fiscal and monetary measures, but proponents of deflationary method of controlling inflation tended to focus on monetary measures. Partly this arose from a widespread view that monetary measures were more important in curtailing booms than inaugurating them. Much more controversially, it arose from the attachment of proponents of deflation to the view that inflation was predominantly a monetary phenomenon, to be curtailed by monetary means, especially control of the money supply.

The latter approach emerged most clearly in policy in 1957. For

[9] Heath's incomes policy was exceptional for being very much part of a 'go' phase of policy.

the first time domestic inflation rather than external pressures were the direct stimulant to monetary restriction, and in this restriction Thorneycroft, the Chancellor, focused attention on the need to control the quantity of money (Kennedy 1962; Dow 1965, pp. 252–61). However, as already noted, this deflationary policy was quickly reversed and for the next decade, whilst deflation was pursued at times, the money supply figured little in policy—though not everyone accepted the Radcliffe Committee's dismissal of its importance (Croome and Johnson 1970).

The money supply re-emerged into policy-making in November 1967 with the Letter of Intent to the IMF from the Labour government. Partly because of the views of the IMF, partly because of the perceived failure of fiscal policy to have the desired deflationary effects, this letter proposed targets for the money supply as a policy instrument. This was followed in May 1969 by a second similar letter, laying out targets for Domestic Credit Expansion, a composite of the domestic money supply and the external balance. Whilst this concept lost ground when the balance of payments improved sharply in 1971, so making it less appropriate, attention to the money supply was never again wholly to disappear, though attention did not amount to anything like a policy of attempted control of the same magnitude. Indeed the Conservative government's policies stimulated a very substantial increase in monetary growth. Partly this resulted from Competition and Credit Control, 1971, which changed the method of monetary control from a focus on lending, typical of the 1960s, to control of the reserves of the banking system (with the implication that lending would be 'rationed by price' i.e. by higher interest rates). It also resulted from the deliberate attempt to go for growth by all means possible from 1972. The growth of the money supply (M3) over this period reached 28 per cent in both 1972 and 1973, but the eventual policy response (in late 1973) was in terms of lending restrictions rather than direct control of the money supply. No targets for this existed between 1971 and 1976 (Tew 1978, pp. 246–57).

Rising inflation, apparent from the late 1960s, brought a new emphasis on monetary instruments. But for most of the long boom the response to the concern with inflation was mainly incomes policies rather than monetary controls. For the period as a whole 'it seems unlikely that monetary policy did very much for good or bad in this period; it did not do very much at all, and was not supposed to' (Artis 1978, p. 303).

Conclusions

The most striking and significant characteristic of the long boom period was the low level of unemployment—few in the 1940s would have predicted that such a low level would have been possible for so long. Slowly in the 1950s this altered policy-makers' perceptions of what was possible and desirable in economic policy: 'high employment has come to be regarded almost as a law of nature; certainly a serious failure to maintain it is one which no government could expect or deserve to survive . . . the domestic threats of poverty and unemployment have been replaced by the threat of inflation' (Rowan 1960, pp. 21, 5).

In retrospect we know that full employment was no law of nature, and government commitment to that end more fragile than many believed in the 1950s and 1960s. The maintenance of full employment for most of this time in fact was unproblematic because it involved few costs. It did not require 'unsound' finance, but was compatible with a surplus on the current budget. And whilst it imparted an inflationary bias to the economy, this was minor—indeed for much of the time Britain's inflation was no higher than countries like the USA where unemployment was much higher. To put the point another way, whilst no one doubts the commitment of governments at the time to full employment, their pursuit of this was rendered easy by the favourable world conditions of the time. High investment, stable exchange rates, and rapidly growing international trade, meant that full employment could be delivered almost painlessly.

In the late 1960s these conditions began to deteriorate. The boom began to run out of steam, the exchange-rate regime came under pressure, inflation accelerated. In these conditions full employment was no longer an easy option, but one whose attainment would require painful adjustments in traditional procedures. At this point the post-war ethos dependent on full employment started to evaporate.

Britain's policy dilemmas in this period were worsened by two features, one passing, one permanent. The passing one was the commitment to restoring sterling's role as an international currency, and the way this led to a focus on the strength of the pound as a policy objective, coupled with over-commitments to 'great power' overseas expenditure. But however absurd and damaging this posture may have been it was clearly in retreat by the late 1960s. Indeed, the worsening economic position at the end of that decade led to the Basle Agreement of 1968 on the sterling balances, and the retreat from East of Suez in the same year, symbolic of the end to this great power dream.

Much more intractable was slow growth—basically a problem of low industrial productivity. The reasons for this will probably be debated as long as economic historians draw breath. But (with hindsight) it is striking how little this problem was seriously investigated by policy-makers in the long-boom period. Slow growth was an important concern from the mid-1950s, but it cannot be said that the sophistication of the analysis of the problem matched the intensity of concern. Simplistic explanations tended to dominate—too low investment, poor industrial relations— and simple policy answers pursued—e.g. industrial concentration, investment grants. Industrial policy became more and more important over the period, but was not crowned with much success.

It may be argued that policy in any case could do little to help— that Britain's problems were so deeply embedded in the social system as to be almost beyond alteration (e.g. Denison 1968). This is surely too pessimistic a conclusion. Recent analyses of Britain's industrial decline (Williams *et al.* 1983; K. Smith 1984; Elbaum and Lazonick 1987), whilst not suggesting any panaceas, do suggest a range of issues over which governments could or did exercise considerable powers. For example the ludicrous concentration of Britains R. & D. resources on nuclear power, military electronics, and aircraft (Smith 1984, ch. 4) was very much a consequence of government policy. The counter-productive merger boom of the 1960s (Williams *et al.*, ch. 6) was not beyond the reach of government, likewise the relation between the City and industry (Elbaum and Lazonick 1987, ch. 9) was not given in Heaven. In other words, there was an 'agenda' of potential reform that could have made a difference, but it was an agenda which scarcely came to light in this period.

Further Reading

Alford, B. W. E. (1988): *British Economic Performance 1945–1975*, London.

Beckerman, W., ed. (1972): *The Labour Government's Economic Record 1964–1970*, London.

Blackaby, F., ed. (1978): *British Economic Policy 1960–1974*, Cambridge.

Brittan, S. (1969): *Steering the Economy*, London.

Cairncross, A., ed. (1971a): *Britain's Economic Prospects Reconsidered*, London.

Caves, R. E., ed. (1968): *Britain's Economic Prospects*, Washington.

Dow, J. C. R. (1965): *The Management of the British Economy 1945–1960*, Cambridge.

Tomlinson, J. (1985): *British Macroeconomic Policy Since 1940*, London.

Van der Wee, H. (1987): *Prosperity and Upheaval: The World Economy 1945–1980*, Harmondsworth, chs. 2, 7, 8, 9, 11.

Worswick, G. D. N., and Ady, P. H., eds. (1962): *The British Economy in the 1950s*, Oxford.

10

1973–1979: From Crisis to Crisis

THE long boom was already breaking up in the late 1960s and early 1970s, but the OPEC oil price rise (from $3.45 to $11.58 per barrel at the end of 1973) heralded the arrival of a wholly new phase in post-war British policy. Whilst the OPEC price rise was far from the only cause of the problems of the 1970s, its effects were serious and widespread. For Britain it meant a sharp deterioration in the trade balance (see Table 10.2) and hence a substantial deflationary pressure, which was reinforced by the effects on exports of similar effects in other oil-importing countries. In addition, the generality of oil use in the economy imparted a sharp upward twist to prices. This latter effect came on top of a pre-existing sudden upward movement in commodity prices in general, brought about by the simultaneous and rapid expansion of demand in the advanced industrial countries in the early 1970s.[1] The resulting 'stagflation' posed economic policy-makers with unprecedented problems and turned the 1970s into a decade of crisis.

Institutions

The Exchange Rate

The break-up of the Bretton Woods system pre-dated the oil crisis. Following the unilateral US decision to end the convertibility of the dollar into gold in August 1971, there followed two years of negotiations between the major financial powers which failed to provide the basis for a new system. By the Smithsonian agreement of December 1971 most major industrial countries revalued their

[1] Winters (1987) suggests that in the long run primary product prices are independent of demand in the advanced industrial (OECD) countries. But in the short run there may be very large effects, with prices rising by up to 2 per cent for every 1 per cent increase in industrial production.

currencies against the dollar, but this was seen by most as only tinkering with the problem. In 1972 the six original EEC members linked their currencies to each other, within the broader band of the Smithsonian parities, creating the 'snake in the tunnel'. Britain was briefly a member, but left in June 1972 in the context of the Heath/Barber 'dash for growth'. For the whole of the 1973–9 period the pound was to float, a position that became general to most of the world's currencies in 1973/4 (Van der Wee 1987, ch. 12).

When the British government announced, in June 1972, that the exchange rate would not be allowed to stand in the way of growth, this obviously meant an expectation that the pound would fall. This indeed happened—the rate fell more or less continuously from June 1972 to November 1976 (Table 10.1). There was a particularly sharp fall in 1976, when the pound's effective rate went from 72.8 in January to 59.1 in November. This pattern was reversed after 1976, and for approximately two years the rate was stable, before beginning to rise sharply from January 1979.

Although the pound was floating, this was very much a 'dirty' float; the authorities intervened substantially. The obvious evidence of the direction of this intervention is the change in the foreign currency reserves held by the authorities. Between 1974 and 1976, annual reserve losses of $1.3b. were incurred to prevent an even more rapid slide of the exchange rate, whilst in 1977 reserves shot up by an unprecedented $16.4b. in attempting to hold the pound down (Green and Metcalfe 1986, p. 168).

Whilst policy-makers intervened in the exchange market their capacity to effect the rate was limited. The 1976 reversal of trend,

Table 10.1   *Effective Exchange Rate for the £ 1972–1979* (1975 = 100)

Year	Rate	Year	Rate
1973	111.8	1977	81.2
1974	108.3	1978	81.5
1975	100.0	1979	87.3
1976	85.7		

Note: The effective exchange rate measures the value of the pound relative to a basket of currencies, weighted according to their importance in international trade.
Source: *Economic Trends Annual Supplement*, 1987.

whilst partly a response to changes in British policy in that year, also reflected a change in financial sentiment about the British economy. Equally, the attempt to hold down the rate was abandoned in 1978 in the face of the strength of market pressures in favour of sterling (see below).

Short-term capital flows have always played a substantial part in British policies on the exchange rate and the balance of payments. But in the 1970s this part of the foreign exchange market became very much more important in determining the exchange rate. This reflected both the long-term trend towards increasing inter-nationalization of world capital markets, and more short-term factors like the 'recycling' of OPEC oil revenues back to Western European financial centres. Capital movement related to direct investment by multinationals was very much less important in this period because, with exchange control, most of such investment was financed either by ploughed-back profits or borrowing in the country where the investment took place.

This is not to say the current account was irrelevant to the exchange rate. This account did see an enormous deterioration as the result of rises in commodity and oil prices coupled with the effects of the boom of 1972–4 (Table 10.2). These figures should

Table 10.2   *The Balance of Payments 1972–1979* (£m.)

	Current balance			Capital transactions	Balance for official financing*
	Visible	Invisible	Total		
1972	−761	+937	+176	−684	−1,265
1973	−2,586	+1,530	−1,056	+166	−771
1974	−5,350	+1,971	−3,379	+1,595	−1,646
1975	−3,333	+1,659	−1,674	+121	−1,465
1976	−3,927	+2,811	−1,116	−3,137	−3,628
1977	−2,279	+1,995	−284	+4,460	+7,362
1978	−1,546	+2,166	+620	−3,518	−1,126
1979	−3,404	+1,541	−1,863	+1,170	+1,710

* Reflects inclusion of balancing item, which was very large in many of these years.

Source: *UK Balance of Payments (Pink Book)*.

be compared with an average visible deficit of £191m. in the preceding years, 1968–71, and an average current balance of £552m. in the same period. However, it is evident from the figures that the current account position was improving after 1974, and that the downward pressure on the exchange rate in 1976 was mainly due to capital outflow.

This outflow caused a major crisis in British policy-making. It seems clear that the initial fall in the pound in that year was triggered by knowledge that the Treasury was keen to see a further fall in the exchange rate to maintain trade competitiveness (e.g. Pliatzky 1984, p. 143). But this downward adjustment got entirely out of the authorities control, and the government had to have recourse to foreign borrowing to try and support the pound. The first borrowings ($5.3b. in June 1976) were from a consortium of central banks, but this was quickly followed by recourse to the IMF. Even before this borrowing had taken place it had become clear that the level of public spending and borrowing were key indicators as far as the financial markets were concerned. Thus the government set about a politically highly charged process of cuts in public expenditure in order to appease financial markets—with obvious parallels to the events of 1931. The approach to the IMF was bound to lead to a loan with conditions, as Britain's unconditional tranche of borrowing had been taken up in 1975. In the event these conditions focused on a reduction in the Public Sector Borrowing Requirement, and the final agreement was a loan of $3.9b. in return for public expenditure cuts of £1.5b. in 1977/8 and 1978/9 (Pliatzky 1984, pp. 142–56; the whole issue of public expenditure and borrowing is discussed more fully in The Public Sector below).

This episode marked the low point in the pound's fortunes, and from late 1976 the pressure was upwards. As already noted, for two years this was offset by substantial intervention by the authorities, aimed at maintaining competitiveness. But this policy was abandoned in late 1977, as the inflow of short-term capital could only be offset by British sales of sterling to purchase foreign currencies, a policy which added unacceptably to the growth of the money supply. The rise in the exchange rate towards the end of this period reflected a number of factors, but probably most of all the effects of North Sea oil, which not only directly improved the current balance and encouraged capital inflow to exploit the resource, but also increased confidence about the future of the pound. This appreciation of the pound went against the purchasing parity theory of the exchange rate; the view that the value of a currency will reflect the inflation rate of a country in comparison with the inflation rate in the countries it trades with. In this period British inflation, though falling most of the time, was faster than in most OECD countries. This 'deviation' reflects the fact that the purchasing power parity theory essentially concerns itself with the current account of the balance of payments, whilst in this period capital flows were more important in determining the level of the pound.

Overall, the period 1972–9 revealed how vulnerable governments had become to changes in financial market sentiment. This was true for the market in government debt as well as that in foreign exchange—but similar movements in 'confidence' tended to appear in both markets. Such problems had always existed for Labour governments, with the exception of 1945–51, when controls were pervasive and powerful enough to largely prevent confidence having much influence. But in the 1970s these problems were compounded by the instability of the world economy, which both manifested itself in, and was probably exacerbated by, floating exchange rates. In 1973 the Bank of England had stated the objective of exchange-rate policy as being 'not to oppose any well-defined trend but merely to smooth excessive fluctuations' (Bank of England 1973, p. 21). This posture reflected a recognition of necessity, a recognition of the weakness of government in the foreign exchange market, and therefore a substantial weakening of the capacity of national policy to manage the economy. However, by the end of the period there was little sign of disillusion with the floating exchange-rate regime, and this was symbolized by Britain's spurning membership of the European Monetary System at its creation in 1979 (Van der Wee 1987, pp. 504–6).

The Trade Regime

During this period Britain's trade position was dominated by the price of commodities and oil. The terms of trade underwent a sharp deterioration (i.e. a given volume of imports cost more in terms of exports) from 1972. In that year the index number for the terms of trade was 106, but by 1974 had fallen to 82 (1980 = 100).

Other things being equal this meant a fall in living standards in Britain, and similarly the growth of oil production would move the position in the opposite direction. The mechanism for bringing these shifts about would be the exchange rate, though, as stressed above, this by no means closely mirrored developments on the current account.

In the context of policy, these fluctuations in living standards have to be seen as an almost unavoidable facet of the economy in this period. Government could (perhaps) mitigate the effects but could not prevent them entirely. Hence this period saw (in post-war terms) an unprecedented cycle in living standards—a sharp fall, and then a sharp revival, though 'sharp' has to be seen in the context of expectations of continous year-by-year increases in the standard of living.

Table 10.3   *Standard of Living 1972–1979* (£ per caput at 1980 prices)

	GDP	Consumers' expenditure	Personal disposable income
1972	3,903	2,165	2,402
1973	3,331	2,271	2,561
1974	3,307	2,238	2,540
1975	3,288	2,226	2,549
1976	3,412	2,233	2,536
1977	3,452	2,223	2,509
1978	3,552	2,346	2,682
1979	3,625	2,447	2,823

Source: Economic Trends Annual Supplement, 1987.

The crisis of the 1970s brought the most sustained attack on the assumptions of free trade since the 1930s. This was related to the view that the 1970s had seen the exacerbation of the long-term trend to 'de-industrialize' the British economy, a process which was making it impossible to combine full employment and balance of payments equilibrium (Singh 1977; Blackaby 1979*b*). Whilst no policy conclusion followed automatically from such a diagnosis, many who supported it proposed import controls as a solution. Most prominent in this were the Cambridge Economic Policy Group and Nicholas Kaldor, one of the government's top economic advisers. Unlike in previous episodes of this kind (in the early 1900s and 1930s) almost all the advocacy of the policy of protection came from the left.

Such arguments had little impact on policy. The reasons were the usual compound of the political and the economic. Politically any recourse to such measures would have cut across both the long-standing commitment to a liberal world economy (and the treaty agreements that embodied this commitment), and the short-term fears of the 1970s crisis inaugurating a round of beggar-my-neighbour trade policies. Equally, there was a strong belief that protectionism would encourage inefficiency rather than be the basis of industrial revival. Most economists argued that devaluation was a better way of improving international competitiveness, and that if policy aimed to help individual industries this was best done by subsidy rather than tariff or quota (Neild 1979; Hare 1980; Greenaway and Milner 1979).

Whilst no import controls as proposed by the CEPG were imposed in the 1970s, protectionism did manifest itself in those years, as it did in other countries. The major form of industrial protectionism was Voluntary Export Restraints—which by 1979 covered textiles, footwear, leather goods, television sets, cars, ball bearings, pottery, and tableware. The main countries affected by these measures were Japan, fast-growing, poor countries like Hong Kong, Singapore, Taiwan, and South Korea, plus India and Pakistan (Van der Wee 1987, pp. 386–90). Coupled with increased subsidies in industries like shipbuilding, these measures reflected the political weight of protectionism in government decisions, even if those governments maintained their public rhetoric of adherence to free trade. Paradoxically, perhaps, the protectionist pattern that evolved was much more geared to the defence of sectors in long-term decline than the proposals for general protection of the Cambridge group.

One reason for the focus of protection on Japan and relatively poor countries was of course Britain's membership of the EEC, which ruled out any such measures against most European competitors. As a consequence of that membership (from January 1973) the long-existing trend towards trading more extensively with other advanced, industrial, European countries has been accentuated (Fetherstone *et al.* 1979). By 1980 over 41 per cent of British imports were from the EEC, compared with 27 per cent in

1970. The comparable figures for exports were 29 and 43 per cent. The main relative declines in trade with Britain over this period were by the White Commonwealth and the non-oil developing countries (Green and Metcalfe 1986, p. 146).

Probably the main effect of Britain's membership of the EEC on trade patterns related to agriculture. Whereas the EEC external tariffs and quotas on industrial goods remained low in the 1970s, agricultural protectionism was, of course, very substantial. This didn't mean Britain immediately shifted its source of supply from outside to inside the EEC. But such a process was set in train, along with the stimulation of domestic output by high Community prices. Little was done in the 1970s to reform the Common Agricultural Policy, which lay behind these trends.

Britain's potential membership of the EEC was a major debate in the early years of the 1974 Labour government, but largely faded away after the referendum in 1975 with its 2 to 1 vote in favour of staying in. The economic consequences of this membership are extremely difficult to assess (Giavazzi 1987). Because of the diversion of import demand on to more expensive EEC sources the 'static' effects of membership on the balance of payments was broadly accepted to be unfavourable. Britain's continued high level of agricultural imports from outside the Community meant large payments to the EEC budget, whilst a relatively efficient domestic agriculture meant much less in payments from the EEC to Britain. The resulting large contribution to the budget was not a focus of attention until after 1979. Advocates of the EEC argued that these static costs of membership would be offset by dynamic gains from belonging to a large and fast-growing free market. Unfortunately, Britain's accession coincided with a slow-down in this growth. But Britain has largely shared in the growth that has been going—per caput GDP fell only slightly from 96 to 94 per cent of the EEC average between 1972 and 1983 (Green and Metcalfe 1986, p. 181).

The basic arguments for joining the Community were essentially political not economic, and it is on political grounds that the decision must be assessed. Nevertheless its implication for economic policy was to highlight the tension between national objectives and instruments of policy and the growing inter-nationalization of the economy. EEC membership meant a loss of formal economic capacity at the national level. The question remains how far that is to be offset by increased capacity *vis-à-vis* the private sector at the European level—not much of this latter was apparent in the 1970s.

The Budget

Public expenditure and public borrowing were at the heart of the economic policy controversies of the mid-1970s. Public expenditure was on a sharply accelerating trend under the Heath government, and this culminated under Labour in the fastest ever yearly increase between 1973/4 and 1974/5 (Table 10.4). This in turn stimulated a major change in the mechanisms for controlling public expenditure. This 'cash limit' system meant planning expenditure on the basis of cash sums, rather than in terms of outputs, where any increase in the cost of providing those outputs would be automatically financed. The change in control mechanisms reflected increased concern with the financial (taxation and borrowing) consequences of public expenditure, rather than its service provision aspect. This concern with the financial aspects of the public sector also focused attention on the Public Sector Borrowing Requirement—that part of public expenditure not financed by taxation.

The initial concern with public expenditure arose in the context of not only an acceleration of the level of that expenditure, but a

Table 10.4   *Public Expenditure 1972/3–1978/9*

	Public expenditure in 1981/2 prices (£b.)	Year on year change (%)	Ratio to GDP	Ratio of expenditure on goods and services to GDP
1972/3	89.4	6.6	38.5	—
1973/4	96.4	7.9	39.9	23½
1974/5	108.8	12.7	45.0	26
1975/6	109.3	0.5	45.4	27
1976/7	106.7	−2.4	43.0	25½
1977/8	99.3	−6.9	39.3	23½
1978/9	105.2	+6.0	40.4	23

Source: Pliatzky (1984), pp. 218, 220.

belief that much of the increase was unplanned. Godley (1975/6) argued that more than half the rise between 1970/1 and 1975/6 (amounting to £5b. in 1975 prices) could not be accounted for by announced policy changes. This led to the argument that public expenditure was 'out of control'. In fact a proportion of the increase was from unannounced policy changes, so did not reflect on the mechanisms of control. But a substantial proportion reflected the workings of the relative price effect, whereby the cost of inputs of the public sector rose faster than the inputs of the economy as a whole, so the public sector required more resources just to stand still. This was a particularly potent force in 1971/2 to 1973/4 with the land and property boom and its impact on public-sector building. Perhaps £1.75b. of Godley's £5b. could be accounted for in this way (Heald 1983, pp. 177–86; Treasury 1975/6).

The controversy over public expenditure in 1975/6 partly reflected the inadequacies of the PESC system as a means of control, especially in circumstances of inflation. PESC planned public expenditure in 'volume' terms and in relation to expected future GDP. Expenditure plans were automatically revalued with the rise in the price index, so that expenditure was discussed in terms of 'funny money' (constant prices), not in terms of actual tax revenues or borrowings to finance it. With rapid inflation, and its differential impact on public- and private-sector costs, PESC offered no means of linking expenditure to these financing considerations (Heald 1983, pp. 174–7).

In 1976 PESC was replaced by cash limits, which involved no automatic link of cost increases to increased expenditure provision. 'Instead of waiting to see what the rate of inflation turned out to be and providing extra cash to cover it when the time came, the government would, in snooker terms, be calling its shots on inflation and declaring in advance what cost increases it would be prepared to finance' (Pliatzky 1984, p. 133). The introduction of this system for 1976/7 contributed greatly to the sharp reversal of the trend in public expenditure in that and the following year,[2] though, as Table 10.4 makes clear, there had already been a very

---

[2] Of themselves cash limits do not, of course, reduce expenditure. But they do make planned cuts effective—indeed, in their early years they seem to have led to undershooting of expenditure targets as Departments were cautious of approaching too close to their limits.

sharp deceleration in the trend in 1975/6, partly reflecting the end of the property boom, partly the cuts in planned expenditure in the 1975 budget.

One other change in the public expenditure area was also of considerable significance—though in this case symbolic and political rather than substantive. This related to the measurement of public expenditure in relation to GDP. The 1976 White Paper on public expenditure suggested this ratio had risen to 60 per cent. This figure was widely quoted, notably by Milton Friedman and Roy Jenkins. In fact in relation to international conventions this figure was greatly exaggerated—by around 15 per cent (Table 10.4). This exaggeration derived from the inclusion of all nationalized industries investment (regardless of source of funds) in the figure; the double counting of debt interest on loans to build public housing; and calculating expenditure at market prices but GDP at factor cost. The 1977 Public Expenditure White Paper brought the British figure into line with international conventions. (It perhaps says something about the public debate on the economy at the time that a Nobel Laureate in Economics and a former Chancellor of the Exchequer could give credence to this exaggeration.)

The Public Sector Borrowing Requirement—the total borrowings of central and local government and the nationalized industries—was calculated from the late 1960s but only entered the policy debates in the 1970s. Through the long boom governments had run current account budget surpluses, but borrowed to finance a proportion of investment expenditure. This yielded a small PSBR, albeit one which rose noticeably from 1971 to 1973 (Table 9.4). From 1974 the figure rose sharply, peaking at 9.6 per cent of GDP in 1975/6 (Table 10.5)

Much of the focus of public debate was on this nominal PSBR. However many economists argued that this figure was a misleading guide to the fiscal stance. A number of possible alternative measures have been canvassed (Heald 1983, pp. 46–53), but the most commonly deployed have adjusted the nominal figure for inflation and the level of economic activity. The first adjustment reflects the fact that whilst the nominal PSBR shows how much the public sector is borrowing, at the same time, with inflation, the value of its outstanding debt is falling. Hence the public sector is usually a net saver. The second adjustment arises from the

Table 10.5   *PSBR 1972–1979*

	(a) Nominal PSBR (£b.)	(b) As % GDP		(c) Cyclically adjusted real surplus (% GDP)
1972/3	2.5	3.7	1972	1.3
1973/4	4.5	6.0	1973	−1.0
1974/5	7.9	8.9	1974	1.4
1975/6	10.6	9.6	1975	1.1
1976/7	8.5	6.6	1976	−0.7
1977/8	5.6	3.8	1977	1.5
1978/9	9.2	5.4	1979	0.9

Sources: (a) and (b) *Economic Progress Report* 160, Sept. 1983; (c) Begg (1987), p. 37.

argument that variations in the PSBR can arise either from policy decisions, or automatically from the effects of variations in the level of activity on government tax receipts and expenditures (called automatic stabilizers). Thus cyclical, or constant-employment adjustments, attempt to show what the level of the deficit is for a constant high level of activity. For most of the 1970s, as Table 10.5 shows, the high levels of inflation and unemployment would transform the positive nominal PSBR into a real surplus.

Such adjustments are controversial. The concern with a growing PSBR arose because of fears of its financial consequences (for the money supply and/or interest rates) whereas these adjustments are broadly Keynesian in character—they are concerned with the impact of fiscal policy on real demand. Whilst the nominal PSBR only became the strategic core of policy in the Thatcher years, under the Labour government it became an object of policy to reduce it, both because of its alleged financial consequences and because of its symbolic significance, a sign of government 'profligacy'. The IMF and private financial institutions focused attention upon this figure, and governments who wanted to borrow money had therefore to respond to this concern.

Agencies

The Treasury

The crisis in policy-making in the 1970s was a crisis for the role of the Treasury. It was the body most clearly responsible for the forms of economic management which now came under challenge. In part these challenges were not uncongenial; the new emphasis on the need to control public expenditure and public borrowing fell well within the Treasury's traditional approach.[3] On the other hand it was still wedded to the management of the demand, whilst accepting this had to take place under new constraints. Thus the 'Treasury line' in this period can be characterized most aptly as a 'financially constrained Keynesianism'. This involved a continuing belief that full employment should be a prime objective, and economic management could and should help to achieve this. On the other hand, it saw that the reduction of inflation was politically very important and might have to take priority over unemployment. Similarly, there was recognition that the views of financial institutions (national and international) and public opinion put severe constraints on public expenditure and finances. Hence the task of economic management had become more difficult, but it was not a task to be given up. The Treasury remained a firm advocate of incomes policy and also favoured intervention in the foreign exchange market and an enlarged industrial policy to supplement traditional policy instruments (Barnett 1982; Pliatzky 1984, ch. 5).

The Treasury in this period has been seen as crucial to the defeat of the Labour Left's Alternative Economic Strategy (e.g. Sedgemore 1980). Whilst no doubt the Treasury played its part in this, the crucial obstacle for proponents of this strategy was at the Cabinet level, where Tony Benn and his small band of supporters were never able to get anywhere near persuading the Cabinet. This strategy was undoubtedly anathema to the Treasury, as it was also to most of the Cabinet, including the Treasury Ministers. Indeed, more generally, this was probably a period when the

---

[3] Holmes (1985, pp. 179–80) says that the Treasury was quite hostile to the idea of cash limits on public expenditure, but was pushed into accepting them by Joel Barnett, the Chief Secretary to the Treasury.

Treasury was most strongly under the control of the Chancellor (Denis Healey), and what has been called the 'Treasury line' above may well be seen as the line of politicians constrained by the exigencies of financial pressures on one side and political pressures on the other.

How far Treasury policy can be called successful in this period is obviously controversial. Clearly 1974/5 was highly unsuccessful in terms of economic management, with accelerating inflation and deteriorating public finances. The Treasury was blamed for the latter in particular—though it may plausibly be argued that the combination of Heath's dash for growth, the oil crisis, and the workings of the relative price effect made the problems of financial control unprecedentedly difficult. Or to put the point another way, financial control could not be a substitute for political management, and the problems of 1974/5 might be more reasonably ascribed to faults in that management rather than Treasury control.

Where the Treasury more clearly failed was in the area of the exchange rate, and in financial and monetary targets. On the exchange rate, the Treasury seems to have greatly underestimated the volatility of the foreign exchange market, and thus failed to anticipate the severe fall in the pound in 1976, that fall being partly stimulated by knowledge of its desire to see the pound fall moderately to aid competitiveness (Holmes 1985, pp. 81–4; Pliatzky 1984, p. 143). Also in 1976 the failure of the Treasury to appreciate how important money supply targets had become to financial confidence meant that they were excluded from the budget of that year, and therefore probably reduced the impact of the government's deflationary stance on the foreign exchange market (Holmes 1985, pp. 179–80).

Overall, it would certainly be wrong to see the Treasury as consisting of simple economic conservatives, as for example Ham (1981) suggests. The Treasury was no longer keen on a strong pound—indeed quite the opposite. Equally it was not the originator of the idea of PSBR and money supply targets, and was never an enthusiast for these devices in the 1970s.

The Bank of England

The traditional role of the Bank of England as defender of the exchange rate disappeared with the floating of the pound in 1972.

Its role in domestic monetary control was reformed in 1971, when Competition and Credit Control aimed to encourage competition by banks and to restrict monetary growth, not by direct controls but by interest rates. However, the impact of this measure, in combination with Heath's dash for growth, was a monetary expansion on an unprecedented scale (Table 10.6).

Table 10.6   *Monetary Growth 1972–1979*

	(a) Increase in £M3 (£m)	(b) PSBR (£m)	(c) % increase in £M3	(d) Inflation rate (RPI)
1972	4,972	2,034	27.2	7.3
1973	6,702	4,195	27.1	9.2
1974	3,255	6.387	11.0	15.8
1975	2,331	10,494	5.8	24.3
1976	3,565	9,152	9.8	16.6
1977	4,132	5,955	9.4	15.8
1978	6,772	8,350	15.6	8.3
1979	6,615	12,620	13.2	13.5

Sources: (a) and (b) Artis and Lewis (1981), p. 69; (c) and (d) Fischer (1987), p. 25.

The Bank's response to this was the reimposition of direct controls on lending by supplementary special deposits (the Corset) and the adoption of unpublicized monetary targets. The adoption of monetary targets is probably best seen as the Bank responding to external sentiment rather than itself being a keen advocate of such targets, though internal work in the Bank (Goodhart and Crockett 1970) had suggested the plausibility of such targeting.

If the foreign exchange and financial markets were beginning to interpret policy changes in monetarist fashion, the Bank would have to take account of that trend by itself watching the behaviour of monetary aggregates. With inflation accelerating, the Bank would have an extra reason to look to money targets as a means of keeping inflation under control, at least in the medium term. The failure to announce the targets suggests a lack of confidence that they could be achieved—or perhaps opposition from the Treasury (Fischer 1987, p. 12).

Two other considerations were of importance. Traditionally the Bank had relied on interest rates as the main indicator of monetary stance, but with higher inflation these rates would be a much harder guide to use. The nominal rate would include an (un-measurable) proportion consequent upon variations in expectations about inflation. Secondly, the departure from a fixed exchange-rate regime left monetary policy without a clear 'anchor', and money supply targets, in some eyes at least, could play such a role (Bank of England 1984, pp. 51–2).

The chosen monetary aggregate—M3—is a broad definition of money embracing cash, current, and deposit accounts. Its choice seems to have been determined by three main considerations. First, the evidence that there was a good relation between this aggregate and inflation rates in the early 1970s. Second, that M3 was compatible with the idea of controlling credit, the traditional focus of monetary policy in Britain, rather than a narrow definition of money, such as cash, which would be involved in directly controlling the supply of money (see further on this issue in Chapter 11). A final and related point was that M3 could be quite easily related (at least in an accounting sense to) the PSBR, by means of a simple equation:

Increase in £M3 = PSBR − gilt sales to non-bank public
+ increase in bank lending
± external flows

This identity makes the link between financing the public sector and monetary growth, which was to be central to the policy debates of the mid- and late 1970s (Bank of England 1984, pp. 45–6).

A public target for £M3 was announced in 1976, not directly at the behest of the IMF, but certainly in response to the pressures on sterling (Walters 1986, p. 107). Public targets, announced in West Germany, Switzerland, and the USA just before being announced in Britain, recognized the importance of maintaining financial confidence, and the attachment of financial bodies to such targeting demonstrated that 'the notion that monetary policy is best conducted in silence and ambiguity has given way to increasingly explicit announcements of operating and ultimate targets of policy' (Fischer 1987, p. 23).

The Bank's hostility to inflation certainly made it embrace monetary targets with some enthusiasm in the mid-1970s. But this does not seem to have marked a fundamental shift towards a belief in money supply control as the sole element of macroeconomic policy. In a speech at the time of the adoption of published monetary targets, the Governor of the Bank said 'Monetary and fiscal policy—and I would add incomes policy—each have their part to play, and should form a coherent whole' (Bank of England 1984, p. 47). This 'pragmatic' stance seems not to have shifted towards a more full-hearted embrace of the overriding significance of monetary targets until the accelerated inflation and failure of incomes policy in the winter of 1978/9.

The Bank, like the Treasury, was still committed in the mid-1970s to an 'activist' management of the economy, albeit its faith in this was slowly being eroded (Bank of England 1984, chs. 3, 4).

The DTI and the NEB

The 1970s saw an enormous growth in the scale and scope of industrial intervention in comparison with the previous two decades, as measured by the amount of money spent under this head (Table 10.7). The basis of much of this was the Heath government's 1972 Industry Act, 'the most comprehensive and most interventionist piece of legislation concerning government assistance to the private sector to have been passed in Britain' (Grant 1982, p. 49).

Most of this industrial policy was carried out under the aegis of the DTI. However, the one big innovation in the agencies of policy-making was the creation of the National Enterprise Board under the 1975 Industry Act. Although the money spent by this body was a small proportion of the total shown in Table 10.7, it was a significant attempt (albeit a failed one) to intervene in the economy in a new way.

The NEB originated in Labour's period in opposition, 1970–4, as a response to the perceived failure of the 1964–70 Labour government to get to grips with Britain's poor industrial performance. The aim was to create a state holding company (the model of the Italian IRI was important here—Holland (1972)) to take over companies in key sectors of the economy. Coupled with this was the idea of planning agreements—contracts made by government agencies with firms, whereby the firms would promise to deliver, for example, investment projects in return for government aid or permission to raise prices. (For the background see Hadfield 1978.)

Table 10.7 *Government Support for Industry, Excluding Nationalized Industries 1974/5–1979/80 (£m. 1980 prices)*

	1974/5	1975/6	1976/7	1977/8	1978/9	1979/80
Regional	878	1,032	1,011	660	731	566
R. & D. (industry and energy	308	373	360	306	299	313
Employment	280	449	720	922	943	945
Investment grants	199	94	31	7	3	2
Selective schemes	497	896	542	682	570	561
Trade	313	264	330	175	279	399
Redundancy	257	269	252	246	243	259
R. & D. (defence and other)	1,400	1,640	2,093	1,962	1,954	2,026
TOTAL	4,132	4,977	5,339	4,960	5,022	5,071

Source: Morris and Stout (1985), p. 863.

The NEB was seen by its proponents as a means of increasing the growth of the economy, by 'picking winners', not as a means of subsidization of declining industries. But as the figures in Table 10.7 suggest, it was the rise in unemployment which was a major reason for the increased scale of intervention in the 1970s. Coupled with the political defeat of Tony Benn as Industry Minister, this circumstance drove the NEB to become predominantly a rescuer of failed companies like British Leyland and Rolls Royce, rather than an agency for intervention in successful companies. The NEB did register some successes—it turned Ferranti round from bankruptcy to viability, and it created the successful silicon chip company INMOS. But these were very small beer in comparison with the ideas of its founders. The basic reason for this was clearly political—most of the Labour leadership believed that the scale of intervention suggested for the NEB would alienate marginal and business opinion, and provide an easy target for the Conservatives. Hence the programme never got off the ground. Most of the increase in industrial intervention in the 1974–9 period therefore followed that of the Heath years in being primarily defensive and reactive, rescuing losers rather than picking winners (Grant 1982, chs. 3, 5).

Doctrine

Economic doctrine does not alter very much in the space of a few years. But in this period the monetarist challenge to post-war Keynesianism, which had been developing over a much longer period, came to a new prominence. What gave monetarism this boost was undoubtedly the parallel sharp rise in both inflation and unemployment (Tables 10.6, 10.8). Whilst this rise may be traced back into the late 1960s, 25 per cent inflation and 1 million unemployed were both unprecedented measures of the failure of the post-war policy consensus.

Theoretically monetarism's most important challenge in this period was to the idea of the Phillips Curve, which embodied the idea of a policy trade-off between inflation and unemployment. Friedman (1975) argued that this Curve showed a fundamental confusion between nominal and real wages. He argued that the level of employment was related to the real wage, and that changes in demand could only raise employment above the level determined by real factors ('natural rate') if people mis-estimated inflation and thereby the real wage. This led to the argument that as people adapted to inflationary trends, employment could only be held above that natural rate by accelerating inflation. This theory was

Table 10.8 *Unemployment 1973–1979**

	%	Numbers
1973	2.6	0.59m.
1974	2.5	0.59m.
1975	4.1	0.9m.
1976	5.6	1.34m.
1977	6.0	1.42m.
1978	6.0	1.33m.
1979	5.6	1.7m.

* On the pre-1982 definition, i.e. those registering for work, not those claiming benefit by reason of unemployment.
Source: Department of Employment Gazette.

used to try and account for the acceleration of inflation of the period. (There was much less attention to the rise in unemployment, and rather bizarrely the estimates of the natural rate in Britain which accompanied Friedman's essay were around 2 per cent (Laidler 1975, p. 45), a long way from the actual rate of 4–5 per cent in 1975/6).

Friedman's argument was clearly an attack on the whole basis of post-war demand management. It suggested that inflation should be the sole concern of macroeconomic policy, because governments were powerless to affect real magnitudes like output and employment by macro-policy. At this stage (i.e. in the mid-70s) this monetarism was not coupled with much discussion of what measures might improve performance in these real magnitudes—'supply-side' economics had not yet been born. One other ramification of Friedman's position was that trade unions were not responsible for inflation. Unions, he argued, 'do an enormous amount of harm . . . We ought to face up to the problem of the correct policy about unions . . . but not on the utterly false and irrelevant grounds that in some way they are manufacturers of money and of inflation' (Friedman 1975, pp. 33–4).[4]

The Keynesian orthodoxy against which Friedman cast his invective was in substantial disarray in this period. The dominant strand of that orthodoxy had prescribed fiscal policy (with a minor accompaniment of monetary policy) to determine output and employment, and incomes policy to counteract inflation. But the combination had failed to arrest either the rise in unemployment (except briefly in 1972/3) or the rise in inflation, where Heath's incomes policy had been a spectacular failure. Keynesians could with reason invoke the wholly exceptional circumstances of the OPEC price rise to account for 'stagflation', but this appeal to circumstance could easily be represented by monetarists as defensive *ad-hoc*ery.

Of course the 'Keynesian orthodoxy' had never been homogeneous. For example Kaldor (1971) had challenged post-war demand management as involving consumption-led rather than export-led growth, and called for a strategy of persistent depreciation of the currency to reverse this. However, like more orthodox Keynesians, Kaldor put his faith in incomes policy to restrain the

---

[4] For a useful summary and discussion see Cross (1982) ch. 8; Backhouse (1985), ch. 26.

inflationary consequences of his policy. Also from Cambridge Keynesianism in the mid-70s came the proponents of the 'New Cambridge' school. The main theoretical novelty of New Cambridge was to emphasize that private-sector expenditure depended on the stock of financial assets as well as on disposable income, that the private sector has a propensity to consume equal to the current and previous year's disposable income, and that therefore changes in fiscal policy would leave private-sector expenditure largely unaffected, and be reflected only in the balance of payments. The main consequence of an expansionary fiscal policy would not therefore be an increase in domestic output and employment, but a balance of payments deficit. In practice the stability of private-sector expenditure invoked by New Cambridge seems to have been fleeting (Cross 1982, ch. 7). At the policy level the New Cambridge main proposal was for import controls—a policy defeated above all for political reasons, as noted in discussion of the 'trade regime' above.

Academic adherents of monetarism were in a small minority in Britain in the 1970s. However the impact of these theories on policy would seem to have been substantial. Backhouse (1985, p. 406) suggests 'force of circumstances, as governments tried to tackle new and unfamiliar problems, was an important factor, if not the major one, behind the change in attitudes. Changes in economic theories were, of course, important . . . but it seems equally fair to say that it was changes in circumstances which were the direct cause of the adoption of new policies'. Whilst fair as far as it goes, this leaves unclear the channels by which changes in circumstances led to increasingly monetarist conclusions.

One channel that would certainly not seem to have been important was official economic advice—the main government economic advisers remained attached to the post-war Keynesian consensus. Probably the most important channel was via the financial markets. With large balance of payments and budget deficits the government had to have regard to opinion in the foreign exchange and debt markets. Here attitude was very much affected by financial journalism, one area of British opinion which did strongly adhere to monetarism. In this way, the financial columns of the quality press provided a major conduit from monetarist theory to governmental practice (Keegan and Pennant-Rea 1979, ch. 4).

Politics and Policies

Inflation and Unemployment

The politics of economic policy-making in this period were dominated by the replacement of unemployment by inflation as the predominant concern. Thus whilst unemployment rose more or less continuously after 1974, inflation policy took priority over the reduction of unemployment. This shift in priorities is clearly registered in Chancellor Healey's House of Commons statement in 1975 (Hansard, 15 April 1975, col. 282):

I fully understand why I have been urged by so many friends both inside and outside the House to treat unemployment as the central problem and to stimulate a further growth in home consumption, public or private, so as to start getting the rate of unemployment down as fast as possible. I do not believe it would be wise to follow this advice today . . . I cannot afford to increase demand further today when 5p. in every pound we spend at home has been provided by our creditors abroad and inflation is running at its current rate.

This priority for inflation can be understood in a number of ways. First of all, of course, the 25 per cent rate reached in 1974/5 was unprecedented since the end of the First World War. Second, inflation did occasion something of a moral panic amongst many commentators. Perhaps this panic found its most extreme spokesman in the Editor of *The Times* (Rees-Mogg) who even before the 1974/5 inflation peak, had justified the coup in Chile (which eventually left 50,000 dead and 1 million in exile) on the grounds that 'there is a limit to the ruin a country can be expected to tolerate' (*The Times*, 17 September 1973).[5]

But perhaps most compellingly, the fear of inflation constrained governments in ways which unemployment did not. Opposition to unemployment levels could manifest itself in electoral opinion— though the impressionistic evidence suggests this opinion was much less sensitive to the mass unemployment of the 1970s than the post-war consensus had assumed would be the case (e.g. Barnett 1982, pp. 49–51). Opposition to inflation could in addition make itself felt via financial opinion. Financiers rarely lose

---

[5] Elsewhere this panic is very much at work in publications of the Institute of Economic Affairs, e.g. Hutton's introduction to Jay (1976).

confidence in a government because of mass unemployment, but inflation is a different matter. Equally, mass unemployment tends to improve the balance of payments, inflation to worsen it, adding extra grounds for loss of confidence when inflation rises.

In sum, governments in the 1970s had little choice but to give priority to defeating inflation. The policy instruments to achieve this end were fiscal and monetary policy on the one hand, and incomes policy on the other. (Incomes policy is discussed in detail in the next section of this chapter.)

On its accession to power in 1974 the Labour government initially hoped to avoid a deflationary response to the oil crisis. There seemed to be an international consensus that if every country deflated to offset the balance of payments consequences of higher oil prices this would lead to a world-wide slump. However, this policy stance was quickly reversed in most countries, especially because of the inflation which accompanied the balance of payments deterioration. Expectations of the future flow of North Sea oil as well as political opposition to deflation may have added to the British government's initial stand on this issue. But it was a stand that nevertheless had to be reversed by late 1974.

The outcome was that whilst extensive borrowings were undertaken to offset the balance of payments consequences of the oil price rise, fiscal policy became broadly neutral in Keynesian terms for most of the Labour government's period in office (Table 10.5). For many monetarists however, the relevant consideration was that the nominal PSBR remained high by historic standards. However, the relation between the PSBR and monetary growth in the form of £M3 broke down in this period (Table 10.6).

Monetary policy in 1973–9 consisted of a combination of the 'Corset'—control of banks' liabilities—lending controls, and monetary targets to be attained mainly by a combination of fiscal and interest-rate policies. Thus monetary policy began to subordinate fiscal policy, in a manner to be central under the Thatcher government.

Monetary targets, as noted above, focused on M3 and then sterling M3, though the 1976 letter of intent to the IMF was framed in terms of Domestic Credit Expansion, which attempts to exclude the external aspects of money supply growth. The most important targets, however, were those for £M3 (Table 10.9).

Table 10.9   *Monetary Targets 1976–1979* (£M3, % increase over financial year)

	Target	Outcome
1976/7	12	10
1977/8	9–13	16
1978/9	8–12	11

Source: Dow and Saville (1988), p. 124.

In 1976/7 the target was reached by a combination of record interest rates (a 15 per cent Minimum Lending Rate), a fall in the PSBR, and heavy gilt sales to the non-bank public (see equation above, The Bank of England). In 1977/8 the target was overshot, especially because of capital inflows. In 1978/9 there was a slower rate of growth as the Corset was reimposed, and higher gilt sales obtained (Hall 1983, pp. 52–4).

All this was not a testimony to the ease of attaining monetary targets—all the elements contributing to £M3 growth were found to be hard to forecast and/or control. Equally the Corset was found to be decreasingly effective over time, as the process of 'disintermediation' took place, i.e. the expansion of financial transactions which did not register in the statistics for £M3 (Hall 1983, pp. 30–43). This pointed to a basic difficulty of monetary targeting which came to be known as Goodhart's Law; that any particular monetary aggregate chosen for targeting will become progressively poorer as a guide to the 'real' stance of monetary policy. This arises from the fundamental clash between the authorities desire to control monetary growth and the banks' incentive to lend, and thus find a way around the controls.[6]

By the end of the 1970s the peculiarly British attempt to control monetary growth by fiscal policy, direct controls, and interest-rate policy was being challenged by monetarists in the name of the greater effectiveness of monetary base control i.e. regulating bank lending by regulating the cash available to them. But this

[6] Other monetary variables perform even less well as predictors of inflation. M1 peaked in 1975, fell sharply in 1976, rose again in 1977, then fell again through 1978 and 1979. M2 reached a trough in 1975, then rose and fell in each successive year (Fischer 1987, p. 25).

argument had little impact before the fall of the Labour government in May 1979 (Dow and Saville 1988, ch. 7).

The Social Contract

The Social Contract was the most systematic attempt ever in
Britain to make an agreement between the governing party and
the trade unions, in line with successful attempts in Scandinavia
and Austria. Substantial impetus was given to the attempt by the
breakdown in government/union relations in Labour's period in
office 1964–70. From the Labour leadership's point of view the
benefit was to be a political claim to 'get on' with the unions, to be
most important in the area of wage bargaining. From the union
point of view the benefits were to be in the form both of specific
legislation (most notably the repeal of the Conservatives 1971
Industrial Relations Act) and a generally policy stance emphasizing
public spending and full employment. The written basis of the
Contract was the 1973 document *Economic Policy and the Cost of
Living* (TUC 1973). But whilst this made noises about trade-union
acceptance of the pointlessness of money wage increases cancelled
by price rises, it embodied no commitment to an incomes policy,
and indeed no commitment was forthcoming before the 1974
General Election (Fishbein 1984, ch. 5). Both the effectiveness
and the desirability on other grounds of the social contract have
been hotly contested.

On the question of effectiveness as a counter-inflation device
during the first 'bargaining' year (1974/5), the Contract was
undoubtedly a failure. The combination of sharp price rises, the
end of the Heath government's incomes policy (especially with its
effect on the public sector), gave a stimulus to wage bargaining
which resulted in average wage increases of around 30 per cent.
On the other hand, the government 'delivered' on its side of the
bargain by introducing the Employment Protection Act and
the Trade Union and Labour Relations Act, which strengthened
the trade unions' legal position, setting up the tripartite Health
and Safety Commission, rescuing BL and (initially) expanding
government expenditure in areas congenial to the TUC.

However the explosion of wages and the deepening balance of
payments and exchange-rate crisis heralded a sharp change of
policy by the spring of 1975. Public expenditure was cut and the

1975 budget clearly put the restraint of inflation above the reduction of unemployment. The government also sought to take a much tighter rein on wage settlements. In the summer of 1975 the government announced a 10 per cent wage target for 1975/6, to be enforced in the public sector directly, and in the private sector by use of the Price Code to stop firms passing on 'excessive' wage increases.

In the event the TUC came up with its own proposals—for a £6-a-week flat-rate increase for workers earning less than £8,500 p.a. Whereas in the first year the government delivered on its side of the Contract and the TUC was unable to, in 1975/6 the boot was on the other foot. The government continued to cut expenditure and allow unemployment to rise, whilst the TUC guidelines were broadly kept to (money wages rose 13.8 per cent). The reason was fundamentally that the TUC and many union members had recognized the fatuity of huge wage increases if prices rose commensurately, and the seriousness of the economic crisis was driven home by the run on the pound in summer 1975.

In 1976/7 the bargain between unions and government had a more specific element—tax cuts, as long as wages were held to a 5 per cent increase. In fact the increase was 8.8 per cent, a striking outcome given that inflation was running at around 15 per cent. A similar deal was struck in 1977/8, this time the target was 10 per cent, and the outcome 17 per cent (Fishbein 1984, ch. 7).

Between 1975 and 1978 the inflation rate fell from 24.3 per cent to 8.3 per cent. How far was this the consequence of wage restraint? The major alternative view is, of course, that the path of inflation is to be explained as a (lagged) response to changes in monetary growth (e.g. Holmes 1985). Inspection of Table 10.6 certainly shows a cycle in both £M3 and inflation. £M3 peaked in 1972, bottomed out in 1975, and then rose again in 1978. Inflation peaked in 1975, bottomed out in 1978, and then rose. However this is hardly a clear indication of the role of £M3. There is only one cycle, the lags seem very variable, and at best the link needs to be explained via another intervening element—the most obvious candidate being the exchange rate. But again, whilst this fell in 1976 and then rose, attempts to link this to monetary variables have not proved very successful (Hacche and Townsend 1981; but see Cobham 1982).

Even amongst those who favour a monetary explanation of the

inflation cycle of the 1970s there are supporters of the incomes policy. Thus the Bank of England's support was based on the argument that, whilst monetary policy would largely determine the inflation rate, the level of unemployment resulting from the monetary slow-down could be reduced by an incomes policy (Bank of England 1984, p. 47). However most proponents of the monetary approach to inflation were also hostile to incomes policy, because they judged it not only ineffective, but also positively harmful—in distorting differentials and therefore reducing the efficiency of the labour market (Brittan and Lilley 1977, chs. 1, 2).

Even for those who put the main emphasis on wage behaviour in explaining inflation, there is still the question of why wage behaviour took the pattern it did. One explanation that does not seem to hold much water is that of unemployment. Unemployment was rising almost continuously whilst inflation first fell and then rose (Blackaby 1978). More persuasive is the view that the exchange rate played a substantial role by its impact on the real wage. Thus the initial TUC acceptance of wage restraint following the crisis of 1975 led to a fall in real wages as the fall in the exchange rate reduced the real standard of living. This was particularly marked in 1976/7 which saw a 7 per cent fall in real wages—the largest one-year fall in the twentieth century (Fishbein 1984, p. 183). This provoked attempts to regain the real wage position, and thus the pressure on the policy in 1977/8 and its breakdown in 1978/9.

This last year of the incomes policy was plainly a disaster. The 5 per cent target for the year seems to have been set not as a realistic estimate of what was achievable, but as part of the run up to the election scheduled for Autumn 1978, but which in the event was postponed until May 1979. The result was a 'winter of discontent' especially manifested in the public sector, where, as in previous incomes policy cycles, workers' remuneration had been relatively worsened by the incomes policy, and they now sought to regain their position (Fallick and Elliott 1981).

Leaving aside questions of effectiveness, the desirability of deals such as the Social Contract has been challenged. The main argument against is that the Social Contract conferred political power on an interest group, the TUC, and therefore undemocratically reduced Parliament's sovereignty (Brittan and

Lilley 1977, pp. 36–9; Fishbein 1984, ch. 8). Two points may be made on this argument. On the empirical question of the capacity of the TUC to get what it wanted from government, this was quite restricted. Whilst it was successful in the labour relations legislation field, in the macroeconomic field (as noted above) and the industrial field (discussed further below) the government conceded little to TUC positions. On the wider question of the constitutional aspects of the social contract, the point can be made that in practice, of course, Parliament is far from sovereign. All kinds of private interests have (variable) capacities to affect decision-making. The most obvious example in the 1970s, alongside the TUC, were financial markets. Particularly in 1976 the 'confidence' of these markets (foreign exchange and gilt-edge) was probably the major constraint on government policy. In this context of a whole cluster of extra-parliamentary bodies impinging on policy there is a case for formalizing such arrangements, so that at least the nature of the 'deals' being done is explicit and public.[7]

The Public Sector

The performance of the public sector was at the centre of economic policy argument in the 1970s. Much of this debate focused on the scale of public expenditure—as already noted this was said to be '60 per cent of national income', but a more appropriate figure would be 45 per cent. Even this figure may be thought to greatly exaggerate the impact of government on decision-making on the economy, as almost half of that 45 per cent represented transfer payments, i.e. transfers of income between households where the recipient households decided what to spend the money on (Table 10.4).

The level of public expenditure in Britain at this time was about average for the advanced capitalist (OECD) countries, and most of these countries showed a similar sharp rise in the mid-1970s (Heald 1983, pp. 30–1). The explanation of the generality of this pattern is that most of these countries tried to some degree to compensate for external instability and deflation by using the budget in a compensatory fashion.

Critics of the level of UK public expenditure who accepted that

[7] In line with this argument, a case can be made for a second chamber of Parliament based on explicit interest representation.

it was not out of line with the OECD argued that, nevertheless, it was particularly harmful in Britain because of the tax structure used to finance the expenditure. In particular, there was the argument that income tax rates were much higher in Britain than in other countries with similar expenditure levels. Certainly the peak marginal rate in this period of 98 per cent (investment income) looks more like an incentive to have a good tax accountant than a way of raising much revenue, and was not matched in other OECD countries. But for the great bulk of tax-payers the burden of income tax plus social security contributions was on a par with OECD countries (Heald 1983, pp. 283–5). But income tax does seem to have been particularly politically sensitive in the UK, and one result of the crisis of 1975/6 was a notable shift from income taxation to indirect taxes (p. 284).

Another attack on the level of public expenditure which had substantial impact in this period was that by the economists Bacon and Eltis (1976). Strictly speaking their work was not about public expenditure but about the ratio of non-marketed to marketed output. The thrust of the argument was that marketed output (including that of nationalized industries in so far as they didn't make losses) had to provide all of the investment and exports of the economy, and that therefore the rising share of non-marketed output in total output would either have to come out of consumption or have serious effects by reducing investment and/or exports. The burden of their argument was that consumers had not been willing·to give up private consumption to offset the rise in public (non-marketed) consumption, so the resources available for exports and investment had been squeezed.

Bacon's and Eltis's approach was criticized on a number of grounds. For example, it assumes that the public sector provides only consumption goods, and ignores the positive economic impact of expenditure on education and health. Its arithmetic, showing a very large shift in the share of non-marketed output, has been criticized (Hadjimatheou and Skouras 1979). And like much of the debate of the 1970s, it seemed to believe Britain's experience was very much out of line with industrial competitors, for which there is little evidence. Nevertheless, the way in which a quite complex piece of academic theorizing was taken up and publicized in the 1970s suggests how far the public sector was seen as the source of Britain's economic difficulties.

Apart from expenditure, a lot of attention was focused on the level of public borrowing. As Table 10.5 shows, this rose to a peak of over £10b. in 1975/6—and it was the nominal figure rather than the economists' 'adjusted' figure which aroused most contention. The cause of this sharp acceleration of public borrowing was partly the unplanned expansion of public expenditure, noted above. To some degree this was financed by borrowing rather than taxation as a deliberate policy choice—the decision not to offset the consequences of OPEC by deflation (a policy stance already partly reversed by late 1974). Partly the failure to tax more heavily arose from the perceived political constraints on taxation. On the one hand, raising indirect taxes was seen as difficult because of their direct impact on the Retail Price Index in a period when governments were trying to pursue wage restraint. In addition, the corporate sector was being squeezed by the recession so it was difficult to raise taxes on companies; in fact they were given substantial relief when Healey stopped them paying tax on the increase in stock values brought about by inflation. Hence income tax seemed the only option in 1974–5—and this did indeed carry the main burden of increases, but not sufficient to offset the increased expenditure (Tomlinson 1981*b*, pp. 394–8).

The debate over the public sector might be seen as a wholly unsurprising, politically inspired fuss, not centrally important to the actuality rather than the rhetoric of policy-making. But in fact the PSBR came to be a crucial index of financial confidence in this period, and financial confidence was a major constraint on governmental action. The collapse in the foreign exchange market in 1976 was very closely linked to fears about 'public profligacy' in the UK. Even more directly, financing the debt itself was a source of leverage over policy. From May to September 1976 the market more or less stopped buying gilts, a 'strike' which forced the government to flood the market with short-term debt, and so boost money supply growth (Keegan and Pennant-Rea 1979, p. 133). Economists often suggest small countries can sell as much public debt as they like as long as they offer high enough returns. But in this period it was not just a case of the markets demanding higher interest rates, because higher interest rates themselves functioned as an index of the failure of government policy on public expenditure (*The Economist*, 25 December 1976, p. 73).

The capacity of financial markets to impact on economic policy was not new in the 1970s—it had been crucial to the 1931 crisis. But what was new was the scale of international financial transactions on the one hand, and the scale of public borrowing on the other. The first aspect meant that any loss of confidence was likely to be very radical in its consequences for the exchange rate. The second meant that, in so far as governments sold that debt on private markets, they had no choice but to take into account market sentiment in setting their policies. Ministers in the 1970s commonly asserted that 'a few young men in stockbrokers' offices are now virtually in charge of economic policy' (Keegan and Pennant-Rea 1979, p. 397). Whilst this was exaggerated, the political frustration it signified was based on a real and important (and unintended) shift of capacity from the public and governmental power to the private.

De-Industrialization and Industrial Policy

The 1970s was a period of general slowing down in growth in the OECD world (Matthews and Bowen 1989). Whilst this pattern was a common one, the events of the 1970s seem to have enhanced the consciousness of economic decline. In particular, the concept of 'de-industrialization' came into public debate for the first time. This concept had no single meaning, and was often used in a confusing manner. For example, total employment in manufacturing was falling from the mid-1960s, but because of productivity increases manufacturing output was still increasing—falling employment *per se* was then not an obvious indicator of a problem (Cairncross 1979; Brown and Sheriff 1979).

However the concept could be given a clear and significant meaning, related to the capacity to finance by exports a full employment level of imports (Singh 1977). The crucial points here were that the role of manufacturing in world trade was much greater than its share in world output, and that Britain was still heavily reliant on manufacturing competitiveness to finance its imports. Whilst all countries had growing levels of import penetration, Britain had particular problems in exporting enough to finance these imports. (One important twist in this argument, new in the policy debates of the 1970s, was the emphasis on 'non-price-factors'—design, quality, after-sales service, etc. in international competition (Stout 1976). This emphasis necessarily cast doubt on the efficacy of exchange rate depreciation, i.e. competition in price, for improving trade performance.)

Even if the problem of de-industrialization was accepted, this implied no obvious solution. Bacon and Eltis, for example, gave a conservative twist to the argument by linking de-industrialization to the growth of the non-marketed sector. The CEPG used the argument to bolster support for their import control strategy. For actual policy-making the debate on de-industrialization does seem to have been partly responsible for a clearly growing emphasis on 'supply-side' policies in the 1970s, though no doubt this was added to the constraints and difficulties of macroeconomic policy.

As already noted, the NEB was the symbol of Labour's new approach to industrial policy, but it was quickly reined back so that it 'did not resemble the instrument of socialist reconstruction envisaged by its progenitors but rather a state merchant bank' (Grant 1982, p. 50). Policy under Labour mainly followed the selective intervention lines set by the Conservatives' 1972 Industry Act. This led to many high-cost job subsidies in the face of rising unemployment, although the focus was on capital subsidies rather than directly on reducing the costs of employment. Regional policy however suffered from cuts in public expenditure, its scope being substantially narrowed in geographical terms (Table 10.7).

Labour did attempt to give its own twist to industrial policy by trying to build up the Sector Working Parties (tripartite bodies under the aegis of the NEDC) as agencies working for industrial progress 'from below'. However, even given its deliberately low-key approach, this policy seems to have had little impact at the company level where the important decisions were made (Grant 1982, pp. 62–71). Nevertheless the SWPs are but one symbol of Ministries' attentiveness to industry in this period. Another sign of this was the tax stock-relief noted above, which seems to have meant that post-tax profit levels stopped falling in the mid-1970s (*BEQB* 1981).

Measures to raise company cash flow and profits may be seen as the most straightforward form of industrial policy. It was also, of course, far more congenial to the private sector than the kinds of policies suggested by the initial creation of the NEB. Government appeasement of the private sector is also apparent in the decision to sack Tony Benn as Industry Minister in 1975. But the dominant elements in the Labour leadership had never believed in the radical industrial strategy of the early 1970s—in part they had only acceded to it to make possible agreement with the TUC (Hadfield 1978, ch. 10). This reluctance to provoke a hostile response from the private sector is also apparent in the government's failure to do anything about the Bullock Report on Industrial Democracy (Cmnd. 6706), or to develop the NEDC to a much more active role in industrial policy. With unemployment rising the government was in a weak position *vis-à-vis* the private sector, so as with the financial markets, it had little choice but to concede substantial ground in its policy-making.

Conclusions

The period in office of the 1974–9 Labour government coincided quite closely with the period from OPEC 1 to OPEC 2. The legacy of OPEC 1 was then the Labour government's starting point. As a hostile commentator has suggested, the government 'inherited an appalling economic situation partly created by the policies of the 1970–4 Heath government and partly created externally by the world oil crisis' (Holmes 1985, p. 1). In particular this legacy included fast-rising prices, money supply, public expenditure, and borrowing.

The specific strategies the new government brought to bear on this situation were first, the Social Contract, and second, the new NEB-led industrial policy. The Social Contract and, indeed, Labour's political survival initially ruled out a deflationary response to OPEC 1. The Barber/OPEC inflation was accommodated and wages grew at record rates. In this sense the Social Contract failed in 1974/5—it could not stand against the inflationary tide. The later phases 1975 to 1978 were (arguably) much more successful. The strongest case for this success has been made by Layard and Nickell (1986, p. 14). 'From 1975–7 the incomes policy was a TUC triumph. It reduced wage inflation by 20 per cent (from 28 to 8) with no further increase in unemployment, whereas Margaret Thatcher faced with a similar crisis rejected incomes policy and used an extra 2 million unemployed to achieve a small reduction in inflation.' However, even if we accept this evaluation of the Social Contract in these years, it is important to note that trade-union acceptance of wage norms was brought about only because of the crisis of 1975. The TUC and constituent unions constantly stressed that their agreement to the policy was temporary, and it also seems clear that there was little sense for most trade-unionists in participating in a deal whereby government provided certain benefits (in legislation or welfare) in return for wage restraint (Fishbein 1984, ch. 9). In other words the ideology of free collective bargaining had barely been undermined by these years.

As already suggested, that ideology was deeply embedded in the institutions and practices of the unions. Hence it may be unrealistic to assert that much more could have been done to build a durable social contract in this relatively short space of time. On the other hand crises seem the best time to set in motion such 'corporatist' arrangements (Katzenstein 1985, ch. 4). In the event the attempt at a 5 per cent wage round in 1978/9 suggests that the government was not seriously addressing how to make the Contract a plausible and long-living feature of management of the economy.

The industrial policy initiative around the NEB was an even weaker response to the crisis of the 1970s. Even if it had had the full-hearted support of the government (which was clearly absent), and whatever its relevance as a long-term response to Britain's economic decline, it had little to offer in the short run, and in the face of rising unemployment and falling profits in 1974–6, the government had little option but to appease the private sector.

The most dramatic and important policy change in this period was the explicit priority given to reducing inflation and reducing unemployment. Healey's April 1975 budget forecast unemployment rising from 750,000 to 1 million with no policy action to reverse this. It therefore may be said to have 'constituted the suspension of the unqualified commitment to the maintenance of full employment which the war-time Coalition government had adopted and which every succeeding government hitherto had honoured' (Fishbein 1984, p. 153).

Coupled with this was the public rejection of the post-war consensus on demand management by fiscal policy, evident in some of the most quoted words of the 1970s, Callaghan's speech to the 1976 Labour Party Conference. In this he asserted that the option of spending our way out of recession 'no longer exists, and that in so far as it ever did exist it only worked on each occasion since the war by injecting a bigger does of inflation into the economy' (Labour Party 1976, p. 188).[8]

In the light of Labour's policies from 1976 onwards it has been much discussed how far we should see the real turning point in post-war policy as being in 1976 rather than in 1979 (e.g. Riddell 1983, pp. 59–60; Allsopp and Mayes 1985, pp. 417–21). Clearly 1976 marked a sharp change, not only in rhetoric but in action, with very large cuts in public expenditure and the adoption of monetary targets, implying a focus on inflation reduction as the central concern of policy, displacing unemployment from that position.

On the other hand, the policy was still one which put the main brunt of counter-inflation policy on incomes restraint. Fiscal policy was broadly neutral (Table 10.5), unlike after 1979 when it was strongly deflationary in the face of the world slump.

By the 1978 Budget the assessment of policy was again very much in terms of the Keynesian analysis of demand and the use of the budget to regulate demand. Finally, and in some ways most importantly, the 'monetarism' of the Labour government was much less the consequence of ideological preference than that of the Thatcher government, but rather the result of *force majeure*. The need to appease financial opinion became in many ways the primary problem of government policy in this period. The capacity of government to manage the national economy has perhaps never seemed so limited.

Further Reading

Bank of England (1984): *Development and Operation of British Monetary Policy 1960–1983*, London, chs. 3, 4.

Caves, R. E., and Krause, L. B., eds. (1980): *Britain's Economic Performance*, Washington.

Dornbusch, R., and Layard, R., eds. (1987): *The Performance of the British Economy*, Oxford.

Fishbein, W. H. (1984): *Wage Restraint by Consensus: Britain's Search for an Incomes Policy Agreement 1965–1979*, London, chs. 5–9.

[8] This oft-quoted statement needs to be put in context. It is often used to suggest a crucial turning point in post-war economic history. But its tactical significance needs to be stressed—it was very much in the context of the Labour leadership trying to 'sell' a restrictive policy to the Labour Party, for which purpose much rhetoric was expended.

Grant, W. (1982): *The Political Economy of Industrial Policy*, London, chs. 3–5.

Hall, M. (1983): *Monetary Policy Since 1971*, London, ch. 4.

Heald, D. (1983): *Public Expenditure: Its Defence and Reform*, Oxford, chs. 2, 3, 7–9, 11, 12.

Pliatzky, L. (1984): *Getting and Spending: Public Expenditure, Employment and Inflation*, 2nd edn., Oxford, ch. 5.

Van der Wee, H. (1987): *Prosperity and Upheaval: The World Economy 1945–1980*, Harmondsworth, chs. 2, 12.

11

1979–1988: Renaissance or Retrogression?

THE rhetoric of the Conservatives under Mrs Thatcher at the time of the election victory of 1979 committed them to a sharp reversal of the whole trend of post-war policy. Attempts to use macroeconomic management to affect real variables like output and employment were to be abandoned as futile; a sharp reduction in inflation via tight control of the money supply was to be central, and the populace's inflationary expectations were to be reversed; the productive potential of the economy was to be unleashed by rolling back the state, reducing government expenditure, borrowing and taxation.

As always, rhetoric and reality did not coincide. The Conservatives' economic strategy, like that of previous governments, was much more qualified, *ad hoc*, and incoherent that its ideologies suggested. Nevertheless, 1979 was a real watershed in economic policy. As already noted in Chapter 10, the previous Labour government had already stepped back from the commitment to full employment, sharply reduced public expenditure, and focused attention on inflation and the need for monetary measures to control it. But these changes were partial and defensive, tactical responses to difficult times rather than a strategic reorientation (Thain 1985, pp. 263–4, compare Walters 1986, p. 10). Whilst it was occasionally politically appealing to the Conservatives to point to Chancellor Healey's policies as precursors of their own, overall the changes heralded by the 1979 election were more fundamental than were the elements of continuity.

This chapter will outline the main policy changes from the first election victory of Mrs Thatcher in 1979 to the third in 1987. These changes, perhaps more than in most periods, need to be set in the context of the international economy whose institutions were crucial to the outcomes of the Thatcher period. By way of conclusion these outcomes will be assessed, to see whether the sharp changes in policy delivered a renaissance of the economy as their protagonists were claiming by 1988.

Institutions

The Exchange-Rate Regime

The regime that emerged from the collapse of Bretton Woods in the early 1970s was one of 'dirty floating', where central banks intervened in the foreign exchange market but without a fixed rate to defend. Such interventions went beyond short-term stabilization around a market-determined trend. In the late 1970s many countries accumulated reserves by holding down their currencies *vis-à-vis* the dollar; in the early 1980s they lost reserves as they tried to hold up the exchange rate to reduce imported inflation (Dunn 1983, pp. 13–16). In other words most governments did not entirely give up the idea of the exchange rate as a policy instrument as the rhetoric of full-blooded floating would suggest. However policy was clearly aimed to influence rather than determine the exchange rate, in most cases the latter was accepted as unrealistic in the world of the late 1970s and early 1980s. As Susan Strange (1983, p. 353) has put the point, the key change in the 1970s was that 'the balance of influence in international capital markets has shifted from public bodies to private operators'. Within this overall picture the European Monetary System operated as a zone of considerable exchange-rate stability (e.g. Masera and Triffin 1984), but this was of relatively minor significance in a system still dominated by the dollar (King 1985; Strange[1] 1985, 1986).

The behaviour of exchange rates has become more erratic and unpredictable since 1973. The broad notion supporting floating rates was that except in the very short run their level would reflect purchasing power parities, i.e. the relative inflation rate in the two countries concerned (see further on this in the section on Doctrine, below). This has not been the pattern. The dollar depreciated in real terms by about 10 per cent 1976/8, then

---

[1] The issue of the status of the dollar in the world economy is a controversial one, on which there is a substantial literature (e.g. Krasner 1985). The view taken here is based on the continuing dominance of the dollar, disproportionate to the relative shrinking of the US real economy, as a reserve currency.

appreciated by over 20 per cent in 1981/2. The Swiss franc rose 30 per cent 1977/8, then fell by 25 per cent in the next two years. The yen rose 30 per cent 1975/8, then fell 25 per cent in 1978/9 (Dunn 1983, pp. 8–9; also Frenkel 1981; Williamson 1985).

Broadly the sharpness of these fluctuations reflected the fact that demand for foreign currencies responded quickly to changes in expectations about the future, expectations which could be affected by political as well as economic events, and where, as in other financial markets, shifts in sentiment seem to feed on themselves (Strange 1986, ch. 1). On the other hand, price levels in most countries were and are much slower to shift, so that substantial disparities could arise between the exchange rate needed to maintain a country's competitiveness and the actual rates. Hence these deviations of the exchange rate from their 'appropriate' level were having major affects on real variables (output and employment), and causing increasing concern amongst governments. This concern led to various high-level international meetings in the mid-1980s culminating in the Louvre agreement in early 1987 which attempted to provide some scheme for more stability, especially of the US dollar. Some co-ordinated action followed, but the agreements seemed fragile and looked likely to be undermined by any substantial shock to the world economy.

It is in this unstable international environment that the policies of 1979 and after must be placed. It seems clear from the pronouncements of major participants in the policy debate that the effects of the Conservatives' policies on the exchange rate were not seen as a central issue in 1979/80. Whilst academic work had already pointed out the problem of exchange-rate 'overshooting' (notably Dornbusch 1976)—and this process had clearly already occurred, notably in Japan and Switzerland in the late 1970s— these facts seem initially to have had little impact on the policy debate or decisions in the UK.

In the Financial Statement and Budget Report for 1979/80 (HC98), the recent appreciation of the pound was noted, but the assumption seems to have been that this would stabilize (para. 12), and there was no sense of the exchange rate as a problem. The FSBR for 1980/81 (HC500 1979/80) which embodied the first version of the Medium Term Financial Strategy (see below), was similarly unexcited by the exchange-rate position. It was not mentioned at all in the outline of the MTFS, and whilst its continuing rise was noted elsewhere in the document, this was not seen as central to the government's strategy. Loss of international competitiveness was likewise noted, but related solely to cost inflation in the UK.

The scale of the appreciation of the exchange rate in 1978–81 (the real rate rose by 37 per cent between 1978 and the first quarter of 1981—50 per cent starting from a 1976 base) seems clearly to have taken the British authorities by surprise. This is reflected in the evidence given by Terry Burns (Chief Economic Adviser) and Charles Goodhart (on behalf of the Bank of England) to the Treasury and Civil Service Committee in 1980. Burns could think of no explanation in terms of traditional economics for the scale of the pound's recent rise, and Goodhart said, 'It is very difficult to understand why the exchange rate is where it is now. Under any of the main theories of exchange-rate determination it is considerably higher than one might have analytically expected' (HC163 1980/ 81, paras. 7.20–7.21; see also Keegan 1984, pp. 148–62).

Whilst later the issue became central to public debate on the economy (see. e.g HC21 1982/3), initially the strength of the rise in the exchange rate was the major unanticipated consequence of Conservative policies. This rise in the real rate for the pound led to a loss of competitiveness without precedent in modern economic history (Emminger, in HC21 1982/3, Q. 827). Currency appreciation was the major transmission belt whereby the change in policy under the Conservatives affected the real economy. For firms in the tradeable goods sector (i.e. those subject to international competition), the rise in the exchange rate meant that unless they reduced their sterling price (and therefore their profits) substantially they would face loss of market share in both domestic and foreign markets. In this situation firms responded in different ways, but for many the only way to survive was to sack workers to save costs and borrow from the banks to maintain cash flow. Hence the sharp rise in both unemployment and bank lending which characterize this period. Firms were relentlessly squeezed between foreign competition and rising domestic costs in a manner which directly contradicted the purchasing-power parity doctrine, which foresaw exchange *depreciation* offsetting fast relative cost increases.

The governmental response to this situation was broadly to argue that the loss of competitiveness was primarily due to the failure of domestic costs to respond to the new policies (e.g.

HC163, Qs. 1345, 1360). Hence the exchange rate was seen not as equilibrating domestic and foreign inflation rates, but as a disciplining force on domestic inflation (i.e. wage costs). Whilst this made little sense in terms of traditional economic theories of the exchange rate, it made perfect sense for a government which saw as a central policy aim the erasing of inflationary expectations.

As a practical policy proposal, however, the offsetting of the loss of competitiveness by wage moderation was a non-starter. Leaving aside for the moment the contentious issue of how far it was plausible to expect that wage-bargainers would respond to macroeconomic signals such as changes in the exchange rate, the scale of changes in wages would have been immense to offset the rise in nominal exchange rates. Wages would have had to fall by up to 20 per cent to offset a rise in the effective rates of 25 per cent, between the beginning of 1979 and the beginning of 1981.

Given the political priority attached to reducing inflation, and the general free-market posture of the government, it is perhaps unsurprising that the government did not intervene to counter the rising exchange rate. The one policy which may have slowed the rise was the abolition of exchange control (given that this operated to hold down outflows of funds) but this seems to have been mainly motivated by a commitment to free international capital flows rather than any consequences for the external value of the pound (HC21 1982/3, Treasury Evidence, para. 16). The authorities rejected the idea of taxing capital inflows, a measure previously used in Switzerland and Germany to try to hold down a rapidly appreciating currency (Higham 1981; Walters 1986, p. 145). In any case the impact of any such measures was likely to be limited if pursued within the context of the overall restrictive policy of the Conservatives. Hence it made a lot of political sense for the government to welcome the exchange rate appreciation as a sign of international confidence in its policies, as aiding the fight against inflation, and as exerting pressure on domestic economic agents to change their price- and wage-setting behaviour.

The pound ended its appreciation at the beginning of 1981, and, mainly in response to US deflationary policies, depreciated strongly especially against the dollar. The rate against the key European currency, the Deutsche Mark, remained high. Further substantial gyrations in exchange rates followed, as shown in Table 11.1. As well as generally tilting governments towards seeking broad co-operation on exchange rates, this pattern raised two major issues for the British government's policies on the exchange rate.

First was the issue of stabilizing the pound within the EMS. This had been rejected early on by the government, primarily because of a desire to reduce inflation and produce thereby a more stable framework before tying the currency down. This view continued through to 1988, though formally policy by then was 'not if, but when'. Advocates of joining the EMS saw it as a way of maintaining low rates of inflation, by tying British policy to West Germany's traditional abhorrence of inflation. To maintain a stable £/DM rate would require British governments to match West German policies. Opponents saw EMS entry as putting the cart before the horse, believing exchange-rate stability to be the consequence of policy co-ordination not vice versa (Walters 1986, ch. 7). The case for the EMS was strengthened by the growing share of Britain's trade with the EEC (over 50 per cent by the early 1980s). On the other hand, it remained the case that it was fluctuations in the value of the dollar which were at the centre of the world exchange-rate regime, and which EMS membership would do little to help.

More important, at least in the short run, was the shifting role of the exchange rate in economic policy. As suggested above, at the time of its accession to power the Thatcher government did not see a key role for the exchange rate, regarding it as at most a signal of how its policies were regarded internationally. Once it became apparent that the appreciation of 1979–81 was having a significant impact it could be seen as a useful instrument of policy. But at the same time as this change was taking place, there was a loss of faith in the key monetary statistic of the MTFS, sterling M3 (see further below, Politics and Policies). This left the government without a clear anchor for its monetary policies—none of the monetary aggregates seemed to show what the authorities saw as the truth about its policies. From 1982 this problem was increasingly addressed by seeing the exchange rate as a good measure of the 'true' monetary stance, which led to an informal exchange-rate target. The logic of this was that if the exchange rate depreciated this would be a good indicator of a lax monetary stance, which could then be tightened by, for example, raising interest rates.

Whilst never the whole monetary target, by the mid-1980s the exchange rate had become the key figure by which government judged its monetary stance, and reacted accordingly. From 1982 until the election of 1987 the sterling effective exchange rate underwent a controlled depreciation at the cost of maintaining variable but relatively high interest rates to match those in the USA. But such a policy stance required a degree of stability in the world economy (particularly relating to the dollar) and thus attempts at international co-operation were a logical correlate of such targeting, but extremely difficult to attain.

The exchange-rate regime was one area where the Thatcher government's initial commitment to free markets was substantially modified by 1988. The belief that the exchange rate was a price that would smoothly adjust between home and foreign inflation levels, and therefore be of no significance in itself, had been lost. Instead, fluctuations in exchange rates were seen as potentially harmful both to real variables and the price level, and something to be regulated both by domestic policy and, it was hoped, stabilized by international agreement. In this as in other areas, policy has substantially shifted in ten years of Conservative rule.

Table 11.1   *Exchange Rates 1979–1987* (1975 = 100)

	Effective rate	DM	$
1979	87.3	3.9	2.12
1980	96.1	4.3	2.33
1981	95.3*	4.6†	2.03‡
1982	90.5	4.2	1.75
1983	83.2	3.8	1.52
1984	78.6	3.8	1.34
1985	78.2	3.8	1.30
1986	72.8	3.2	1.47
1987	72.6	2.9	1.64
1988 October	76.3	3.2	1.74

* peak at 103.2 in Jan. 1981
† peak at DM 4.8 in Jan. 1981
‡ peak at $2.4 in Jan. 1981.

Source: *Financial Statistics*, (HMSO).

The Trade Regime

The Conservatives inherited a trade regime which was largely determined by Britain's EC membership and adherence to the GATT. Within this framework Britain was a low tariff country, with free trade with the EC and EFTA, and tariffs of perhaps 4.7 per cent round the EC (Thompson 1986*a*, p. 112). However, more significant than overt tariffs in recent years have been various 'voluntary export restraints' (VERs) whereby exporting countries are persuaded to limit their exports to a fixed ceiling, e.g. Japanese cars and videotape recorders.

Whilst strongly committed to the rhetoric of free trade, the Conservative government has not ushered in a sharp change of policy in this area: 'It has certainly not gone in for a full scale and radical dismantling of existing trade barriers. If anything it has cautiously encouraged and supported the status quo' (Thompson 1986*a*, p. 115). So whilst pursuing subsidy reduction and deregulation at home, internationally the Conservatives have been party to a renewal of the Multi-Fibre Agreement (MFA.), which regulates trade in textiles, and extensions of VERs. The latter have been mostly negotiated by the EC rather than at national level (Jones 1987).

Policy has largely gone along with the European fears about Japanese competition, and unlike in the case of agricultural subsidies, Britain has not disagreed with her European partners. Perhaps this is politically understandable, as cuts in the Common Agricultural Policy have a directly favourable impact on the British budget, whilst open entry for Japanese products has obvious short-term losers amongst domestic producers whatever its longer-term consequences. (Import controls have also had the significant effect of encouraging Japanese direct investment in Britain and the EEC.) In the case of services rather than manufactured goods, Britain has followed the USA in pressing for deregulation, on the basis of Britain's assumed[2] comparative advantage in financial services. Domestic deregulation of financial

[2] There is good ground for believing that this claim of comparative advantage in financial services was ill-founded—Britain's share of the world market in such services fell as far as her share of world trade in manufactured goods 1974–84 (*BEQB* Sept. 1985). Indeed, the 'Big Bang' of 1986, when the Stock Exchange was deregulated, might be interpreted as an attempt to restore Britain's weakening position in this area.

services has followed, but little has moved internationally, even within the EC where further liberalization waits upon 'harmonization' of legal, accounting, and other institutional conditions.

The absence of a comprehensive free trade offensive by the Conservatives is understandable, even if somewhat in contradiction to their rhetoric. The underlying position is that in manufactures (which account for most of Britain's trade) the scope of existing protection is small—most of Britain's imports came from the EC without any restriction. Whilst free-traders may rail against the MFA and VERs their economic impact on the UK is small, and the short-term political cost of abandoning them could be high, given the likely displeasure of both domestic producers currently protected and international partners to these agreements.

The Budgetary Framework

As discussed in Chapter 10, the budgetary system had undergone a severe crisis in the mid-1970s. This had been precipitated by the sharp increases in both public expenditure and borrowing which occurred in the years from 1972 to 1975. Public expenditure had been propelled to its highest-ever level both in absolute (real) terms and as a share of output (see Table 10.1). The succeeding years 1976/7 and 1977/8 saw a sharp reversal in this trend with very sharp falls in public expenditure, in turn reversed in 1978/9.

The Conservatives thus inherited an upward trend in public expenditure, but where the level was substantially below the peak of 1975/6. In addition they inherited a composition of public expenditure which had previously proved difficult to alter in its fundamental shape. Seventy-five per cent of expenditure went on five broad programmes—health and social services, social security, defence, education, and the Scottish, Welsh, and Northern Irish Offices. The largest of these, social security, was exempt from the cash-limits system introduced by Labour. The Conservative commitment to reduce public expenditure in absolute terms thus implied some combination of significant cuts in these major areas of expenditure, or deep cuts in some of the remaining much smaller programmes.

The difficulty in broad terms was that demand for public expenditure on education and the NHS is substantially demographically determined (Levitt and Joyce 1987). In addition, defence was a political priority for the Conservatives who were committed to a real increase of expenditure in that area, along with law and order. So although cash limits had proved their efficacy as an instrument of cuts in the mid-1970s, they had not of course reduced the political problems associated with such exercises. The inherited structure of public expenditure and their political commitments substantially 'boxed in' Conservative decision-making in this area.

As regards public borrowing, the pattern of a sharp fall from a mid-seventies peak followed by a more gentle upward trend by the time of the Conservative accession is repeated. On the tax side the Conservatives inherited a structure which had been moving for a long time towards a higher incidence of income tax, coupled with lower receipts from indirect and company taxes. In addition they had the growing revenues from North Sea oil, which were destined to reach their peak in 1985/6.

It was within this framework that the Conservatives had to pursue their policies of simultaneous cuts in public borrowing, taxes, and spending. Clearly this was an ambitious programme given the framework outlined here. The Conservatives' actual achievements in this area are returned to below (Politics and Policies).

Agencies

The Treasury

The strategy of the 1979 Conservative government focused on public finance. It simultaneously downgraded the importance of the government's (direct) role in determing what happened in the real economy, and emphasized the centrality of a sound financial framework. Such a posture clearly fits well with the Treasury's traditional role, a role akin to a Ministry of Finance rather than an economics ministry, with a focus on public finance and public expenditure. Hence the post-1979 period saw a 'natural' enhancement of the Treasury's role *vis-à-vis* other Whitehall Ministries.

The Treasury also gained in influence from the centralization of decision-making into small committees of Cabinet Ministers, usually dominated by the Prime Minister and including the

Chancellor or other Treasury Ministers. This increase in power should not, however, be exaggerated. The Treasury conspicuously failed to deliver the cuts in public expenditure that the Conservatives had aimed for, actual spending increasing throughout the early 1980s (Table 11.2; Pliatzky 1984, pp. 190–207; Thain 1985, pp. 279–81).

In the initial discussions of the MTFS from late 1979, the Treasury seems to have evinced some scepticism over the policy. This seems to have focused on the dangers of committing the government to such long-term targets, as well as doubts about the supposed effects of the policy on wage-bargainers' expectations (Thain 1985, pp. 265–6). On the other hand the MTFS was seen as useful from a Treasury viewpoint as a bargaining weapon with the spending Departments to keep public expenditure down, though in retrospect this seems to have been an exaggerated hope.

Table 11.2   *Public Expenditure under The Conservatives 1979/80–1987/88*

	Absolute spending (in 1987/8) prices Excluding privat- ization proceeds £b.	As share of GDP (%) Including privat- ization proceeds	Excluding privat- ization proceeds
1979/80	158.6	43.25	43.5
1980/81	161.5	45.75	46.0
1981/82	163.3	46.25	46.5
1982/83	167.6	47.75	46.75
1983/84	170.5	45.5	45.75
1984/85	175.2	45.5	46.25
1985/86	175.0	43.75	44.5
1986/87	177.8	42.75	43.75
1987/88	176.7	40.5	41.5

Source: *Autumn Statement*, Nov. 1988 (HC695).

As Thain (1985, p. 269) argues, the Treasury was never able to persuade other departments, local authorities, or nationalized industries that the MTFS was an immutable framework. Public expenditure discussions therefore continued on the old horse-trading basis, and ultimately this meant the targets of the MTFS could not be met. Something had to give if cuts in public expenditure could not finance both tax cuts and cuts in borrowing.

A similar dilemma was resolved in the USA by going ahead with tax cuts and allowing borrowing to multiply; in Britain the opposite occurred, borrowing was reduced and taxes increased. 'In practice the British priority has been fiscal rectitude rather than gambling on the impact of tax cuts in the manner of the Reagan administration' (Riddell 1985, p. 241). This choice probably partly reflected the Treasury's traditional concern with reducing public borrowing, coupled with some scepticism about the at best long-term benefits of tax-cutting on economic growth.

The MTFS embodied the principle of fixed rules both for public borrowing and monetary expansion. Such fixed rules are aimed to narrow the scope of political discretion in policy-making, in the belief that such discretion is likely to respond to pressures in the 'political market-place' rather than any objective notion of the health of the economy. But such a lack of room for manœuvre must be anathema to a government Ministry charged with day-to-day management of the economy and operating within a highly political framework. It is unsurprising, then, that the Treasury, whilst willing to make tactical use of the MTFS, worried about the implied loss of discretion for the Treasury Ministers.

In the event the MTFS did not provide that kind of rigid framework; its targets were largely exceeded. This was most striking in the monetary field (see below), but was also true for the level of public borrowing. However it is right to say that the PSBR is relatively more controllable by the authorities than any money supply target. As Table 11.3 shows, the PSBR targets were exceeded, but not as grossly as the M3 targets. The reasons for this pattern included tax increases noted above, plus such ploys as

Table 11.3   *The First MTFS: Targets and Outcomes*

	1980/81	1981/82	1982/83	1983/84
Sterling M3 (% p.a.)				
Target	7–11	6–10	5–9	4–8
Actual	17.9	13.6	11.7	8.2
PSBR (% GDP)				
Target	3.75	3.0	2.25	1.5
Actual	5.4	3.3	3.1	3.2

Sources: Financial Statement and Budget Report 1980 (HC500, 1979/80).

public asset sales (privatization) which, counting as 'negative public expenditure' thereby reduced public borrowing for any given level of expenditure and taxation. Whilst the politicians could rejoice at this extension of people's capitalism, the Treasury could take credit for an imaginative way of bridging the public finance gap.

From 1982 the aim of reducing public spending was given up. This strategy change resulted above all from the realization that such cuts would have to mean a substantial cut-back in welfare state provision, which a majority of the Cabinet found unpalatable (Riddell 1985). The target then became to reduce the share of public expenditure in national income, thus making possible tax cuts with continuing increases in absolute levels of expenditure. By the mid-1980s this was firmly established as the new strategy, and a successful one in its own terms. The share of public expenditure in national income peaked in 1982/83 and then fell, making possible both a lower level of public borrowing and lower taxes. This was almost Utopia for the Treasury, though tax levels for the mass of the population were no lower than in the last year of the Labour government.

Ham (1981) has pictured the Conservatives' economic policies as a triumph for the Treasury's attachment to obscurantist economic theory and its unconcern with the real economy. The particular question of doctrine is returned to below, but the general theme of Ham's argument raises the question, how important was the Treasury in bringing the MTFS into being? The broad answer must be 'not very'. The MTFS was largely dreamt up outside official circles; it was pushed through by (a small number of) Ministers rather than imposed upon them. The Treasury welcomed certain aspects of it and worried about others, as noted above. Some Treasury civil servants were enthusiasts for the policy, but Ham surely exaggerates their significance. The MTFS was above all a political strategy, to be understood best as the outcome of certain political calculations, not as the imposition of a Treasury undergoing a renewed attachment to 'pre-Keynesian' theory.

The Bank of England

The role of the Bank of England has been enhanced by recent changes in the environment of policy-making. Above all, the growing focus on financial confidence as the economy has become more open to international pressures has unavoidably enhanced the status of a body, one of whose central concerns is to tell governments about the state of such confidence. The Bank has always functioned as a conduit for presenting the prevailing state of City opinion to the government, and City opinion has come to matter more and more to governments, that opinion seeming to function as an 'objective' assessment of government policy in some accounts (Walters 1986).

In addition the Bank has the expertise in the areas highlighted by recent policy discussions, such as the exchange rate, monetary control and government borrowing. Finally, the Bank has close links with international bodies like the IMF, OECD, and the World Bank, whose own roles have mattered more with the internationalization of the economy (Thain 1984, p. 593).

These had been trends pre-dating the Conservatives' accession to power in 1979, but strongly reinforced after that date. The Bank seems to have played a limited role in the actual formulation of the MTFS (Thain 1985, p. 267) but its monetary targeting in particular accorded with well-established Bank of England desires (see Chapter 10 above). In the event monetary targeting in the early years of the MTFS was a fiasco, and this appears to have been blamed to some extent on the Bank. Certainly it seems to have been the case that the Bank began earlier than the Treasury or the government as a whole to worry about the exchange-rate consequences of policy (Walters 1986, pp. 135, 144; Keegan 1984, pp. 145–7). This accompanied some scepticism about the technical merits of focusing on the £M3 target. However, insider accounts (notably Fforde 1983) suggest that these technical difficulties were initially seen by the Bank as outweighed by the benefits of a simple monetary target in conveying to the public the government's anti-inflationary intentions.

Even before the MTFS period the Bank was conducting examinations of possible alternative targets for monetary policy. However once the initial shock to expectations had been delivered, the Bank argued strongly against replacing the M3 target with any other single measure. In particular it resisted monetary-base control, i.e. a very narrow measure of the money supply, as an alternative, mainly because it believed such a policy would lead to sharp fluctuations in interest rates in the attempt to control this magnitude (*BEQB* 1979; Cmnd. 7858; Keegan 1984, pp. 153–6).

Like the Treasury, the Bank of England favoured the firm anti-inflationary stance of the Thatcher government, and accepted that this meant involve a clear 'no U-turn' posture emphasized in the Medium Term aspect of policy. But its knowledge of monetary behaviour, and above all its attachment to discretion in monetary management, made it wary of the kind of 'fixed-rule' policy that the MTFS could be seen to suggest. Thus the bank played a considerable role in the retreat from the initial 'hard' monetary targeting of 1980 to the much more pragmatic policies of 1981 onwards. These involved an attention to a wide variety of monetary indices, but especially the exchange rate. Unacceptable movements in these indices were to be responded to on an *ad hoc* basis mainly via variations in interest rates. Such a role was extremely congenial to the Bank, combining as it did a focus on its major concern (inflation) with a wide degree of day-to-day discretion on how this concern was to be translated into policy measures.

Doctrine

The ferment in economic theory evident in the mid-1970s reached a crescendo in the years around the election of the Conservative government. In many accounts of this period the policies pursued by the government are seen as a direct application of new monetarist theories—in Galbraith's often-quoted words, 'Britain has, in effect, volunteered to be the Friedmanite guinea-pig' (cited Keegan 1984, Frontispiece).

There is no doubt that economic theory, especially macro-economics, underwent a profound crisis in the 1970s, paralleled only by the original Keynesian revolution in doctrine in the 1930s. There also can be no doubt that Conservative policy after 1979 could and did draw on economic theory as a defence for its objectives and instruments. However this conjunction of theoretical and policy revolution should not be treated as proof of causation. To try and assess the extent and nature of this link some brief account must be given of the various strands of theoretical argument used to discuss macroeconomics in the late 1970s and early 1980s.

Four main elements in contemporary macroeconomic theory are conveniently distinguished in the Treasury and Civil Service Committee on Monetary Policy in 1980 (HC163 1980/81, ch. 4). The four are gradualists, new classicals, pragmatists, and anti-monetarists. The label monetarist could crudely cover both of the first two of these. Both built on the work of Friedman, especially his argument that inflation was 'always and everywhere' a monetary phenomenon that could only be ended by slowing the growth of the money supply; that traditional demand management only worked in so far as economic agents were misled about future inflation rates; and that therefore macroeconomic policy should be centrally concerned with sound money, leaving real variables to be determined by the private sector.

Both these sub-groups of 'monetarism' also accepted that central to any counter-inflationary strategy was the need to break the expectation of inflation that people had come to build into their wage- and price-setting behaviour. Once these expectations were destroyed, a slow-down in monetary expansion would have no effects on real variables, only on the price level. Where gradualists and new classicals differed was over the speed at which expectations could be expected to adjust. The former saw expectations as 'sticky' and therefore advocated a gradual deceleration of monetary growth and slow squeeze on inflation. New Classicals advocated a 'short sharp shock' to break this expectation with one blow.

The New Classicals approach was based on a new (or newly applied) theoretical development, that of rational expectations. Simply put, this argued that, in making decisions, private economic agents would not make systematic errors, because they would have strong incentives to seek the correct information on which to base their decisions. Hence they would learn to behave as if they had a true model of how the economy worked, rather than continually making errors. This approach had been best developed in discussions of financial markets, but its application to macroeconomics carried a highly significant message. Private economic agents would not be fooled by government policy; if they saw money supply expanding they would know that this meant that inflation was about to rise and would adjust their behaviour accordingly. (Obviously this approach assumed the true model of the link between money supply and inflation was the Friedmanite one.)

This rather arcane theory ws of immense significance to any counter-inflation policy, because it suggested that the transition to low inflation would be quite painless—people's behaviour would adjust with little impact on real variables like output and employment. Gradualists on the other hand would be worried that a rapid slow-down in the growth of the money supply would be followed only slowly by changes in expectations, and this would mean high costs in terms of lost output and employment.

In 1980 both schools of thought welcomed the monetary squeeze embodied in the MTFS, and both schools believed that the impact on output and employment would be small. Friedman (HC720 1980/81, p. 61), a gradualist, argued that 'only a modest reduction in output and employment will be a side effect of reducing inflation to single figures by 1982', and Minford (HC720 1980/81, p. 142), a new classical, concurred 'on the assumption that policies are properly understood when they are announced and implemented, the disturbance to output and employment from reduction in the money supply and in the PSBR would be minimal'. Some monetarist proponents of the 1979 strategy have retrospectively accepted that they underestimated its consequences, 'Though some of us did expect the implementation of a monetary strategy designed finally to bring the great inflation of the 1970s to an end to have significant adverse effects, none of us expected the deep and prolonged depression that ensued.' (Laidler 1985*a*, p. 36.)

The two monetarist views are obviously those most closely related to the policies of the post-1979 period. Opposition within economic theory could also be divided into two camps, pragmatists and anti-monetarists. Pragmatists broadly saw the single-minded focus on inflation and the money supply as inappropriate. They believed these should be one, but only one, facet of government macro-policy. They believed government could (and should) affect real variables in the economy especially employment, and that in pursuit of its policies it should use the full range of fiscal, monetary, and (some argued) incomes policy. This school provided some of the best academic critiques of Conservative policy (e.g. Buiter and Miller 1981, 1983).

The other school of opponents of the Conservatives' policy, the anti-monetarists, argued that the central theory of the monetarists, the impact of the money supply on inflation, was wrong. The most active proponent of this view was Kaldor (1982, 1983) who argued that in a credit-money as opposed to a gold-based system there was no such thing as a definable entity, money, which could be controlled by the authorities.[3] Rather, money supply responded to money demand. Coupled to this analysis was a strongly asserted view that monetarist policy in Britain was the direct (and dire) consequence of the bad economic theory provided by the monetarists. If the anti-monetarists were Keynesians in economic theory, they were also Keynesians in their belief that economic policy linked directly to economic theory. In this version, Mrs Thatcher had been as ill-advised by the theorists as Mr Churchill had been half a century earlier (Chapter 3, above).

Some scepticism about this close link between policy and theory seems to be justified. The policies prescribed and pursued did not fit easily the prescriptions of either monetarist school. Friedman especially was sceptical about the design of the MTFS, arguing that its focus on the PSBR was misplaced because it suggested trying to control the money supply via the demand for money rather than directly, via monetary base control. He was all in favour of cutting back the public sector, but saw this as a quite distinct policy from monetary control. This focus on the PSBR as a means of reducing monetary growth in fact could find little warrant in economic theory. It was the product of the desire to reduce public borrowing *per se*, the passing stable relationship between PSBR and M3 in the early 1970s, and the accounting link between these two quantities (Fforde 1983). As noted above, the Bank vigorously resisted Friedman's proposal for monetary base control.

If the grand design of the MTFS was some distance from pure monetarism, the actual policies pursued were even further. The kind of economic management that emerged from 1981 onwards, using interest rates to respond to a varying set of indicators, was the kind of discretionary approach that monetarists anathematized.

Undoubtedly it was useful for the Conservatives to be able to draw upon academic economics literature to defend their policies. To cite the support of eminent professors helps governments pursuing controversial policies, albeit in other contexts the views of academics were not seen as something to be taken very

---

[3] When the arguments had died away, Hendry and Ericsson (1983) subjected Friedman and Schwartz's (1982) historical work on this relationship to a devastating econometric critique.

seriously.[4] But can we not explain Conservative policies quite well without recourse to a causative influence from economic theory?

Hostility to inflation and a belief that this could be defeated by monetary stringency were, as Conservative politicians in the late 1970s and early 1980s never tired of saying, mere common sense. And yet this was about as far as the fit between monetarist ideas and actual policies went.[5] The corollary that unemployment could not be affected by government action also accorded well with traditional Conservative distrust of government. In addition, the more recent growth in influence of financial markets over policy was a powerful inducement to governments to pursue 'sound' financial policies, irrespective of doctrinal allegiance, as the Labour Party had found in the mid-1970s.

The closest parallel to the 1979–82 episode in British economic history is the policies of 1920–1. In both cases a highly deflationary policy was pursued on the basis of fears about inflation. (In both cases the consequences for output and employment were much greater than expected, partly because of the coincidence of a world-wide downturn.) In both cases the central calculation underlying policy was that the defeat of inflation was a political priority which would outweigh any (assumed transitory) costs in employment. That the key was a change in political calculation— i.e. what could be got away with without massive loss of electoral support—is more evident in 1920, when the change of policy took place without change of government. The biggest difference between the two periods is that no one has attempted to explain the 1920 episode by reference to economic theory, whose role in policy-making at this time was minimal (Chapter 3, above). On similar lines we can argue that the role of economic theory in the 1980s 'monetarist experiment' has been much exaggerated.

After all the excitement of the early 1980s, economists and economic doctrine never figured so highly in discussions of the government's economic policy. As macro-policy became more *ad hoc*, attention increasingly switched to microeconomic issues. Here economists had rather less to contribute. Most striking perhaps was the absence of serious evidence on two issues

---

[4] Hence the disparaging response to the public letter of the 361 economists who in 1981 attacked the government's policies.

[5] The question of why governments worry about inflation is a difficult one to answer. See discussion in Chapter 10, and Higham and Tomlinson 1982.

increasingly central to the government's policies—the importance of low taxes and privatization for economic efficiency. On both these issues economists have rather little to say. They have mainly been content to point out the theoretical problems and difficulties of empirical work in both areas—in the first case because of the conflicting impact of the income and substitution effects, in the second, because of belief in the importance of levels of competition rather than ownership for efficiency.[6] Despite this absence of much in the way of evidence, the government's policies have focused more and more on these concerns. The lack of academic support for these policies has not been crippling, if only because they fit well within the traditional predilections of the Conservative right, and do not face the same political hostility as 'monetarism' did in the years before and after the 1979 election.

Politics and Policies

The victory of the Conservatives in 1979 mainly reflected the perceived failures of Labour in economic management, including the relationship to the trade unions. It was not a positive endorsement of 'New Right' or 'Thatcherite' policies so much as disbelief in Labour's capacity to manage what had become widely perceived as Britain's growing economic crisis (Butler and Kavanagh 1980, ch. 7).

Nevertheless the emphasis on controlling inflation, and in some vague sense reducing the role of the state, reflected widespread popular concerns. The problem for the Conservatives was to translate these concerns into effective policies. Politically, this was what the MTFS clearly did. Its prime strategic objective was to reduce inflation; it suggested that this could only be done successfully by reducing public borrowing. This was coupled to an explicit desire to cut government spending, which the government

---

[6] On the first issue see Brown (1983, 1988). The income effect suggests that the higher incomes from tax cuts will reduce the desire to work. The substitution effect operates the other way, by making working relatively more attractive than leisure. On the second, Pryke (1981) argues for the inefficiency of nationalized industries, but his earlier book (1971) had made the opposite case. The government's privatization programme did stimulate a growth in the 'economics of regulation', as many of the privatized corporations continued to be regulated in a variety of ways, e.g. Kay and Vickers (1988).

argued was 'at the heart of Britain's economic difficulties' (Cmnd. 7746).

At one level this initial programme was a failure. Sterling M3 and the PSBR overshot their targets (Table 11.3). The major reason for the failure to attain M3 targets was the growth of 'distress borrowing' to companies, as they attempted to respond to the loss of competitiveness and the squeeze on demand that the MTFS brought about (Hall 1982, pp. 101–9). The failure to attain the PSBR targets (albeit by a narrower margin than M3) was largely the consequence of a failure to cut public expenditure (Table 11.2).

This rise in public expenditure resulted largely from the government's own political commitments (to maintain expenditure on health, and increase it on defence and law and order), and the effects of the recession on the demand for social welfare benefits and also on the finances of nationalized industries. Coupled with these was higher public-sector pay, as proposed by the Clegg Commission set up by the previous Labour government, and accepted by the Conservatives.

The failure of policy by those indices to a substantial extent reflected the depth of recession which Britain experienced. The second quarter of 1979 was the peak of the cycle, and from then on output fell for two years. As Table 11.4 shows, Britain was the only one of the 'Big 6' in the OECD area to experience a fall in output in 1980 and 1981[7] (though several of the smaller OECD countries experienced a fall in 1981).

The necessary consequence of this fall in output was a rise in unemployment. As Table 11.5 shows, this doubled in under two years from the turning point of spring 1979. On the left this rise was regarded as both the major condemnation of economic policy, and a revelation of the true objectives of the Conservatives. These objectives were seen as the reduction of wages and the weakening of trade unions by creating mass unemployment (Tomlinson 1985, ch. 10 for discussion of this). However there seems good reason to doubt the latter proposition. The Conservatives were taken by surprise by the rise in unemployment, as they were taken by

---

[7] The OECD 'Big 6' seem the most reasonable comparisons for Britain in this period—the number of countries is manageable, the data readily available, and the countries included broadly represent those with which Britain normally compares herself.

Table 11.4   *GDP in the OECD 'Big 6', 1979–1988* (Annual changes in real GDP)

	1979	1980	1981	1982	1983	1984	1985	1986	1987	1988*
UK	2.2	−2.3	−1.2	1.0	3.8	2.2	3.7	2.7	4.5	3.5
USA	2.0	0.0	3.7	−2.5	4.0	6.7	3.0	2.5	2.9	2.75
Japan	5.2	4.4	3.9	2.8	3.2	5.0	4.5	2.5	4.2	4.25
W. Germany	4.2	1.4	0.2	−0.6	1.5	2.7	2.6	2.4	1.7	2.25
France	3.3	1.1	0.5	1.8	0.7	1.5	1.1	2.0	1.9	2.0
Italy	4.9	3.9	0.2	−0.5	−0.2	2.8	2.3	2.7	3.1	2.5

 * Forecasts at June 1988.

Sources: *OECD Economic Outlook and OECD Main Economic Indicators.*

Table 11.5   *Unemployment in the OECD 'Big 6' 1979–1988* (% of total labour force on standardized basis)

	1979	1980	1981	1982	1983	1984	1985	1986	1987	1988 (July)
UK	5.0	6.4	9.8	11.3	12.5	11.7	11.3	11.5	10.2	8.2
USA	5.8	7.0	7.5	9.5	9.5	7.4	7.1	6.9	6.1	5.4
Japan	2.1	2.0	2.2	2.4	2.6	2.7	2.6	2.8	2.8	2.5
W. Germany	3.2	3.0	4.4	6.1	8.0	7.1	7.2	6.9	6.5	6.6
France	5.9	6.3	7.4	8.1	8.3	9.7	10.2	10.4	10.6	10.5
Italy	7.6	7.5	8.3	9.0	9.8	10.2	10.5	n/a	n/a	n/a

n/a = Not available.

Sources: as Table 11.4.

surprise by the major mechanism which produced that rise, the appreciation of the exchange rate. Like the economists cited above, they believed that any rise in unemployment brought about by their policies would be small and transient. They also believed that a return to mass unemployment would be a political death-knell for the Party.

In this second calculation they were wrong. Whilst the rise in unemployment hit the poll-ratings of the Conservatives, the Labour opposition fell into disarray, with the split with the SDP, the role of Militant, and the replacement of Callaghan by Foot as party leader. How far these purely political factors plus the Falklands War affected the Conservatives' position remains controversial, given that from 1982 onwards a rise in the living standards of the employed began, which is the best economic prediction of party political fortunes.

Thus in a short period one of the key assumptions of the post-war consensus was shattered—that governments must manage the economy to preserve full employment or suffer disastrous political consequences. For a period in the early 1980s this assumption was held on to, and the focus on unemployment in the public policy debate was intense. But especially after the Conservative victory in 1983 the issue became much less prominent. Academic arguments were produced to demonstrate that unemployment was not the consequence of recent policy (notably Minford 1983; also Matthews and Minford 1987), but rather was to be explained by the inefficiencies of the labour market, especially the trade unions, and the provision of income support for the unemployed, both of which were argued to prevent supply and demand in the labour market clearing at full employment. Support for this view amongst economists was very limited, but such views served to give an economists' gloss to a political *fait accompli*—the abandonment of full employment as a key goal of government policy.

This negative aspect of the government's policies was matched by a belief that microeconomic policy could do more to improve economic performance. Microeconomic policy in this context meant not the 'corporatist' interventionism of the Labour party, but policies aimed at reducing the obstructions to the working of free markets. Such was the rationale for limiting trade-union powers, reducing public control of wage levels (e.g. Wage Councils), and reducing employee protection (e.g. in maternity leave and unfair dismissals). These policies both built upon and reinforced the change in the balance of power in the labour market brought about by mass unemployment.

The most striking innovation among the Conservative microeconomic policies was the privatization programme, which covered a number of policy areas, but focused upon the sale of public assets (Kay *et al.* 1986; Brittain 1986). In 1979 the government had committed itself to a general programme of rolling back the state, and specific programmes for cutting public borrowing and expenditure. But privatization only came into prominence later, as its many benefits were realized. First, it could be used to reduce the PSBR for any given level of public expenditure, privatization receipts counting as 'negative public expenditure'. Second, in the context of a bull market it offered a way of expanding private shareholding by offering short-term capital gains to buyers.[8] Third, it reduced the scale of the public sector in line with the arguments about the inefficiency of that sector. Economists evinced considerable scepticism about the efficiency consequences of these changes in ownership unless accompanied by enhanced competition, but the political benefits clearly outweighed such objections.[9]

Broadly one can say that the focus of policy switched increasingly from macro to micro economic issues after the second election victory of 1983. Partly this reflected the fact that it was realized that macroeconomic failure in traditional terms, i.e. mass unemployment, need not be politically disastrous. It also reflected the fact that the primary macroeconomic target seemed in the mid-1980s to have been achieved—a sharp reduction in inflation, as shown by Table 11.6, though by 1988 inflation was clearly re-emerging as a significant concern. The focus on micro-policy might be seen as a partial shift of objective—from inflation to growth. Like most governments in the post-war period the Conservatives saw that growth would solve conflicts in policy goals—more especially the desire to reduce taxation and borrowing against the political problems of reducing public expenditure.

This shift in focus did not mean a retreat from the format of Medium Term Financial Strategies. These were produced annually from 1980 onwards. However they proved more flexible than their initial presentation suggested was the intention. As early as October 1980 doubts were being publicly expressed by the Governor of the Bank of England about the sense of targeting M3: 'The lesson, perhaps, is the need to avoid attaching undue importance to short-term developments in any single monetary aggregate; it is sounder to take into account, as we in fact do, the underlying developments both in the aggregates as a whole and in the real economy' (*BEQB* 1980, p. 458).

These suggestions that monetary policy was much tighter than was indicated by the explosion of sterling M3 were taken up by the

---

[8] There are obvious parallels here with the sale of council houses, which in the context of sharply rising house prices and large discounts for sitting tenants, meant large capital gains as incentives for those wishing to join the 'property-owning democracy'.

[9] In some areas, e.g. British Telecom, there was a direct conflict between maximizing asset values by maintaining the public monopoly in private hands, and introducing competition for reasons of efficiency.

government and interest rates were reduced in November 1980. However to show that the MTFS was still be taken seriously, this monetary loosening was followed by a fiscal tightening in the budget of 1981. Indeed this budget is probably a key point in the evolution of Conservative policy. Despite the rising tide of unemployment and bankruptcies it signalled that the deflationary stance of policy was to be maintained. Nevertheless the monetary loosening in Britain and the tightening of monetary policy in the USA led to a sharp fall in the exchange rate, as shown by Table 11.1. By late 1981 the authorities believed this fall had gone far enough, and intervened on a large scale. Thus emerged the exchange rate as a key concern of the authorities. However the MTFS itself continued to have £M3 targets until 1986, but they were joined by narrow money figures from 1984.

This continuity of format was misleading, however, as the whole idea of monetarism putting the economy on a pre-defined and automatic course had been abandoned as early as 1980. In one sense the anti-monetarists had won the argument; simple monetary growth rules would be unattainable and if pursued would have serious effects on the real economy. However the government could (from 1981) point to the achievement of its primary goal of a reduction in inflation, and argue that the MTFS had delivered that prize despite the technical problems.

The acid test of monetary policy is its record in reducing inflation. Those who wish to join in the debate about the intricacies of different measures of money and the implications they may have for the future are welcome to do so. But at the end of the day the position is clear and unambiguous. The inflation rate is judge and jury (Lawson, cited D. Smith 1987, p. 125).

What, then, is the status of monetarism with the Conservatives' economic policy? As noted above, the MTFS can only with substantial qualification be seen as a pure monetarist strategy, because of its focus on the PSBR. Nevertheless it did see reductions in money supply growth as the main instrument, and consequential reductions in inflation as the main objective of policy. In that sense 'monetarist' is appropriate (Laidler 1985*b*).

However the MTFS, as a set of fixed parameters for economic policy, never got off the ground, and quickly became the setting for pragmatic fiscal and monetary adjustments within a framework of a declining PSBR and falling inflation. We have already suggested that to interpret this disparity between the rhetoric of 1979/80 and events thereafter as simply a disguise for anti-Labour policies is unhelpful.[10] Another interpretation is offered by Fforde (1983). He distinguishes between the 'political economy' of a money-supply strategy and the 'practical macroeconomics' of a money-supply policy. The former means the perceived need to persuade the public of the government's intentions to stick to a counter-inflationary strategy, and thus change price and wage behaviour. The second aspect is the more narrowly economic concern to actually control the monetary aggregates. In this view the crucial point about the MTFS was not that it was a viable policy in the latter sense, but that it was the only basis for so determined a counter-inflationary strategy.

. . . it would have been possible to initiate such a strategy with a familiar 'Keynesian' exposition about managing demand down-wards . . . but this would have meant disclosing objectives for, *inter alia*, output and employment. This would have been a very hazardous exercise, and the objectives would either have been unacceptable to public opinion or else inadequate to secure a substantial reduction in the rate of inflation, or both. Use of strong intermediate targets, for money supply and government borrowing, enabled the authorities to stand back from output and employment as such and to stress the vital part to be played in respect of these by the trend of industrial costs (Fforde 1983, p. 207).

In this highly political sense, it might be remarked, monetarism was very successful. But its period of significance was fairly short, and certainly by the Conservatives' second period of office it had little purchase on what was going on. By their third period the re-emergence of inflation was being combated by discretionary use of interest rates which owed little to the monetarist programmes of the 1970s. Rather a return to 'stop-go' seemed to have taken place, but with the differences that the sole economic instrument was now interest rates, and unemployment was several times as high as in the stop-go era of the 1950s and 1960s.

---

[10] Though clearly, once it was realized that unemployment could, politically, be tolerated, it was seen that it could be used as a policy instrument e.g. in pushing through deregulation in the labour market, and of course arguing for 'wage moderation'.

Conclusions: Renaissance or Retrogression?

It is, of course, impossible to say what the course of economic events would have been had a non-Conservative government been elected in 1979. Hence any assessment of the consequences of the first two Thatcher periods of office must be crude and at best indicative. One way of reducing the crudity is to provide some amount of international comparison—at least this provides some check on exaggerating the impact on *any* individual national government in a highly integrated world economy.

Strong supporters of Mrs Thatcher's policies argued that the government's main economic objectives were threefold—to reverse the pattern of chronic inflation, low productivity growth, and rising unemployment (Matthews and Minford 1987, p. 60). These would seem to provide the main indices of which it would seem reasonable to assess the record.

On inflation the record is set out in Table 11.6. Two points are immediately apparent; inflation is very much an international phenomenon, with roughly similar peaks and troughs in most countries; Britain has always been near the top of the inflation league, and that relative position has been quite stable over the variations in absolute rates.

Table 11.6   *Inflation in the OECD 'Big 6', 1979–1988* (annual changes in consumer prices %)

	1979	1980	1981	1982	1983	1984	1985	1986	1987	1988*
UK	13.4	18.0	11.9	8.6	4.6	5.0	6.1	3.4	4.2	5.9
USA	11.3	13.5	10.4	6.1	3.2	4.3	3.5	2.0	3.7	4.2
Japan	3.6	8.0	4.9	2.7	1.9	2.2	2.1	0.4	−0.2	0.5
W. Germany	4.1	5.5	6.3	5.3	3.3	2.4	2.2	−0.2	0.2	1.4
France	10.8	13.6	13.4	11.8	9.6	7.4	5.8	7.7	3.1	3.0
Italy	15.7	21.1	18.7	16.3	15.0	10.6	8.6	6.1	4.6	5.0

 * 12 months to September 1988

Source: *OECD Economic Outlook and OECD Main Economic Indicators.*

Clearly then it is difficult to argue that British policy by itself has been notably successful in the inflation field. This would seem to throw doubt on explanations of the fall in inflation which put great weight on the 'shock' of 1979–81 in destroying 'inflation psychology' (e.g. Minford 1987, pp. 61–2).

Why does inflation have this pattern of world-wide falls after 1980? Three possible answers may be suggested. The one most obviously 'international' in scope is the fall in commodity prices which took place over this period. Beckerman and Jenkinson (1986) have pointed out that between 1980 and 1982 primary product prices fell 50–60 per cent, and that given that 45 per cent of the imports of OECD countries are primary commodities, this factor can account for the deceleration in prices in this period. They argue that this collapse in commodity prices reflected the collapse of demand in the OECD world, and conclude (p. 39) that 'the recession in the industrialized world did not . . . slow down the inflation by acting directly on the labour market . . . it worked by inducing a collapse of commodity prices'.

Beckerman and Jenkinson thus explicitly explore and reject the hypothesis that it was the mass unemployment in the early 1980s which produced the fall in inflation via its effect on wage bargaining (e.g. Grubb 1986). For them the impact of recession on wages operates not through the demand for labour but through the inflation rate, determined in turn by import prices. Certainly in the British case it seems that unemployment has had surprisingly little impact on wage bargaining (e.g. Muellbauer 1986, pp. xvi–xviii; *Oxford Economic Policy Review*, Summer 1985). In manufacturing, where job losses were heaviest so too were wage rises (see below).

The third explanation would look for a simultaneity of policy actions in the OECD countries—a tightening of either fiscal or monetary policy. The best evidence for this is on the fiscal side, where undoubtedly a common policy response to the oil shock of the end of the 1970s was a fiscal tightening—as shown in Table 11.7. All the countries shown, except the USA, tightened their fiscal policy in this period, though actual changes were much smaller than the announced policy because of the effects of falls in economic activity and increased interest payments on reducing government receipts and increasing expenditure.

Most countries also adopted restrictive monetary policies at about the same time—see Table 11.8. If we leave aside theoretical arguments about the direction of causation between monetary contraction and falls in activity, there is plainly a prima-facie case that the fall in price trends was due to a similar monetary response

Table 11.7   *Fiscal Tightening in the OECD 'Big 6' Changes in Budget Balances 1979–1982 (% GDP; – = movement towards deficit)*

	Actual	Effect of changes in economic activity	Effect of increased interest payments	Apparent 'ex ante' change
UK	1.1	−4.4	0.5	6.0
USA	−4.3	−3.5	−0.6	−0.2
Japan	1.5	−0.7	−1.2	3.4
W. Germany	−1.4	−2.8	−0.7	2.1
France	−2.2	−2.5	−0.9	1.2
Italy	−2.9	−2.3	−1.8	1.2

Source: 'Retrospect & Prospect' *OECD Economic Outlook*, December 1982, no. 32, p. 9.

Table 11.8   *Rate of Monetary* Growth in the OECD 'Big 6', 1978–1982 (% change on previous year)*

	1978	1979	1980	1981	1982
UK	20.3	12.2	4.4	11.4	17.3
USA	8.2	8.0	6.3	7.1	6.6
Japan	10.8	9.9	0.8	3.7	7.1
West Germany	13.5	7.2	2.4	0.9	3.2
France	11.1	12.1	7.9	12.1	15.6
Italy	23.8	23.9	15.9	11.1	11.5
(All industrial countries)	11.2	9.8	5.8	6.8	8.2

* Currency in circulation, deposits of clearing banks, and demand deposits of non-government bodies.

Source: International Financial Statistics.

by OECD governments to the inflationary surge of 1979/80. The scale of both the fiscal and monetary shocks seems to have been relatively severe in Britain, and the fall in output similarly sharp.

In sum, the explanation of the fall in inflation cannot be seen as lying with marked differences in Mrs Thatcher's policies from those in other major economies. Inflation in Britain earlier in the

1970s had similarly followed the OECD with relatively little impact from different national policies.

Manufacturing productivity is the second area where, by 1987, the Conservatives were claiming a substantial improvement, and Table 11.9 shows the basis for these claims. It suggests that, at least, Britain had stopped being the laggard, in the rate of income in manufacturing productivity, that it had been over most of the post-1945 period.

Table 11.9   *Manufacturing Productivity Growth in the OECD 'Big 6',*
1979–1985 (% p.a.)

	Hourly	Per employed person
UK	3.9	3.4
USA	3.4	3.6
Japan	6.2	6.3
Italy	3.3	2.9
France	3.5	2.5
West Germany	3.1	2.4

Source: 'Total Factor Productivity', *OECD Economic Outlook* 42, p. 42.

Manufacturing productivity matters. It feeds directly into living standards and, other things equal, helps competitiveness and thus indirectly raises living standards. Manufacturing also provides two-thirds of Britain's exports of goods and services. However whilst productivity matters, it is only an unambiguously 'good thing' if it goes along with full employment i.e. so that it is not diluted in its impact by the fact that many are not producing at all. If one looks simply at the manufacturing sector, not only is there of course very heavy unemployment, but this is reflected in the fact that total output did not reach its 1979 level until after the 1987 election, and is still (in 1988) only just above the previous peak of 1973.

As regards competitiveness, one of the peculiarities of the British scene in the mid-1980s was the fact that, despite fast-rising manufacturing productivity, competitiveness was weak because of fast increases in manufacturing wages (Rossi *et al.* 1986, Muellbauer 1986). Whilst obviously beneficial to those directly employed in manufacturing, this pattern meant that manufacturing trade performance continued to deteriorate, a theme returned to below.

One final point about manufacturing productivity in this period is simply to note that the reasons for its growth are unclear. Changes in workplace labour practices are perhaps the obvious explanation in the context of weak trade unions and mass unemployment—though this fits poorly perhaps with the rise in manufacturing wages. Evidence on these practices is inconclusive, and the whole issue of the relation between labour and productivity is highly problematic (Batstone 1986; MacInnes 1987). Some have argued that in Britain the idea that 'labour' is the key to productivity is mistaken (Nichols 1986; Williams *et al.* 1986). Evidence on other practices in manufacturing throws little light on the productivity increases; New's and Myers's (1987) survey of manufacturing operations suggests strikingly few changes in the organization of production between 1975 and 1985. However the data in Table 11.10 suggests the gains have largely been in capital productivity. It would be much easier to assess the long-term significance and especially the substainability, of these productivity shifts if we had a clearer idea of their cause (see also Muellbauer 1986; Meen 1988).

The level of unemployment (Table 11.6) shows that Britain remained close to the top of the league in 1988, though with the trend downwards. Britain's relative position improved in the period after 1981 as other countries caught up—unemployment, like inflation, is plainly an international phenomenon. However this does not mean that its existence cannot in part be related to individual government's actions. Britain led the way into the recession of the early 1980s, and her deflationary policies, via the impact on imports, made some contribution to the world-wide recession, as perhaps did her example of how to deal with inflationary pressures. Of course, the impact was much smaller than that of the USA, whose own deflationary policies from late 1979 significantly contributed to the generality of unemployment.

Unemployment clearly helped one indicator of economic policy attainment—the balance of trade. Three million unemployed, via the proportionate reduction in household income, reduce imports very significantly, especially given British consumers' high-income elasticity of demand for imports. Bradshaw and Morgan (1987) have calculated that a family with two children on Supplementary Benefit spent just £6.68 per week on import-intensive clothing, footwear, and durable household goods, whereas the all-household

Table 11.10   *Private-Sector Productivity Trends in OECD 'Big 6',*
1979–1989

	UK	USA	Japan	Italy	France	West Germany
Total Factor productivity						
1960–73	1.9	1.5	6.3	4.8	4.3	2.6
1973–9	0.2	−0.1	1.8	1.6	2.1	1.8
1979–86	1.0	0.1	1.7	0.7	1.2	0.8
1986–9*	2.0	0.2	1.9	0.9	1.3	0.7
Labour productivity						
1960–73	3.3	2.2	8.8	6.6	5.9	4.7
1973–9	1.3	0.3	3.2	2.4	3.5	3.4
1979–86	1.0	0.6	2.8	1.3	2.3	2.0
1986–9*	2.4	0.7	3.1	1.7	2.2	1.6
Capital productivity						
1960–73	−0.9	0.3	−2.0	0.6	0.6	−1.2
1973–9	−2.0	−0.8	−2.9	−0.3	−1.1	−1.0
1979–86	−0.8	−1.0	−2.0	−0.6	−1.3	−1.3
1986–9*	1.2	−0.6	−2.2	−0.8	−0.8	−1.0

* 1987–9 based on estimates and forecasts.

Source: OECD Economic Outlook.

average in the Family Expenditure Survey is £36.20. Despite this the current account of the balance of payments was in the red to the extent of £15b. in 1988 (Table 11.11).

It may be argued that this is of no significance, because if the level of demand for imports had been higher because unemployment was lower (without a parallel rise in exports) the exchange rate would have fallen and maintained balance. This may be so, but the point here is simply that, as of 1988, it was far from clear that the traditional British problem of trade uncompetitiveness had been reversed, i.e. that Britain could hold its own in world trade without a continually depreciating exchange rate. (Note that the effective rate has fallen about 25 per cent since its peak in 1981— Table 11.1.)

Worries on this score in the 1980s focused on trade in manufactures, where 1983 saw the first import surplus since the industrial revolution, which rose to £20b. by 1988. This issue received some official attention (HC461 1983/4; House of Lords 1985). The general government view was that there is nothing special about manufactures; that logically a deficit in one sector must be matched by a surplus elsewhere (especially in invisibles); and that any problem of competitiveness would be automatically solved by exchange-rate changes (e.g. Tebbitt in HC461 1983/4, Qs. 1–96). The alternative view was that manufacturing remained the largest single element in world trade; that Britain had no clear comparative advantage in trade in services; and that as supplies of North Sea oil ran down, the loss of manufacturing capacity would mean a very tight foreign trade constraint (Keegan 1985; Cutler *et al.* 1986, ch. 4; Rowthorn and Wells 1987, ch. 13).

Table 11.11 shows Britain's current account position in the period 1977–88. Clearly North Sea oil made a major contribution to the current account in those years, but this peaked in 1985. The manufacturing balance declined continuously, very much in line with the trends of the last 25 years. The key question in the assessment of the success of Conservative policy by 1988 is how far this North Sea oil balance could be plausibly offset by an improved balance on services and manufacturing, in the context of a sterling depreciation, as suggested would happen by the Chancellor in 1985 (House of Lords 1985, p. 554). K. Smith (1987, pp. 24–8) summarizes the arguments on this question. He concludes that given the evidence of low price elasticities for Britain's trade, and low investment manufacturing and R. & D. in the early and mid-1980s, the prospects are gloomy. In sum (p. 28):

depreciation will indeed expand export volumes, but it will be most effective in product areas which are in general slow-growing and in which competition, especially from developing-country producers, is increasingly strong. Britain is very unlikely to be able to compete in the innovation-intensive product groups which form the fast growing categories of world trade, especially among the OECD economies, who carry out the bulk of such trade.

For the period up to the end of 1988 the argument that Britain had undergone an economic renaissance looks decidedly shaky. Above all, the ability to combine full employment with current

Table 11.1 *Britain's Current Balance of Payments 1979–1988 (£m.)*

	1979	1980	1981	1982	1983	1984	1985	1986	1987	1988*
Oil balance	−731	+315	+3,111	+4,643	+6,976	+6,947	+8,105	+4,057	+4,184	+1,558
Manufacturing balance	+1,697	+5,468	+4,583	+2,371	−2,268	−3,879	−3,000	−4,491	−7,490	−10,365
Visible balance	−3,449	+1,361	+3,360	+2,331	−835	−4,384	−2,178	−8,463	−10,162	−8,386
Invisible balance	+2,778	+1,555	+2,952	+1,704	+4,173	+5,858	+5,097	+7,483	+7,658	+2,629
Current balance	−661	+2,916	+6,312	+4,035	+3,388	+1,474	+2,919	−980	−2,504	+5,756

* First half of year only.

Source: *UK Balance of Payments (Pink Book)*, and *Monthly Digest of Statistics*, HMSO.

account balance seems to be further away than ever. In the long run manufacturing competitiveness remains vital to Britain, yet despite gains on the productivity front, the overall picture remained gloomy. And as Nickell (1987, p. 93) emphasized, any assessment must take into account that Britain in this period 'had the truly enormous advantage of North Sea oil, something which . . . will surely figure very heavily in the deliberations of future economic historians'.

Further Reading

Buiter, W. H., and Miller, M. (1983): 'Changing the Rules: Economic Consequences of the Thatcher Regime', *Brookings Papers in Economic Activity* 2, pp. 305–79.

Cutler, A., Williams, K. and Williams. J. (1986): *Keynes, Beveridge, and Beyond*, London, ch. 4.

Kaldor, N. (1982): *The Scourge of Monetarism*, Oxford.

Keegan, W. (1984): *Mrs Thatcher's Economic Experiment*, Harmondsworth.

Matthews, K. G. P., and Minford, P. (1987): 'Mrs Thatcher's Economic Policies 1979–1987', *Economic Policy* 5, pp. 59–92.

Maynard, G. (1988): *The Economy Under Mrs Thatcher*, Oxford.

Smith, D. (1987): *The Rise and Fall of Monetarism*, Harmondsworth.

Smith, K. (1984): *The British Economic Crisis*, Harmondsworth.

Thompson, G. (1986a): *The Conservatives' Economic Policy*, London.

Walters, A. A. (1986): *Britain's Economic Renaissance*, Oxford.

References

Addison, P. (1977): *The Road to 1945*, London.

Ady, P. H. (1952): 'The Terms of Trade' in G. D. N. Worswick and P. H. Ady (eds.), *The British Economy in the 1950s*, Oxford, 147–72.

Aldcroft, D. H. (1977): From Versailles to Wall Street 1919–1929, London.

—— (1986): *The British Economy* i. *The Years of Turmoil 1920–1951*, Brighton.

Alford, B. W. E. (1988): *British Economic Performance 1945–1975*, London.

Allen, G. C. (1951): 'The Concentration of Production Policy' in D. N. Chester (ed.), *Lessons of the British War Economy*, Cambridge, 167–81.

Allsopp, C., and Mayes, D. (1985): 'Demand Management in Practice', in D. Morris (ed.), *The Economic System in the UK*, 3rd edn., Oxford 398–443.

Amery, J. (1969): *The Life of Joseph Chamberlain* vol. vi, London.

Andrzejewski, S. (1954): *Military Organisation and Society*, London.

Arkes, H. (1972): *Bureaucracy, the Marshall Plan, and the National Interest*, Princeton.

Armitage, S. (1969): *The Politics of Decontrol of Industry: Britain and the USA*, London.

Arndt, H. W. (1978): *The Rise and Fall of Economic Growth*, Melbourne.

Artis, M. (1972): 'Fiscal Policy for Stabilisation', in W. Beckerman (ed.), *The Labour Government's Economic Record 1964–1970*, London, 262–99.

—— (1978): 'Monetary Policy—Part 2', in F. T. Blackaby (ed.), *British Economic Policy 1960–1974*, Cambridge, 258–303.

—— and Lewis, M. K. (1981): *Monetary Control in the United Kingdom*, Deddington.

Atkin, J. (1970): 'Official Regulation of British Overseas Investment 1914–1931', *Economic History Review* 23, pp. 324–35.

Backhouse, R. (1985): *A History of Modern Economic Analysis*, Oxford.

Bacon, R., and Eltis, W. (1976): *Britain's Economic Problem: Too Few Producers*, London.

Balfour, A. (1929): *Committee on Industry and Trade: Survey*, Part i.

Balogh, T. (1940): 'The Drift towards a Rational Foreign Exchange Policy', *Economica* 7, pp. 248–79.

—— (1949): *The Dollar Crisis: Causes and Cure*, Oxford.

—— (1948): 'Britain's Foreign Trade Problem: A Comment', *Economic Journal* 58, pp. 74–85.

—— (1952): 'The International Aspect', in G. D. N. Worswick and P. H. Ady (eds.), *The British Economy 1945–1950*, Oxford, 476–510.

—— (1960*a*): *Oral Evidence to the Radcliffe Committee: Minutes of Evidence*, Qs. 11025–66.

—— (1960*b*): 'Memorandum of Evidence' to Radcliffe Committee: *Memoranda of Evidence* iii, paras. 33–47.

Bank of England (1973): *Annual Report* 1972/3.

—— (1984): *Development and Operation of British Monetary Policy 1960–1983*, London.

Barna, T. (1949): 'Those "Frightfully High Profits" ', *Bulletin of the Oxford University Institute of Statistics* 11, pp. 213–26.

Barnett, C. (1986): *The Audit of War*, London.

Barnett, J. (1982): *Inside the Treasury*, London.

Barratt-Brown, M. (1988): 'Away with All the Great Arches: Anderson's History of British Capitalism', *New Left Review* 167, pp. 22–51.

Batstone, E. (1986): 'Labour and Productivity', *Oxford Review of Economic Policy* 2, pp. 32–43.

Baysinger, B., and Tollison, R. (1980): 'Chaining Leviathan: The Case of Gladstonian Finance', *History of Political Economy* 12, pp. 206–13.

Beck, M. (1979): 'Public Sector Growth: A Real Perspective', *Public Finance* 34, pp. 313–56.

Beckerman, W., and Jenkinson, T. (1986): 'What Stopped Inflation? Unemployment or Commodity Prices?', *Economic Journal* 96, pp. 39–54.

Beckerman, W., ed. (1972): *The Labour Government's Economic Record 1964–1970*, London.

Beenstock, M., Capie, F., and Griffiths, B. (1984): 'Economic Recovery in the UK in the 1930s', Bank of England Panel of Academic Consultants, *Panel Paper* 23.

Beer, S. (1982): *Modern British Politics*, 3rd edn., London.

Begg, D. (1987): 'Fiscal Policy', in R. Dornbusch and R. Layard (eds.), *The Performance of the British Economy*, Oxford, 29–63.

Beloff, M. (1975): 'The Role of the Higher Civil Service', in G. Peele and C. Cook (eds.), *The Politics of Reappraisal*, London, 209–31.

Benjamin, D. K., and Kochin, L. A. (1979): 'Searching for an Explanation of Unemployment in Inter-War Britain', *Journal of Political Economy* 87, pp. 441–78.

—— (1982): 'Unemployment and Unemployment Benefits in Twentieth-Century Britain: A Reply to our Critics', *Journal of Political Economy* 90, pp. 410–36.

Bentley, M. (1985): *Politics Without Democracy*, Oxford.

BEQB (1979): 'Monetary Base Control', *Bank of England Quarterly Bulletin* 19, pp. 149–59.

—— (1980): 'Governor's Speech', 16 Oct., *Bank of England Quarterly Bulletin* 20, pp. 457–9.

—— (1981): 'Profitability and Company Finance', *Bank of England Quarterly Bulletin* 21, pp. 228–31.

—— (1985): 'Services in the British Economy', *Bank of England Quarterly Bulletin* 25, pp. 405–14.

Best, M., and Humphries, J. (1986): 'The City and Industrial Decline', in B. Elbaum and W. Lazonick (eds.), *The Decline of the British Economy*, Oxford, 223–39.

Beveridge, W. H. (1909): *Unemployment: A Problem of Industry*, London.

—— (1944): *Full Employment in a Free Society*, London.

Beveridge Report (1942): *Social Insurance and Allied Services*, Cmd. 6404, London.

Blackaby, F. T. (1978): 'Narrative, 1960–1974', in F. T. Blackaby (ed.), *British Economic Policy 1960–1974*, Cambridge, 11–76.

—— (1979a): 'The Economics and Politics of Demand Management: The British Experience', in S. T. Cook and P. Jackson (eds.), *Current Issues in Fiscal Policy*, Oxford, 185–97.

—— ed. (1979b): *De-Industrialisation*, London.

Blaug, M. (1985): *Economic Theory in Retrospect*, 4th edn., Cambridge.

Bleaney, M. (1985): *The Rise and Fall of Keynesian Economics: An Investigation of its Contribution to Capitalist Development*, London.

Bloomfield, A. (1968): 'Rules of the Game of International Adjustment', in C. R. Whittlesey and J. S. Wilson (eds.), *Essays in Honour of R. S. Sayers*, Oxford, 26–46.

Booth, A. (1978): 'An Administrative Experiment in Unemployment Policy in the Thirties', *Public Administration* 56, pp. 139–57.

—— (1982): 'The Second World War and the Origins of Modern Regional Policy', *Economy and Society* 11, pp. 1–21.

—— (1983): 'The "Keynesian Revolution" in Economic Policy-Making', *Economic History Review* 36, pp. 103–23.

—— (1984): 'Defining a "Keynesian Revolution"', *Economic History Review* 37, pp. 263–8.

—— (1985a): 'The "Keynesian Revolution" in Economic Policy-Making: A Reply', *Economic History Review* 38, pp. 101–6.

—— (1985b): 'Economists and Points Rationing in the Second World War', *Journal of European Economic History* 14, pp. 297–317.

—— (1986a): 'Simple Keynesianism and Whitehall 1936–1947', *Economy and Society* 15, pp. 1–22.

—— (1986*b*): 'Economic Advice at the Centre of British Government, 1939–1941', *Historical Journal* 29, pp. 655–75.

—— (1987*a*): 'Britain in the 1930s: A Managed Economy?', *Economic History Review* 40, pp. 499–522.

—— (1987*b*): 'Unemployment and Inter-War Politics', in S. Glynn and A. Booth (eds.), *The Road to Full Employment*, London, 43–56.

—— and Coats, A. W. (1980): 'Some Wartime Observations on the Role of the Economist in Government', *Oxford Economic Papers* 32, pp. 177–99.

—— and Pack, M. (1985): *Employment, Capital, and Economic Policy*, Oxford.

Bordo, M. (1981): 'The Classical Gold Standard: Some Lessons for Today', *Federal Reserve Bank of St Louis Review* 63, pp. 2–17.

—— (1984): 'The Gold Standard: The Traditional Approach', in M. Bordo and A. Schwartz (eds.), *A Retrospective of the Classical Gold Standard 1821–1931*, Chicago, 23–119.

Boyce, R. W. D. (1987): *British Capitalism at the Crossroads*, Cambridge.

Bradshaw, J., and Morgan, J. (1987): *Budgeting on Benefit: The Consumption of Families on Social Security*, Family Policy Studies Centre.

Bristow, J. A. (1968): 'Taxation and Income Stabilisation', *Economic Journal* 78, pp. 299–311.

Brett, T., Gilliatt, S., and Pople, A. (1982): 'Planned Trade, Labour Party Policy, and US Intervention: The Successes and Failures of Post-War Reconstruction', *History Workshop* 13.

Britain's Industrial Future (1928): *Report of the Liberal Industrial Enquiry*.

Brittan, S. (1964): *The Treasury under the Tories*, London.

—— (1969): *Steering the Economy*, London.

—— (1978): *The Economic Consequences of Democracy*, London.

—— (1986): 'Privatisation: A Comment on Kay and Thompson', *Economic Journal* 96, pp. 33–8.

—— and Lilley, P. (1977): *The Delusions of Incomes Policy*, London.

Broadberry, S. (1984): 'Fiscal Policy in the Nineteen Thirties: A Reappraisal', *Economic History Review* 37, pp. 95–102.

—— (1986): *The British Economy between the Wars: A Macroeconomic Survey*, Oxford.

—— (1987): 'Purchasing Power Parity and the Pound–Dollar Rate in the 1930s', *Economica* 54, pp. 69–78.

Brown, A. J. (1972): The Framework of Regional Economics in the UK, London.

Brown, C. J. F., and Sheriff, T. D. (1979): 'De-industrialisation: A

Background Paper', in F. T. Blackaby (ed.), *De-Industrialisation*, 233–62.

Brown, C. V. (1983): *Taxation and the Incentive to Work*, 2nd edn., Oxford.

—— (1988): 'Will the 1988 Income Tax Cuts either Increase Work Incentives or Raise More Revenue?', *Fiscal Studies* 9, pp. 93–107.

Brown, K. (1971): *Labour and Unemployment, 1900–1914*, Newton Abbot.

Browning, P. (1986): *The Treasury and Economic Policy 1964–1985*, London.

Buchanan, J. M., and Wagner, R. E. (1977): *Democracy in Deficit: The Political Legacy of Lord Keynes*, London.

—— Burton, J., and Wagner, R. E. (1978): *The Consequences of Mr Keynes*, London.

Buiter, W., and Miller, M. (1981): 'The Thatcher Experiment: The First Two Years', *Brookings Papers on Economic Activity*, 315–67.

—— (1983): 'Changing the Rules: Economic Consequences of the Thatcher Regime', *Brookings Papers on Economic Activity*, 305–79.

Bullock, A. (1967): *The Life and Times of Ernest Bevin* ii. *Minister of Labour 1940–1945*, London.

—— (1983): *Ernest Bevin: Foreign Secretary*, London.

Burk, K. (1979a): 'Great Britain and the US, 1917–1918: The Turning Point', *International History Review* 1, pp. 228–45.

—— (1979b): 'J. M. Keynes and the Exchange-Rate Crisis of July 1917', *Economic History Review* 32, pp. 405–16.

—— (1981): 'The Mobilisation of Anglo-American Finance during World War I', in N. Dreisziger (ed.), *Mobilisation for Total War*, Ontario, 25–42.

—— ed. (1982): *War and the State: The Transformation of British Government 1914–1919*, London.

Butler, D., and Kavanagh, M. (1980): *The British General Election of 1979*, London.

Butler, R. A. (1971): *The Art of the Possible*, London.

C. 5512 (1888): *Final Report of the Royal Commission on Recent Changes in the Values of the Precious Metals*, London.

Cd. 4499 (1909): *Report of the Royal Commission on the Poor Laws*, London.

Cd. 9182 (1918): *First Interim Report of the Committee on Currency and Foreign Exchanges after the War*, London.

Cmd. 3331 (1929): *Memorandum on Certain Proposals Relating to Unemployment*, London.

Cmd. 3920 (1930): *Report of (May) Committee on National Expenditure*, London.

Cmd. 6311 (1942): *Correspondence Respecting the Policy of HM Government in Connexion with the Use of Materials under the Lend Lease Act*, London.

Cmd. 6437 (1943): *Proposals for an International Clearing Union*, London.

Cmd. 6519 (1944): *Joint Statement by Experts on the Establishment of an International Monetary Fund*, London.

Cmd. 6527 (1944): *Employment Policy*, London.

Cmd. 9725 (1956): *The Economic Consequences of Full Employment*, London.

Cmnd. 1432 (1961): *Control of Public Expenditure*, London.

Cmnd. 6706 (1977): *Report of the Committee of Enquiry into Industrial Democracy*, London.

Cmnd. 7746 (1979): *The Government's Expenditure Plans 1980/81*, London.

Cmnd. 7858 (1980): *Monetary Control*, London.

Cmnd. 9474 (1985): *Employment: The Challenge for the Nation*, London.

Cairncross, A., ed. (1971*a*): *Britain's Economic Prospects Reconsidered*, London.

—— (1971*b*): *Essays in Economic Management*, London.

—— (1979): 'What is De-Industrialisation?', in F. T. Blackaby (ed.), *De-Industrialisation*, 5–17.

—— (1981): 'The Post-War Years 1945–1977', in R. Floud and D. McCloskey (eds.), *The Economic History of Britain since 1700*: ii. *1860 to the 1970s*, Cambridge, 370–416.

—— (1984): 'An Early Think-Tank: The Origins of the Economic Section', *Three Banks Review* 144, pp. 50–9.

—— (1985): *The Years of Recovery: British Economic Policy 1945–1951*, London.

—— and Eichengreen, B. (1983): *Sterling in Decline*, Oxford.

Calder, A. (1971): *The People's War*, London.

Capie, F. (1983): *Depression and Protectionism*, London.

—— (1987): 'Unemployment and Real Wages', in S. Glynn and A. Booth (eds.), *The Road to Full Employment*, London, 57–69.

Carew, A. (1987): *Britain under the Marshall Plan*, Manchester.

Carroll, B. (1968): *Design for Total War*, The Hague.

Casson, M. (1983): *Economics of Unemployment: An Historical Perspective*, Oxford.

Caves, R. E., ed. (1968): *Britain's Economic Prospects*, Washington.

—— and Krause, L. B., eds. (1980): *Britain's Economic Performance*, Washington.

Chamberlain, J. (1904): *Tariff Reform and the Agricultural Industry*, Birmingham.

Checkland, S. (1957): 'The Mind of the City', *Oxford Economic Papers* 9, pp. 261–78.

—— (1983): *Public Policy and the Economy since 1750*, London.

Chester, D. N., ed. (1951): *Lessons of the British War Economy*, Cambridge.

—— (1952): 'Machinery of Government and Planning', in G. D. N. Worswick and P. H. Ady (eds.), *The British Economy 1945–1950*, 336–64.

—— (1975): *The Nationalisation of British Industry 1945–1951*, London.

Chick, M. (1986): 'Economic Planning, Managerial Decision-Making, and the Role of Fixed Capital Investment in the Economic Recovery of the UK 1945–1955, Ph.D. thesis (LSE).

Chick, V. (1983): *Macroeconomics after Keynes*, Deddington.

Clapham, J. (1944): *The Bank of England: A History*, vol. ii, Cambridge.

Clark, C. (1937): *National Income and Outlay*, London.

Clarke, P. (1988): *The Keynesian Revolution in the Making 1924–1936*, Oxford.

Clarke, R. W. B. (1978): *Public Expenditure, Management, and Control*, ed. A. Cairncross, London.

—— (1982): *Anglo-American Collaboration in War and Peace 1942–1949*, ed. A. Cairncross, Oxford.

Clarke, S. V. O. (1967): *Central Bank Co-operation 1924–1931*, New York.

Clay, H. (1929): 'The Public Regulation of Wages in Great Britain', *Economic Journal* 39, pp. 323–43.

—— (1957): *Lord Norman*, London.

Clower, R. W. (1965): 'The Keynesian Counter-Revolution: A Theoretical Appraisal', in F. Hahn and F. Breckling (eds.), *The Theory of Interest Rates*, London, 103–25.

Coats, A. W. (1964): 'The Role of Authority in the Development of British Economics', *Journal of Law and Economics* 4, pp. 85–106.

—— (1968): 'Political Economy and the Tariff Reform Campaign of 1903', *Journal of Law and Economics* 11, pp. 181–229.

—— ed. (1981): *Economists in Government: A Comparative Study*, Durham, North Carolina.

Cobham, D. (1982): 'Domestic Credit Expansion, Confidence, and the Foreign Exchange Market: Sterling in 1976', *Kredit und Kapital* 15, pp. 434–53.

Colwyn, F. H. (1927): *Royal Commission on National Debt and Taxation*, Cmd. 2800, London.

Costigliola, F. (1977): 'Anglo-American Financial Rivalry in the 1920s', *Journal of Economic History* 37, pp. 911–34.

Cowling, M. (1971): *The Impact of Labour 1920–1924*, Cambridge.

Crafts, N. (1987): 'Long-Term Unemployment in Britain in the 1930s', *Economic History Review* 40, pp. 418–32.

Crofts, S. W. (1986): 'The Attlee Government's Economic Information Propaganda', *Journal of Contemporary History* 21, pp. 453–71.

Cronin, J. E. (1988): 'The British State and the Structure of Political Opportunity', *Journal of British Studies* 27, pp. 199–231.

Croom, D. R., and Johnson, H. G., eds. (1970): *Money in Britain 1959–1969*, London.

Cross, R. (1982): *Economic Theory and Policy in the UK*, Oxford.

Crowther, A. (1988): *British Social Policy 1914–1939*, London.

Currie, R. (1979): *Industrial Politics*, Oxford.

Cutler, A., Hindess, B., Hirst, P., and Hussain, A. (1977, 1978): *Marx's Capital and Capitalism Today*, vols. i. ii, London.

Cutler, A., Williams, K., and Williams, J. (1986): *Keynes, Beveridge, and Beyond*, London.

Cuyvers, L. (1983): 'Keynes' Collaboration with Edwin Rothbarth', *Economic Journal* 93, pp. 629–36.

Dalton, H., ed. (1934): *Unbalanced Budgets: A Study of the Financial Crisis in Fifteen Countries*, London.

Davidson, R. (1972): 'Llewellyn Smith, the Labour Department, and Government Growth 1886–1909', in G. Sutherland (ed.), *Studies in the Growth of Nineteenth Century Government*, London, 227–62.

—— (1985a): *Whitehall and the Labour Problem in Late Victorian and Edwardian Britain*, London.

—— (1985b): 'Treasury Control and Labour Intelligence in Late Victorian and Edwardian Britain', *Historical Journal* 28, pp. 719–26.

Davis, L. E. (1974): *The Cold War Begins: Soviet–American Conflict over Eastern Europe*, Princeton.

Deacon, A. (1976): *In Search of the Scrounger: The Administration of Unemployment Benefit in Britain 1920–1931*, London.

—— (1977): 'Concession and Coercion: The Politics of Unemployment Insurance in the 'Twenties', in A. Briggs and J. Saville (eds.), *Essays in Labour History 1918–1939*, 9–35.

—— (1987): 'Systems of Inter-War Unemployment Relief', in S. Glynn and A. Booth (eds.), *The Road to Full Employment*, London, 31–42.

de Cecco, M. (1974): *Money and Empire*, Oxford.

Denison, E. F. (1968): 'Economic Growth', in R. Caves (ed.), *Britain's Economic Prospects*, Washington, 231–78.

Department of Employment Gazette (monthly), London.

Devons, E. (1951): 'The Problem of Co-ordination in Aircraft Production', in D. N. Chester (ed.), *Lessons of the British War Economy*, Cambridge, 102–21.

—— (1970): 'Planning by Economic Survey', in *Planning and Economic Management*, ed. A. Cairncross, Manchester, 67–83.

de Vries, M. G. (1987): *Balance of Payments Adjustment, 1945–1986: The IMF Experience*, Washington.

Diebold, W. (1952*a*): *The End of the ITO*, Princeton Essays in International Finance no. 16, Princeton.

—— (1952*b*): *Trade and Payments in Western Europe: A Study in Economic Co-operation 1947–1951*, New York.

Dimand, R. (1988): *The Origins of the Keynesian Revolution*, Aldershot.

Dimsdale, N. H. (1981): 'British Monetary Policy and the Exchange Rate 1920–1938', *Oxford Economic Papers* 33, pp. 306–49.

—— (1984): 'Employment and Real Wages in the Inter–War Period', *National Institute Economic Review* 110, pp. 94–103.

Dintenfass, M. (1984): 'The Politics of Producers' Co-operation', in J. Turner (ed.), *Businessmen and Politics*, 76–92.

Donovan, (1968): *Report of the Royal Commission on Trade Unions and Employers' Organizations*, London.

Dornbusch, R. (1976): 'Expectations and Exchange Rate Dynamics', *Journal of Political Economy* 84, pp. 1161–76.

—— and Layard, R. (1987): *The Performance of the British Economy*, Oxford.

Dow, J. C. R. (1965): *The Management of the British Economy 1945–1960*, Cambridge.

—— and Saville, I. D. (1988): *A Critique of Monetary Policy: Theory and the British Experience*, Oxford.

Downs, A. (1957): *An Economic Theory of Democracy*, New York.

Drobny, A. (1988): *Real Wages and Employment: Keynes, Monetarism and the Labour Market*, London.

Drummond, I. (1972): *British Economic Policy and the Empire*, London.

—— (1974): *Imperial Economic Policy 1917–1939*, London.

—— (1981): *The Floating Pound and the Sterling Area 1931–1939*, Cambridge.

—— (1987): *The Gold Standard and the International Monetary System 1900–1939*, London.

Dunn, R. M. (1983): *The Many Disappointments of Flexible Exchange Rates*, Princeton University Essays in International Finance, No. 154.

Durbin, E. (1985): *New Jerusalems: The Labour Party and the Economics of Democratic Socialism*, London.

Dutton, J. (1984): 'The Bank of England and the Rules of the Game under the International Gold Standard: New Evidence', in M. Bordo and A. Schwartz (eds.), *A Retrospective on the Classical Gold Standard 1821–1931*, Chicago, 173–202.

Economic Progress Report (bi-monthly), London

Economic Trends (monthly), London.

Eichengreen, B. (1981): *Sterling and the Tariff, 1929–1932, Princeton Studies in International Finance*, no. 48.

—— (1984): 'Keynes and Protection', *Journal of Economic History* 44, pp. 363–73.

—— ed. (1985): *The Gold Standard in Theory and History*, London.

—— (1987a): *Hegemonic Stability Theories of the International Monetary System, Centre for Economic Policy Research Discussion Paper* no. 193.

—— (1987b): 'Unemployment in Inter-War Britain: Dole or Doldrums?', *Oxford Economic Papers* 39, pp. 597–623.

Elbaum, B., and Lazonick, W., eds. (1987): *The Decline of the British Economy*, Oxford.

Emy, H. V. (1972): 'The Impact of Financial Policy on English Party Politics before 1914', *Historical Journal* 15, pp. 103–31.

Evans, P., Rueschmayers, D., and Skocpol, T., eds. (1985): *Bringing the State Back In*, Cambridge.

Fallick, J. L., and Elliott, R. F. (1981): 'Incomes Policies, Inflation, and Relative Pay: An Overview', in J. L. Fallick and R. F. Elliott (eds.), *Incomes Policies, Inflation, and Relative Pay*, London, 246–63.

Feinstein, C. H. (1972): *National Income, Expenditure, and Output of the UK 1855–1965*, Cambridge.

Fetherstone, M., Moore, B., and Rhodes, J. (1979): 'EEC Membership and UK Trade in Manufactures', *Cambridge Journal of Economics* 3, pp. 399–407.

Fetter, F. (1965): *The Development of British Monetary Orthodoxy*, Harvard, Mass.

Fforde, J. S. (1983): 'Setting Monetary Objectives', *Bank of England Quarterly Bulletin* 23, pp. 200–8.

Financial Statistics (monthly), London.

Fischer, S. (1987): 'Monetary Policy', in R. Dornbusch and R. Layard (eds.), *The Performance of the British Economy*, Oxford, 6–28.

Fishbein, W. H. (1984): *Wage Restraint by Consensus, Britain's Search for an Incomes Policy Agreement, 1965–1979*, London.

Flanders, A. (1952): 'Industrial Relations' in G. D. N. Worswick and P. H. Ady (eds.), *The British Economy 1945–1950*, Oxford, 101–24.

—— (1970): *Management and Unions*, London.

Floud, R. and McCloskey, D. (1981): *The Economic History of Britain since 1700* ii. *1860 to the 1970s*, Cambridge.

Ford, A. (1962): *The Gold Standard 1880–1914: Britain and Argentina*, Oxford.

—— (1969): 'British Economic Fluctuations 1870–1914', *The Manchester School* 37, pp. 99–130.

Foreman-Peck, J. (1981): 'The British Tariff and Industrial Protection in the 1930s: An Alternative Model', *Economic History Review* 34, pp. 132–9.

—— (1983): *A History of the International Economy 1850–1970*, Brighton.

Freeden, M. (1978): *The New Liberalism: An Ideology of Social Reform*, Oxford.

French, D. (1982): *British Economic and Strategic Planning 1905–1915*, London.

Frenkel, J. (1981): 'The Collapse of Purchasing Power Parities in the '1970s', *European Economic Review* 16, pp. 145–65.

Friedman, M. (1953): 'The Methodology of Positive Economics', in *Essays in Positive Economics*, Chicago.

—— (1968): 'The Role of Monetary Policy', *American Economic Review* 58, pp. 1–17.

—— (1975): *Unemployment Versus Inflation*, London.

—— and Schwartz, A. J. (1982): *Monetary Trends in the United States and the UK*, Chicago.

Gamble, A., and Walkland, S. A. (1984): *The British Party System and Economic Policy 1945–1983*, Oxford.

Gardner, R. (1969): *Sterling–Dollar Diplomacy* (expanded edition), New York.

Garside, W. R. (1980): *The Measurement of Unemployment*, Oxford.

—— (1985): 'The Failure of the Radical Alternative: Public Works, Deficit Finance, and British Inter-War Unemployment', *Journal of European Economic History* 14, pp. 537–55.

—— (1987): 'The Real Wage Debate in British Inter-War Unemployment', in S. Glynn and A. Booth (eds.), *The Road to Full Employment*, London, 70–81.

—— and Hatton, T. (1985): 'Keynesian Unemployment and British Unemployment in the 1930s', *Economic History Review* 38, pp. 83–8.

Giavazzi, F. (1987): *The Impact of EEC Membership*, in R. Dornbusch and R. Layard (eds.), *The Performance of the British Economy*, Oxford, 97–130.

Gilbert, B. (1966): *The Evolution of National Insurance in Great Britain*, London.

Gilpin, R. (1987): *The Political Economy of International Relations*, Princeton.

Gimbel, J. (1976): *The Origins of the Marshall Plan*, Stanford.

Glynn, S., and Booth, A. (1983): 'Unemployment in Inter-War Britain: A Case for Relearning the Lessons of the 1930s?', *Economic History Review* 36, pp. 329–48.

—— (1985): 'Building Counterfactual Pyramids', *Economic History Review* 36, pp. 89–94.

—— eds. (1987): *The Road to Full Employment*, London.

Glynn, S., and Howells, P. (1980): 'Unemployment in the 1930s: The Keynesian Solution Reconsidered', *Australian Economic History Review* 20, pp. 28–45.

Godley, W. H. (1975/6): *1st Report from the Expenditure Committee: The Financing of Public Expenditure*, HCP 69 II.

Goodhart, C. (1986): *The Business of Banking, 1890–1914*, Aldershot.

—— and Crockett, A. D. (1970): 'The Importance of Money', *Bank of England Quarterly Bulletin* 10, pp. 159–98.

Gowing, M. (1972): 'The Organisation of Manpower in Britain during the Second World War', *Journal of Contemporary History* 7, pp. 147–67.

—— (1974): *Independence and Deterrence: Britain and Atomic Energy 1945–1952* vol. i, London.

Grant, W. (1982): *The Political Economy of Industrial Policy*, London.

Green, C. J., and Metcalfe, J. S., (1986): 'Foreign Trade and the Balance of Payments', in M. J. Artis (ed.), *The UK Economy: A Manual of Applied Economics*, London, 130–202.

Green, E. (1985): 'Radical Conservatism: The Electoral Genesis of Tariff Reform, *Historical Journal* 28, pp. 667–92.

Greenaway, D., and Milner, C. (1979): *Protectionism Again . . .?*, London.

Grove, J. W. (1962): *Government and Industry in Britain*, London.

Grubb, D. (1986): 'Topics in the OECD Phillips Curve', *Economic Journal* 96, pp. 55–79.

Hacche, G., and Townsend, J. (1981): 'Exchange Rates and Monetary Policy: Modelling Sterling's Effective Exchange Rate', in W. A. Eltis and P. J. N. Sinclair (eds.), *The Money Supply and the Exchange Rate*, Oxford, 201–47.

Hadfield, M. (1978): *The House the Left Built*, London.

Hadjimatheou, G., and Skouras, A. (1979): 'Britain's Economic Problem: The Growth of the Non-Marketed Sector?', *Economic Journal* 89, pp. 392–401.

Hague, D. C., and Wilkinson, G. (1983): *The IRC: An Experiment in Industrial Intervention*, London.

Hall, H. D., and Wrigley, C. C. (1956): *Studies of Overseas Supply*, London.

Hall, M. (1952): 'Monopoly Policy', in G. D. N. Worswick and P. H. Ady (eds.), *The British Economy 1945–1950*, Oxford, 399–423.

—— (1983): *Monetary Policy since 1971*, London.

Hall, P. (1986): *Governing the Economy*, Oxford.

—— (1987): 'The State and Economic Decline' in B. Elbaum and W. Lazonick (eds.), *The Decline of the British Economy*, Oxford, 266–302.

Hall, R. L. (1955): 'The Place of the Economist in Government', *Oxford Economic Papers* 7, pp. 119–35.

—— (1959): 'Reflections on the Practical Application of Economics', *Economic Journal* 69, pp. 639–52.

—— (1965): Foreword to J. C. R. Dow, *The Management of the British Economy*, Cambridge.

—— (1982): 'The End of Full Employment', in C. Kindleberger and G. di Tella (eds.), *Economics in the Long View* iii. *Applications and Cases*, Part 2, London, 155–74.

Ham, A. (1981): *Treasury Rules*, London.

Hancock, K. J. (1960): 'Unemployment and Economists in the 1920s', *Economica* 27, pp. 305–21.

—— (1970): 'The Reduction of Unemployment as a Problem of Public Policy', in S. Pollard (ed.): *The Gold Standard and Employment Policies between the Wars*, London, 99–121.

Hancock, W. K., and Gowing, M. (1949): *British War Economy*, London.

Hare, P. (1980): 'Import Controls and the CEPG Model of the UK Economy', *Scottish Journal of Political Economy* 27, pp. 183–96.

—— (1985): *Planning the British Economy*, London.

Hargreaves, E. L. (1930): *The National Debt*, London.

—— and Gowing, M. (1952): *Civil Industry and Trade*, London.

Harris, J. (1972): *Unemployment and Politics*, Oxford.

—— (1975): 'Social Planning in Wartime: Some Aspects of the Beveridge Report', in J. Winter (ed.), *War and Economic Development*, Cambridge, 239–56.

—— (1977): *William Beveridge: A Biography*, Oxford.

—— (1981): 'Some Aspects of Social Policy in Britain during the Second World War', in W. J. Mommsen (ed.), *The Emergence of the Welfare State in Britain and Germany 1850–1959*, London, 247–62.

Harrison, M. (1988): 'Resource Mobilisation in World War Two: The USA, UK, USSR, and Germany 1938–1945', *Economic History Review* 41, pp. 171–92.

Harrod, R. F. (1947): *Are these Hardships Really Necessary?* Oxford.

—— (1952): *The Life of John Maynard Keynes*, London.

Hatton, T. (1985): 'Unemployment in the 1930s and the "Keynesian Solution": Some Notes of Dissent', *Australian Economic History Review* 25, pp. 129–48.

—— (1986): 'Structural Aspects of Unemployment in Britain between the Wars', *Research in Economic History* 10, pp. 54–92.

—— (1987): 'The Outlines of a Keynesian Solution', in S. Glynn and A. Booth (eds.), *The Road to Full Employment*, London, 82–94.

Hawtrey, R. (1913): *Good and Bad Trade*, London.

Hay, J. (1975): *The Origins of the Liberal Welfare Reforms*, London.

Hayek, F. (1935): *Collectivist Economic Planning*, London.

HC98 (1979/80): *Financial Statement and Budget Report 1979*, HMSO.

HC500 (1979/80): *Financial Statement and Budget Report 1980*, HMSO.

HC720 (1979/80): *Treasury and Civil Service Committee: Memoranda on Monetary Policy*, HMSO.

HC163 (1980/1): *3rd Report from the Treasury and Civil Service Committee: Monetary Policy*, HMSO.

HC21 (1982/3): *4th Report from the Treasury and Civil Service Committee: International Monetary Arrangements*, HMSO.

HC461 (1983/84): *2nd Report from the Trade and Industry Committee: The Growth in the Imbalance of Trade in Manufactured Goods Between the UK and Existing and Prospective Members of the EEC*, HMSO.

HC695 (1987/8): *Autumn Statement*, HMSO.

Heald, D. (1983): *Public Expenditure: Its Defence and Reform*, Oxford.

Heath, T. L. (1927): *The Treasury*, London.

Heclo, H., and Wildavsky, A. (1981): *The Private Government of Public Money*, 2nd edn., London.

Heim, C. (1983): 'Industrial Organization and Regional Development in Inter-War Britain', *Journal of Economic History* 43, pp. 931–52.

Henderson, H. (1947): *The Uses and Abuses of Economic Planning*, Cambridge.

—— (1955): *The Inter-War Years and Other Essays*, ed. H. Clay, Oxford.

—— and Keynes, J. M. (1929): *Can Lloyd George Do It?*, in J. M. Keynes, *Essays in Persuasion*, Collected Writings, vol. ix, London.

Henderson, P. D. (1952): 'Development Councils: An Industrial Experiment', in G. D. N. Worswick and P. H. Ady (eds.), *The British Economy 1945–1950*, 452–62.

—— (1962): 'Government and Industry', in G. D. N. Worswick and P. H. Ady (eds.), *The British Economy in the 1950s*, Oxford, 326–77.

Hendry, D., and Ericsson, N. R. (1983): *Assertion Without Empirical Basis: An Econometric Appraisal of Friedman and Schwartz, Bank of England Panel Paper* 22, 45–101.

Henry, S. G. B., and Ormerod, P. (1978): 'Incomes Policy and Wage Inflation: Empirical Evidence for the UK 1961–1977', *National Institute Economic Review* 85, pp. 31–9.

Hicks, U. K. (1953): 'The Budget as an Instrument of Policy, 1837–1953', *Three Banks Review* 18, pp. 16–34.

—— (1958): *British Public Finance 1880–1952*, Oxford.

—— (1970): *The Finance of British Government 1920–1936*, 2nd edn., Oxford.

Higham, D. (1981): 'Strong Currencies and Economic Performance', *Three Banks Review* 130, pp. 3–22.

—— and Tomlinson, J. (1982): 'Why Do Governments Worry about Inflation?', *Three Banks Review*, 2–13.

Hindess, B. (1977): *Philosophy and Methodology in the Social Sciences*, Brighton.

—— (1984): 'Rational Choice Theory and the Analysis of Political Action', *Economy and Society* 13, pp. 255–77.

—— (1988*a*): *Politics and Class Analysis*, Oxford.

—— (1988*b*): *Choice, Rationality, and Social Theory*, London.

Hirsch, F. (1965): *The Pound Sterling: A Polemic*, London.

Hirschman, A. O. (1951): 'The EPU', *Review of Economics and Statistics* 33, pp. 49–55.

Hoffman, S. and Maier, C., eds. (1984): *The Marshall Plan: A Retrospective*, Boulder, Colorado.

Hogan, M. (1987): *The Marshall Plan: America, Britain, and the Reconstruction of Europe 1947–1952*, Cambridge.

Holland, S., ed. (1972): *The State as Entrepreneur*, London.

—— (1975): *The Socialist Challenge*, London.

—— (1983): *Out of Crisis*, Nottingham.

Holmes, M. (1985): *The Labour Government 1974–1979: Political Aims and Economic Reality*, London.

Hotten, K. (1988): 'The Labour Party and the Enterprise', Ph.D. dissertation, Birkbeck College.

House of Lords (1985): *Select Committee on Overseas Trade* i. *Report*; ii. *Evidence*, HMSO.

Howson, S. (1973): 'A Dear Money Man? Keynes on Monetary Policy, 1920', *Economic Journal* 83, pp. 456–64.

—— (1975): *Domestic Monetary Management in Britain 1919–1938*, Cambridge.

—— (1980*a*): *Sterling's Managed Float: The Operations of the Exchange Equalisation Account 1931–1939*, Princeton Studies in International Finance no. 46.

—— (1980*b*): 'The Management of Sterling 1932–1939', *Journal of Economic History* 40, pp. 53–60.

—— (1981): 'Slump and Unemployment', in R. Floud and D. McCloskey (eds.), *The Economic History of Britain Since 1700* ii. *From 1860 to the 1970s*, Cambridge, 265–85.

—— (1987): 'The Origins of Cheaper Money, 1945–1947', *Economic History Review* 40, pp. 433–52.

—— (1988): ' "Socialist" Monetary Policy: Monetary Thought in the Labour Party in the 1940s', *History of Political Economy* 20, pp. 543–64.

—— and Winch, D. (1977): *The Economic Advisory Council 1930–1939: A Study of Economic Advice during Depression and Recovery*, Cambridge.

Hume, D. (1985): 'On the Balance of Trade', in B. Eichengreen (ed.), *The Gold Standard in Theory and History*, London, 39–48.

Hume. L. (1970): 'The Gold Standard and Deflation: Issues and Attitudes in the 1920s', in S. Pollard (ed.), *The Gold Standard and Employment Policies between the Wars*, London, 122–45.

Hutchison, T. W. (1953): *A Review of Economic Doctrines 1870–1929*, Oxford.

—— (1968): *Economics and Economic Policy in Britain 1946–1966*, London.

—— (1977): *Knowledge and Ignorance in Economics*, Oxford.

—— (1978): 'Review of Howson and Winch (1977)', *Economic History Review* 31, pp. 155–6.

ILO (1944): *Joint Production Machinery in British Industry*, Geneva.

Inman, P. (1957): *Labour in the Munitions Industries*, London.

In Place of Strife, (1969): Department of Employment and Productivity, London.

Jahoda, M. (1982): *Employment and Unemployment: A Social Psychological Analysis*, London.

Jay, D. (1980): *Change and Fortune: A Political Record*, London.

Jay, P. (1976): *Employment, Inflation, and Politics*, London.

Jeffreys, K. (1987): 'British Politics and Social Policy during the Second World War', *Historical Journal* 30, pp. 123–44.

Jessop, B. (1982): *The Capitalist State*, Oxford.

Jewkes, J. (1948): *Ordeal by Planning*, London.

—— (1978): 'A Defence of the White Paper on Employment Policy', in *A Return to Free Market Economics?*, London, 39–52.

Johnson, H. G. (1972): 'Keynes and British Economics', in M. Keynes (ed.), *Essays on John Maynard Keynes*, Cambridge, 108–122.

Johnson, P. B. (1968): *Land Fit for Heroes: The Planning of British Reconstruction*, Chicago.

Jones, C. D. (1987): *Tariff and Non-Tariff Barriers to Trade*, Government Economic Service Working Paper no. 97.

Jones, K. (1978): 'Policy Towards the Nationalised Industries', in F. T. Blackaby (ed.), *The British Economy 1960–1974*, Cambridge, 484–514.

Jones, M. E. F. (1985): 'Regional Employment Multipliers, Regional Policy and Structural Change in Inter-War Britain', *Explorations in Economic History* 22, pp. 417–39.

Jones, R. (1987): *Wages and Employment Policy 1936–1985*, London.

Joseph, K. (1975): *Reversing the Trend*, London.

Kaldor, N. (1971): 'Conflicts in National Economic Objectives', *Economic Journal* 81, pp. 1–16.

—— (1982): *The Scourge of Monetarism*, Oxford.

—— (1983): *The Economic Consequences of Mrs Thatcher*, London.

Kareken, J. H. (1968): 'Monetary Policy', in R. E. Caves (ed.), *Britain's Economic Prospects*, Washington, 68–103.

Katzenstein, P. (1985): *Small States in World Markets*, Ithaca NY.

Kay, J., and Vickers, J. (1988): 'Regulatory Reform in Britain', *Economic Policy* 7, pp. 28–43.

Kay, J., Mayer, C., and Thompson, D. (1986): *Privatisation and Regulation: The UK Experience*, Oxford.

Keegan, W. (1984): *Mrs Thatcher's Economic Experiment*, Harmondsworth.

—— (1985): *Britain without Oil*, Harmondsworth.

—— and Pennant-Rea, R. (1979): *Who Runs the Economy?*, London.

Kennedy, C. (1962): 'Monetary Policy', in G. D. N. Worswick and P. H. Ady (eds.), *The British Economy in the 1950s*, Oxford, 301–25.

Keynes, J. M. (1939): 'Relative Movements in Real Wages and Output', *Economic Journal* 49, pp. 34–51.

—— (1971): *A Tract on Monetary Reform, Collected Writings*, vol. iv, London.

—— (1972): *Essays in Persuasion, Collected Writings*, vol. ix, London.

—— (1973): *The General Theory, Collected Writings*, vol. vii, London.

—— (1978): *Activities 1939–1945: Internal War Finance, Collected Writings*, vol. xxii, London.

—— (1979*a*): *Activities 1940–1943: External War Finance, Collected Writings*, vol. xxiii, London.

—— (1979*b*): *Activities 1944–1946: The Transition to Peace, Collected Writings*, vol. xxiv, London.

—— (1980*a*): *Activities 1940–1946: Shaping the Post-War World: Employment and Commodities, Collected Writings,* vol. xxvii, London.

—— (1980*b*): *Activities 1940–1944: Shaping the Post-War World: The Clearing Union, Collected Writings*, vol. xxv, London.

—— (1980*c*): *Activities 1941–1946: Shaping the Post-War World: Bretton Woods and Reparations, Collected Writings*, vol. xxvi, London.

—— (1981): 'Evidence to Macmillan Committee', in *Collected Writings*, vol. xx, London.

—— (1982): *Activities 1931–1939: World Crises and Policies in Britain and America, Collected Writings*, vol. xxi, London.

Kindleberger, C. P. (1973): *The World in Depression*, London.

—— (1987): *Marshall Plan Days*, London.

King, K. (1985): *US Monetary Policy and European Responses in the 1980s, RIIA Chatham House Papers*, 16.

Kirby, M. W. (1977): *The British Coal Mining Industry 1870–1946: A Political and Economic History*, London.

—— (1987): 'Industrial Policy', in S. Glynn and A. Booth (eds.), *The Road to Full Employment*, London, 125–39.

References 365

Kolko, J., and Kolko, G. (1972): *The Limits of Power: The World and US Foreign Policy 1945–1954*, New York.

Krasner, S., ed. (1985): *International Regimes*, Princeton.

Kuisel, R. F. (1981): *Capitalism and the State in Modern France*, Cambridge.

Kunz, D. B. (1987): *The Battle for Britain's Gold Standard in 1931*, London.

Labour Party (1945): *Let Us Face the Future*, London.

—— (1976): *Report of the Annual Conference of the Labour Party*, London.

Laidler, D. (1975): 'The End of Demand Management: How to Reduce Unemployment in the 1970s', in M. Friedman, *Unemployment Versus Inflation?*, London, 36–48.

—— (1985*a*): 'Monetary Policy in Britain: Success and Shortcomings', *Oxford Review of Economic Policy* 1, pp. 35–43.

—— (1985*b*): *The Demand for Money: Theories, Evidence, and Problems*, 3rd edn, New York.

Lange, O. (1939): *On the Economic Theory of Socialism*, ed. B. Lippincott, Minnesota.

Layard, R., and Nickell, S. (1986): *An Incomes Policy to Help the Unemployed*, London.

Lee, J. M. (1980): *The Churchill Coalition 1940–1945*, London.

Leijonhufvud, A. (1968): *On Keynesian Economics and the Economics of Keynes*, Oxford.

Leruez, J. (1975): *Economic Planning and Politics in Britain*, Oxford.

Levacic, R. (1987): *Economic Policy-Making*, Brighton.

Levering, R. B. (1982): *The Cold War 1945–1972*, Arlington Heights.

Levitt, M., and Joyce, M. (1987): *The Growth and Efficiency of Government Spending*, Cambridge.

Lewis, W. A. (1949): *The Principles of Economic Planning*, London.

—— (1978): *Growth and Fluctuations 1870–1913*, London.

Leyland, N. H. (1952): 'Trade Associations', in G. D. N. Worswick and P. H. Ady (eds.), *The British Economy 1945–1950*, 87–100.

Little, I. (1952): 'Fiscal Policy', in G. D. N. Worswick and P. H. Ady (eds.), *The British Economy 1945–1950*, 159–87.

Llewellyn-Smith, H. (1928): *The Board of Trade*, London.

Lowe, R. (1978*a*): 'The Erosion of State Intervention in Britain 1917–1924', *Economic History Review* 31, pp. 270–286.

—— (1978*b*): 'The Failure of Consensus in Britain: the NIC 1919–21', *Historical Journal* 21, pp. 649–75.

—— (1980): 'The Ministry of Labour: Fact and Fiction', *Bulletin of the Society for the Study of Labour History* 4, pp. 23–7.

—— (1982): 'The Ministry of Labour, 1916–1919; A Still, Small Voice?', in K. Burk (ed.), *War and the State*, London, 108–34.

—— (1986): *Adjusting to Democracy: The Role of the Ministry of Labour in British Politics 1916–1939*, Oxford.

McCord, N. (1968): *The Anti-Corn Law League* 2nd edn., London.

McDonald, G. W. and Gospel, H. F. (1973): 'The Mond–Turner Talks, 1927–1933', *Historical Journal* 16, pp. 807–29.

MacInnes, J. (1987): *Thatcherism at Work*, Milton Keynes.

McKibbin, R. (1975): 'The Economic Policy of the Second Labour Government', *Past and Present* 68, pp. 65–123.

Macmillan, H. P. (1931a): *Committee on Finance and Industry: Report*, Cmd. 3897.

—— (1931b): *Committee on Finance and Industry: Minutes of Evidence.*

Maddison, A. (1987): 'Growth and Slowdown in Advanced Capitalist Economies: Techniques of Quantitative Assessment', *Journal of Economic Literature* 25, pp. 649–98.

Mallett, B. (1913): *British Budgets 1887–1913*, London.

—— and George, C. (1929): *British Budgets 1913/14 to 1920/21*, London.

Marris, R. (1954): *The Machinery of Economic Policy*, Fabian Society Research Series no. 168, London.

Marshall, A. (1926): *Official Papers*, London.

Marwick, A. (1964): 'Middle Opinion in the Thirties: Planning, Progress, and Political Agreement', *English Historical Review* 79, pp. 285–98.

—— (1965): *The Deluge: British Society and the First World War*, London.

Masera, R., and Triffin, R. (1984): *Europe's Money*, Oxford.

Matthews, K. G. P. (1986): 'Was Sterling Overvalued in 1925?', *Economic History Review* 39, pp. 572–87.

—— and Minford, P. (1987): 'Mrs Thatcher's Economic Policies 1979–1987', *Economic Policy* 5, pp. 59–92.

Matthews, R. C. O. (1968): 'Why has Britain had Full Employment since the War?', *Economic Journal* 78, pp. 555–69.

—— (1971): 'The Role of Demand Management', in A. Cairncross (ed.), *Britain's Economic Prospects Reconsidered*, London, 13–35.

—— and Bowen, A. (1989): 'Keynesian and Other Explanations of Britain's Post-War Economic Trends' (forthcoming).

—— Feinstein, C. H., and Odling-Smee, J. (1982): *British Economic Growth 1856–1973*, Oxford.

Maynard, G. (1988): *The Economy under Mrs Thatcher*, Oxford.

Meade, J. (1948): *Planning and the Price Mechanism*, London.

—— (1988): *Collected Economic Papers* vol. i, ed. S. Howson, Cambridge.

Meadows, P. (1978): 'Planning', in F. T. Blackaby (ed.), *British Economic Policy 1960–1974*, Cambridge, 402–17.

Meen, G. (1988): 'International Comparisons of the UK's Long-Run Economic Performance', *Oxford Review of Economic Policy* 4, pp. xxii–xli.

Metcalf, D., Nickell, S., and Floros, N. (1982): 'Still Searching for an Explanation of Unemployment in Inter-War Britain's, *Journal of Political Economy* 90, pp. 386–99.

Middlemas, K. (1979): *Politics in Industrial Society*, London.

—— (1981): 'Unemployment: The Past and Future of a Political Problem', in B. Crick (ed.), *Unemployment*, London, 135–51.

—— (1986): *Power, Competition, and the State* i. *Britain in Search of Balance 1940–1961*, London.

Middleton, R. (1983): 'The Treasury and Public Investment: A Perspective on Inter-War Economic Management', *Public Administration* 61, pp. 351–70.

—— (1985): *Towards the Managed Economy: Keynes, the Treasury, and the Fiscal Policy Debate of the 1930s*, London.

—— (1987): 'Treasury Policy on Unemployment', in S. Glynn and A. Booth (eds.), *The Road to Full Employment*, London, 109–24.

Miller, F. M. (1976): 'The Unemployment Policy of the National Government 1931–1936', *Historical Journal* 19, pp. 453–76.

Milward, A. S. (1965): *The German Economy at War*, London.

—— (1984): *The Reconstruction of Western Europe 1945–1951*, London.

—— (1985): *The Economic Effects of the World Wars on Britain*, 2nd edn., London.

—— (1987): *War, Economy, and Society 1939–1945*, Harmondsworth.

Minford, P. (1983): *Unemployment: Causes and Cure*, Oxford.

Mitchell, J. (1966): *Groundwork to Economic Planning*, London.

Moggridge, D. E. (1972): *British Monetary Policy 1924–1931: The Norman Conquest of $4.86*, Cambridge.

—— (1976): *Keynes*, London.

Moore, B., and Rhodes, J. (1973): 'Evaluating the Effects of British Regional Policy', *Economic Journal* 83, pp. 87–110.

Morgan, E. V. (1943): *The Practice of Central Banking*, Cambridge.

—— (1952): *Studies in British Financial Policy, 1914–1925*, London.

Morgan, K. (1979): *Consensus and Disunity: The Lloyd George Coalition Government 1918–1922*, Oxford.

Morley, J. (1903): *Life of Cobden*, vol. i, London.

Morris, D., and Stout, D. (1985): 'Industrial Policy', in D. Morris (ed.), *The Economic System in the UK*, 3rd edn., Oxford, 851–96.

Mosley, P. (1984): The Making of Economic Policy, Brighton.

Mottershead, P. (1978): 'Industrial Policy', in F. T. Blackaby (ed.), *British Economic Policy 1960–1974*, Cambridge, 418–83.

Mowery, D. (1986): 'Industrial Research, 1900–1950', in B. Elbaum and

W. Lazonick (eds.), *The Decline of the British Economy*, Oxford, 189–222.

Muellbauer, J. (1986): 'Productivity and Competitiveness in British Manufacturing', *Oxford Review of Economic Policy* 2, pp. i–xxv.

Munby, D. L. (1962): 'The Nationalised Industries', in G. D. N. Worswick and P. H. Ady (eds.), *The British Economy in the 1950s*, Oxford, 378–428.

Murray, B. (1980): *The People's Budget 1909/10*, Oxford.

Musgrave, R. A., and Musgrave, P. B. (1968): 'Fiscal Policy', in R. Caves (ed.), *Britain's Economic Prospects*, Washington, 21–67.

Neild, R. (1979): 'Managed Trade between Industrialised Countries', in R. L. Major (ed.), *Britain's Trade and Exchange Rate Policy*, London, 5–36.

New, C. C., and Myers, A. (1987): *Managing Manufacturing Operations in the UK 1975–1985*, Cranfield.

Newton, C. C. S. (1984): 'The Sterling Crisis of 1947 and the British Response to the Marshall Plan', *Economic History Review* 37, pp. 391–408.

Newton, C., and Porter, D. (1988): *Modernisation Frustrated: The Politics of Industrial Decline in Britain since 1900*, London.

Nichols, T. (1986): *The British Worker Problems*, London.

Nickell, S. (1987): 'Discussion of Matthews and Minford (1987)', *Oxford Review of Economic Policy* 5, pp. 93–5.

Niskanen, W. (1971): *Bureaucracy and Representative Government*, Chicago.

O'Brien, P. K. (1987): 'Britain's Economy between the Wars: A Counter-Revolution in Economic History', *Past and Present* 115, pp. 107–30.

OECD, *Economic Outlook* (bi-annually), Paris.

OECD, Main Economic Indicators (monthly), Paris.

Olson, M. (1965): *The Logic of Collective Action*, Cambridge, Mass.

Ormerod, P., and Worswick, G. D. N. (1982): 'Unemployment in Inter-War Britain', *Journal of Political Economy* 90, pp. 400–9.

Overy, R. J. (1982): 'Hitler's War and the German Economy: A Reinterpretation', *Economic History Review* 35, pp. 272–91.

Panitch, L. (1976): *Social Democracy and Industrial Militancy*, Cambridge.

Parker, H. M. D. (1957): *Manpower: A Study of Wartime Policy and Administration*, London.

Parker, R. A. C. (1983): 'The Pound Sterling, the American Treasury, and British Preparations for War, 1938–1939', *English Historical Review* 98, pp. 261–79.

Parsons, D. W. (1986): *The Political Economy of British Regional Policy*, Beckenham.

Peacock, A. (1979): *The Economic Analysis of Government*, Oxford.

—— and Wiseman, J. (1967): *The Growth of Public Expenditure in the UK*, 2nd edn., London.

Peden, G. (1979): *British Rearmament and the Treasury 1932–1939*, Edinburgh.

—— (1980): 'Keynes, the Treasury, and Unemployment in the Later Nineteen-Thirties', *Oxford Economic Papers* 32, pp. 1–18.

—— (1983): 'Sir Richard Hopkins and the "Keynesian Revolution" in Employment Policy 1929–1945', *Economic History Review* 36, pp. 281–96.

—— (1984): 'The Treasury View on Public Works and Employment in the Inter-War Period', *Economic History Review* 37, pp. 167–81.

—— (1985): *British Economic and Social Policy: Lloyd George to Margaret Thatcher*, Deddington.

—— (1988): *Keynes, the Treasury, and Economic Policy*, London.

Phelps, E. (1967): 'Phillips Curves, Expectations of Inflation, and Optimum Unemployment over Time', *Economica* 34, pp. 254–81.

Phelps Brown, E. H., and Browne, M. (1968): *A Century of Pay*, London.

Phillips, G., and Whiteside, N. (1985): *Casual Labour: The Unemployment Question in the Port Transport Industry 1880–1970*, Oxford.

Pigou, A. C. (1904): *The Riddle of the Tariff*, London.

—— (1929): 'Wage Policy and Unemployment', *Economic Journal* 37, pp. 355–68.

Pimlott, B. (1985): *Hugh Dalton*, London.

Pliatzky, L. (1984): *Getting and Spending: Public Expenditure, Employment, and Inflation*, 2nd edn., Oxford.

Pollard, S., ed., (1970): *The Gold Standard and Employment Policies Between the Wars*, London.

—— (1982): *The Wasting of the British Economy*, London.

—— (1983): *The Development of the British Economy 1914–1980*, 3rd edn., London.

Postan, M. M. (1952): *British War Production*, London.

Pressnell, L. S. (1986): *External Economic Policy since the War* i. *The Post-War Financial Settlement*, London.

Prest, A., and Coppock, D. (1974): *The UK Economy: A Manual of Applied Economics*, 5th edn., London.

Price, R. W. R. (1978): 'Budgetary Policy', in F. T. Blackaby (ed.), *British Economic Policy 1960–1974*, Cambridge, 135–217.

Pringle, R. (1977): *The Growth Merchants: Economic Consequences of Wishful Thinking*, London.

Pryke, R. (1971): *Public Enterprise in Practice*, London.

—— (1981): *The Nationalised Industries: Policies and Performance since 1968*, Oxford.

Radcliffe, C. J. R. (1959): *Committee on the Working of the Monetary System: Report* (Cmnd. 827), London.

Radcliffe, C. J. R. (1960): *Memoranda and Minutes of Evidence to the Committee on the Workings of the Monetary System*, London.

Reddaway, W. B. (1951): 'Rationing', in D. N. Chester (ed.), *Lessons of the British War Economy*, Cambridge, 182–99.

Redmond, J. (1980): 'An Indicator of the Effective Exchange Rate of the Pound in the Nineteen-Thirties', *Economic History Review* 33, pp. 83–91.

Rees, J. F. (1921): *A Short Fiscal and Financial History of England 1815–1918*, London.

Reid, D. J. (1977): 'Public Sector Debt', *Economic Trends* 283, 100–9.

Riddell, P. (1985): *The Thatcher Government*, Oxford.

Robbins, L. (1947): *The Economic Problem in Peace and War*, London.

—— (1971): *Autobiography of an Economist*, London.

Roberts, R. (1984): 'The Administrative Origins of Industrial Diplomacy: An Aspect of Government–Industry Relations', in J. Turner (ed.), *Businessmen and Politics*, London, 93–104.

Robinson, E. A. G. (1951): 'The Overall Allocation of Resources', in D. N. Chester (ed.), *Lessons of the British War Economy*, Cambridge, 34–57.

—— (1986): 'The Economic Problems of the Transition from War to Peace', *Cambridge Journal of Economics* 10, pp. 165–85.

Rogow, A. A., and Shore, P. (1955): *The Labour Government and British Industry 1945–1951*, Oxford.

Rollings, N. (1985): 'The "Keynesian Revolution" in Economic Policy-Making: A Comment', *Economic History Review* 38, pp. 95–100.

—— (1988): 'British Budget Policy, 1945–1954: A "Keynesian Revolution"?', *Economic History Review* 41, pp. 283–98.

Roseveare, H. (1969): *The Treasury*, London.

Rossi, V., Walker, J., Todd, D., and Lennan, K. (1986): 'Exchange Rates, Productivity, and International Competitiveness', *Oxford Review of Economic Policy* 3, pp. 56–73.

Rowan, L. (1960): *Arms and Economics*, Cambridge.

Rowland, B. M., ed. (1976): *Balance of Power or Hegemony: The Inter-War Monetary System*, New York.

Rowthorn, R. E., and Wells, J. R. (1987): *De-Industrialisation and Foreign Trade*, Cambridge.

Ruggie, J. H. (1982): 'International Regimes, Transactions, and Change: Embedded Liberalism in the Post-War Economic Order', *International Organisation* 36, pp. 379–415.

Sabine, B. E. V. (1970): *British Budgets in Peace and War 1932–1945*, London.

Sargent, J. R. (1952): 'Britain and the Sterling Area', in G. D. N. Worswick and P. H. Ady (eds.), *The British Economy 1945–1950*, Oxford, 531–49.

Sayers, R. S. (1936): *Bank of England Operations 1890–1914*, London.

—— (1956): *British Financial Policy 1939–1945*, London.

—— (1957): *Central Banking after Bagehot*, Oxford.

—— (1970): 'The Return to Gold, 1925', in S. Pollard (ed.), *The Gold Standard and Employment Policies between the Wars*, London, 85–98.

—— (1976): *The Bank of England 1891–1944* vols i and ii, Cambridge.

Scammell, W. M. (1975): *International Monetary Policy: Bretton Woods and After*, London.

—— (1983): *The International Economy since 1945*, 2nd edn., London.

Schott, K. (1982): 'The Rise of Keynesian Economics: Britain 1940–64', *Economy and Society* 11, 292–316.

Scott, M. FG (1962): 'The Balance of Payments Crises', in G. D. N. Worswick and P. H. Ady (eds.), *The British Economy in the 1950s*, Oxford, 133–46.

—— (1963): *A Study of UK Imports*, Cambridge.

Sedgemore, B. (1980): *The Secret Constitution*.

Semmel, B. (1960): *Imperialism and Social Reform*, London.

Shackle, G. L. S. (1967): *The Years of High Theory*, Cambridge.

Shonfield, A. (1959): *British Economic Policy since the War*, Harmondsworth.

—— (1965): *Modern Capitalism*, Oxford.

Singh, A. (1977): 'UK Industry and the World Economy: A Case of De-industrialisation?', *Cambridge Journal of Economics* 1, pp. 113–36.

Skidelsky, R. (1970): *Politicians and the Slump*, Harmondsworth.

—— (1975): 'The Reception of the Keynesian Revolution', in M. Keynes (ed.), *Essays on John Maynard Keynes*, Cambridge, 89–107.

Smith, D. (1987): *The Rise and Fall of Monetarism*, Harmondsworth.

Smith, H. L. (1984): 'The Womanpower Problem in Britain during the Second World War', *Historical Journal* 27, pp. 925–45.

Smith, K. (1984): *The British Economic Crisis*, Harmondsworth.

—— (1987): *The UK Economy in the Late 1980s: Trends and Prospects*, University of Keele, Department of Economics and Management Science, Working Paper 87–6.

Snowden, P. (1920): *Labour and National Finance*, London.

Southall, H. R. (1988): 'The Origins of the Depressed Areas: Unemployment, Growth, and Regional Structure in Britain before 1914', *Economic History Review* 41, pp. 236–58.

372 References

Stafford, G. B. (1970): 'Full employment since the War: Comment', *Economic Journal* 80, pp. 165–72.

Stedman-Jones, G. (1971): *Outcast London*, Oxford.

Stewart, M. (1972): *Keynes and After*, Harmondsworth.

—— (1983): *Controlling the Economic Future*, Brighton.

—— (1986): *Keynes and After*, 3rd edn., Harmondsworth.

Stone, R. (1951): 'The Use and Development of National Income and Expenditure Estimates', in D. N. Chester (ed.), *Lessons of the British War Economy*, Cambridge, 83–101.

—— (1977): *Inland Revenue Report on National Income 1929*, Cambridge.

Stout, D. (1976): *International Price Competitiveness, Non-Price Factors and International Trade*, London.

Strange, S. (1971): *Sterling and British Policy*, Oxford.

—— (1983): '*Cave! hic dragones*: A Critique of Regime Analysis', in S. Krasner (ed.), *International Regimes*, Princeton, 337–54.

—— (1985): 'Interpretation of a Decade', in L. Tsoukalis (ed.), *The Political Economy of International Money*, London, 1–43.

—— (1986): *Casino Capitalism*, Oxford.

Stubbs, J. (1975): 'The Impact of the Great War on the Conservative Party', in G. Peele and C. Cook (eds.), *The Politics of Reappraisal 1918–1939*, London, 14–38.

Summerfield, P. (1984): *Women Workers in the Second World War*, London.

Supple, B. (1986): 'Ideology or Pragmatism? The Nationalisation of Coal, 1916–1946', in N. McCendrick and R. B. Outhwaite (eds.), *Business Life and Public Policy*, Cambridge, 228–50.

Sutherland, G. ed. (1972): *Studies in the Growth of Nineteenth-Century Government*, London.

Swenarton, M. (1981): *Homes Fit for Heroes*, London.

Tawney, R. H. (1943): 'The Abolitions of Economic Controls 1918–1921, *Economic History Review* 12, pp. 1–30.

Taylor, I. H. (1978): 'War and the Development of Labour's Domestic Programme 1939–1945', Ph.D. dissertation, London.

Tew, B. (1978): 'Monetary Policy—Part I', in F. T. Blackaby (ed.), *British Economic Policy 1960–1974*, Cambridge, 218–57.

Thain, C. (1984): 'The Treasury and Britain's Decline', *Political Studies* 32, pp. 581–95.

—— (1985): 'The Education of the Treasury: the MTFS 1980–1984, *Public Administration* 63, pp. 261–85.

Thane, P., ed. (1978): *The Origins of British Social Policy*, London.

—— (1984): 'Welfare Reform and the Working Class in Edwardian England', *Historical Journal* 27, pp. 877–900.

Thomas, T. (1981): 'Aggregate Demand in the UK 1918–1945', in

R. Floud and D. McCloskey (eds.), *The Economic History of Britain since 1700* ii. *1860 to the 1970s*, Cambridge, 332–46.

Thompson, G. (1986*a*): *The Conservatives' Economic Policy*, London.

—— (1986*b*): *Economic Calculation and Policy Formation*, London.

—— (1987): 'The "New Institutionalism" and Political Analysis', *Economy and Society* 16, pp. 252–73.

Titmuss, R. M. (1976): *Problems of Social Policy* (annotated edition; 1st edition 1950), London.

Tolliday, S. (1984): 'Tariffs and Steel, 1916–1934: The Politics of Industrial Decline', in J. Turner (ed.), *Businessmen and Politics*, 50–75.

—— (1986): 'Steel and Rationalisation Politics 1918–1950', in B. Elbaum and W. Lazonick (eds.), *The Decline of the British Economy*, Oxford, 82–108.

—— and Zeitlin, J., eds. (1985): *Shop Floor Bargaining and the State*, Cambridge.

Tomlinson, J. (1978): 'The Rupee/Pound Exchange in the 1920s', *Indian Economic and Social History Review* 15, pp. 133–50.

—— (1981*a*): *Problems of British Economic Policy 1870–1945*, London.

—— (1981*b*): 'The Economics of Politics and Public Expenditure: A Critique', *Economy and Society* 10, pp. 383–402.

—— (1982): *The Unequal Struggle? British Socialism and the Capitalist Enterprise*, London.

—— (1984): 'A Keynesian Revolution in Economic Policy-Making?', *Economic History Review* 37, pp. 258–62.

—— (1985): *British Macroeconomic Policy since 1940*, London.

—— (1987*a*): *Employment Policy: The Crucial Years 1939–1955*, Oxford.

—— (1987*b*): 'The Politics of Economic Measurement: Causes and Consequences of the Rise of the "Productivity Problem" in the 1940s', Brunel University, Department of Economics Discussion Paper 8706.

—— (1987*c*): 'Industrial Democracy and the Labour Government 1945–1951', Brunel University, Department of Economics Discussion Paper 8702.

—— (1988): 'Can Governments Manage the Economy?', *Fabian Pamphlet* no. 524, London.

—— (1989): 'Labour's Management of the National Economy 1945–1951: Survey and Speculations', *Economy and Society* 18, pp. 1–24.

Toye, T. J. (1976): 'Economic Theories of Politics and Public Finance', *British Journal of Political Science* 6, pp. 433–47.

Treasury (1975/6): *1st Report from the Expenditure Committee*, HCP 69-I and 69-II.

Tsoukalis, L., ed. (1985) *The Political Economy of International Money*, London.

TUC (1967): 'Trade Unionism: The Evidence of the TUC to the Royal Commission on Trade Unions and Employers Associations', London
—— (1973): *Economic Policy and the Cost of Living*, London.
UK Balance of Payments (annually), London.
Van der Wee, H. (1986): *Prosperity and Upheaval: The World Economy 1945–1980*, Harmondsworth.
Van Dormael, A. (1978): *Bretton Woods: Birth of a Monetary System*, London.
Walters, A. A. (1986): *Britain's Economic Renaissance*, Oxford.
Ward, S. V. (1988): *The Geography of Inter-War Britain: The State and Uneven Development*, London.
Webster, C. (1988): *The NHS since the War* i. *Problems of Health Care: The NHS Before 1957*, London.
We Can Conquer Unemployment (1929), Liberal Party.
Wexler, I. (1983): *The Marshall Plan Revisited*, Westport, Conn.
Whiting, A. (1976): 'An International Comparison of the Instability of Economic Growth', *Three Banks Review* 66, pp. 26–46.
Williams, K. (1979): *From Pauperism to Poverty*, London.
—— and Williams, J., eds. (1987): *A Beveridge Reader*, London.
—— Williams, J., and Haslem, C. (1986): *The Breakdown of Austin Rover*, Leamington Spa.
—— Williams, J., and Thomas, D. (1983): *Why Are the British Bad at Manufacturing?*, London.
Williams, P., ed. (1983): *The Diary of Hugh Gaitskell 1945–1956*, London.
Williamson, J. (1985): *The Exchange Rate System*, Washington DC.
Williamson, P. (1982): 'Safety First: Baldwin, The Conservative Party, and the 1929 General Election', *Historical Journal* 25, pp. 385–409.
—— (1984): 'Financiers, the Gold Standard, and British Politics 1925–1931', in J. Turner (ed.), *Businessmen and Politics*, London, 105–29.
Wilson, T. (1952): 'Manpower', in G. D. N. Worswick and P. H. Ady (eds.), *The British Economy 1945–1950*, Oxford, 224–52.
—— (1982): 'The Recommendations of J. M. Keynes', in A. P. Thirlwall (ed.): *Keynes as a Policy Adviser*, London, 39–67.
Winch, D. (1972): *Economics and Policy*, London.
Winters, L. (1987): 'Models of Primary Price Indices', *Bulletin of the Oxford University Institute of Statistics* 49, pp. 307–22.
Wintringham, T. (1942): *People's War*, London.
Wood, J. (1983): *John Maynard Keynes: Critical Assessments*, 4 vols., London.
Wright, J. F. (1981): 'The Inter-War Experience', *Oxford Economic Papers* 33 (Supplement), 282–305.

Wright, M. (1972): 'Treasury Control 1854–1914', in G. Sutherland (ed.), *Studies in the Growth of Nineteenth-Century Government*, London, 195–226.

Wrigley, C. (1976): *Lloyd George and the British Labour Movement*, Hassocks.

Zebel, S. (1967): 'Joseph Chamberlain and the Genesis of Tariff Reform', *Journal of British Studies* 7, pp. 131–157.

Zeitlin, J. (1985): 'Shop Floor Bargaining and the State: A Contradictory Relationship', in S. Tolliday and J. Zeitlin (eds.), *Shop Floor Bargaining and the State*, Cambridge, 1–45.

—— (1987): 'From Labour History to the History of Industrial Relations', *Economic History Review* 40, pp. 159–184.

Index

AACP 224, 229
agriculture 108–9, 206, 252, 284
aircraft industry 265
Atlantic Charter 174–5

balance of payments 15, 19, 71–2
  in 1930s 127
  1940–5 136–9, 175
  1945–50 199, 205–7, 209–12
  in 1950s and 1960s 220–3, 241–2
  in 1970s 279–80
  in 1980s 344–6
Baldwin, S. 91
Balfour Committee 82–3
Balogh, T. 198, 220, 222
Bank of England 10, 18, 25–8, 48, 51,
  53–5, 79–84, 117–19, 216–17,
  251–2, 290–3, 325–7
  industrial role 83–4
Bank Rate 15, 26–7, 45–6, 73–4, 79,
  82, 258
Barnett, C. 168–9, 228
Beveridge, W. H. 39, 162, 168
  Report 163–5
  Full Employment in a Free Society
  170
Bevin, E. 94, 145–9, 154, 193, 197
Board of Trade 30–2, 150, 152, 158,
  169, 217–18
Bretton Woods 175–80, 185–6,
  186–7, 239–40, 277
budgets
  before 1914 21–4
  in 1920s 45, 76–8
  in 1930s 110–13
  in 1940s 140–4, 212–15
  in 1950s and 1960s 245–9
  in 1970s 285–8
  in 1980s 321–2
Butler, R. 257
Butskellism 257

Cairncross, A. 256
Callaghan, J. 310–11
capitalism 4, 5–6, 12–13
capital flows 15, 72–3, 279, 280–1, 307
  controls on 81

car industry 206
CEPG 282–3
CEPS 207, 216
Chamberlain, J. 20, 35–6, 106
Chamberlain, N. 106
cheap money
  in 1930s 117, 124–5, 132
  in war 156
  in late 1940s 216, 233
Churchill, W. 77, 85, 91
  coalition 1940–5 135, 144–5,
  149–50, 153–4, 162, 175
City of London 223, 243, 251–2, 275
class 4–5
Clay, H. 89, 96
coal industry 206–7, 231
Colwyn Commission 52
Commonwealth 193, 200, 243
  see also Empire
Conservative Government
  in 1920s 77, 91
  in 1930s 106, 125–6, 131–2
  in 1950s 196
  in 1960s 252–3, 257, 261–2, 270–1,
  272–3
  in 1970s 253, 263–4
  in 1980s 313–47
Conservative Party 20, 36–7, 75, 106
consumer rationing 152, 204
corporatism 65, 130–1, 154, 234
cotton industry 265
Cripps, S. 215–16, 218
Cunliffe Committee 27, 43–4, 53
  see also gold standard

Dalton, H. 213–14, 218
DEA 250, 252–3, 262
de-industrialization 282, 307–8
de-rating 92–3
devaluation
  1949 210–12
  1967 241–3
Development Councils 236, 264
Distribution of Industry Act (1945) 217
  see also regional policy
domestic investment 227–30, 260

Donovan Commission 27
DTI 253, 293

EAC 90, 124–5
EC 196, 244–5, 283–5, 320–1
economic controls 145–50, 156–8,
     203–7, 215
   see also economic planning
economic growth 223, 255, 261–4, 275
Economic Implications of Full Employ-
     ment 269–70
economic planning 144–5, 205–7, 236
Economic Planning Board 207, 216
Economic Section 151–3, 165–8, 170,
     218, 256
economic theory 32–4, 60–1, 89–90,
     121–5, 151–3, 219–20, 254–6,
     295–7, 327–32
   influence on economic policy 32–4,
     47–8, 59–61, 90, 123–5, 151–3,
     220, 255–6, 297, 330–2
   see also Keynesianism; monetarism
ECSC 195–6
EEA 101–2, 105, 117, 118–19
   see also exchange rate
Empire 20, 35–6, 49–50, 75–6, 106,
     174, 182, 185, 193, 197–8, 222
Employment Policy White Paper 153,
     163, 165–8
EMS 314, 318
EPU 195, 196, 239
Essential Work Order 147, 204
exchange rate 98–105, 131, 134–6,
     239–44, 277–81, 290, 314–19
   see also devaluation; floating
     exchange rate
exchange controls 134–6, 205, 209–10
exchange convertibility 173–80, 182–6

floating exchange rate 243, 278–9,
     280–1
France 104, 119, 195, 206–7, 218, 220,
     227, 230, 232, 262
free trade 9–10, 18–21, 23–4, 48–50,
     75–6, 175, 244–5
full employment 220–3, 234, 255,
     257–9, 274, 335
   see also unemployment

Gaitskell, H. 220, 232, 233, 257
GATT 189, 196, 197, 244
Geddes axe (1922) 52, 58, 59, 65, 67,
     76

general strike 91, 123
   see also trade unions; TUC
Germany 155–6, 192
Giffen, R. 31
Gladstone 24–5, 246
'gold devices' 26–7
gold standard 9, 14–18, 24, 42–8, 70–4
   restoration in 1925, 42, 53–5
government borrowing 30, 50–2, 74,
     77, 115–16, 140–4, 306–7, 321–2
   see also PSBR
government expenditure 21–4, 28–9,
     50–2, 77–8, 110–11, 140–4,
     212–14, 246–8, 285–7, 304–5,
     321–2, 323–4

Haldane Committee (1919) 56, 59
Hall, R. 220, 256
Hawtrey, R. 33, 60
Hayek, F. 151
Henderson, H. 90, 166, 180–1, 219
Hopkins, R. 87, 102, 165–6

IBRD 180, 191
IDAC 108
IMF 178–80, 187, 273, 280, 292
Imperial Preference 20, 35–6, 49–50,
     75–6, 106, 174, 182, 185
incomes policy, *see* wages policy
Independent Labour Party 67, 95
industrial policy 130–1, 169–70,
     252–3, 264–8, 293–5, 307–9
   see also rationalization
In Place of Strife 271
Industrial Transference Act (1928) 92,
     120
inflation 17–18, 43, 46–7, 61, 99,
     159–60, 232–4, 263, 268–74, 296,
     298–9, 331, 339–42
IRC 252–3, 266–7
IRI 293
ITO 188–90

Jewkes, J. 219, 227
JPCs 154, 225

Kaldor, N. 329–30
Keynes, J. M. 3, 47, 48, 54, 57, 60–1,
     87, 88, 103, 105, 114, 124, 126,
     162, 164, 175–80, 181, 183–6,
     221–2
   Economic Consequences of the Peace
     47

Tract on Monetary Reform 48
Means to Prosperity 114
General Theory 121–3
How To Pay For The War 141–3, 159
Keynesianism 11, 47–8, 112, 114–17, 123, 127–9, 143–4, 214–15, 219, 246, 254–6, 257, 259–60, 264, 296–7

Labour Government
1924 49, 67
1929–31, 12, 74, 77–8, 83–4, 94–7
1945–51 12, 184, 196, 203–37
1964–70 241–3, 253, 255–6, 261, 271, 273
1974–9 298–304
Labour Party 63–4, 66, 92, 126, 162, 164, 197
Lend Lease 137–9, 174–5, 182–6
Liberal Government of 1906, 32, 36–9
Liberal Party 62, 92, 126
We Can Conquer Unemployment 86, 90, 93, 197
Yellow Book 93
Lloyd George coalition 44–5, 57, 62–3

Macdonald, R. 67
Macmillan Committee 80–1, 87, 89–90
manpower planning 148, 156–7, 218
Marshall, A. 34
Marshall Aid 188, 190–7
Marxism 3–7, 13
May Committee 77
McKenna duties (1915) 49
Meade, J. 142, 151, 165–6, 180, 213, 219, 220, 227, 230
Ministry of Labour 57–9, 119–20, 145–9, 218
Ministry of Technology 253, 267
monetarism 254–6, 295–7, 327–32, 337–8
see also economic theory
monetary policy 44–6, 55, 124–5, 216–17, 245–6, 257, 272–3, 290–3, 299–301, 324, 325–7, 336–8
money supply 15, 25, 43, 254–5, 272–3, 290–3, 299–301, 336–8, 341
Monopolies and Mergers Act (1965) 266

Mosley, O. 88, 95
MTFS 315, 318, 323–5, 326–7, 329–30, 332–3, 336–8
multilateralism 173, 175–90, 192–3, 199–201
see also free trade

National Debt 21–4, 25, 50–2, 246
see also government borrowing
national economy 8–10, 13, 41, 131–3
National Incomes Commission 271
National Insurance 39, 68, 163–5, 230–1
National Investment Bank 207
nationalization 224, 231–2, 265–6, 267–8
National Plan 250, 263
NEB 293–5, 308
NEDO 252–3, 262, 309
new classical economics 328–9
see also economic theory; monetarism
Norman, M. 73, 80–1, 83

OEEC 194–6
OPEC 277, 279, 296, 306, 309
Ottawa Conference 103, 109–10, 118

'people's budget' (1909) 23, 35, 36–7
PESC 248, 286
Phillips Curve 254–5, 295
see also Keynesianism; monetarism
Pigou, A. 34, 60, 89, 122, 123
postwar reconstruction 160–70
poverty 38–9, 163–5
privatization 335–6
productivity 155, 223–7, 342–4
protection 49–50, 105–10, 245, 282–3, 320
effective 107
see also trade controls
PSBR 246–7, 263, 287–8, 306–7
public choice theory 1–3, 248
public spending
see government expenditure
public works 39, 86–7, 89–90, 93, 114–16, 127–8
purchasing power parity 57, 71, 101

Radcliffe Report 251
rationalization 75, 83–4, 169
see also industrial policy

rearmament
   in 1930s 115, 126
   in 1940s 155, 232–3
regional policy 120, 127, 217, 264–5,
   266–7
   see also Distribution of Industry Act
Relative Price Effect 248, 286
Robbins, L. 151, 219
Royal Commission on the Poor Laws
   (1905–9) 38

Salisbury, Lord 29
Sinking Fund 23
Snowden, P. 66, 77, 95, 98–100, 106
Social Contract 301–4, 309
social reform 23, 35, 37–9
Special Areas Act (1937) 120
standard of living 223, 261, 282
Stone, R. 142–3
Sterling Area 102–3, 193, 198–201,
   240–1
sterling balances 200, 241
'stop-go' 257–61, 272
supply-side policies 335–6

Tariff Reform 19–21, 34, 35–6
taxation 21–4, 50–2, 77, 142–3, 302,
   332
textile industry 206–7
Titmuss, R. 161–2
trade controls 136–9, 180–2, 204–5,
   208–9, 221–2, 224–5
trade unions 64, 65, 89, 144–9, 154,
   233–4, 270, 301–4, 309–10

Treasury 10, 12, 28–30, 31, 48, 51,
   55–7, 58–9, 85–9, 113–17,
   144–5, 166–8, 215–16, 218–19,
   249–51, 289–90, 322–5
Treasury View 60–1, 85–8, 89–90,
   114–16
TUC 167, 224, 270, 271, 301–4, 309

UAB 119–20
UGC 67, 85
unemployment
   before 1914 19–20, 31–2, 37–40
   between the wars 46, 60–1, 66–8,
      84–7, 89–90, 99
   1939–45 146–7
   after 1945 213, 258, 263, 295, 298–9,
      310–11, 333–6, 338, 343
   see also full employment
USA 54, 73–4, 119, 137–9, 172–202,
   208–9, 221–2, 239–40
   and dollar exchange rate 103–5,
      211–12, 314
US loan 182–6, 198

wage policy 16–17, 129, 146–8, 159,
   232–4, 260, 317
wages 233–4, 263–4, 268–74, 301–4,
   309–10, 340
Wall Street crash (1929) 75, 79
White, H. 176–8
Wilson, H. 215, 225
women's employment 148–9
World Economic Conference 103, 104,
   118

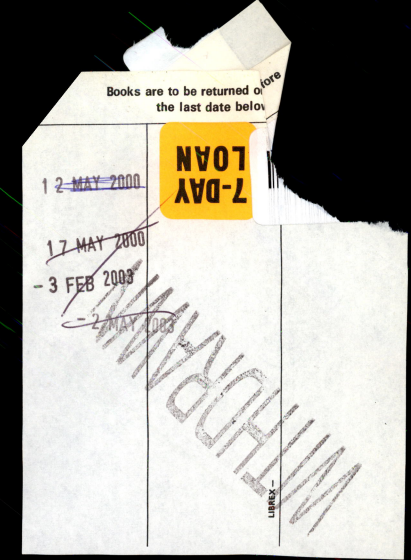

A SOURCEBOOK OF AFRICAN-AMERICAN PERFORMANCE

A Sourcebook on African-American Performance: Plays, People, Movements is the first volume to consider African-American performance between and beyond the Black Arts Movement of the 1960s and the New Black Renaissance of the 1990s.

The Sourcebook consists of writings previously published in *The Drama Review* (*TDR*) as well as newly commissioned pieces by notable scholars, writers and performers including Annemarie Bean, Ed Bullins, Barbara Lewis, John O'Neal, Glenda Dicker/sun, James V. Hatch, Warren Burdine, Jr, and Eugene Nesmith. Included are articles, essays, manifestos and interviews on

- theatre on the professional, revolutionary and college stages
- concert dance
- community activism
- step shows
- performance art previously published in *TDR*.

The volume also includes the plays *Sally's Rape* by Robbie McCauley and *The America Play* by Suzan-Lori Parks, and comes complete with an Introduction by Annemarie Bean.

Annemarie Bean is an assistant professor of theatre at Williams College, Williamstown, Massachusetts. She was managing editor of *The Drama Review* for three years, and is the co-editor, with James V. Hatch and Brooks McNamara, of *Inside the Minstrel Mask: Readings in Nineteenth-Century Blackface Minstrelsy* (Wesleyan University Press/University Press of New England, 1996), winner of the 1997 Errol Hill Award given by the American Society for Theatre Research for outstanding scholarship in African-American theatre studies. Her current project is a study of gender impersonation by white and African-American nineteenth-century minstrels.

Worlds of Performance
General Editor: Richard Schechner

WORLDS OF PERFORMANCE

What is a "performance"? Where does it take place? Who are the participants? Not so long ago these were settled questions, but today such orthodox answers are unsatisfactory, misleading, and limiting "Performance" as a theoretical category and as a practice has expanded explosively. It now comprises a panoply of genres ranging from play, to popular entertainments, to theatre, dance, and music, to secular and religious rituals, to "performance in everyday life", to intercultural experiments, and more.

For nearly forty years, *The Drama Review* (*TDR*), the journal of performance studies, has been at the cutting edge of exploring these questions. The Worlds of Performance Series is designed to mine the extraordinary riches and diversity of TDR's decades of excellence, bringing back into print important essays, interviews, artists' notes, and photographs. New materials and introductions bring the volumes up to date. Each World of Performance book is a complete anthology, arranged around a specific theme or topic. Each World of Performance book is an indispensable resource for the scholar, a textbook for the student, and an exciting eye-opener for the general reader.

Richard Schechner
Editor, *TDR*
Series Editor

Other titles in the series:

Acting (Re)Considered edited by Phillip B. Zarrilli
Happenings and other Acts edited by Mariellen R. Sandford
A Sourcebook of Feminist Theatre and Performance: On and Beyond the stage edited by Carol Martin
The Grotowski Sourcebook edited by Richard Schechner and Lisa Wolford